Essentials of Social Work Management and Leadership

Essentials of Social Work Management and Leadership

A COMPETENCY-BASED APPROACH

RICHARD HOEFER AND LARRY D. WATSON

University of Texas—Arlington

SAN DIEGO

Bassim Hamadeh, CEO and Publisher
Amy Smith, Project Editor
Casey Hands, Associate Production Editor
Emely Villavicencio, Senior Graphic Designer
Stephanie Kohl, Licensing Coordinator
Natalie Piccotti, Director of Marketing
Kassie Graves, Vice President of Editorial
Jamie Giganti, Director of Academic Publishing

3970 Sorrento Valley Blvd., Ste. 500, San Diego, CA 92121

For Paula Homer and Sharon Hoefer, who lift my spirits daily. —RH

To Judy—my wife, my love, my best friend, and proofreader extraordinaire. —LW

BRIEF CONTENTS

DETAILED CONTENTS

PART II   LEADERSHIP AND COMMUNICATION   61

CHAPTER 4   Leadership   63

CHAPTER 7   Program Planning, Logic Models, and Program Evaluation   124

CHAPTER 8   Budgeting and Finance   144

PREFACE

Social work education is always in a time of transition, but the last decade has seen unusually significant changes in the environment of social work administration and management. Some of this has occurred inside academia, but the bulk is in the practice arena. For social work education–based programs, perhaps the most consequential shifts include the continued movement (which was codified in 2008 with revised Educational Policy and Accreditation Standards [EPAS] statements) toward expecting students to graduate with competency in, rather than only knowledge of, the necessary skills (Council for Social Work Education [CSWE], 2015). This book embraces the competency-based approach in order to provide a book on social work leadership and management that fits neatly into any social work education program.

CSWE (2018) defines competency as "the ability to integrate and apply social work knowledge, values, and skills to practice situations in a purposeful, intentional, and professional manner to promote human and community well-being" (p. xv). As students work through this book, they will find a strong foundation in social work values, knowledge development in leadership and management, and opportunities to develop skills under the supervision of their instructor. While the text is grounded in social work, we incorporate information and material from a multitude of disciplines and sources, because that reflects the world that social work leaders and managers operate in.

Another aspect of social work education that has continued to evolve is the need to balance providing textbooks that are multifaceted, incorporating a variety of ways for students to access information, with the need for the instructor and text to provide a curated map of a field of study. Our book orients readers with an overarching conceptualization of leadership and management in social work and provides a considerable amount of information directly. It also points out additional resources for instructors to use and ways for students to deepen their knowledge. Skills building exercises are part of every chapter.

It is impossible for any book, or any one learning experience, to allow students to demonstrate skills in all nine of the 2015 EPAS competencies. This book is designed to be used in conjunction with other courses and a student's field education experiences so that students have the chance to demonstrate educational outcomes. Instructors will be able to identify how the book best fits within their educational programs and coursework. We believe that instructors will find this book helpful in generalist programs (BSW or MSW) that need material on leadership and management, even if they do not have time enough to cover every chapter.

As described in CSWE (2018), "specialized practice for macro social work builds on generalist practice but augments and extends social work knowledge, values, and skills to engage, assess, intervene, and evaluate within administration and management practice" (pp. xvii-xviii). This book can be used in its entirety to achieve this standard. The text is especially designed to be a core textbook for any course on social work leadership and management at a specialized or advanced level. This text provides depth in each chapter and gives a solid basis for developing practice competencies through exercises and assignments, as well.

Austin and Kruzich (2004) noted a number of shortcomings when they reviewed 11 human services administration textbooks a decade and a half ago. They stated that almost all the texts emphasized content over application or skills building; that learning through case-based and problem-centered exercises was minimal; that transmitting content was seen as more important than providing learning strategies for content integration; that descriptions of managerial practice took the place of social environment theory; and that none of the textbooks reviewed empirical research on what managerial practice is. This set of five conclusions powerfully indicted the texts available at the time, most of which still exist in updated editions that have not been radically revised to meet the challenge of contemporary social work leadership and management. Other texts have been developed, but they have not fully heeded the lessons that Austin and Kruzich described, nor the similar issues found by Au (1994) a decade earlier.

We made three decisions while planning our text: to focus on developing practice competence as much as substantive content, to connect *all* chapters to skill development and competency, and to use a comprehensive conceptual overview. We believe these decisions make the book particularly compelling both for instructors of contemporary social work administration and leadership courses and for instructors of generalist macro practice courses looking for a book on essential topics in administration and leadership within human services. We explicitly link the material to the CSWE 2015 EPAS to provide a strong connection between coursework and competencies. Practitioners looking for an accessible overview of essential knowledge combined with exercises that can be completed individually or in groups at the office will also find the book engaging and indispensable.

Decision 1: Focus on Developing Practice Competence as Much as Substantive Content

Our first decision to develop a "better book" was to focus as much on the development of competence in practice skills as on substantive content. Each chapter contains hands-on experiential exercises (including a substantial in-basket case exercise) and additional assignments. The exercises provide opportunities for readers to apply the substantive information in the chapter and to better internalize how the ideas can be used in practice.

Most other administration texts in social work management and leadership have discussion questions in them. We do not. Students and readers generate *their own* discussion questions when they are faced with *applying* concepts in addition to *reading* about them. The addition of these exercises (which include activities, small-group or paired discussion, responding to YouTube videos, and other approaches to application) marks this book as substantially different from other texts in the field. It places students in the center of learning, allowing the instructor to "flip the classroom."

Students are more likely to come to class ready to interact with the concepts and each other when they know that they will be called on to apply the ideas in class. This is good training, because that is more similar to what they will need to do in the field. Having exercises ready to use encourages students to come to class sessions prepared to take part and develop their competencies. In our book, both substantive content and competency development are central.

Decision 2: Connect *All* Chapters to Skill Development and Competency

Almost all textbooks about social work leadership recognize the importance of context. These other books tend to take only an expository view of the topics of sector history, values and ethics, and administrative and organizational theories. We think these other texts miss an important point. Thus, the second major decision we made as we wrote this book was to present these contextual topics as areas ripe for skills development, equal to the more traditional areas such as planning, evaluation, fund development, and so on. We believe, for example, that administrators must be able to look outside of their organization to discover the larger picture of the contemporary political, economic, and social environment whenever needed. We describe *our* ideas on key current trends, but others (including students and practitioners reading this book) will have access to different pockets of information and will perhaps focus on entirely different trends that make a difference to them. Thus, learning to find one's own context is important to social work and nonprofit organization leaders.

We also emphasize applying values and ethics in practice situations and the importance of understanding administrative and organizational theory *in situ*. Too often, the obligatory chapters on "ethics" and "theory" are merely skimmed and forgotten by students, instead of being seen as unique sets of tools to increase understanding and action. For example, ethics must underlie administrators' behavior, or else the scandals that have harmed the reputations of many organizations will continue to erode public trust in the nonprofit sector as a whole. Theory points the way, in many cases, to solutions to dilemmas about how social work leaders should act. However, if none of these foundational topics are seen as skills-related, part of their worth is left untapped. In our book, *everything* connects to knowledge and skills to enhance competency.

Decision 3: Use a Comprehensive Conceptual Overview

Our third decision in designing this book that separates it from many others is to use a comprehensive conceptual overview of human service administration. This overview is based on original work by Schmid (2006) and was expanded and linked to skills and theories by Hoefer (2010). The overview is depicted in Figure 0.1 and is developed more fully throughout our book. This conceptual overview places administrative skills into four quadrants derived from two continua: task vs. people orientation and internal vs. external orientation. While ethics surrounds and underlies the use of all leadership and administrative skills, other skills that are in the literature can be placed (more or less) neatly into one of the four resulting quadrants: internal and task orientation (Quadrant

I); external and task orientation (Quadrant II); internal and people orientation (Quadrant III); or external and people orientation (Quadrant IV).

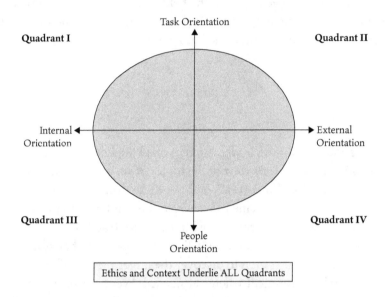

FIGURE 0.1. The Four-Quadrant Model of Social Work Leadership and Management (adapted from Schmid, 2006)

We believe the use of a conceptual approach such as this is quite beneficial. First, the model is empirically tested as having validity, and it comports with the reality seen by social work leaders, administrators, and managers. Giving readers a peek at the overall field in this way provides scaffolding for their continuing to learn specific knowledge and develop competencies. What they learn from this text, its exercises, and its assignments can be put into a framework to be filled in with additional knowledge and experiences they claim from other sources.

The four quadrants are ideal for mapping administrative skills and will be discussed in later chapters. While there is perhaps some debate over which list of skills for social work leaders is most useful, Hoefer (2010) has drawn from multiple skills lists and mapped the skills to this four-quadrant conceptual overview. In this book, we have chosen skills from each of the quadrants to provide coverage of essential skills from all aspects of the social work administrator's world. In our book, all the pieces (knowledge and skills) can be linked into a conceptual framework, showing readers how to think of the broad arena of competencies, as well.

Who is This Book For?

This book is not for everyone. It has two primary audiences that we feel will be well served by the approach we take and the elements we have included.

The first audience we see comprises instructors (and their students) who want a *social work leadership and administration* text that provides essential information in a concise format. Not everyone needs or wants a full-scale, comprehensive, all-in-one *macro social work* text. This may be because some are teaching on a quarter system, have only a portion of a semester to devote to administration and leadership, or have other materials that cover other topics in a longer course. This text does not cover community organization and discusses policy practice only in the sense that social work leaders need to know how to conduct advocacy, which is only one element of policy practice. At the same time, we cover the range of material needed for a long semester course dedicated to social work leadership, administration, and management.

While this text focuses almost exclusively on administrative practice (and not the larger arena of macro practice), students in macro social work courses will still gain much from reading it. We believe, as do the authors of the *Specialized Practice Curricular Guide for Macro Social Work Practice* (CSWE, 2018), that combating social injustice as a professional commitment requires building effective organizations and social work leadership within them. We assert that the competencies of leaders and administrators in human service organizations cross over and are vital to being effective community workers and policy practitioners.

A way to conceptualize administrative practice that differentiates it from community work and policy practice is provided in the macro competencies guide (CSWE, 2018), wherein the authors state that administration and management practitioners should "understand leadership behaviors, performance management, organizational behavior, evidence-based or promising practices, finances, and budgeting and know how these features of organizational life interconnect and influence service effectiveness and talent management" (p. xxviii).

The second audience that would benefit from this text is anyone seeking a text that connects experiential learning exercises, case studies, and carefully crafted assignments with essential substantive information. This book is ideal for increasing student and practitioner competency. This second audience may overlap considerably with the first but also expands beyond it. We know that adult learners seek to learn from experience and practice as well as from reading. We also know that one of the main issues in human services administration is that good clinicians are promoted to supervisory (and higher) positions without having the opportunity to receive training or education in management or leadership skills.

For both our target audiences, having a text that combines exercises with substantive information accelerates learning and retention of knowledge and, ultimately, competency in essential social work leadership and administrative skills. The exercises in this book, when combined with the essential ideas and facts around each topic, assist readers as they grapple with the ideas and skills needed for competent human services leadership. If we can help students and current practitioners develop more skills through cases, assignments, and exercises, these ideas and skills will be more quickly integrated into practice and at a higher level of achievement. By arming them with a conceptual view of the roles of social work leaders and a larger repertoire of skills, we may anticipate larger cohorts of new leaders staying in the field for a longer career. Ultimately, this can lead to better outcomes for service recipients.

CSWE's 2015 EPAS and Competencies

If you are a social work educator, you already know about the Council on Social Work Education's Educational Policy Accreditation Standards and the need to link coursework to achieving competencies for social work graduates. This book has been designed to assist you in meeting those standards. As noted in CSWE documents (such as CSWE, 2017), "Competence in *real or simulated practice* can only be demonstrated by behavior and behavior cannot be demonstrated without incorporation of the knowledge, values, skills and cognitive and affective processes associated with the competency" (p. 1). Instructors may thus desire to ensure that the knowledge described in each chapter is linked with social work values (see chapter 2), skill-building exercises (such as provided here or in the CSWE [2018] macro guide) and "debriefing processing" of the material and exercises. Each educational competency is listed below, and the sections or elements of this book that apply are described afterward (see Table 0.1 for the overview of this material).

TABLE 0.1   Connections Between CSWE 2015 EPAS Competencies and Chapters

2015 CSWE Competency	Related Chapter in this Book
Competency 1: Demonstrate Ethical and Professional Behavior	Chapter 2: Values and Ethics in Administration
Competency 2: Engage Diversity and Difference in Practice	Chapter 4: Leadership Chapter 5: Personal Communication Chapter 11: Human Resources and Supervision
Competency 3: Advance Human Rights and Social, Economic, and Environmental Justice	Chapter 2: Values and Ethics in Administration Chapter 4: Leadership Chapter 6: Strategic Planning Chapter 13: Persuasion Chapter 14: Advocacy
Competency 4: Engage in Practice-Informed Research and Research-Informed Practice	Chapter 3: Administrative and Organizational Theories Chapter 6: Strategic Planning Chapter 7: Program Planning, Logic Models, and Program Evaluation Chapter 14: Advocacy
Competency 5: Engage in Policy Practice	Chapter 13: Persuasion Chapter 14: Advocacy
Competency 6: Engage with Individuals, Families, Groups, Organizations, and Communities	Chapter 1: The Context of Social Work Leadership and Administration Chapter 3: Administrative and Organizational Theories Chapter 4: Leadership Chapter 5: Personal Communication Chapter 13: Persuasion Chapter 14: Advocacy
Competency 7: Assess Individuals, Families, Groups, Organizations, and Communities	Chapter 4: Leadership Chapter 6: Strategic Planning Chapter 7: Program Planning, Logic Models, and Program Evaluation Chapter 8: Budgeting and Finance Chapter 10: Marketing Chapter 11: Human Resources and Supervision Chapter 12: Boards Chapter 13: Persuasion Chapter 14: Advocacy

COMPETENCY 1 Demonstrate Ethical and Professional Behavior

Social workers understand the value base of the profession and its ethical standards, as well as relevant laws and regulations that may impact practice at the micro, mezzo, and macro levels. Social workers understand frameworks of ethical decision-making and how to apply principles of critical thinking to those frameworks in practice, research, and policy arenas. Social workers recognize personal values and the distinction between personal and professional values. They also understand how their personal experiences and affective reactions influence their professional judgment and behavior. Social workers understand the profession's history, its mission, and the roles and responsibilities of the profession. Social workers also understand the role of other professions when engaged in inter-professional teams. Social workers recognize the importance of life-long learning and are committed to continually updating their skills to ensure they are relevant and effective. Social workers also understand emerging forms of technology and the ethical use of technology in social work practice. Social workers:

- make ethical decisions by applying the standards of the NASW Code of Ethics, relevant laws and regulations, models for ethical decision-making, ethical conduct of research, and additional codes of ethics as appropriate to context;
- use reflection and self-regulation to manage personal values and maintain professionalism in practice situations;
- demonstrate professional demeanor in behavior; appearance; and oral, written, and electronic communication;
- use technology ethically and appropriately to facilitate practice outcomes; and
- use supervision and consultation to guide professional judgment and behavior. (CSWE, 2015, p. 7)

This book provides a thorough grounding in how students may know about and demonstrate ethical and professional behavior. Chapter 2 (Values and Ethics in Administration) presents a detailed explanation of the values of and ethical basis for human services administration and leadership, drawing on the National Association of Social Workers' Code of Ethics and other ethics writings. Readers see how to resolve issues and are provided case studies to apply abstract concepts to practice. They learn to tolerate ambiguity as they apply strategies of ethical reasoning to arrive at their decisions. Along with the material in Chapter 2, additional material is integrated throughout the book, because ethics informs behaviors in all aspects of social work leadership and administration. The many exercises and assignments provide opportunities for readers to practice personal reflection and self-correction as they learn about proper professional roles and boundaries. Material is presented regarding professional behavior, appearance, and communication in the processes of communication and persuasion.

COMPETENCY 2 Engage Diversity and Difference in Practice

Social workers understand how diversity and difference characterize and shape the human experience and are critical to the formation of identity. The dimensions of diversity are understood as the intersectionality of multiple factors including but not limited to age, class, color, culture, disability and ability, ethnicity, gender, gender identity and expression, immigration status, marital status, political ideology, race, religion/spirituality, sex, sexual orientation, and tribal sovereign status. Social workers understand that, as a consequence of difference, a person's life experiences may include oppression, poverty, marginalization, and alienation as well as privilege, power, and acclaim. Social workers also understand the forms and mechanisms of oppression and discrimination and recognize the extent to which a culture's structures and values, including social, economic, political, and cultural exclusions, may oppress, marginalize, alienate, or create privilege and power. Social workers:

- apply and communicate understanding of the importance of diversity and difference in shaping life experiences in practice at the micro, mezzo, and macro levels;
- present themselves as learners and engage clients and constituencies as experts of their own experiences; and
- apply self-awareness and self-regulation to manage the influence of personal biases and values in working with diverse clients and constituencies. (CSWE, 2015, p. 7)

Chapter 4 (Leadership) explicitly addresses these topics, as does Chapter 5 (Personal Communication). Chapter 11 (Human Resources and Supervision) discusses at length the necessity for social work leaders and administrators to understand best practices regarding the many types of diversity that exist within human services organizations. The chapter includes exercises to foster self-awareness and self-regulation as learners understand better the influence of their personal biases and values.

Additionally, the underpinnings of this book are set in understanding diversity and difference and the ways that leaders and managers must address them to maximize their positive impact. Leaders should strive to be the leader of everyone in the organization, and the book provides readers with the skills to do so, regardless of age, class, color, culture, disability status, ethnicity, gender, gender identity and expression, immigration status, political ideology, race, religion, sex, or sexual orientation.

COMPETENCY 3 Advance Human Rights and Social, Economic, and Environmental Justice

Social workers understand that every person regardless of position in society has fundamental human rights such as freedom, safety, privacy, an adequate standard of living, health care, and education. Social workers understand the global interconnections of oppression and human rights violations, and are knowledgeable about theories of human need and social justice and strategies to promote social and economic justice and human rights. Social workers understand strategies designed to eliminate oppressive structural barriers to ensure that social goods, rights, and responsibilities are distributed equitably and that civil, political, environmental, economic, social, and cultural human rights are protected. Social workers:

- apply their understanding of social, economic, and environmental justice to advocate for human rights at the individual and system levels; and

- engage in practices that advance social, economic, and environmental justice. (CSWE, 2015, pp. 7–8)

Chapter 2 (Values and Ethics in Administration) shows how these principles should be integrated into agency work. Chapter 4 (Leadership) asks the question, "What is leadership for?" and is answered with a challenge for social work leaders to work for greater equity and a just distribution of resources so that civil, political, environmental, economic, social and cultural human rights are protected. Chapter 6 (Strategic Planning) recalls the values and ethics material from earlier in the book. Finally, Chapters 13 (Persuasion) and 14 (Advocacy) build on information regarding social, economic, and environmental justice to present a step-by-step process for effectively engaging in efforts to achieve these vital social work goals. The exercises in these chapters are practices that students can engage in to develop competency in advocacy skills advancing human rights and social, economic, and environmental justice.

COMPETENCY 4 Engage in Practice-Informed Research and Research-Informed Practice

Social workers understand quantitative and qualitative research methods and their respective roles in advancing a science of social work and in evaluating their practice. Social workers know the principles of logic, scientific inquiry, and culturally informed and ethical approaches to building knowledge. Social workers understand that evidence that informs practice derives from multi-disciplinary sources and multiple ways of knowing. They also understand the processes for translating research findings into effective practice. Social workers:

- use practice experience and theory to inform scientific inquiry and research;

- apply critical thinking to engage in analysis of quantitative and qualitative research methods and research findings; and

- use and translate research evidence to inform and improve practice, policy, and service delivery. (CSWE, 2015, p. 8)

Many chapters relate to this competency. Chapter 3 (Administrative and Organizational Theories), Chapter 6 (Strategic Planning), Chapter 7 (Program Planning, Logic Models, and Program Evaluation), and Chapter 14 (Advocacy) show clearly the importance of these topics. Research for social work leaders is a tool and a resource. Data, whether gathered from quantitative or qualitative methods, need to be analyzed and interpreted to apply to the situations that clients, organizations, and communities face. While we do not delve deeply into research methods (because this material is included in mandatory research courses), we stress the techniques of translating and using research evidence. As in other chapters, the exercises we present will test and stretch student knowledge and ability to turn knowledge into competency in practical skills.

COMPETENCY 5 Engage in Policy Practice

Social workers understand that human rights and social justice, as well as social welfare and services, are mediated by policy and its implementation at the federal, state, and local levels. Social workers understand the history and current structures of social policies and services, the role of policy in service delivery, and the role of practice in policy development. Social workers understand their role in policy development and implementation within their practice settings at the micro, mezzo, and macro levels and they actively engage in policy practice to effect change within those settings. Social workers recognize and understand the historical, social, cultural, economic, organizational, environmental, and global influences that affect social policy. They are also knowledgeable about policy formulation, analysis, implementation, and evaluation. Social workers:

- identify social policy at the local, state, and federal level that impacts well-being, service delivery, and access to social services;

- assess how social welfare and economic policies impact the delivery of and access to social services;

- apply critical thinking to analyze, formulate, and advocate for policies that advance human rights and social, economic, and environmental justice. (CSWE, 2015, p. 8)

This competency is addressed primarily in Chapter 13 (Persuasion) and Chapter 14 (Advocacy), which build on information regarding social, economic, and environmental justice in this text and across the reader's knowledge base to present a step-by-step process for engaging in advocacy. The exercises we present are practices that students can engage in to develop competency in advocacy skills advancing social, economic, and environmental justice.

COMPETENCY 6 Engage with Individuals, Families, Groups, Organizations, and Communities

Social workers understand that engagement is an ongoing component of the dynamic and interactive process of social work practice with, and on behalf of, diverse individuals, families, groups, organizations, and communities. Social workers value the importance of human relationships. Social workers understand theories of human behavior and the social environment, and critically evaluate and apply this knowledge to facilitate engagement with clients and constituencies, including individuals, families, groups, organizations, and communities. Social workers understand strategies to engage diverse clients and constituencies to advance practice effectiveness.

Social workers understand how their personal experiences and affective reactions may impact their ability to effectively engage with diverse clients and constituencies. Social workers value principles of relationship-building and inter-professional collaboration to facilitate engagement with clients, constituencies, and other professionals as appropriate. Social workers:

- apply knowledge of human behavior and the social environment, person-in-environment, and other multidisciplinary theoretical frameworks to engage with clients and constituencies; and

- use empathy, reflection, and interpersonal skills to effectively engage diverse clients and constituencies. (CSWE, 2015, p. 8–9)

Theories of human behavior and the social environment are presented in Chapter 1, (The Context of Social Work Leadership and Administration), Chapter 3 (Administrative and Organizational Theories) and Chapter 4 (Leadership). Leaders must be skilled in interacting with and valuing each staff member and client, along with external constituencies who support their organization. Chapter 4, Chapter 5 (Personal Communication), Chapter 13 (Persuasion), and Chapter 14 (Advocacy) provide in-depth information on engaging with people, groups, organizations, and communities to provide readers with the skills to engage around social, economic, and environmental justice issues. Readers have the opportunity to improve on these skills through participating in the exercises at each chapter's end.

COMPETENCY 7 Assess Individuals, Families, Groups, Organizations, and Communities

Social workers understand that assessment is an ongoing component of the dynamic and interactive process of social work practice with, and on behalf of, diverse individuals, families, groups, organizations, and communities. Social workers understand theories of human behavior and the social environment, and critically evaluate and apply this knowledge in the assessment of diverse clients and constituencies, including individuals, families, groups, organizations, and communities. Social workers understand methods of assessment with diverse clients and constituencies to advance practice effectiveness. Social workers recognize the implications of the larger practice context in the assessment process and value the importance of inter-professional collaboration in this process. Social workers understand how their personal experiences and affective reactions may affect their assessment and decision-making. Social workers:

- collect and organize data, and apply critical thinking to interpret information from clients and constituencies;

- apply knowledge of human behavior and the social environment, person-in-environment, and other multidisciplinary theoretical frameworks in the analysis of assessment data from clients and constituencies;

- develop mutually agreed-on intervention goals and objectives based on the critical assessment of strengths, needs, and challenges within clients and constituencies; and

- select appropriate intervention strategies based on the assessment, research knowledge, and values and preferences of clients and constituencies. (CSWE, 2015, p. 9)

Chapter 6 (Strategic Planning), Chapter 7 (Program Planning, Logic Models, and Program Evaluation), Chapter 8 (Budgeting and Finance), Chapter 10 (Marketing), Chapter 11 (Human Resources and Supervision), Chapter 12 (Boards), Chapter 13 (Persuasion), and Chapter 14 (Advocacy) bring this competency to the fore, as they show how to apply knowledge of human behavior, the social environment, and other theoretical frameworks to community and agency issues. The multitude of practice exercises and skill-building exercises across these chapters provide many ways to demonstrate competency in assessing needs and programs to improve the quality of social, economic, and environmental justice in communities.

COMPETENCY 8 Intervene with Individuals, Families, Groups, Organizations, and Communities

Social workers understand that intervention is an ongoing component of the dynamic and interactive process of social work practice with, and on behalf of, diverse individuals, families, groups, organizations, and communities. Social workers are knowledgeable about evidence-informed interventions to achieve the goals of clients and constituencies, including individuals, families, groups, organizations, and communities. Social workers understand theories of human behavior and the social environment, and critically evaluate and apply this knowledge to effectively intervene with clients and constituencies. Social workers understand methods of identifying, analyzing and implementing evidence-informed interventions to achieve client and constituency goals. Social workers value the importance of interprofessional teamwork and communication in interventions, recognizing that beneficial outcomes may require interdisciplinary, inter-professional, and inter-organizational collaboration. Social workers:

- critically choose and implement interventions to achieve practice goals and enhance capacities of clients and constituencies;

- apply knowledge of human behavior and the social environment, person-in-environment, and other multidisciplinary theoretical frameworks in interventions with clients and constituencies;

- use inter-professional collaboration as appropriate to achieve beneficial practice outcomes;

- negotiate, mediate, and advocate with and on behalf of diverse clients and constituencies; and

- facilitate effective transitions and endings that advance mutually agreed-on goals. (CSWE, 2015, p. 9)

Chapters throughout the book address the competencies for intervening. Chapter 3 (Administrative and Organizational Theories) relays information on creating change in organizations, which is often necessary to introduce new interventions or alter existing ones. Chapter 4 (Leadership) and Chapter 5 (Personal Communication), as well as Chapter 13 (Persuasion), discuss building support for organizational change and motivating staff members in adopting new practices and interventions, in addition to fostering success in interprofessional collaborations. Chapter 6 (Strategic Planning) and Chapter 7 (Program Planning, Logic Models, and Program Evaluation) provide the foundation for planning interventions at every level. Chapter 8 (Budgeting and Finance) and Chapter 9 (Fund Development and Grantwriting) help readers acquire and distribute resources needed to complete interventions once they have been chosen according to evidence-based principles for effectiveness, as does Chapter 10 (Marketing). Chapter 13 (Persuasion) and Chapter 14 (Advocacy) inform on the topics of persuading others, negotiating, mediating, and advocating on behalf of diverse clients and constituencies, both within the leader's organization and among the broader community. Exercises throughout the book are useful in addressing this competency.

COMPETENCY 9 Evaluate Practice with Individuals, Families, Groups, Organizations, and Communities

Social workers understand that evaluation is an ongoing component of the dynamic and interactive process of social work practice with, and on behalf of, diverse individuals, families, groups, organizations and communities. Social workers recognize the importance of evaluating processes and outcomes to advance practice, policy, and service delivery effectiveness. Social workers understand theories of human behavior and the social environment, and critically evaluate and apply this knowledge in evaluating outcomes. Social workers understand qualitative and quantitative methods for evaluating outcomes and practice effectiveness. Social workers:

- select and use appropriate methods for evaluation of outcomes;
- apply knowledge of human behavior and the social environment, person-in-environment, and other multidisciplinary theoretical frameworks in the evaluation of outcomes;
- critically analyze, monitor, and evaluate intervention and program processes and outcomes; and
- apply evaluation findings to improve practice effectiveness at the micro, mezzo, and macro levels. (CSWE, 2015, p. 9)

Chapter 7 (Program Planning, Logic Models, and Program Evaluation) is an obvious resource in developing this competency. The exercises and assignments help students develop both clarity on the information and skill in the competency area.

Conclusion

We believe one of the primary directives of social work and nonprofit leaders is the advancement of human rights and social and economic justice. We equip readers to fulfill this directive by helping them develop knowledge, skills, and competencies relating to effective administrative practice. The competent social work leader and administrator can then apply these to promote services that seek to end oppression and discrimination and to improve the life chances of marginalized populations.

Leadership and administration are, ultimately, processes designed to change the behavior and thinking of humans. Social workers should understand theories and conceptual frameworks as they look at improving the world at all levels of intervention. Assessment for, intervention by, and evaluation of programs, interventions, and policies requires the ability to understand, critique, and apply knowledge of decision-making and other administrative tasks, all of which take place in a dynamic social, economic, and political context. This book provides readers with considerable information, coming from many academic disciplines, relating to human behavior in an organizational and social context.

This text combines in one book the essential knowledge needed to be effective in social work leadership, personal communication, planning, program evaluation, budgeting, fund development, marketing, advocacy, and more—all vital topics of social work leaders in the 21st century.

By providing information related to the context of human services leadership linked to the values and ethics of social work, this book is able to show readers how to assess new trends and developments. Readers will grasp and show leadership across the gamut of human services issues that stand in the way of improving the quality of social services across the United States and internationally. All of these topics and subtopics are addressed in this book in conjunction with the specialty area of administrative practice. Readers learn how to engage others, assess agency- and community-level concerns, intervene when problems occur, and evaluate the impacts of programs, interventions, and policies.

Anyone who completes this book will have an excellent grounding in the nine competencies required by the Council on Social Work Education (CSWE, 2015) within the context of administration and leadership of human services organizations. An instructor who adopts this book will be able to provide students with a clearly enunciated connection to all of the core competencies of social work administrative practice. The program or school of social work that adopts this book may find the reaffirmation process a bit easier.

As We Begin ...

Leadership, administration, and management in the social work and human services arenas depend a great deal on practitioners' ability to begin, cultivate, and maintain meaningful personal relationships with those around them. While it may at times be difficult and full of challenges, we know that the satisfactions and joys of the work are abundant. We present this book to all students of social work leadership—past, present, and future—and to those dedicated social work leaders we have had the pleasure of working with over the years.

Reference List

Au, C. (1994). The status of theory and knowledge development in social welfare administration. *Administration in Social Work, 18*(3), 127–157.

Austin, M. J., & Kruzich, J. M. (2004). Assessing recent textbooks and casebooks in human services administration. *Administration in Social Work, 28*(1), 115–137.

Council on Social Work Education (CSWE). (2015). *2015 educational policies and accreditation standards for baccalaureate and master's social work programs.* Retrieved from https://cswe.org/getattachment/Accreditation/Standards-and-Policies/2015-EPAS/2015EPASandGlossary.pdf.aspx

Council on Social Work Education (CSWE). (2017). *2015 EPAS overview: Accreditation updates and resources.* Retrieved from https://cswe.org/Accreditation/Standards-and-Policies/2015-EPAS

Council on Social Work Education (CSWE). (2018). *Specialized practice curricular guide for macro social work practice: 2015 EPAS curricular guide resource series.* Alexandria, VA: Author.

Hoefer, R. (2010). Basic skills of nonprofit leadership. In K. A. Agard (Ed.), *Leadership in nonprofit organizations: A reference handbook* (pp. 321–328). Thousand Oaks, CA: Sage.

Schmid, H. (2006). Leadership styles and leadership change in human and community service organizations. *Nonprofit Management & Leadership, 17*(2), 179–194.

Image Credits

Fig. 0.1: Adapted from Hillel Schmid, "The 4-Quadrant Model of Social Work Leadership and Management," Nonprofit Management and Leadership, vol. 17, no. 2. Copyright © 2006.

Context

We begin this book by providing you with a view of the territory of social work leadership and management. We want you to see that this field of study does not exist in a vacuum. Environment affects every element of a social work leader's job. As leaders, you need to understand what the forces outside of your organization are, because they influence nearly everything that goes on inside your organization. Chapter 1 builds on the four-quadrant model of social work management work introduced in the preface by discussing one current trend for each quadrant. In this way, we look at the current broader context of social work leadership.

Social work administrators also need to approach their positions with a firm value structure in place. No one in a social work job, including the leaders, managers and supervisors this book is written for, will avoid ethical challenges for long. Decisions that seem clearly wrong when seen at a distance suddenly become more complex when staring at them up close. It is best to have clear ideas based on deep thinking about the sort of person you are and what you believe is right. You must know already where the "bright red line" is that you will not cross. If you are tempted to step over it, you can rely on your calm reflections taken beforehand to help you stop yourself. The point of Chapter 2, which is about values and ethics, is to help you reach that decision point long before it is needed. You will be able to work more effectively and with less stress if you have your mind made up about what you will not do. You will be more able to focus on what you can and will do to help make the world a better place than if you were not prepared. Chapter 2 readies you for the profession of social work by presenting common ethical issues in the realms of leadership, administration, and management.

Chapter 3 presents theories of management. While it may sound daunting, theory is really a choice of how to approach others—are you someone who prefers to pay close attention to everyone's feelings, or do you perhaps believe you must have a tough exterior persona in order to be perceived as "in charge"? These two approaches actually relate to different theories of management. While you may prefer one of them (or one of any number of other theories), what you will learn from Chapter 3 is that you must be familiar with many different understandings of leadership. You must be adept at selecting the correct management approach for each situation that you face. The analogy you can use to understand this is that being a leader is like playing Frisbee golf. Beginning players may use the same ordinary Frisbee they had when they were young for each of the throws. More skillful players, however, have learned about and practiced with different sizes and weights of Frisbees for drives, approaches, and, finally, putts. Having a variety of options (and the skills to use them well) allows the player to match the situation being faced with the techniques and skills required.

As you work through the chapters in this section and the related competency-building exercises, we want you to gain an appreciation of the broad nature of social work leadership and management. As you read this material, you are standing on the leadership mountaintop, seeing the entire landscape. Enjoy the experience and retain this knowledge as you learn more in later sections of the details needed to become proficient in the field of social work administration.

The Context of Social Work Leadership and Administration

The larger context of social work administration must be considered before reading chapters on any other topic. When you think about leadership, your thinking must extend beyond the limits of your program or organization. Just as individuals are affected by their environment, so too are agencies and the individual programs within them. By understanding the "big picture," you will be able to fit your individual knowledge and competencies into a larger framework so that their importance is clearer. Human service agencies operate as part of society, and the natures of the broader culture and trends have considerable impact on what individual nonprofit managers and leaders can accomplish and how they go about their work.

Understanding what is happening in the environment and the context for practice allows social workers of all types to understand how to do their work better, whether it is with individuals, families, groups, organizations or communities. Organizational leaders will be especially able to use their knowledge and understanding to work at a broader level, but everything that influences the organization and community has ramifications for individuals, families, and groups in the community.

Examples of how the environment affects social service agencies are all around us. When the AIDS crisis began, for example, the need for social and support services to those with the disease, nearly all of whom were dying, was paramount. Much of the initial funding came from nongovernmental sources. At length, the federal government provided assistance through discretionary grants. As medical treatments became available and more

effective, services provided became more medical in nature and were funded through entitlement spending programs such as Medicare and Medicaid. Social service agencies saw fewer grant opportunities for nonmedical services, such as prevention, which has been funded at much the same level between 2013 and 2019 (Kaiser Family Foundation, 2019). The decline in AIDS death rates is to be celebrated, of course. The point is that the context changed, funding shifted, and human service agencies in the field had to adapt to these changes.

Another example of contextual change is due to political changes, not medical advances. In this case, services to refugees and immigrants into the United States have been affected by policy changes that cause fewer refugees and immigrants to enter the country. Refugee- and immigrant-serving organizations have found funding streams cut deeply for some services, while those providing assistance to incarcerated people and their children have found more funding available. Some agencies have struggled to balance their devotion to providing services to individuals in need with being associated with policies that many social workers find abhorrent.

Social agency context is not confined to medical and political factors. It is also impacted by changing demographics, shifts in technology, alterations in fundraising patterns, and modifications in communication approaches (among other things). These swirling environmental currents impact human service organizations' ability to provide appropriate and effective services. Social work leaders must constantly be looking at their organization's current situation, as well as doing their best to foresee what is around the corner. Forecasting is important so that agencies can position themselves to take advantage of positive change and blunt the impact of negative shifts.

Change in human service organizations' context is a constant. A decade or two ago, the literature was also full of information about how social work managers needed to be aware of, and deal with, changes in their agencies' worlds. Important issues at that time included managed care (Jones, 2006; McBeath & Meezan, 2006), an uncertain political and economic climate (Golensky & Mulder, 2006; Hopkins & Hyde, 2002; Schmid, 2004), policy reform (Regehr, Chau, Leslie & Howe, 2002; Reisch & Sommerfeld, 2003), requirements for outcome budgeting (Martin, 2000), and the introduction of performance measurement systems (Zimmermann & Stevens, 2006). Most of these topics are still relevant today.

Social work leaders are expected to have more competencies at higher skill levels than in the recent past. Challenges are greater now for human service agencies than ever before (Hopkins & Hyde, 2002; Perlmutter, 2006). The range of skills needed to cope with this difficult environment is also greater than what was needed previously (Golensky & Mulder, 2006). Administrators need to be competent not only at internally oriented

activities, such as budgeting, supervision, and human resources, but also in externally oriented capacities, such as advocacy, community collaboration, and fundraising (Alexander, 2000; Golensky & Mulder, 2006; Hoefer, 2003; Hopkins & Hyde, 2002; Menefee, 2000; Menefee & Thompson, 1994). Increasingly, cross-sector partnerships involving the government, business, and nonprofit sectors are used to achieve progress on social issues (Selsky & Parker, 2005), which shows the need for staying abreast of new topics and skills. One example is the expansion in use of the term *social enterprise*, which has arisen as a way to incorporate for-profit principles into nonprofit operations (Fernando, 2017; Gray, Healy & Crofts, 2003; see Box 1.2 for more information on social enterprise.) Social work leaders must respect and understand how to collaborate with counterparts in other sectors who have different perspectives. The most important skill of all, given the rapidly evolving landscape of human services, may be the ability to manage change.

BOX 1.2 **What is Social Enterprise?**

Social enterprise is a management practice that integrates principles of private enterprise with social-sector goals and objectives. Social enterprise is a relatively new type of social work macro practice and includes a variety of sustainable economic activities designed to yield social impact for individuals, families, and communities. Despite the increased popularity of social enterprise scholarship, social work is visibly absent from it. Social enterprise is a field that promises to harness the energy and enthusiasm of commercial entrepreneurship combined with macro practice to address many long-standing social issues. Despite being a popular practice phenomenon, empirical research on social enterprise is still quite nascent; indeed, only a few empirical articles on the subject have thus far appeared in academic journals, and even fewer in social work journals.

Source: Fernando, R. (2017).

In this chapter, we touch on four current trends that are having the most significant impact on social work leaders and administrators. One trend is listed for each of the four quadrants described in the preface and illustrated in Figure 1.1. After reading about these trends, you will understand better why specific preparation for being an administrator is important and how working through practical exercises and assignments like those in this book will be valuable for your learning process.

Quadrant I: Increasing Importance of Planning

Given the current level of unpredictability in the world of human service organizations, you may wonder if planning makes much sense. When political leaders make decisions that change human services funding on a whim rather than according to thoughtful analysis, what can social work leaders count on? Or when the amount of available philanthropic funding swings wildly, depending on how many natural disasters have occurred recently, how can development plans last more than a month or two? In other words, some might ask "Why bother planning, when nothing is stable or

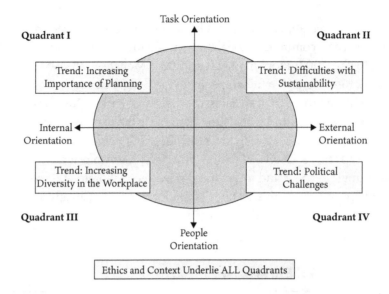

FIGURE 1.1. The Four-Quadrant Leadership Model with Trends

predictable anymore?" As Allison and Kaye (2015) state, "defining the direction and activities of an organization in an ever-changing environment is daunting and can almost seem futile" (p. 2).

Perhaps counterintuitively, the rapid changes we see in the human services world indicate that careful planning is more important than ever. The key words here are "careful planning." Careful strategic planning, for example, focuses on "big questions" and "big issues" that are often stable over longer periods, such as five to 10 years. In fact, some of the big questions have been the same for decades, if not hundreds of years. Examples include, "How do we define social justice?" and "What are the societal problems we most want to work to eliminate?" These questions can never be ultimately answered, but the struggle to seek answers within the current environment is what propels organizations to continue striving.

Most organizations keep the same mission (or something closely aligned) for many years. The American Red Cross's mission statement, for example, is "Prevents and alleviates human suffering in the face of emergencies by mobilizing the power of volunteers and the generosity of donors" (American Red Cross, n.d.). The purpose of strategic planning is not always to change the mission

or vision but to get better at achieving them. If an organization seeks to tackle big problems, they need to put in time and energy to plan their responses. They do this by creating strategic goals and operationalizing them with program planning to achieve measurable desired outcomes. Planning includes creating sets of action steps that translate resources (such as funds, staff and volunteer time, physical space, and so on) into concrete actions that achieve outcomes. Procedures to measure achievements are needed to show how well the agency is doing. Only by doing the work of planning can organizations continue to meet the increasing demands for accountability, the difficulties of sustaining operations, and attacks from political figures.

Planning is more important than ever, because it is the only way to overcome the seeming chaos of the world and the desire to achieve more. When an organization plans, it crafts options (Allison & Kaye, 2015). It may seek to do more of the same things it is currently doing to have a larger impact. Given the constant financial constraints facing human service organizations, simply "doing more by growing bigger" may not be possible. Fortunately, Allison and Kaye provide three alternative ways to have a greater impact:

- Improve processes: do the same work more efficiently, thus achieving more at the same cost;
- Improve design: do the same work with a novel approach to achieve more; and
- Improve strategically: do different things to get better results. (p. 3)

In many ways, planning is more important now than ever because of the other trends we will discuss.

Quadrant II: Difficulties with Sustainability

Put simply, social work administrators operate in an environment of increasingly scarce resources and increased competition for those resources. Funding from government at local, state, and federal levels is strained due to political pressure to lower tax rates (or at least keep them steady, despite inflation). Many states and localities have delayed contracted payments to nonprofit organizations for months, causing those nonprofits to face cash-flow problems and undermining the service providers' fiscal health. Some nonprofits have found that getting a government contract causes more harm than benefit because the amount they are paid is lower than the cost of providing the services required to fulfill the terms of the contract.

Getting a contract or grant is more difficult than ever. While numbers fluctuate depending on the source chosen and years of comparison, there is no dispute that the number of nonprofits has grown. According to McKeever (2019), approximately 1.56 million nonprofits existed in the United States in 2015. This number of nonprofits grew by over 10% between 2005 and 2015. Additionally, a greater number of nonprofits are turning to foundations and government grants for support, even though funding from those sources is unsteady.

Foundation funding has had ups and downs in the past decade, but even in its good years, increases in this type of philanthropy simply cannot equal the amount of funding lost at the governmental level. Research shows that foundation funding accounts for approximately 24% of all philanthropic giving (McGill, 2018). It totaled approximately $69 billion in 2016, an increase over 2015 and an impressive amount, to be sure, but not enough to meet all unmet social services needs. Over half of this amount went to two areas: health (30%) and education (25%), a statistic that has been true since at least the 1960s (McGill, 2018).

A number of subtrends affect individual giving. The economy is a major one, and during the recession of 2007–2009, giving fell. Some rebound occurred as the economy improved, but we are now seeing an impact from an increasing income and wealth divide separating the well-to-do from lower income individuals. Household-level giving has decreased for many nondisaster related human service nonprofits (Bicoy, 2018), although some types of nonprofits have seen individual donations increase in recent years. More generally, a smaller percentage of households are giving at all (in 2008, 56.5% of US households gave to nonreligious institutions, and in 2014, this was down to 47.1% of households), and the average amount of donations by Americans is decreasing (Rooney, 2018). The ability of middle-class, middle-aged donors to give has been impacted by uncertainty over home values, long-term employment situations, and volatility in the value of retirement nest eggs. Increasingly, these families have had increased financial responsibilities toward young adult children and parents with medical and other issues. This "sandwich generation" has been hard-pressed to keep their giving to charity at the same level as in prior years. Nonprofits are thus relying more on wealthy people who are able to give large amounts of funding. Some researchers believe a giving gap is following the wealth gap (Callahan, 2018, Johnson Center at Grand Valley University, 2019).

Concentration in donations can lead to problems, as a more limited set of well-to-do donors, sometimes with clear ideological and policy intentions, control which organizations receive and which do not (Levine, 2019). An increasing number of larger donors put their donations into donor-advised funds, in which they personally influence which entities receive funding rather than leaving it to a more transparent process (Rooney, 2018). Observers anticipate that the growth in donor-advised funds will continue (Forbes Nonprofit Council, 2018; Rooney, 2018).

A final drag on individual giving is the Tax Cuts and Jobs Act of 2018, which decreased taxes and changed the ability of taxpayers to deduct donations to charities. One estimate is that 21 million families will no longer be able to deduct their giving to nonprofits. Economists on both the right and the left believe the change in the tax code will decrease the amount of giving that will occur, although disagreement exists as to the level of decrease that should be expected (Bicoy, 2018).

Another important aspect of the difficulties in sustainability is that evidence-based practice and research/program evaluation are becoming more important to funders and other stakeholders. As the need to compete for resources intensifies, human service agencies must become more effective. One way to accomplish this is to use service technologies that have the research to support their claims of helping solve client problems. The movement toward evidence-based practice, while compelling theoretically, may require culture change within agencies (Johnson & Austin, 2006). As difficult as this is to accomplish, some grant-providing agencies, such as the federal Substance Abuse and Mental Health Services Administration (SAMHSA), provide strong incentives and greater funding opportunities for agencies willing to use program models that have been tested empirically and have evidence of effectiveness. Interventions that have received research validation are listed by the Evidence-based Practices Resource Center (available online at https://www.samhsa.gov/ebp-resource-center). Additional reviews of evidence-based social work practice are located on the website for the Campbell Collaboration (https://www.campbellcollaboration.org/) and elsewhere.

Similarly, program evaluation within agencies is usually required as a condition of receiving a grant. Agencies struggle with how to cope with such demands, having neither the staff time nor the knowledge base to analyze the data they collect (Stoecker, 2007). Performance measurement, within the context of program evaluation and accountability, is a salient example of the need for additional research skills for nonprofit managers (Zimmermann & Stevens, 2006). Salipante and Aram (2003) argue that nonprofit managers must move beyond being *users* of knowledge to becoming *generators* of knowledge. Education for nonprofit administration should stress the ability to collect, manage, and analyze data to make management decisions.

Quadrant III: Increasing Diversity in the Workplace

Considerable attention has been given to the decreasing percentage of people in the United States who are of European ancestry and the increasing percentage of people from Hispanic, African American, and Asian backgrounds. For example, half the growth in the American population from 1990 to 2010 (30 million people) was among Hispanics (El Nasser & Overberg, 2011). Hispanics now account for about one in six of all Americans and have had larger numbers than African Americans since 2003. The Asian population doubled between 1990 and 2010 and now comprises nearly 5% of Americans. Of considerable importance over the long term is the increase in the number of people who identify as multiracial, a category available on the U.S. Census since only 2010 (El Nasser & Overberg, 2011).

This type of diversity, racial and ethnic, is extremely important for the running of non-profits, particularly in terms of leadership style. But other types of diversity exist as well and need to be included when we think about the topic (Kozan, 2019). Women in the age range of 25–29 are more likely than before to have earned a baccalaureate degree or higher, regardless of race, and have been for at least a decade (Semuels, 2017). They should thus be expected to occupy more top leadership positions in the nonprofit sector (and elsewhere). Unfortunately, not only are women seriously underrepresented in the leadership of nonprofits (particularly large ones), but when they are promoted, they are paid less (Alexander, 2017). The debates about "male" and "female" styles of leadership have softened over the past few decades, with a consensus emerging that leaders must have a variety of skills, including those skills historically seen as male traits, such as financial shrewdness, and those traits historically seen as female, such as listening and nurturing.

Human service organization leaders are also challenged to be able to relate to differences between younger workers (Generations X and Y, Millennials, and so on) and their older counterparts (members of the Boomer and Bust generations). Maintaining relationships is important not only within the organization, in terms of supervision and leadership styles, but also among donors. For example, gay, lesbian, bisexual, and transgendered persons have distinct viewpoints about many human services issues, and their communities often are strong stakeholders of and donors to certain types of nonprofits (Dale, 2018).

This type of discussion can often seem as if diversity were a problem, when in fact, it is definitely a positive aspect of today's nonprofit workforce! The range of ideas and experiences in the workplace may now be broader than at any other time in history. Still, having a larger variety of people in the workplace is an issue that must be addressed and sometimes "managed" so that various stakeholder groups, with their unique perspectives, see value in the differences that can sometimes cause misunderstanding or even conflict. One way to remove at least some of the unconscious bias in the hiring process may be to use artificial intelligence to screen applications, though this process is not without pitfalls of its own (Biswas, 2018). Another approach is to ensure that the leadership within social work nonprofits is reflective of the larger society, especially the stakeholders of an agency, including the local community, staff, clients, and other supporters.

Quadrant IV: Political Challenges

Nonprofit social service organizations tend to want to avoid becoming deeply involved in partisan battles and instead to build bridges to government officials and other stakeholders regardless of their political affiliation. Social work leaders may privately agree with the policy direction of Democrats and disagree with those of Republicans, but they, like all social workers, must start

where the client is. Given that the political party of the moment may be out as soon as the next election, wisdom dictates avoiding making enemies of the "other" party. This standard advice is generally good, but what happens when one party becomes antagonistic to the very core of the social work profession?

Political polarization now seems to be a fact of life in the United States, with less overlap in policy positions between Republicans and Democrats, making compromise less achievable. Some elements of the Republican party are hostile to human services programs that vulnerable populations depend on for their life and livelihoods. Programs such as Social Security, Medicare, Food Stamps, housing assistance, and direct cash payments have been targeted for decreases in support (Stein, 2017). Legal asylum seekers have been vilified as a group by a Republican president who is supported by large numbers of elected officials. On the other hand, Democrats tend to support the social-work-held position of keeping abortion rights legal, a position at odds with the religious views of many people, including social workers. Some agencies end up on different sides of the political spectrum depending on the issue being discussed. Catholic Charities, for example, provides considerable assistance to refugees but is also against abortion (Catholic Charities, n.d.). Secular agencies can face similar conflicts. How do social work leaders operate ethically in such environments, balancing their sense of ethical behavior and policy with the demands to promote the interests of their organizations?

The Importance of Education for Leaders and Administrators

All of these trends influence the ability of social work leaders to achieve high results. Yet research tells us it is important for nonprofit administrators to perform well. Poertner's (2006) literature review links higher social administration skills with better client outcomes. Ritchie and Eastwood (2006) show that a nonprofit's financial performance is improved if its executives have appropriate experience. In short, supervisors, managers, and leaders clearly have tangible and lasting effects on their organizations and, ultimately, clients' lives. A well-led organization will achieve more, and at higher levels, than an organization with poor leadership. It is up to the future leaders themselves to learn and apply the necessary skills to their jobs, but this process can be made easier if supported by well-designed educational programs. We believe that students need to learn from experiential cases and assignments that take them beyond the classroom, in addition to learning from lectures, books, videos, discussions, and other means. That is why we put this book together—to provide information (supplemental to other sources), along with exercises, assignments, and recommendations for additional resources for learning. This book will help you become more competent as social work leaders and administrators, and we invite you to join the ranks of the profession in those capacities.

Conclusion

This chapter highlights four trends that are shaping the world of human services administrators and leaders. Each is a challenge to handle on its own, but in combination, they can become overwhelming. These trends are evolving and will never be truly "solved" in a permanent way. We believe that only skilled practitioners, armed with ethics, theory, knowledge, and experience, have a chance to deal with their repercussions successfully. This book is our effort to bring insight and experiential learning to the classroom by focusing on practical application of concepts and developing competency for readers to meet their needs and goals.

The trends identified in this chapter (the increasing need for planning, difficulties in remaining sustainable, diversity in staff members and clientele, and political challenges) must not be examined in isolation, because a nonprofit executive does not face these trends sequentially—rather, they come forward simultaneously, with varying strength, each day. As difficult as the job of a social work leader may be, it is also extremely rewarding. Prepared with commitment to clients, appropriate job competencies, practical experience, and the will to move forward, social work leaders make an important difference in their organizations and communities every day.

Reference List

Alexander, J. (2000). Adaptive strategies of nonprofit human service organizations in an era of devolution and new public management. *Nonprofit Management & Leadership, 10*(3), 287–303.

Alexander, L. B. (2017, September 6). Why women are still underrepresented in nonprofit leadership and what we can do about it. Retrieved from Nonprofit HR website: https://www.nonprofithr.com/women-underrepresented-nonprofit-leadership/

Allison, M., & Kaye, J. (2015). *Strategic planning for nonprofit organizations: A practical guide for dynamic times.* New York, NY: John Wiley & Sons.

American Red Cross. (n.d.). Mission statement. Retrieved from https://www.redcross.org/about-us/who we are/mission-and-values.html

Bicoy, B. (2018, Sep. 7). Commentary: The impending decline of charitable giving. *Peninsula Pulse.* Retrieved from https://doorcountypulse.com/commentary-the-impending-decline-in-charitable-giving/

Biswas, S. (2018, October 12). Can Artificial Intelligence eliminate bias in hiring? *HR Technologist.* Retrieved from https://www.hrtechnologist.com/articles/recruitment-onboarding/can-artificial-intelligence-eliminate-bias-in-hiring/

Callahan, D. (2018, January 7). Philanthropy forecast 2018: Trends and issues to watch. *Inside Philanthropy.* Retrieved from https://www.insidephilanthropy.com/home/2018/1/7/philanthropy-forecast

Catholic Charities. (n.d.). Catholic Charities is committed to helping immigrants & refugees. Retrieved from https://www.catholiccharitiesusa.org/our-ministry/immigration-refugee-services/

Dale, E. J. (2018). Financial management and charitable giving in gay and lesbian households. *Nonprofit and Voluntary Sector Quarterly, 47*(4), 836–855. doi:10.1177/0899764018768715

El Nasser, H., & Overberg, P. (2011, August 10). Census tracks 20 years of sweeping change. *USA Today.* Retrieved from http://usatoday30.usatoday.com/news/nation/census/2011-08-10-census-20 -years-change_n.htm

Fernando, R. (2017). Social enterprise. In C. Franklin (Ed.), *Encyclopedia of social work* (Online ed.). Retrieved from https://oxfordre.com/socialwork/view/10.1093/acrefore/9780199975839.001 .0001/acrefore-9780199975839-e-1027

Forbes Nonprofit Council. (2018, December 27). *Seven trends that may impact charitable giving in 2019.* Retrieved from https://www.forbes.com/sites/forbesnonprofitcouncil/2018/12/27/seven-trends-that-may-impact-charitable-giving-in-2019/#4c017ae7148e

Golensky, M., & Mulder, C. A. (2006). Coping in a constrained economy: Survival strategies of nonprofit human service organizations. *Administration in Social Work, 30*(3), 5–24.

Gray, M., Healy, K., & Crofts, P. (2003). Social enterprise: Is it the business of social work? *Australian Social Work, 56*(2), 141–154.

Hoefer, R. (2003). Administrative skills and degrees: The "best place" debate rages on. *Administration in Social Work, 27*(1), 25–46.

Hopkins, K. M., & Hyde, C. (2002). The human service managerial dilemma: New expectations, chronic challenges and old solutions. *Administration in Social Work, 26*(3), 1–15.

Johnson Center at Grand Valley University. (2019, January 15). *11 trends in philanthropy for 2019: Anticipate and embrace what's coming next.* Retrieved from http://johnsoncenter.org/11-trends-for-2019/

Johnson, M., & Austin, M. J. (2006). Evidence-based practice in the social services: Implications for organizational change. *Administration in Social Work, 30*(3), 75–104.

Jones, J. M. (2006). Understanding environmental influence on human service organizations: A study of the influence of managed care on child caring institutions. *Administration in Social Work, 30*(4), 63–90.

Kaiser Family Foundation. (2019, March 5). *US federal funding for HIV/AIDS: Trends over time.* Retrieved from https://www.kff.org/hivaids/fact-sheet/u-s-federal-funding-for-hivaids-trends-over-time/

Kozan, K. (2019, February 13). 6 best workplace diversity trends for 2019 [Web log post]. Retrieved from https://ideal.com/workplace-diversity-trends/

Levine, M. (2019, March 12). Saying "no" to donor demands should be a core competency. *Nonprofit Quarterly*. Retrieved from https://nonprofitquarterly.org/2019/03/12/saying-no-to-donor-demands-should-be-a-core-competency/?utm_source=Weekly+Newsletter+%28Most+Popular+of+the+Week%29&utm_campaign=ad7fd049ab-EMAIL_CAMPAIGN_2018_06_01_03_21_COPY_01&utm_medium=email&utm_term=0_eab3e5d534-ad7fd049ab-12832169&mc_cid=ad7fd049ab&mc_eid=2e9fc66ac2

Martin, L. L. (2000). Budgeting for outcomes in state human agencies. *Administration in Social Work, 24*(3), 71–88.

McBeath, B., & Meezan, W. (2006). Nonprofit adaptation to performance-based, managed care contracting in Michigan's foster care system. *Administration in Social Work, 30*(2), 39–70.

McGill, L. (2018, October 29). Current trends in philanthropy: The big picture [Web log post]. Retrieved from https://pndblog.typepad.com/pndblog/2018/10/current-trends-in-philanthropy-the-big-picture.html

McKeever, B. (2019, January 3). *The nonprofit sector in brief.* Retrieved from Urban Institute, National Center for Charitable Statistics website: https://nccs.urban.org/project/nonprofit-sector-brief

Menefee, D. (2000). What managers do and why they do it. In R. J. Patti (Ed.), *The handbook of social welfare management* (pp. 247–266). Thousand Oaks, CA: Sage.

Menefee, D. T., & Thompson, J. J. (1994). Identifying and comparing competencies for social work management: A practice driven approach. *Administration in Social Work, 18*(3), 1–25.

Perlmutter, F. D. (2006). Ensuring social work administration. *Administration in Social Work, 30*(2), 3–10.

Poertner, J. (2006). Social administration and outcomes for consumers: What do we know? *Administration in Social Work, 30*(2), 11–24.

Regehr, C., Chau, S., Leslie, B., & Howe, P. (2002). An exploration of supervisor's and manager's responses to child welfare reform. *Administration in Social Work, 26*(3), 17–36.

Reisch, M., & Sommerfeld, D. (2003). Welfare reform and the future of nonprofit organizations. *Nonprofit Management & Leadership, 14*(1), 19–46.

Ritchie, W. J., & Eastwood, K. (2006). Executive functional experience and its relationship to the financial performance of nonprofit organizations. *Nonprofit Management & Leadership, 17*(1), 67–82.

Rooney, P. M. (2018, November 21). The growth in total household giving is camouflaging a decline in giving by small and medium donors. What can we do about it? *Nonprofit Quarterly*. Retrieved from https://nonprofitquarterly.org/2018/11/21/total-household-growth-decline-small-medium-donors/

Salipante, P., & Aram, J. D. (2003). Managers as knowledge generators: The nature of practitioner-scholar research in the nonprofit sector. *Nonprofit Management Leadership, 14*(2), 129–150.

Schmid, H. (2004). Organization-environment relationships: Theory for management practice in human service organizations. *Administration in Social Work, 28*(1), 97–113.

Selsky, J. W., & Parker, B. (2005). Cross-sector partnerships to address social issues: Challenges to theory and practice. *Journal of Management, 31*(6), 849–873.

Semuels, A. (2017, November 27). Poor girls are leaving their brothers behind. *The Atlantic*. Retrieved from https://www.theatlantic.com/business/archive/2017/11/gender-education-gap/546677/

Stein, J. (2017, December 6). Republican officials say targeting welfare programs will help spur economic growth. *The Washington Post*. Retrieved from https://www.washingtonpost.com/news/wonk/wp/2017/12/06/house-republicans-welfare-restrictions-are-needed-for-the-economy-to-grow/?utm_term=.95d3349166ec

Stoecker, R. (2007). The research practices and needs of non-profit organizations in an urban center. *Journal of Sociology and Social Welfare, 34*(4), 97–119.

Zimmermann, J. M., & Stevens, B. W. (2006). The use of performance measurement in South Carolina nonprofits. *Nonprofit Management & Leadership, 16*(3), 315–327.

Additional Resources

Council on Social Work Education (CSWE). (2018). *Envisioning the future of social work: Report of the CSWE Futures Task Force.* Washington, DC: Council on Social Work Education. Retrieved from https://www.cswe.org/About-CSWE/Governance/Board-of-Directors/2018-19-Strategic-Planning-Process/CSWE-FTF-Four-Futures-for-Social-Work-FINAL-2.aspx

Germak, A. J., & Singh, K. K. (2009). Social entrepreneurship: Changing the way social workers do business. *Administration in Social Work, 34*(1), 79–95.

Social Enterprise Alliance. (n.d.). *What's a social enterprise?* (https://www.se-alliance.org/what-is-social-enterprise)

Wareing, T. & Hendrick, H. H. (2013). Toward the next frontier: Trends driving the future of human services. *Policy & Practice, 71*(1), 10–13, 37.

HELPFUL TERMS

Artificial Intelligence—the ability of computers to imitate intelligent human behavior, such as to locate patterns in data, screen resumes, and adapt to changing conditions.

Competency-based education—an approach to education that emphasizes student outcomes, that is, that graduates should know how to perform tasks well. This approach to education contrasts with that focusing on the inputs of the education process, such as number of teachers, amount spent per student, and so on.

Council on Social Work Education (CSWE)—the sole accrediting body for social work programs in the United States, which sets and maintains educational standards at the bachelors and masters levels.

Evidence-based practice—a (controversial) movement within social work to more closely tie interventions to a scientific research base to ensure that the practices are effective in achieving positive and anticipated client outcomes.

Foundation—an organization that has been established according to law to receive donations and to disburse funds in accordance with its founding documents. There are several different types of foundations, such as corporate foundations, family foundations, and community foundations.

Government grant—funding provided by local, state, and federal government agencies to nonprofits to achieve certain purposes, such as decreasing homelessness or preventing the transmission of HIV/AIDS. Nonprofits compete to receive these awards.

Individual giving—donations of money to charities by individuals and families. This category does not include donations by corporations or foundations.

Program evaluation—a type of applied research that determines the ability of a program to achieve its stated goals. Program evaluation is often divided into process evaluation, which evaluates how well the program operates and was implemented, and outcome evaluation, which examines the extent to which program goals were achieved.

Social enterprise—"a management practice that integrates principles of private enterprise with social-sector goals and objectives. (*Fernando, R., 2017*).

Stakeholder—any person or group of persons or organization that has an interest in the workings and activities of an organization. Examples of stakeholders for nonprofit organizations include funders, clients, staff members, and the general public.

Workplace diversity—"understanding, accepting, and valuing differences between people of different races, ethnicities, genders, ages, religions, disabilities, and sexual orientations, as well as differences in personalities, skill sets, experiences, and knowledge bases" (Kozan, 2019).

EXERCISES

1. In-Basket Exercise

Directions

You are Oscar Cervantes, director of planning at a United Way. . Read the following memo from your boss, Jaylynn Banks, the CEO of your United Way. She is asking you to provide her with information so she can be a panelist at a roundtable discussion attended by many of your community's movers and shakers. She wants a page of talking points, a backup memo of three to five pages, and an oral briefing from you on the answers you have developed. Additional details are in the memo. [NOTE: for the purposes of this exercise, find real information about the area where you actually live.]

> **Memo**
>
> Date: August 21, 20XX
>
> To: Oscar Cervantes, Director of Planning
>
> From: Jaylynn Banks, CEO, United Way of Metropolitan Gotham
>
> Subject: Roundtable Presentation
>
> I have been asked to be part of a roundtable presentation at a local University in two weeks' time. The topic is "Current Context and Future Possibilities for Nonprofits."
>
> I am simply too busy to do the necessary preparation for such a roundtable, but all the heavy hitters in the funding, business, and civic sectors of our city will be there, so I need to do this.
>
> I need your help. Below are the questions that will be asked of each panelist. I need you and your team to come up with answers relating to our community.
>
> 1. How has the recent (last two to three years) economic situation affected the nonprofit sector here?
>
> 2. What does the near-term (five years) future funding picture look like for nonprofits in general in our community?
>
> 3. What feasible policy changes would have the most positive or negative impacts on nonprofits?

I know this isn't much time to prepare, but you and your team work with these types of questions all the time, so I know I can count on you for an oral briefing, talking points, and three to five pages of background information so that I can represent the United Way well.

2. Become a Nonprofit Futurist

In ancient times and up to now, people who claim to know what is going to happen can influence others (and make a very good living at it!). The purpose of this exercise is to make yourself an expert in one aspect of the future context of human service agencies.

Examine the history of one aspect of the nonprofit sector in your community. This may be an area of practice, such as child welfare, health, the arts, or any other part of the nonprofit world in your area. Or you may wish to predict the future of something else, such as the effect of global climate change on the nonprofit sector where you live. Those with a political perspective might wish to address a subject such as "Nonprofits in a Right-wing (or Left-wing) Political Environment." Think carefully about the trajectory and possible future of your chosen subject.

After choosing your topic, prepare three scenarios as to what will happen in the next five years, writing each up in no more than two to three pages. Make one scenario purposely gloomy, another particularly positive, and the third representing what you think will be the most likely future. Be prepared to present your thoughts to others in your class or at work to get their reaction to your predictions.

3. Host a Roundtable Discussion

In order to gain additional insight, you can connect with local nonprofit leaders to learn their views about the current context and future of nonprofits in your community.

One way to do this is to invite three or four current or past nonprofit leaders from your community together for a roundtable discussion. They may be from similar or varied parts of the nonprofit world, including human services, arts, museums, or others, depending on your community. This could be done several times in a semester, with different leaders. You may wish to send them a set of questions that will be asked so they may prepare answers, although you may also wish to have a mix of prepared questions and "pop" questions that emerge from the conversation. It would be a plus if this panel discussion could be filmed and even posted to the web (only with signed releases from the participants, of course).

ASSIGNMENTS

1. One task of nonprofit managers is to gather additional information on topics important to their organization. This assignment asks you to "curate" information for yourself and others in your class or group. Be willing to post the results of these assignments to a class or group wiki or other method of dissemination.

   a. Find two or three blogs that address topics of interest to the nonprofit sector. Look over their posts of the past few months. What do they discuss that supports, supplements, or contradicts what is discussed in this chapter? What evidence do the blog posters provide?

    b.   If possible, post to one of the blogs a comment on something you've found interesting from this chapter or from your own thoughts. What type of response do you get from the blog author and others who read it?

2.   Search through academic literature databases or other locations to find two to three articles that describe trends affecting the nonprofit sector. Compare the trends you find with those found by others in your class or group. Which are mentioned often, and which are spotted only once or twice? Select one of the most commonly mentioned and one of the least mentioned trends to discuss with your colleagues in class or at your work or internship. What thoughts do others have about these trends and their importance?

3.   Choose one of the trends you've identified or read about. Prepare a one-minute oral presentation to share with your class or another group. It is best to be able to present this conversationally and without notes, as if you were in a meeting where it is important for others to know this information because of its impact on your organization.

Image Credits

2

Values and Ethics in Administration

To be a successful social work administrator, you must have knowledge in many different areas of administration. These areas of needed expertise include knowledge of the political and economic dimensions of social services administration coupled with the leadership skills necessary to move an organization forward. You will also need to know and understand different theories of administration, as well as practical skills, such as governance strategies, employee relations, supervision, management strategies, and agency–environment relations. However, all of these skills and expertise are not enough to be a successful administrator. As an administrator, you must also have skills in recognizing and dealing with ethical issues and questions. An administrator must understand the ethical issues and dilemmas of administration and be able to analyze situations using moral reasoning and decision-making strategies. Ethical risk management is a way to avoid complaints and even possible lawsuits. It is vitally important to practice in a manner that engenders trust and respect for the institution that you have been entrusted to administer and also strengthens the public trust in human services. As you learned earlier, there are nine competencies that every social work administrator should demonstrate. This chapter outlines the competencies related to values and ethics.

Values, ethics, and professional behavior are part of everything social work administrators and leaders do. This chapter provides the foundation of all the skills outlined in the following chapters, and ethical practices are highlighted throughout this book.

Making Ethical Decisions

Social work administrators make ethical decisions by applying the standards of the National Association of Social Workers (NASW) Code of Ethics, relevant laws and regulations, models for ethical decision-making, ethical conduct of research, and additional codes of ethics as appropriate to context. Before examining the social work code of ethics and codes of ethics from other disciplines, it is important to understand the nature of ethical dilemmas you will face and the theoretical basis that informs the development of professional codes of ethics. In this section, you will learn the competencies required of social work administrators, learn how to recognize an ethical dilemma, examine classical theories of ethics, and review several major codes of ethics that guide administrators. Finally, you will learn how to apply a model of ethical decision-making and understand the connection between ethical practice and public trust.

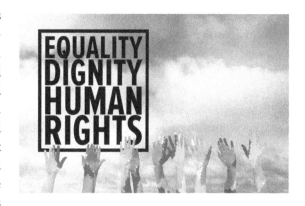

Ethical Dilemmas

An ethical dilemma "is that situation in which an action is required that reflects only one of two values or principles that are in opposition to one another" (Beckerman, 1997, p. 6). Ethical dilemmas arise when administrators must make decisions of conflicting ethical responsibility. For example, think about decisions that must be made about the use of agency resources. If you are facing budget cutbacks, how do you decide how to use the funds available? Do you use the remaining resources to help as many people as possible before the money runs out, or do you use the limited resources to help those most in need over a longer time period (Reamer, 2000)? Both directions are admirable. It is good to want to help as many people as possible with the resources of the organization, but there is also a strong case to be made that resources should be directed to those with the most need.

Classical Theories of Ethics

For you to develop a framework for ethical decision-making, it is important that you have a basic understanding of the theories of ethics. As you will learn in Chapter 3, theories are the lens through which we view the world and, in this case, how we make ethical administrative decisions. Two classical approaches to ethics are the *deontological* theories and the *teleological* theories: "Deontological ethics are ethics of duty or principle, while teleological ethics are ethics of results or consequences" (Chandler, 2001, p. 179).

Deontological Theories

Deontological theories claim that certain actions or behaviors are inherently right or wrong and that actions are either good or evil. These theories are based on the idea that there are higher-order principles. From a religious standpoint, this approach is based on the belief that God has determined what is right and what is wrong.

Teleological Theories

Teleological theories assume that individuals faced with an ethical dilemma should measure the moral rightness of their actions based on the moral goodness of the consequences. In other words, one should act in a manner that produces the most favorable outcome. Fox (1994) described this set of theories as being based on the idea that the ends justify the means. Teleological theories are based on the belief that decisions should be made that will do the most good and impose the least harm. It is the result that is important, regardless of any inherent right or wrong, as proposed in deontological theories.

Utilitarianism

Utilitarianism is a subset of the teleological theories. This approach holds that the proper actions are those that promote the greatest good for the greatest number in society (Solomon, 1992). Two applications of utilitarianism are *act utilitarianism* and *rule utilitarianism* (Mill & Gorovitz, 1971). In *act utilitarianism*, the rightness of an action is determined by the goodness of its consequences in

that individual case. This approach would look only at the individual case at hand and would not be concerned with its impact on other cases. In contrast, *rule utilitarianism* requires one to anticipate long-term consequences and act accordingly in all similar situations (Grobman, 2011). Think about the implications of these two approaches from the standpoint of a social work administrator. Can you make a decision based only on the situation at hand, or must you consider that you will need to apply the decision to future similar cases that will arise? Will your decision in one instance set a precedent for future cases?

Three Core Concepts of Ethics

More recent theories focus on the core concepts of ethical behavior. Denhardt (1991) outlines three core concepts of ethical behavior: honor, benevolence, and justice. *Honor* is defined as adherence to the highest standards of responsibility, integrity, and principle and denotes a quality of character in which the individual exhibits a high sense of duty, pursuing good deeds as ends in themselves, not because of any benefit or recognition that might be accrued because of the deeds. *Benevolence* is the disposition to do good and to promote the welfare of others and implies not only actions that promote good and the welfare of others but also motivation to pursue those ends. *Justice* signifies fairness and regard for the rights of others, which includes, most fundamentally, respect for the dignity and worth of each individual. Justice further involves a commitment to developing and preserving rights for individuals that will ensure that their dignity and worth will not be violated by others in society.

Codes of Ethics

Codes of ethics are systematic efforts to define acceptable conduct (Plant, 1994). Many professions have codes of ethics, and they range from being very general to very specific and prescriptive. Human service administrators come from a variety of disciplines and backgrounds, but their individual codes of ethics are often very similar. If you think about it, this is not surprising, since codes of ethics are based on many of the theories, concepts, and principles outlined above.

Three of the most common degrees held by administrators are Master of Social Work (MSW), Master of Business Administration (MBA), and Master of Public Administration (MPA). Look at the codes of ethics (or oaths) of each of these and see how they are similar and how they are different. In the "Resources" section at the end of this chapter, there are links to each code discussed in the following sections.

Social Work Administrators (MSW)

Social work administrators are guided by the NASW Code of Ethics. The current edition of the NASW Code of Ethics includes four major sections: Preamble, Purpose of the Code, Ethical Principles, and Ethical Standards. The NASW Code of Ethics (2017) is included in this book as Appendix A, and a link to the code is provided in the additional resources section at the end of this chapter. The current code of ethics includes new and expanded standards for social work administrators. Social work administrators are to advocate within and outside their agencies for adequate resources to meet clients' needs and provide appropriate staff supervision; they must also promote resource allocation procedures that are open and fair. A major requirement of standards is that the administrator ensures that the working environment for which they are responsible is consistent with and encourages compliance with the NASW Code of Ethics, and they should provide or arrange for continuing education and staff development for all staff for whom they are responsible (Reamer, 2018). Look at the preamble, purpose, and principles in the code and think about how the code can be a guide to you as a social work administrator.

Codes of Ethics in Other Disciplines

As a social work administrator, you will work in collaboration with administrators from other disciplines that operate under different codes of ethics. It is also probable that you will have staff members from other disciplines that have their own codes. A competency required for social work administrators is to understand the role of other professions when engaged in interprofessional teams. If you are a social worker, it is important to remember that your primary obligation is to work within the framework of the NASW Code of Ethics (NASW, 2017). In this section, we will examine the codes of two of the most common disciplines engaged in human services administration: MBA administrators and MPA administrators. We will then turn to several other disciplines often involved in the direct delivery of services and, sometimes, the administration of those services.

MBA Administrators

There is not a standard code of ethics for administrators holding an MBA degree. However, even though there is not a formalized code of ethics, there have been attempts to move toward a standard of ethical conduct by the development of an "oath." The mission for the oath is to facilitate a widespread movement of MBAs who aim to lead in the interests of the greater good and who have committed to living out the principles articulated in the oath. The oath is a voluntary pledge for graduating and current MBAs to create value for responsibly and ethically based practice. Those supporting the oath have formed a coalition of MBA students, graduates, and advisors. Over 10,000 students representing more than 100 schools around the world have taken the MBA Oath, creating a community of MBAs with a shared standard for ethical and professional behavior. See additional resources at the end of this chapter for links to the MBA Oath.

MPA Administrators

The code of ethics for the American Society for Public Administration (ASPA) calls for administrators to serve the public interest, respect the constitution and the law, demonstrate personal integrity, promote ethical organizations, and strive for professional excellence. See additional resources at the end of this chapter for links to the ASPA Code of Ethics.

Other Professions and Their Codes

Of course, there are also professionals from many other disciplines that hold positions as administrators in human service organizations. Different fields of service seem to attract administrators from different professions. It is impossible to cover all the different professions and their codes of ethics, but the following studies of ethical codes has implications for human services administration regardless of the area of practice.

In a study of adoption services, Babb (1998) "identified the professions most often involved in this area of practice, such as social work, law, medicine, nursing, and mental health, including psychology, counseling, and marriage and family therapy" (p. 124). The codes of ethics of these groups have major implications in the provision of services and in protecting the rights of clients. In reviewing the codes of these professional groups and surveying 75 organizations, Babb found that shared standards for ethical practices could be identified and categorized. Shared standards were found in the areas of the professional's role in society, client–employee relations, nondiscrimination, diligence and due care, communication, objectivity and independence, fees, what constitutes the best interest of the child, contract relationships, and some aspects of confidentiality. The overlapping principles in professional groups are significant and, in many ways, very reassuring. There is a great deal of commonality when evaluating ethical practice as it relates to providing human services.

Watson and Cobb (2012), building on the work of Babb, examined the codes of ethics for each of these groups in more detail. For social workers, the basic ethical standards are prescribed by the NASW (2017). These ethical principles are based on social work's core values of service, social justice, importance of human relationships, integrity, competence, and the dignity and worth of human beings. Similarly, the guiding principles for psychologists include beneficence and nonmaleficence, fidelity and responsibility, integrity, justice, and respect for people's rights and dignity (American Psychological Association, 2010). A fundamental principle that underlies all nursing practice is respect for the inherent worth and dignity of patients and the human rights of every individual. Furthermore, nurses take into account the needs and values of all persons in all professional relationships (American Nurses Association, 2011). The American Counseling Association's (2005) code of ethics asserts that responsible professional counselors should advocate for clients' access to services at the individual, group, institutional, and societal levels. They also should examine potential barriers and obstacles to clients' growth and development. Marriage and family therapists' code of ethics calls for respect for the rights of clients to make decisions and understand the consequences of these decisions, including cohabitation, marriage,

divorce, separation, reconciliation, custody, and visitation (American Association for Marriage and Family Therapy, 2001). Regardless of the affiliation of the major professions involved in the administration of human services, adequate guidance exists for ethical practice in social work.

It is reassuring to know that there is a great deal of overlap in the codes of ethics of professions most often involved in human services. However, as social workers and social work administrators, we function under a code of ethics that is much more detailed and specific than the codes of most other professions. While we are obligated to respect and understand the ethics of other professions, our primary duty and responsibility is to uphold and practice within the bounds of the NASW Code of Ethics.

Aspirational Ethics

Whereas professional codes of ethics detail the basic standards of behavior, some codes express aspirational goals for higher levels of ethical standards. For example, the social work code describes professional behavior as behavior to which all professionals should aspire. Corey, Corey, and Callanan (2003) suggested that all professional groups should look beyond their codes of ethics and endorse the larger issue of aspirational ethics that describe the highest level of ethical functioning and do more than just meet the letter of the ethics code. Candilis and Martinez (2006) affirmed aspirational ideals as "a higher standard for professionals than any minimalist legal requirements. Aspirational ethics are concerned with what the profession ought to be" (p. 244). They conceptualize the professional duty as providing a "structurally stabilizing, morally protective presence" (p. 244). Many ethicists point to Aristotle's emphasis on the "ultimate good" as a principle to which professionals should aspire (Souryal, 1992).

Reamer (2000, p. 76) presents Solomon's (1992) assertion that administrative actions should be based on six core values from Aristotle's writings:

1. Community: "We are, first of all, members of organized groups, with shared histories and established practices governing everything from eating and working to worshiping" (Solomon, 1992, p. 146).
2. Excellence: "It is a word of great significance and indicates a sense of mission to a commitment beyond profit potential and the bottom line. It is a word that suggests 'doing well' but also 'doing good'" (Solomon, 1992, p. 153).
3. Membership: "The idea that an employee or executive develops his or her personal identity largely through the organizations in which he or she spends most of their adult waking life" (Solomon, 1992, p. 161).
4. Integrity: "Integrity is essentially *moral courage,* the will and willingness to do what one knows one ought to do" (Solomon, 1992, p. 168).
5. Judgment: "Aristotle thought that it was 'good judgment' or *phronesis* that was of the greatest importance in ethics" (Solomon, 1992, p. 174).
6. Holism: "The ultimate aim of the Aristotelian approach to business is to cultivate whole human beings, not jungle fighters, efficiency automatons, or 'good soldiers' … But one of the problems of traditional business thinking is our tendency to isolate our business or professional roles from the rest of our lives" (Solomon, 1992, p. 180).

According to Solomon, these six values "form an integrative structure in which the individual, the corporation, and the community, self-interest and the public good, the personal and the professional business and virtues all work together instead of against one another" (p. 145).

A Model of Ethical Decision-Making

There is no one model to guide administrators in making ethical decisions. From the material presented above, you can see that there are many different views to determine what is "ethi-

cal." Cottone and Clause (2000) conducted a comprehensive review of the literature on ethical decision-making models from the counseling profession. They found the literature rich with decision-making models, but few had been assessed empirically. There was a great deal of consistency across the models. Using several of the models presented and borrowing heavily from the model presented by Forester-Miller and Davis (1996), we present the following model as a starting place for you as you develop your own model of ethical decision-making:

1. Identify the problem. What are the facts, as opposed to the assumptions, suspicions, or rumors? Is it a legal problem? Do you need to seek legal advice or involve law enforcement?

2. Apply the code of ethics of your professional association. Be clear about your professional obligations, and be sure that you are upholding the principles of your organization. Be sure you truly understand your code of ethics. Seek consultation from your professional organization if you need help interpreting your specific code of ethics.

3. What is the nature of the ethical dilemma? Is it in fact a dilemma, or is it so clear-cut that there are not competing values? Remember that an ethical dilemma "is that situation in which an action is required that reflects only one of two values or principles that are in opposition to one another" (Beckerman, 1997, p. 6). If there is not an ethical dilemma, you can move forward and make the decision that the situation demands.

4. Generate several scenarios of potential decisions. What are all the different decisions that you might make? Consult with a colleague if you can do so without violating confidentiality of the people involved.

5. Consider the potential consequences of all the options and determine a course of action. What will the impact of your decision be on the individuals involved, on the people you serve, on the organization, and on the community? What will the impact be on you and your career? Would you be willing to make the obvious ethical decision (or refuse to make an obviously unethical decision) if it meant you would lose your job?

6. Choose the course of action and evaluate it. Stadler (1986) proposes several questions to evaluate the chosen course of action. Is it just? Does it meet the standard of your own sense of fairness? Would you expect to be treated the same way in the same situation? How would your action look if reported on the six o'clock news or on the front page of the newspaper? Finally, would you recommend the same action to a colleague dealing with the same situation?

7. Implement the action. Many times, implementing the action is difficult. In most cases, the stakes are high whether the involved parties be clients, staff, volunteers, or board members. After some time has passed, it is good practice to go back and review the situation to see if there are things you would do differently in the future.

The Council on Social Work Education Competency requires that the decision-making process apply the standards of the NASW Code of Ethics, relevant laws and regulations, models for ethical decision, ethical conduct of research, and additional codes of ethics as appropriate to context.

Use Reflection and Self-Regulation to Manage Personal Values

How does a social work administrator know when it is necessary to utilize the ethical decision-making process or even recognize that an ethical question exists? How do you practice ethical administration? The answer to these questions is found in the concept of reflective practice. Reflective practice is a core concept in social work and probably the most well-known theoretical perspective across the entire applied professions of teaching, health, and social services. In social work literature, reflection is often tied in with the "use of self" and "emotional intelligence" (Ferguson, 2018). Sheppard (2007) argues that the reflective social work practitioner shows a high degree of self-awareness, role awareness and awareness of the assumptions underlying their practice. Much of the social work literature on the subject has its origins in Schon's (1983) concept of how professionals engage in reflection. Redmond (2006) further refined the concept to include "reflection on action" to think about and link practice to knowledge.

Schon (1983) reported in his book *The Reflective Practitioner: How Professionals Think in Action* that the most skilled and effective professionals have the ability to pay critical attention to the way they conduct their work at the same time that they do their work. Based on his research, he developed the concepts of "knowing-in-action" and "reflection-in-action." Put simply, this describes the situation in which a professional can analyze what they are doing and reflect on it while they are doing it. This concept is particularly applicable to administrators, who must make dozens of decisions daily and oftentimes must make the decisions "on the fly." Schon's concept is wholly compatible with social work and the well-known concept of "use of self" (Schon, 1983; Reamer, 2018).

Frederic G. Reamer (2013) has suggested that social workers should have a refined "ethics radar" that increases their ability to detect and respond to ethical issues. In explaining this concept, he states,

> Ordinarily the concepts of knowing-in-action and reflection-in-action are applied to practitioners' cultivation and use of technical skill, whether in surgery, architecture, town planning, engineering, dentistry, or psychotherapy. In my view, social workers would do well to extend the application of these compelling concepts to their identification and management of ethical issues in the profession. Ideally, effective practitioners would have the ability to recognize and address ethical issues and challenges as they arise in the immediate context of their work, not later when someone else points them out. Put another way, social workers would have a refined "ethics radar" that increases their ability to detect and respond to ethical issues. (Reamer, 2013)

According to Reamer (2013), ethics-related reflection-in-action entails three key elements:

- **Knowledge:** The social work administrator must have the knowledge base for ethical practice. It is imperative to have an extensive knowledge of the social work code of ethics. The administrator must set the example of ethical practice for the agency and be able to interpret ethical practice both on the administrative and on the direct practice level. The administrator must also have extensive knowledge of agency policies and practices and/or the laws and regulations related to the agency's area of practice.
- **Transparency:** Social work administrators should practice in an open and straightforward manner. To develop and maintain the trust of the community, board, staff, volunteers, and clients, the administrator must operate in the "light of day." When ethical issues or potential ethical issues arise, it is important that every effort be made to deal with the issue professionally and responsibly. Transparency requires the administrator to be open and informative about the agency's financial performance, goals, history, outcomes, and operations.

  A recent study in the business sector (Alton, 2017) found that up to 94% of consumers surveyed indicated that they were more likely to be loyal to a brand that offers transparency, while 73% said they were willing to pay more for a product that offers complete transparency. Internal transparency in maintaining open lines of communication with employees and being honest about company operations is positively correlated with higher employee morale and, therefore, productivity. Transparency in this internal context will build trust and make employees feel that they're working for an organization with high ethical standards (Alton, 2017).

- **Process:** Reamer (2013) states, "Although some ethical decisions are clear-cut, many are not. What I have learned is that many ethical decisions are not simple events; they require a considerable, often painstaking, process. During the course of the profession's history, social workers have refined the art of reflective practice. Historically, these skills have been applied primarily to clinical, policy, advocacy, and administrative functions. Clearly, reflective practice should extend to ethics as well" (p.1)

Demonstrate Professional Demeanor in Behavior, Appearance, and Oral, Written, and Electronic Communication

What does it mean to act professionally and have a professional demeanor? Penny Clarke (n.d.), of the Manchester Business School, says that professionalism cannot be taught, because it is not a skill but a collection of attributes that need to be developed over time. We borrow from her list of professional attributes for accountants and apply them to social work administrators. Several standards in the NASW Code of Ethics relate to the ethical responsibilities that social workers have as professionals. Reamer (2018) outlines the standards related to professionalism as: professional competence (Standard 4.01); discrimination (Standard 4.02); private conduct (Standard 4.03); dishonesty, fraud, and deception (Standard 4.04); social worker impairment (Standard 4.05); misrepresentation (4.06); solicitation of clients (Standard 4.07); and acknowledgment of work done by social workers and others (Standard 4.08).

Competency

Social work administrators must practice within their level of professional competence and should seek positions for which they have the education, training, knowledge, and skills. Also, the social work administrator is bound by the code of ethics to base their practice on recognized knowledge, including empirically based knowledge, relevant to social work and social work ethics. Social workers and social work administrators base their practice on specialized knowledge and skills that are backed up by their social work degrees and their level of licensure. Social work administrators are required by the code of ethics to become and remain proficient in professional practice by keeping current with emerging knowledge, routinely review the professional literature, and participate in continuing education relevant to their practice and social work ethics (NASW, 2017, Standard 4.01b). It is expected and required that they will keep their knowledge and skills up to date throughout their careers so that they can always deliver work of the highest quality in accordance with social work standards and relevant laws and regulations.

Reliability and Accountability

True professionals plan in advance and never turn up unprepared. This attribute is critical for the competent social work administrator. It is crucial to set the example for staff that you will do what you say and that they can confidently rely on you for support. Line-level social workers, supervisors, and directors must have the confidence that if they act ethically and thoughtfully in the best interest of their clients, they can count on the backing of the administrator. They must know that you are willing to do anything that you ask them to do and that you are committed to their best interest and the interest of their clients. It must be clear to the staff, volunteers, and clients that you are ultimately responsible for the functioning of the agency and that you accept that responsibility. If mistakes are made, you must accept responsibility for the part you played.

Honesty and Integrity Versus Dishonesty, Fraud, and Deception

Social worker administrators must not participate in dishonest, fraudulent, or deceptive activities. In a later section, we will examine the elements of trust. As the administrator of an organization, you have been "entrusted" with that organization for a period of time. To the public and stakeholders of the organization, you become the "face" of the organization. Any lapse in professionalism related to dishonesty mars not only your reputation and credibility but also the reputation of the organization. To be a professional is to be viewed as a person who is honest, personally accountable, and overall a person of impeccable integrity. Professionals tell the truth and never compromise their values.

Self-Control and Private Conduct

Self-control is a professional attribute in both the professional setting and the social work administrator's personal life. A large part of your job as a social work administrator is to solve problems. Often, those problems are presented to you in the form of unhappy people making a complaint to you. Such complaints may come from staff members, clients, board members, donors, community leaders, or just about anyone else you can imagine. The good news is that social work administrators are well equipped to deal with these issues. Faced with an irate person, you will have the skills to act like a professional, stay calm, and do what you can to understand and help resolve the issue. As a social worker first (and then an administrator), you will have the training and natural ability to consider the emotions and needs of the person before you. A high degree of emotional intelligence and your training in human behavior and emotions will serve you well in this area of professionalism.

As mentioned earlier, as the administrator of an organization, you are the "face" of that organization to many, and as such, you must consider your private conduct as part of your professional identity. In general, what a social work administrator does in their free time is their own business, but they must avoid behaviors or activities that reflect poorly on them and their organization (Reamer, 2018). This includes the use of technology and online behavior, as will be discussed later. Regarding private conduct, Reamer (2018) states the following:

> As a guiding principle, social workers should attempt to distinguish between private conduct that directly interferes with the performance of professional functions and private conduct that, although perhaps distasteful, disturbing, or distracting, is tangential to professional obligations. The former cannot be permitted; the latter may need to be tolerated. (p. 206)

We believe that social work administrators must be held to a higher standard. Behavior that is distasteful, disturbing, or distracting should not be tolerated or condoned for a social work administrator. Being the face of an organization brings a higher standard of expected conduct and behavior, even in your personal life.

Respect for Others and Nondiscrimination

Social workers (and therefore social work administrators) should not practice, condone, facilitate, or collaborate with any form of discrimination on the basis of race, ethnicity, national origin, color, sex, sexual orientation, gender identity or expression, age, marital status, political belief, religion, immigration status, or mental or physical ability (NASW, 2017, Standard 4.02).

Treating all people with respect and kindness is part and parcel of being professional. One of the first concepts social work students learn is "unconditional positive regard" for others (Rogers, 1951). Social work administrators are in a unique position to practice this tenet. On any given day, you may interact with elected officials, wealthy donors, board members, staff, volunteers, clients and client families, other agency administrators, and members of the community. You may interact in one day with both the donor who has given your agency hundreds of thousands of dollars and the person who vacuums your office. A professional will treat all people with the same level of respect, regardless of their station in life and their contributions to the organization.

Professional Image

What does it mean to "look the part" of a professional? A quick Google search will provide you with unlimited fashion advice on how to dress professionally. But what does that mean within the context of social work values and ethics? We are obligated as social workers to understand culture and its function in human behavior and society, recognizing the strengths that exist in all cultures (NASW, 2017, Standard 1.05). Couple this with our requirement to not practice, condone, facilitate, or collaborate with any form of discrimination on the basis of race, ethnicity, national origin, color, sex, sexual orientation, gender identity or expression, age, marital status, political belief, religion, immigration status, or mental or physical ability (NASW, 2017, Standard 4.02), and we have a complicated task to determine what it is to have a "professional image." As administrators, you should promote agency policies that honor the diversity of the staff.

Tom Peters (1997), a highly respected management expert, coined the phrase "personal branding" in a 1997 article in the magazine *Fast Company*. Personal branding is a marketing phenomenon related to the marketing effort that a person adopts in order to promote oneself and to establish his or her image and reputation. Khedher (2015) conceptualizes personal branding in three stages: Developing a personal brand identity involves (1) investing in cultural capital and social capital within established organizational fields, (2) managing a brand's position by actively seeking to manage impressions through artifactual, nonverbal behaviors and verbal strategies, and (3) assessing the personal brand by engaging in a reflexivity-in-action and reflexivity-on-action approach. Personal branding is a useful concept for social work administrators in projecting a professional image. Building on Khedher's concepts, social work administrators will take into account the organizational norms of their agency and the community in which the organization exists. The personal brand includes not only dress but manner of speaking and written communication. Finally, the concept takes into account reflexivity-in-action to allow for flexibility depending on the situation in which administrators find themselves to present themselves appropriately. Personal branding also extends to external emails, written documents, texts, social media, and other online platforms where you present yourself to others.

Use Technology Ethically and Appropriately to Facilitate Practice Outcomes

A core competency for social work administrators is to use technology ethically and appropriately. When the NASW Code of Ethics was revised in 2017, the revisions focused explicitly on ethical challenges pertaining to social workers' and clients' increased use of technology (Reamer, 2018). These standards have major implications for social work administrators in shaping agency policy regarding the use of technology. Social work administrators should become familiar with several key additions to the NASW Code of Ethics.

The most significant updates to the code have to do with the use of technology (Reamer, 2018). Clients should be informed about how social workers use technology in service delivery and in communications between social workers and their clients. If records are stored online, clients should be given information on how this sensitive information is stored and protected. Social workers should consider the use of encryption, firewalls, and secure passwords to protect the confidentiality of electronic communications and develop policies and procedures for notifying clients of any breach of confidential information.

The revised code encourages social workers to obtain client consent to use technology at the beginning of the professional relationship. This may be done through the signed form in which the client agrees to consent to receive services. Social workers using technology to conduct evaluation or research should obtain clients' informed consent for the use of such technology. Social workers should assess the clients' technological skills and offer alternative methods of service delivery or research if the use of technology is inappropriate or a barrier to quality services or participation.

Social workers must be able to verify the identity and location of clients who receive services through remote technology to comply with the laws and licensure requirements of the client's jurisdiction. Verification is also important in case of emergency. If a social worker uses technology, he or she must comply with the laws of both the jurisdiction where the social worker is regulated and located and that where the client is located.

There are several potential boundary issues to avoid in the use of technology in a social work setting. Social workers should not conduct online searches for information about clients without their consent (unless there is an emergency) or communicate with clients using technology for personal or non-work-related purposes. Care should be taken to prevent client access to social workers' personal social networking sites and personal technology to avoid the possibility of developing dual relationships. Posting personal information on professional websites or other media has the potential to cause boundary confusion and inappropriate dual relationships. It is very likely that clients may discover personal information about the social worker based on their personal affiliations and use of social media. To limit this potential issue, social workers should avoid accepting friend requests from clients in online social networks. Social workers need to be aware of and respond to cultural, environmental, economic, disability, linguistic, and other social diversity issues that may affect delivery or use of services through technology (NASW, 2017; Reamer, 2018).

Use Supervision and Consultation

To assure ethical practice, social work administrators must use supervision and consultation to guide professional judgment and behavior. It is easy to understand how this required competency applies to direct-practice social workers, but it is a bit more complicated when we apply the concept to social work administrators. This is especially true when we apply the concept to the social work administrator who is the chief operating officer of an organization and responsible to the Board of Trustees. As a social work administrator, you must have the skills to supervise others and to guide agency middle managers in their supervision of staff. In Chapter 11 (Human Resources), we will discuss your responsibilities to provide supervision, and in Chapter 12 (Boards), we will explore how you will use supervision and consultation in your own practice. As a competent social work administrator, it is your responsibility to define the relationship between yourself and the board and to be clear about your needs for supervision and support. Much of this activity revolves around the board's responsibility to evaluate the CEO, as you will see in Chapter 12.

Public Trust and Social Capital

It is a moral obligation for a social work administrator to protect and enhance public trust in their organization and in the human services sector generally. Ethical practice is key to developing and maintaining trust. Unfortunately, there is currently a crisis of trust in the United States that extends to the nonprofit and human services sectors. The Edelman Trust Barometer (Edelman Trust, 2018) reveals that trust in the United States has suffered the largest recorded drop in the survey's history among the general population. The Edelman measure, which for 18 years has been asking people around the world about their level of trust in various institutions, has never recorded such steep drops in trust in the United States. Only a third of Americans now trust their government to do what is right. In terms of trust in nonprofit organizations, among the adult (18 years or older) general population, the trust percentage dropped 9 points from 58% in 2017 to 49% in 2018. In terms of the "informed public" (ages 25–64, college educated, significant media consumption, and in top 25% of household income), trust in nonprofits dropped even more—22 points, from 73% in 2017 to 51% in 2018.

Social Capital

Level of trust has a direct impact on the level of social capital in a society. Social capital is defined as a network of relationships that produce a culture of norms, communication, obligations, and sanctions. Social capital is important because it affects our quality of life, including our employment, income, civic participation, health, fear of crime, and community involvement. In 1961, Jane Jacobs used the term *social capital* in her book, *The Life and Death of Great American Cities.* In this work, she decried the isolation of the American family due to the development of urban structures. However, it was Robert Putnam (2000) who brought the term into wide use in several works related to social capital. The title of his book *Bowling Alone: The Collapse and Revival of American Community,* popularized the term social capital. The title emerged from his finding that while there had been an increase in the number of individual bowlers, there had been a decrease in the number of organized bowling leagues. His catchy title has become a popular metaphor to express the phenomenon of the decline of social capital in America. Two important elements of social capital are trust and civic engagement. It is this relationship that makes trust so important to human services administration.

Trust

There are two dimensions to trust. The first is trust in others, and the second is trust in institutions. These have been characterized as horizontal trust (trust in family, neighbors, coworkers, etc.) and vertical trust (trust in institutions, government, etc.). Almond and Verba (1963) reported a difference in the levels of trust in different countries. In their study, they found that Americans had a relatively high level of trust in each other. They reported that 55% of Americans viewed other people as trustworthy and believed in the basic goodness of mankind. Unfortunately, for the past several years, trust has been in decline. Putnam (2000) found the greatest level of trust to have occurred around the time of World War II, but since that time, he finds a decline in associational memberships of 25% and an overall decrease in trust levels by 30%.

Why do we care? We care because people who trust government will vote and participate in the political process, and they will engage in activities such as volunteering their time and donating to charity. They will pay their taxes and support programs that provide for the vulnerable populations in our society. Nye, Zelikow, and King (1997) argue that trust is important because if there is a lack of trust, then citizens become disenchanted on five levels: (1) with their elected officials, (2) with the electoral process, (3) with institutions, (4) with democracy, and (5) with the country. Trust is important because we need to make sure that future generations do not become disenchanted with our precious democracy. Social work administrators must safeguard and build trust in their organizations and the larger institution of human services delivery.

Conclusion

Human services administrators are often required to make decisions that involve two values or principles that are in opposition to one another. Such situations constitute ethical dilemmas. In this chapter, we have reviewed classic as well as more recent theories of ethics. We have also reviewed a model of decision-making for you to use as you face ethical dilemmas in your administrative practice. Having a good understanding of the theories of ethics and an example of a decision-making process will help you as you face these difficult decisions. You should also be aware of the cultural and diversity issues as they relate to ethical decision-making. As in all cases, you must be careful not to impose your own cultural or religious beliefs on others but be mindful and respectful of cultural differences that come into play in many ethical dilemmas. Finally, we have explored the link between ethical practice and trust and the sacred responsibility that administrators assume when they become the face of an organization.

Reference List

Almond G. A., & Verba, S. (1963). *The civic culture: political attitudes and democracy in five nations.* Princeton, NJ: Princeton University Press.

Alton, L. (2017, June 14). How transparency became a top priority for businesses, and why you should care. *Entrepreneur.* Retrieved from https://www.entrepreneur.com/article/295739

American Association for Marriage and Family Therapy. (2001). Code of ethics. Retrieved from http://www.aamft.org/imis15/content/legal_ethics/code_of_ethics.aspx

American Counseling Association. (2005). *ACA code of ethics.* Retrieved from https://www.counseling.org/docs/default-source/library-archives/archived-code-of-ethics/codeethics05.pdf

American Nurses Association. (2011). Ethics and human rights. *Nursingworld.* Retrieved from http://nursingworld.org/MainMenuCategories/EthicsStandards/CodeofEthicsforNurses

American Psychological Association. (2010). *Ethical principles of psychologists and code of conduct, including 2010 amendments.* Retrieved from http://www.apa.org/ethics/code/index.aspx

Babb, L. A. (1998). Ethics in contemporary American adoption practice. In V. K. Groza & K. F. Rosenberg (Eds.), *Clinical and practice issues in adoption: Bridging the gap between adoptees placed as infants and as older children* (pp. 105–155). Westport, CT: Bergin & Garvey.

Beckerman, N. (1997). Advanced medical technology: The ethical implications for social work practice with the dying. *Practice, 8(3),* 5–18.

Candilis, P. J., & Martinez, R. (2006). Commentary: The higher standards of aspirational ethics. *The Journal of the American Academy of Psychiatry and the Law Online, 34(2),* 242–244.

Chandler, R. C. (2001). Deontological dimensions of administrative ethics revisited. In T. Cooper (Ed.), *Handbook of administrative ethics* (2nd ed., pp. 179–193). New York, NY: Marcel Dekker.

Clarke, P. (n.d.). What it means to be professional. *NCCA Student Magazine.* Retrieved from https://www.accaglobal.com/us/en/student/sa/features/being-professional.html

Corey, G., Corey, M. S., & Callanan, P. (2003). *Issues and ethics in the helping professions* (6th ed.). Pacific Grove, CA: Brooks/Cole.

Cottone, R. R., & Clause, R. E. (2000). Ethical decision-making models: A review of the literature. *Journal of Counseling & Development, 78(3),* 275–283.

Denhardt, K. G. (1991). Unearthing the moral foundations of public administration: Honor, benevolence, and justice. In J. S. Bowman (Ed.), *Ethical frontiers in public management: Seeking new strategies for resolving ethical dilemmas* (pp. 91–113). San Francisco, CA: Jossey-Bass.

Edelman Trust. (2018). *2018 Edelman trust barometer: Executive summary.* Retrieved from https://www.edelman.com/sites/g/files/aatuss191/files/2018-10/2018_Edelman_TrustBarometer_Executive_Summary_Jan.pdf

Ferguson, H. (2018). How social workers reflect in action and when and why they don't: The possibilities and limits to reflective practice in social work. *Social Work Education, 37*(4), 415–427. doi:10.1080/026 15479.2017.1413083

Forester-Miller, H., & Davis, T. E. (1996). *A practitioner's guide to ethical decision making.* Retrieved from American Counseling Association website http://www.counseling.org/resources /pracguide.htm

Fox, C. J. (1994). The use of philosophy in administrative ethics. In T. Cooper (Ed.), *Handbook of administrative ethics* (pp. 105–130). New York, NY: Marcel Dekker.

Grobman, G. M. (2011). *Introduction to the nonprofit sector: A practical approach for the 21st century* (3rd ed.). Harrisburg, PA: White Hat Communications.

Jacobs, J. (1961). *The death and life of great American cities.* New York, NY: Vintage Books.

Khedher, M. (2015). A brand for everyone: Guidelines for personal brand managing. *Journal of Global Business Issues. 9*(1), 19–27.

Mill, J. S., & Gorovitz, S. (Ed.). (1971). *Utilitarianism.* Indianapolis, IN: Bobbs-Merrill.

National Association of Social Workers (NASW). (2017*). Code of ethics of the National Association of Social Workers.* Washington, DC: NASW.

Nye, J. S., Jr., Zelikow, P. D., & King, D. C. (Eds.). (1997). *Why people don't trust government.* Cambridge, MA: Harvard University Press.

Peters, T. (1997, August–September). The brand called you. *Fast Company, 10,* 37–46.

Putnam, R. D. (2000). *Bowling alone: The collapse and revival of American community.* New York, NY: Touchstone Books/Simon & Schuster.

Reamer, F. G. (2000). Administrative ethics. In R. J. Patti (Ed.), *The handbook of social welfare management* (pp. 69–86). Thousand Oaks, CA: Sage

Reamer, F. G. (2013). Eye on ethics: Reflective practice in social work—the ethical dimension. *Social Work Today.* Retrieved from https://www.socialworktoday.com/news/eoe_042513.shtml

Reamer, F. G. (2018). *The social work ethics casebook: Cases and commentary* (2nd ed.). Washington, DC: NASW Press.

Redmond, B. (2006). *Reflection in action: Developing reflective practice in health and social services.* London, UK: Routledge.

Rogers, C. R. (1951). *Client-centered therapy: Its current practice, implications, and theory.* Boston, MA: Houghton Mifflin.

Schon, D. A. (1983). *The reflective practitioner: How professionals think in action.* New York, NY: Basic Books.

Sheppard, M. (2007). Assessment: From reflexivity to process knowledge. In J. Lishman (Ed.), *Handbook for practice learning in social work and social care* (2nd ed., pp. 128–137). London, UK: Jessica Kingsley.

Solomon, R. C. (1992). *Ethics and excellence: Cooperation and integrity in business.* New York, NY: Oxford University Press.

Souryal, S. S. (1992). *Ethics in criminal justice: In search of the truth.* Cincinnati, OH: Anderson.

Stadler, H. A. (1986). Making hard choices: Clarifying controversial ethical issues. *Counseling & Human Development, 19,* 1–10.

Watson, L. D., & Cobb, N. H. (2012). Ethical issues in the use of putative father registries in infant adoption: Implications for administrators and practitioners. *Adoption Quarterly, 15*(3), 206–219.

Additional Resources

American Society for Public Administrators (ASPA) Code of Ethics (https://www.aspanet.org/ASPA/Code-of-Ethics/Code-of-Ethics.aspx).

Loera, A. Introduction to the NASW Code of Ethics (2017 Revision) [Video file]. Retrieved from https://www.youtube.com/watch?v=wOfx4Gcv9EU

MBA Oath (http://mbaoath.org/).

NASW Code of Ethics online (https://www.socialworkers.org/About/Ethics/Code-of-Ethics/Code-of-Ethics-English).

HELPFUL TERMS

Aspirational ideals—a higher standard for professionals than any minimalist legal requirements.

Benevolence—disposition to do good and to promote the welfare of others, implying not only actions that promote good and the welfare of others but also motivation to pursue those ends.

Code of ethics—a systematic effort to define acceptable conduct (Plant, 1994).

Deontological theories—claim that certain actions or behaviors are inherently right or wrong, and that actions are good or evil. These theories are based on the idea that there are higher-order principles. From a religious standpoint, this approach is based on the belief that God has determined what is right and what is wrong.

Ethical dilemma—"that situation in which an action is required that reflects only one of two values or principles that are in opposition to one another" (Beckerman, 1997, p. 6).

Honor—adherence to the highest standards of responsibility, integrity, and principle; denotes a quality of character in which the individual exhibits a high sense of duty, pursuing good deeds as ends in themselves, not because of any benefit or recognition that might be accrued because of the deeds.

Justice—sense of fairness and regard for the rights of others, which includes, most fundamentally, respect for the dignity and worth of each individual. Justice further involves a commitment to developing and preserving rights for individuals that will ensure that their dignity and worth will not be violated by others in society.

Teleological theories—based on the assumption that individuals faced with an ethical dilemma should measure the moral rightness of their actions based on the moral goodness of the consequences. In other words, one should act in a manner that produces the most favorable outcome.

Trust—comprises two dimensions: the first is trust in others, and the second is trust in institutions, characterized as horizontal trust (trust in family, neighbors, coworkers, etc.) and vertical trust (trust in institutions, government, etc.).

Utilitarianism—a subset of the teleological theories. This approach holds that the proper sets of actions are those that promote the greatest good for the greatest number in society (Solomon, 1992).

Utilitarianism (act)—the rightness of an action is determined by the goodness of its consequences in that individual case (Grobman, 2011).

Utilitarianism (rule)—requires one to anticipate long-term consequences and act accordingly in all similar situations (Grobman, 2011).

EXERCISES

Below, you will find three ethical dilemmas that demand your attention as a human services administrator. Sit with three or four of your classmates and discuss one of the following scenarios. Your instructor will assign you one or more of the scenarios to discuss. Select a spokesperson from your group and report your findings to the class. Use the Model of Ethical Decision-Making to frame your answer.

1. Service Delivery

You are sitting in your office when the director of family services comes into your office. She has received a request from a couple who had previously adopted a child from your agency. The request is that the agency assist them in their process to adopt an embryo. The couple has found an agency on the Internet that places embryos for adoption. The couple asking your agency for help has learned that the agency they found on the Internet stores embryos produced through fertility treatment because they believe it is morally wrong to destroy the embryos. The couple is requesting that your agency provide the home study for the adoption of the embryo and provide ongoing supervision once the baby is born. Your agency does home studies and provides ongoing supervision but has no experience with embryo adoption. Your agency is religiously affiliated and is pro-life. However, some of the staff members are opposed to providing the service because they believe that fertility treatments are morally wrong.

Can your agency help?

2. Agency Functioning

You are sitting in your office when the phone rings. It is Mr. Warbucks, who is the community relations director of the Acme Tobacco Company, the largest tobacco company in America. Acme has selected your agency to receive a $100,000 check to remodel the agency's youth services complex. You have recently had the Board of Directors approve a policy that all facilities in the agency will be smoke-free. Some of the employees are very angry that they must leave the property to smoke, and a few have resigned. Since the smoke-free policy has been adopted, you find that fewer of the clients are smoking. Mr. Warbucks would like to come to the next board meeting with his camera crew to present the check. The board will need to agree to have the film footage used in national advertising for the Acme Tobacco Company. The agency is experiencing financial difficulties, and the youth services complex is badly in need of repair.

Do you accept the donation and have your agency featured in the advertising campaign?

3. Relationships

You are sitting in your office when two clerks from the business office come in and tell you that the director of finance is stealing money from the petty cash drawer. You consider the director a dear friend and would trust him with your personal money. You do not believe that this could be true, but to be on the safe side, you call the independent auditor to come and check out the allegation. After the auditor completes his work, he asks to meet with you and the director. As the auditor begins to discuss several questionable transactions, the director asks to speak to you alone. The director tells you that it is true that he has been taking money from petty cash. He used the money to buy tires and make repairs on his personal automobile. On one occasion, he gave some of the money, about $200, to the two employees who are making the allegations. The director states that he did this because they had worked so hard and were underpaid for what they do. The total amount taken was $1,200, which he says he will pay back immediately. The employee has been with the organization for 18 years.

What will you do with the three employees involved?

ASSIGNMENTS

1. Examine the code of ethics for your discipline and compare and contrast it to two of the other codes mentioned in this chapter. Discuss the similarities and the differences in the codes of ethics between the disciplines.

2. Describe an ethical dilemma from either your own experience or a current event. In dealing with the ethical dilemma, would you use a deontological approach or a teleological approach? Why did you choose this approach? What actions would you take based on the approach you find to be the most appropriate? Use the steps in the Model of Ethical Decision-Making presented in this chapter to describe how you would deal with the ethical dilemma.

3. Conduct a telephone or a face-to-face interview with a human services administrator. Ask them if they can share an ethical dilemma that they have faced in their administrative practice and describe the process used to arrive at the decision.

Image Credits

Img. 2.1: Copyright © 2015 Depositphotos/Wavebreakmedia.
Img. 2.2: Copyright © 2014 Depositphotos/Stuartmiles.
Img. 2.3: Copyright © 2014 Depositphotos/IzelPhotography.
Img. 2.4: Copyright © 2016 Depositphotos/HstrongART.
Img. 2.5: Copyright © 2014 Depositphotos/Klublub.

3

Administrative and Organizational Theories

How can theory be helpful and meaningful to an administrator? Why should you care about theory? For theory to be of practical use to you, it must have three critical elements: the capacity to describe, to explain, and to predict (Frederickson & Smith, 2003). Theory attempts to *describe* a phenomenon in abstract terms rather than attempting to describe a specific situation, setting, or case. The description cannot be highly specific without losing the ability to describe a general phenomenon. To build on a general description, a strong theory will also attempt to *explain*. The explanatory elements of a theory will explain "why" something happened or is happening. The most important part of a theory is its ability to *predict*. No theory could be expected to explain every situation, but it should have the ability to describe a range of outcomes that can be expected when applying the theory to real-life situations. This chapter will give you an overview of some of the most important theories that shape administrative practice. You will then have the opportunity to apply each of the theories to a real-world situation.

Few administrators can describe which theories they use in their work and in their decision-making processes, but all administrators, over time, will develop their own theory of administration and will use different theories of organization and administration, depending on their particular values, beliefs, and administrative styles. Therefore, to shape and inform your administrative practice, it is important for you to have a working knowledge of the major theories of administration. At the end of this section, you will be asked to imagine that you have been appointed as the administrator of an organization and to list three of the most important things you would do in your first 100 days based on each theoretical perspective presented in this chapter.

There are many approaches to the study of organization and administrative theory. Some typologies place the different theories on a chronological time line, while others divide the literature into different approaches or "schools." The history of organization and administration theory cannot be easily divided into clearly delineated periods, and therefore, each period must be viewed from the perspective of chronology, subject orientation, and issue orientation, since each period of theory development has built on the work of earlier theorists. Some theorists appeared to be far ahead of their times and gave glimpses of

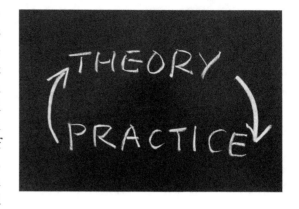

work that was to be further developed many years in the future. There are limits to any classification system, but we will approach the history of organization and administration theory in the following categories: Rational Approach Theories, Human Relations Perspectives, Contingency Theory, Political Economy Perspective, Population Ecology, Institutional Perspective, Organizational Culture and Sense Making, Postmodernism, and Critical Theory (Hasenfeld, 2000).

This chapter provides only a brief overview of several theories of organization and administration. Each of the sections below is a "thumbnail sketch" of the theory presented. There are numerous books written on each of these approaches, and the references at the end of this chapter will guide you to some of these books. This list is by no means complete, but hopefully, it will give you a sense of the use of theory in administrative practice and will lead you to a further in-depth study of the theories that will shape your practice.

Historical Theories

Rational Approach Theories

Rational Approach Theories have their roots in the classical theory of the late 1800s and early 1900s and are, therefore, strongly influenced by the European values of the time. Max Weber identified the elements of bureaucracy as the ideal method of organization (Weber, Gerth, & Wright, 1946). This highly structured, chain-of-command approach was the model for this period. During this period of time, management viewed workers as intellectually and socially subordinate, and for the most part, management was indifferent to the human needs of the workforce. Workers needed to be controlled.

In this view, organizations existed to accomplish production and to achieve economic goals. As the scientific approach of this time gained acceptance, it was thought that there was one best way to organize work for maximum production and that people and organizations act in accordance with rational economic principles. Workers were viewed not as individuals but interchangeable parts. From this perspective, the organization was seen as a machine, with interacting, interdependent parts, and workers were seen as incidental "cogs" in the machinery. This orientation was referred to as *mechanistic* by later theorists. Frederick Taylor's (1911) *Principles of Scientific Management* and Henry Fayol's (1949) *General and Industrial Management* (originally published in 1916

as *Administration industrielle et générale*) were major works of this period. Taylor designed a mechanical way to do a job and concentrated on the mechanics of what was performed rather than who was performing the work. Fayol's approach was to look at methods to promote effectiveness and efficiency. He also put forth the proposition that a university education had implications for one's ability as a manager and, from this position, developed career-development schemes.

Papers on the Science of Administration, edited by Luther Gulick and L. Urwick (1937), brought together in one volume articles of the leading theorists of the time. Many of the concepts from that work still have great influence on management practices today. For example, the work of V. A. Graicunas on "span of control" studied the number of subordinates that a supervisor should supervise (Gulick & Urwick, 1937). This work still has influence on the design of organizations today. It was also in this publication that Gulick introduced POSDCORB, or the seven major functions of executive management: Planning, Organizing, Staffing, Directing, Co-Ordinating, Reporting, and Budgeting.

In the mid-1940s Herbert A. Simon wrote "The Proverbs of Administration" (1946), which questioned the relevance of principles of administration and challenged the approach. He proposed that the idea of principles was a myth, and that for every principle there was a contradictory principle. Simon's work was the beginning of a challenge to the Rational Approach Theories and led to the development of other approaches.

Human Relations Perspective

In keeping with the classical approach, the management of Western Electric Company contracted with a group of Harvard professors to perform a study to improve effectiveness and efficiency. These studies, known as the Hawthorn Studies (Greenwood & McDonald, 1994), observed production rates while controlling variables such as lighting, work group membership, and physical position. The researchers were surprised to find that there were many variables other than physical space and lighting that impacted productivity. While it seems obvious to us today, they discovered that interpersonal relationships, supervisory relationships, and informal groups within the organization all had influences on productivity. These studies led to new thinking about work environments, worker motivation, supervision, and influences on productivity. This was a major event in the development of the social/psychological approaches, even though the studies were completed in 1932 and the social/psychological approaches were still several years in the future.

In view of this, management began to view worker relationships as important factors in the work environment, and the power of both formal and informal groups was recognized. Dynamics of group conformity and group loyalty became the new topic of investigation and theory development. Some began to question the bureaucratic structures of the workplace and to view the Industrial Revolution as removing the meaning from work. Human Relations Perspectives theory held that workers were more responsive to social pressure of peer groups than to the demands, or even incentives, of management.

In "A Theory of Human Motivation," Abraham Maslow (1943) described his hierarchy of needs: physical security, self-esteem, and self-actualization. Figure 3.1 identifies these needs as physiological, safety, belonging/love, self-esteem, and self-actualization. The human relations perspective brought about a major shift in the view of workers. Management began to view workers as capable of growth, as needing choices to grow, and as adaptive. Managers also began to recognize that motivation was important and that the sources of motivation would change over time.

FIGURE 3.1. Maslow's Hierarchy of Needs

In *The Human Side of Enterprise*, Douglas McGregor (1957) proposed a framework to examine administrative styles that he called *Theory X* and *Theory Y*. The traditional approach to management he labeled as Theory X management. He proposed a Theory Y as an alternative approach, in which the task of management was to arrange organizational conditions and methods of operation so that people could achieve their own goals by directing their efforts toward organizational objectives.

Contingency Theory

What is the best structure for a human services organization? Some of the work in the Human Relations models, such as Theory X and Theory Y, would lead us to the conclusion that an organization with little structure and maximum flexibility would lead to the highest levels of efficiency and effectiveness. Contingency Theory challenges this notion.

Contingency Theory moves toward an open-system perspective as opposed to the closed-system view of the Rational Approach. In Contingency Theory, the structure of an organization is variable and contingent on the characteristics of the organization's environment, including environmental heterogeneity and stability, technological certainty, organizational size, and power (Mintzberg, 1979). In this theory, the task of the administrator is to create the right "fit" between the contingency and the internal structure of the organization as a strategy to promote effectiveness and efficiency.

A study by Burns and Stalker (1994) examined over 20 firms in the United Kingdom. The purpose of this study was to see what types of management methods and procedures produced the highest level of productivity. They found that the determining factor is the nature of each organization's demands from the environment and the types of tasks and functions necessary to meet those demands. From this work, they developed a new typology of organizations they called mechanistic organizations and organic organizations (Kettner, 2002).

Mechanistic organizations are defined as organizations that were fixed and somewhat rigid, with predictable tasks and relatively stable

environments. *Organic organizations* are defined as being less structured. The supervisors in these organizations function more as consultants rather than supervisors. In the organic organization, workers are given expected outcomes to achieve rather than specific tasks. Burns and Stalker found that these organizations function best in an unstable environment in which inputs are unpredictable and the organization is expected to respond to changing environmental conditions.

What are the implications for the human services administrator? Because we are in the human services field, the tendency may be to lean more toward an unstructured and informal organizational structure that appears more equalitarian and participatory, but Contingency Theory says this is not always the best arrangement. The administrator taking the Contingency Theory approach will look at the inputs to the organization and the expected outcomes and develop structures to maximize positive outcomes. The administrator will seek to achieve the best fit for the organization.

Political Economy Perspective

Political Economy Perspective states that for organizations to survive and to produce services, they must secure legitimacy and power, as well as production or economic resources. From this perspective, *political economy* refers to a system of distribution not only of resources but also of status, prestige, power, legitimacy, and related social amenities. The Political Economy Perspective views the organization as a collectivity that has multiple and complex goals, paramount among them being survival and adaptation to the environment (Hasenfeld, 2000). The capacity of the organization to survive and to provide services depends on its ability to mobilize power, legitimacy, and economic resources—for instance, money, personnel, and clients (Wamsley & Zald, 1976).

Most organizations are dependent on resources that are controlled by others in the external environment. In this approach, the greater the organization's dependence on these resources, the stronger the influence of external interest groups on processes within the organization (Schmid, 2000).

The social work administrator must manage the environment the organization exists in at least as well as the organization itself to ensure an adequate resources supply. In this respect, managing the environment may be even more important than managing the organization itself (Aldrich & Pfeffer, 1976). Pfeffer (1992) notes that changes in the external and internal political economies will result in changes within the organization. Internal power relations shape internal structure and resource allocation.

Population Ecology

Population Ecology views the organization within the context of the community of organizations and services. In this view, dynamics of the founding and survival of organizations—that is, the founding and failure of organizations—are explained by population dynamics and density dependence. Population dynamics is seen as a factor in stimulating the founding of new organizations. For example, if there is an identified community need and there is the perception that there are resources to meet this need, then chances are that groups will work to develop a new organization or service to meet this need. Conversely, as new organizations or services are founded, then there is a perception of competition, and therefore, new foundings are discouraged. The concept of density dependence means that an increase in the density of organizations or services signals legitimacy of the services being provided and that resources are available for such services. In this view, the administrator must employ macro strategies to position the organization within the larger community of organizations and services and recognize that environmental forces set limits on the success of administrative practice (Hasenfeld, 2000).

Institutional Perspective

According to the Institutional Perspective, survival depends on the degree that structure reflects and reinforces the institutional rules shared by the community of organizations. The more the organization adheres to rules, the greater its legitimacy and chances of survival. The social work administrator using this approach will focus on the critical relations between the organization and cultural institutions, as well as the values and norms these institutions are expected to promote (Scott, 1995). In this theory, the more closely the organization mirrors the values of the community, the more likely it is that there will be financial and political support for the organization.

Organizational Culture and Sense Making

This theory posits that organizational culture enables members of the organization to make sense of their work and construct common understanding of their internal and external environments. Sense making is the process that ties together the beliefs and actions of the organization and the individuals in the organization. This approach recognizes that powerful subcultures exist in organizations and have a powerful socializing function. When new employees enter the organization, they must be socialized into the culture or, alternatively, leave the organization. Services will be organized to accommodate the culture, and therefore, productivity is strongly influenced by culture. An important task of administrators is to influence organizational culture through the messages they give and their behavior (Weick, 1995).

Postmodernism

For many administrators, Postmodernism is very difficult to understand, yet alone explain. The term *postmodern*, put simply, implies a reaction against the modern condition. There is, however, a deeper meaning that attempts to move to a higher level of social thought. The common denominator to the many meanings of postmodernism is the idea that individuals and societies today have lost the capacity to represent the "real" (Denhardt, 2004). One of the tools of postmodernism is "deconstruction," or the process of finding the historical and cultural flaws that mold our thinking and our institutions.

Postmodernists argue against the concepts of rationality or "scientific" knowledge. In this approach, it is the culture that defines and objectifies the values, norms, and knowledge of those in power. Since the culture is defined by those in power, the culture perpetuates the patterns of dominance that exist in the society. Postmodernists examine how things come into being and become self-ratifying. The administrator taking a postmodern approach will attempt to uncover practices that maintain and reinforce patterns of domination over staff and clients while excluding alternative perspectives. The major limitation of the postmodern approach is that it does not provide a specific model for administration.

Critical Theory

Critical Theory is similar to Postmodernism in that it views organizations as repressive systems. All Critical Theory is historical, in the sense that it tries to analyze the long-term development of oppressive arrangements in society (Turner, 1986). The foundation of Critical Theory is Marxist theory, which says that the very structure of organizations, including hierarchical structures and division of labor, is designed to disenfranchise workers.

According to Marxist theory, human service organizations play a special role in a capitalist economy. In this view, the organization serves as a buffer between the capitalist and the working classes. "The benefits and services they provide are designed to maintain a compliant and complacent working class while defining and isolating as deviant those who might challenge the capitalist system" (Hasenfeld, 2000, p. 105). While this is not a popular notion with social work administrators, it does force an administrator to, at least, examine this proposition. Administrators strive to be agents of positive change, not agents of oppression. While administrators are engaged in "hands-on" service provision, critical theorists are focused on the purpose of their research—to achieve social change. Social work administrators committed to social change as well as service provision will draw on the lessons of the critical theorists.

Theories of Sector Relationships

The brief overview of classical theories presented in this chapter provides a foundation to understand modern theories of sector relationships. As you examine the framework presented in this section, reflect on the theories presented above and how they have influenced the development of each of the sectors in which social work administrators are employed.

Social work administrators practice in every sector of society. Whether working in a nonprofit agency, a governmental program, a for-profit enterprise, or a hybrid organization, social work administrators function in highly developed, networked environments, where the lines of the governmental, business, and nonprofit sectors cross. The effective administrator must possess skills in mediating, reconciling, and influencing the expectations of multiple external constituencies and must also have the skills not only to direct an agency but to manage the complex environmental context in which the organization exists (Patti, 2000; Schmid, 2004).

Watson (2007) developed a framework to examine the unique role of the nonprofit sector within the context of a theory of governance. Watson & Hegar (2013) expanded and refined that framework to demonstrate the model's utility to aid social work administrators in understanding the theoretical concepts and reform movements that shape the environment of contemporary social work administration. Social work administrators are well positioned to provide leadership in each of the three sectors in which their agencies and programs deliver social services.

The relationships between the nonprofit, government, and business sectors are complicated, multidimensional, and fluid. Unfortunately, popular stereotypes of the sectors can disguise the complex nature of their interrelationships (Brinkerhoff & Brinkerhoff, 2002). The public often views governments as monolithic, bloated bureaucracies in need of an injection of the types of business practices and market solutions preferred by the for-profit sector. Although many see practices such as downsizing as the most effective ways to allocate resources and provide cost-effective solutions, the business sector may simultaneously be viewed as uncaring or more concerned with enriching private interests than with promoting societal good. According to Brinkerhoff and Brinkerhoff (2002), the public image of nonprofits involves being value-driven, softer, kindhearted, and able to mobilize voluntary efforts. A more balanced assessment reveals the many connections and linkages among the sectors and examines both their differences and interrelationships.

Scholars have demonstrated growing research interest in the ties and relationships linking government, the private sector, and the nonprofit sector, including the emergence of hybrid organizations. Several forces have reshaped social work administration. In this chapter, we present a framework to illustrate and explain the dynamic forces impacting administrators in each of the three sectors. The framework not only illuminates the structural realities of contemporary administrative practice in social work, but also highlights opportunities to strengthen democratic administration by recognizing characteristics unique to social work, including the profession's historical emphasis on relationship building, use of authority, and professional values.

Much of the theoretical literature on government–nonprofit relations concerns political ideology, the proper role of government, preferences for free-market approaches, and values of fairness, equity, and equality.

Ryan, Furneaux, and Lewis (2006) identify three typologies relevant to their research on partnerships among government, business, and nonprofit sectors. The first, Coston's (1998) model, builds on the work of Salamon (1987) in conceptualizing the relationship between government and nonprofit agencies as a continuum, with one extreme being repression and rivalry, the middle of the continuum indicating completion and contracting, and the other extreme being third-party government, cooperation, and complementarity (Ryan, Furneaux, & Lewis, 2006).

Young (1998) uses exchange as the basis for exploring the relationships between government and nonprofits. He observes that these relations in the United States are not one dimensional, but complex, and that they must be viewed on multiple levels. In his view, economic theories support three views of government–nonprofit relationships: supplementary, complementary, and adversarial. In the supplementary model, nonprofits are seen as fulfilling a demand for public goods left unsatisfied by the government, while in the complementary view nonprofits are partners to government, helping to deliver public goods largely financed by the government.

From Young's adversarial view, nonprofits prod government into making changes in public policy and into maintaining accountability to the public. Reciprocally, government attempts to influence the behavior of nonprofit organizations by regulating their services and responding to their advocacy initiatives (Young, 1998, p. 33). Much of the literature of government-nonprofit relationships takes its perspective from either the governmental or nonprofit standpoint. Young (1998) is one of few who look at both sides of the equation and acknowledge that relationships are reciprocally based on decisions made by both governmental and nonprofit administrators (Najam, 2000).

The Framework

A theoretical framework (Watson, Rycraft, & Hernandez, 2006) that was originally developed to demonstrate the role of the nonprofit sector in theory development integrates several of the major forces that have shaped social work management over the past 30 years and that continue to impact both seasoned and new social work administrators. Contingency Theory identifies the task of the administrator as creating the right "fit" between circumstances in the environment and the internal structure of the organization as a strategy to promote effectiveness and efficiency. It uses an open-system perspective as opposed to the closed-system view of the bureaucratic or Rational Approach. In Contingency Theory, the structure of an organization is variable and contingent on the characteristics of the organization's environment, including environmental heterogeneity and stability, technological certainty, organizational size, and power (Mintzberg, 1979). An important dimension of managing within a network environment is an understanding of both the internal and external politics at work in such environments (Agranoff & McGuire, 1999).

This framework gives the social work administrator a conceptual model for the many forces that shape the environment in which a human service agency must function. From this perspective, the administrator can evaluate structural and political forces as they seek the "best fit" for their organization while maintaining a commitment to democratic ideals.

Traditionally, the public, private, and nonprofit sectors have been viewed as distinct entities with clearly defined functions. The private or business sector is driven primarily by market forces surrounding the exchange of goods and services. The public or governmental sector is built on the foundation of authority, as only government can tax or exercise police powers of enforcement. The nonprofit sector can be viewed as a mechanism for cooperation through which government and business intersect and foster the cooperation of local communities to achieve public purposes (Swanstrom, 1997). Within the framework, the three sectors are depicted as independent but intersecting circles (Watson, 2007).

Sector Tasks

Savas (1987) identified the strengths of each of the three sectors, and Osborne and Gaebler (1993) built on Savas's work to propose a separate set of tasks or operations for which each sector is suited (see Figure 3.2).

They propose that policy management and regulation are tasks best suited to the public sector. Additionally, they view enforcement of equity, prevention of discrimination, prevention of exploitation, and promotion of social cohesion as tasks best suited to the public sector. In the private sector, the operations identified are economic tasks, investment tasks, profit generation, and promotion of self-sufficiency. Finally, Osborne and Gaebler (1993) propose that the nonprofit sector is best suited to perform social tasks, those requiring volunteer labor, and operations that generate little profit. The promotion of community, individual responsibility, and commitment to the welfare of others are all seen as tasks appropriate for the nonprofit sector (Osborne & Gaebler, 1993). The tasks or operations presented do not represent an exhaustive list, and arguments can be made concerning their respective assignment to each sector, but the value of this approach is that it begins the work of determining the appropriateness of allocating each task to one of the three sectors (Watson, 2007). None of the tasks can be viewed as exclusive to one sector or another. The use of contracting to deliver public services has resulted in greater "blending" of tasks across sectoral lines.

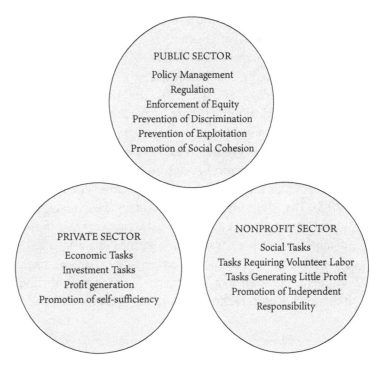

FIGURE 3-2. Savas's (1987) Sector Tasks

New Public Management

As the role of government has changed over the past 30 years, a cluster of reform initiatives known collectively as new public management (NPM) has been a force driving many of the changes. As a part of these reform initiatives, numerous traditional government functions have shifted to the private and nonprofit sectors (Kettl, 2000). Frederickson and Smith (2003) identify common elements in the various forms of this movement as, "1) adoption of market-based management and resource allocation techniques, 2) increased reliance on private sector organizations to deliver public services, and 3) a deliberate and sustained effort to downsize the decentralized government's role as the central policy actor in society" (p. 208).

The advent of market-based management brings the values and techniques of the private sector into the public and nonprofit sectors by introducing competition into the marketplace for social services. The NPM goal of downsizing and decentralizing the government's role has been accomplished by shifting many functions to either the private or the nonprofit sectors. This trend has been highly controversial, both in the United States and in Europe, where observers in countries such as Sweden characterize NPM as an undesirable turning away from universal, public-sector responsibility for social welfare (e.g., Blomberg & Jan, 2010; Höjer & Forkby, 2011).

Governance Theory

Many administrative theories are based on concepts of cooperation, networking, and governance (Frederickson, 1999). In some instances, the term *governance* is used interchangeably with *public management* (Garvey 1992; Kettl, 2000; Peters & Pierre, 1998; Salamon, 1989). Frederickson and Smith (2003) propose governance theory as one "that accounts for lateral relations, inter-institutional relations, the decline of sovereignty, the diminishing importance of jurisdictional borders, and a general institutional fragmentation" (p. 222). They propose a theory of administrative conjunction, defined as "the array and character of horizontal formal and informal association between actors representing units in a networked public (including the nonprofit sector) and the administrative behavior of those actors" (p. 223). Administrative conjunction conceptualizes professionals, including social work administrators, as performing diplomatic functions across jurisdictional lines to accomplish public purposes where an administrator's claim to authority comes not from a hierarchical position, but rather from knowledge and ability to work within a network. The connections between administrators develop around specific policy domains, and by establishing relationships in networks, administrators are linked across jurisdictional and sector lines (Frederickson & Smith, 2003). The administrator's task becomes the management of network relationships. A key concept in network theory is that participants retain their individual characteristics while moving from competitive to cooperative relationships (Salamon, 2002).

Frahm and Martin (2009) conceptualize changes affecting the three sectors as moving from a "government" paradigm to a "governance" paradigm. In their view, this new paradigm has emerged from the policy debates of the 1980s and 1990s that revolved around preference for either the government paradigm or the market paradigm (Frederickson & Smith, 2003; Kettl, 2000; Osborne & Gaebler, 1993). From the dichotomous government versus market debate, the new "governance" paradigm has emerged (Agranoff, 2003; Salamon, 2002; Frederickson & Smith, 2003). Governance suggests the possibility of transcending old dichotomies to build on the relationship between the government and the governed. From the governance perspective, solutions to social problems will be found at the intersection of all disciplines and all sectors—governmental, nonprofit, for-profit, faith-based, and others (Johansson, 2004)—a perspective consistent with the emergence of hybrid organizations, as discussed in the next section.

In the framework presented here, social work administrators from the nonprofit, private, and public sectors are centered at the intersection of the three sectors, represented by a small circle at the midpoint of the graphic model. This placement illustrates the position from which administrators work across sector lines and play an important role in governance. From this position, social work administrators not only advance the mission of their agencies, but they also become participants in governance and in the promotion of democratic administration.

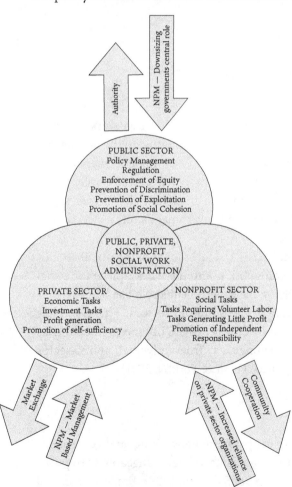

FIGURE 3.3. Social Work Administrators and the Three Sectors

Hybrid Organizations

In some human services fields, such as foster care of children, nonprofits, for-profits, and government, institutions all provide similar services. Handy (1997) contends that each sector attracts a share of the market because consumers (or funders) are willing to trade perceived quality in one sector for anticipated efficiency and lower costs in another. Handy (1997) goes on to suggest this tradeoff as the reason that organizations from each of the three sectors can coexist in the same industry, a reality that has led many agencies to seek alternative organizational structures.

Traditionally, private organizations in the United States are divided into for-profit and nonprofit groups. In seeking new organizational forms, administrators operating between the two categories have used creative partnerships, subsidiaries, or joint ventures to accomplish their goals (Gottesman, 2007). The desire to function between the for-profit and nonprofit sectors has also led to new organizational forms: hybrid organizations. These organizations are not classified as subsidiaries or partnerships but instead represent new organizational types that function at the intersection of the traditional nonprofit and for-profit sectors (Gottesman 2007).

Hasenfeld and Gidron (2005) list several fields of service that have developed hybrid organizations. These include some racial, ethnic, and gender-based organizations (Minkoff, 1995), religious charitable organizations (Allahyari, 2000), women's nonprofit organizations (Bordt, 1998), peace and conflict resolution organizations (Gidron, Katz, & Hasenfeld, 2002), and social influence organizations (Knoke & Wood, 1981).

Social work administrators may discover that the traditional for-profit–nonprofit dichotomy has less relevance in today's environment than it did in the past. The overlapping circles in the model represent the blurring of boundaries between the sectors and the emergence of hybrid organizational forms.

Implications for Social Work Administrators

Frahm and Martin (2009) suggest that social work administrators may be uniquely positioned to play a key role in society's shift to a governance paradigm. The framework presented here demonstrates the central role that social workers can play in developing new administrative models of practice. Relying on foundations of social work practice, recognizing the forces at work in the current environment, and utilizing the best management skills are the challenge for today's social work administrators.

Hoefer (2009) identified 37 skills, attitudes, and elements of knowledge needed for human services administration and used several groups of professionals to place these into four categories: people skills, attitudes and experiences, substantive knowledge, and management skills. His pool of raters included human services administrators and later social work educators, government program managers, and educators in public administration. For respondents at all levels, "people skills" were the most important, and "management

skills" were the least important (Hoefer, 2009). While it is important for social work administrators to have the management skills necessary to compete and be technically competent, these competencies are not a substitute for the interpersonal skills and core values of the social work profession.

Social work administrators must also find the balance between market-driven new public management concepts and foundational social work principles, such as social justice. Efficiency and effectiveness are not enough. They must be coupled with principles of participation, trust, fairness, honesty, and reciprocity. The model presented here highlights several tasks that demand the attention of social work administrators: building relationships, understanding the forces influencing each sector, adopting management ideas that work, and focusing on issues of social justice and inclusion. Sections below elaborate on each of these.

Building Relationships

The model framework places social work administrators at the intersection of the three sectors to emphasize the importance of their role in building relationships across the sectors. Social work administration is about forming relationships with funding sources, regulatory agencies, the general public, boards and commissions, referral sources, staff, clients, and all other stakeholder groups related to the organization. *Relationship* is a term of great historical significance in social work (Johnson & Yanca, 2010). While it is often used with reference to the social worker–client dyad, it is of equal importance in administrative practice. Perlman (1979) describes relationship as "a catalyst, an enabling dynamism in the support, nurture, and freeing of people's energies and motivation toward problem solving and the use of help" (p. 2). This definition describes well the administrative task illustrated in this model.

Understanding the Forces Influencing Each Sector

The framework presented here provides social work administrators with a graphic representation of the forces being exerted on human service organizations. The outward forces are those that make each sector unique. For example, the public sector is based on the authority of the state. Some social work functions require authority for the prevention of discrimination and exploitation, such as protection of children, the elderly, and people with disabilities. Authority also is required for the enforcement of regulations that protect vulnerable populations and set standards of care for the provision of services.

Like relationship, *authority* is a construct with longstanding salience in social work. Deschweintz and Deschweintz elaborated for the profession what it means to use in disciplined and conscious ways the authority inherent in many public sector roles to help recipients of services (Deschweintz & Deschweintz, 1946; Yelaja, 1965). The professional obligation and tool of authority is not limited to direct services; it applies equally well to interorganizational relationships in which one party carries statutory responsibilities. Social work administrators who are well grounded in the meaning and use of authority are particularly well prepared to work at the intersection of the three sectors, where one of the forces at work is the authority vested in the public sector. Market exchange is the defining force of the private or business sector. Whether in private practice or in a for-profit company, social work administrators can balance the need to generate profit with the obligations of equity and fairness. The key element in the nonprofit sector is the force of community cooperation. It is in the nonprofit setting that social work administrators engage the community, encourage cooperation between the sectors, and build community strengths. Like boards of directors of nonprofit agencies, social work administrators are trustees holding "in trust" the organizations that in reality belong to the larger community.

Adopting Management Ideas That Work

Research by Watson (2012) reports that social service administrators have, to a large extent, embraced many core elements of the various organizational reform movements discussed above. Most of the agency administrators (70.3%) agreed that the private (business) sector is more efficient and effective than government and that the nonprofit sector should adopt market-based management and resource allocation techniques. They further agreed with statements that the government should rely more on the business and nonprofit sectors to deliver public services, and that government should be downsized and decentralized. There was high agreement with the idea that business practices should be employed to reduce costs.

Social work administrators practice in an environment of accountability and evidence-based practice and should evaluate and implement management practices that further the mission of the organization. If NPM concepts are found to be effective, they can be incorporated into administrative practice. Many scholars take issue with the tenets of NPM approaches, but even the harshest critics concede that there are parts of the model that hold promise. Even though NPM seldom reduces costs, it has produced numerous innovative ways to accomplish public or collective purposes. Frederickson and Smith (2003) examine the theoretical underpinnings of NPM and conclude that NPM is very influential in administrative literature and can be understood as an acceptable doctrine of management. Wamsley and Wolf (1996) posit that NPM has done much good, and few would wish to detract from its accomplishments. Others contend that, while NPM principles can result in selective and short-run increases in efficiency, NPM is silent on issues of fairness, equity, or justice (Frederickson & Smith, 2003). It is in this arena that social work administrators can make a great contribution to the use of NPM practices, which with their leadership need not exclude attention to issues of social justice.

Some have criticized social work's move toward evidence-based practice as little more than a hidden managerialist agenda (e.g., Pease, 2007). Most social work administrators would agree that there is a need to strive constantly for improved efficiency and effectiveness. However, social work administrators need not abandon their core values in favor of a managerial approach based solely on an instrumental, depoliticized, and competence-based approach (Houston, 2001).

Focusing on Issues of Social Justice and Inclusion

Regardless of the sectoral setting or the management approach, social work administrators are well situated to focus their practice on issues of social justice and democratic participation. As with the unique social work perspectives on use of relationship and authority discussed above, social justice is a value for which social work administrators are prepared by their profession. The NASW Code of Ethics includes social justice among the "core values, embraced by social workers throughout the profession's history," that form "the foundation of social work's unique purpose and perspective" (NASW, 2017). Social work authors Dolgoff, Loewenberg, and Harrington (2005) offer an ethical principles screen to guide professional decision-making in which the value of "fair and equal treatment" is superseded only by basic human survival needs.

Administrators with social work backgrounds bring these and other core professional values to their work within and between the three sectors. Contracting arrangements, hybrid organizations, and other alliances across sectors offer new opportunities to strengthen professional values and democratic principles by developing service networks based on participation, trust, fairness, honesty, and reciprocity. Relationships are key to deepening and strengthening democratic participation and administration based on such social justice concepts (Wamsley & Wolf, 1996). For the social work administrator, entering into contract arrangements also means accepting specific performance requirements that may have no emphasis on issues of social justice, such as equitable access to services. It is therefore critical that social work administrators advocate social justice in contract negotiations, in policy advocacy, and in their administrative practice.

While much of NPM focuses on the roles of service providers, the civil society perspective emphasizes citizen participation and community building (Anheier, 2009). Social work administrators can balance the aspects of their practice that emphasize provision of services with those that work to strengthen the fabric of our society by promoting policy and practice based on fair and equal treatment.

Practice at the Intersection of the Three Sectors

The theoretic framework presented here is based on the contemporary environments in which social work administrators practice. The framework examines management theory, as well as the reform movements that have impacted social work administrative practice. It is important for social work administrators to recognize the forces that have pushed the three sectors in which they practice closer together, as well as the historical and economic forces that keep them separate and distinct.

As social work administrators engage in practice at the intersection of the three sectors, including new hybrid organizational forms, they are in a position to apply and advance concepts that are the bedrock of the profession: relationships based on understanding, trust, and respect; disciplined use of professional authority; and the values of equity and justice. Through application of these concepts in work across the three sectors, social work administrators can demonstrate that market-oriented values such as efficiency and effectiveness are not enough.

Putting Theories into the Four-Quadrant Model

This chapter includes a considerable number of theories. Until you examine them closely, it may be difficult to differentiate them and understand their unique details. Figure 3.4 is an effort to map most of the theories presented onto the four-quadrant model introduced earlier. This is not an easy task, and you may disagree with where we have placed them. Reasonable people can place them in different locations. Just be sure to think clearly about why you locate the theories where you do.

As you can see from Figure 3.4, Theory X and Rational Approach theories are placed in Quadrant I, where task orientation combines with an internal orientation. Critical Theory and the Institutional Perspective are in Quadrant II, where the task and external orientations combine. Quadrant III

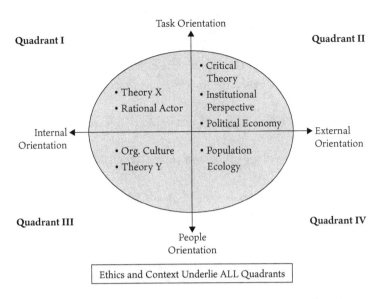

FIGURE 3.4. The Four-Quadrant Model and Management Theories

(people and internal orientations) has the Organizational Culture and Theory Y theories embedded. Finally, Quadrant IV has the Resource Dependence Theory, to explain what happens when a people orientation meets with an external orientation. A few theories described in the chapter have not been included. Where do you think they would best fit?

Conclusion

The challenge for social work administrators is to embrace the elements of theory and practice that promote efficiency and effectiveness while holding fast to concepts and ideals fundamental to social work practice. In this chapter, we have examined both classical theories and more modern theories influencing the government, for-profit and nonprofit sectors. Social work administrators are uniquely positioned to function in each of the sectors and to develop critical relationships across sectoral lines in order to accomplish the purposes of their organizations in the context of a democratic society.

Reference List

Agranoff, R. (2003). *Leveraging networks: A guide for public managers working across organizations.* Washington, DC: IBM Endowment for the Business of Government.

Agranoff, R., & McGuire, M. (1999). Managing in network settings. *Review of Policy Research, 16*(1), 18–41.

Aldrich, H. E., & Pfeffer, J. (1976). Environments of organizations. *Annual Review of Sociology, 11*(2), 79–105.

Allahyari, R. A. (2000). *Visions of charity: Volunteer workers and moral community.* Berkeley: University of California Press.

Anheier, H. K. (2009). What kind of nonprofit sector, what kind of society?: Comparative policy reflections. *American Behavioral Scientist, 52*(7), 1082–1094.

Blomberg, S., & Jan, P. (2010). The increasing importance of administrative practices in the shaping of the welfare state. *Social Work & Society, 8*(1). Retrieved from https://socwork.net/sws/article/view/24/67

Bordt, R. L. (1998). *The structure of women's non-profit organizations.* Bloomington: Indiana University Press.

Brinkerhoff, J. M., & Brinkerhoff, D. W. (2002). Government–nonprofit relations in comparative perspective: Evolution, themes and new directions. *Public Administration & Development, 22*(1), 3–18. doi:10.1002/pad.202

Burns, T., & Stalker, G. M. (1994). *The management of innovation* (Rev. ed.). New York, NY: Oxford University Press.

Coston, J. M. (1998). A model and typology of government-NGO relationships. *Nonprofit and Voluntary Sector Quarterly, 27*(3), 358–382.

Denhardt, R. B. (2004). *Theories of public organization* (4th ed.). Belmont, CA: Thomson Wadsworth.

Deschweintz, E., & Deschweinitz, K. (1946). The place of authority in the protective function of the public agency. *Child Welfare League Bulletin, 25*, 1–6.

Dolgoff, R., Loewenberg, F. M., & Harrington, D. (2005). *Ethical decisions for social work practice* (7th ed.) Belmont, CA: Brooks/Cole.

Fayol, H. (1949). *General and industrial management.* London, UK: Sir Isaac Pitman and Sons.

Frahm, K. A., & Martin, L. L. (2009). From government to governance: Implications for social work administration. *Administration in Social Work, 33*(4), 407–422.

Frederickson, H. G. (1999). The repositioning of American public administration. *PS: Political Science & Politics, 32*(4), 701–712.

Frederickson, H. G., & Smith, K. B. (2003). *The public administration theory primer.* Boulder, CO: Westview Press.

Garvey, G. (1992). *Facing the bureaucracy: Living and dying in a public agency.* San Francisco, CA: Jossey-Bass.

Gidron, B., Katz, S. N., & Hasenfeld, Y. (2002). *Mobilizing for peace: Conflict resolution in Northern Ireland, Israel/Palestine, and South Africa.* New York, NY: Oxford University Press.

Gottesman, M. D. (2007). From cobblestones to pavement: The legal road forward for the creation of hybrid social organizations. *Yale Law & Policy Review, 26*(1), 345–358.

Greenwood, R. G., & McDonald, J. F. (1994). Preface. *International Journal of Public Administration, 17*(2), xvii–xxi.

Gulick, L. H., & Urwick, L. (Eds.). (1937). *Papers on the science of administration.* New York, NY: Institute of Public Administration, Columbia University.

Handy, F. (1997). Coexistence of nonprofit, for-profit and public sector institutions. *Annals of Public & Cooperative Economics, 68*(2), 201–223.

Hasenfeld, Y. (2000). Social welfare administration and organizational theory. In R. J. Patti (Ed.), *The handbook of social welfare management* (pp. 89–112). Thousand Oaks, CA: Sage.

Hasenfeld, Y., & Gidron, B. (2005). Understanding multi-purpose hybrid voluntary organizations: The contributions of theories on civil society, social movements, and non-profit organizations. *Journal of Civil Society, 1*(2), 97–112.

Hoefer, R. (2009). Preparing managers for the human services. In R. J. Patti (Ed.), *The handbook of human services management* (2nd ed., pp. 483–501). Thousand Oaks, CA: Sage.

Höjer, S., & Forkby, T. (2011). Care for sale: The influence of new public management in child protection in Sweden. *British Journal of Social Work, 41*(1), 93–110. doi:10.1093/bjsw/bcq053

Houston, S. (2001). Beyond social constructionism: Critical realism and social work. *British Journal of Social Work, 31*(6), 845–861.

Johansson, F. (2004). *The Medici effect: Breakthrough insights at the intersection of ideas, concepts, and cultures.* Boston, MA: Harvard Business School Press.

Johnson, L. C., & Yanca, S. J. (2010). *Social work practice: A generalist approach.* Boston, MA: Allyn & Bacon.

Kettl, D. (2000). Public administration at the millennium: The state of the field. *Journal of Public Administration Research and Theory, 10*(1), 7–34.

Kettner, P. M. (2002). *Achieving excellence in the management of human service organizations.* Boston, MA: Allyn & Bacon.

Knoke, D., & Wood, J. R. (1981). *Organized for action: Commitment in voluntary associations.* New Brunswick, NJ: Rutgers University Press.

Lewis, J. A., Lewis, M. D., Packard, T. R., & Souflee, F., Jr. (2001). *Management of human service programs* (3rd ed.). Belmont, CA: Brooks/Cole.

Lewis, J. A., Packard, T., & Lewis, M. D. (2011). *Management of human service programs* (5th ed.). Belmont, CA: Brooks/Cole.

Maslow, A. (1943). A theory of human motivation. *Psychological Review, 50,* 370–396.

McGregor, D. (1957). *The human side of enterprise.* New York, NY: McGraw-Hill.

Minkoff, D. C. (1995). *Organizing for equality: The evolution of women's and racial-ethnic organizations in America, 1955–1985.* New Brunswick, NJ: Rutgers University Press.

Mintzberg, H. (1979). *The structuring of organizations.* Englewood Cliffs, NJ: Prentice Hall.

Najam, A. (2000). The four C's of third sector–government relations. *Nonprofit Management & Leadership, 10*(4), 375–396.

National Association of Social Workers. (2017). Code of ethics. Retrieved from http://www.socialworkers.org/pubs/code/code.asp

Osborne, D., & Gaebler, T. (1993). *Reinventing government: How the entrepreneurial spirit is transforming the public sector.* Reading, MA: Addison-Wesley.

Patti, R. (2000). The landscape of social welfare management. In R. Patti (Ed.), *The handbook of social welfare management* (pp. 3–26). Thousand Oaks, CA: Sage.

Pease, B. (2007). Critical social work theory meets evidence-based practice in Australia: Towards critical knowledge-informed practice in social work. In K. Yokota (Ed.), *Empowering people though emancipatory social work* (pp. 103–138). Koyoto, Japan: Sekai Shisou-sa.

Perlman, H. H. (1979). *Relationship: The heart of helping people.* Chicago, IL: University of Chicago Press.

Peters, B. G., & Pierre, J. (1998). Governance without government? Rethinking public administration. *Journal of Public Administration Research and Theory, 8*(2), 223–243.

Pfeffer, J. (1992). *Managing with power: Politics and influence in organizations.* Boston, MA: Harvard Business School Press.

Ryan, N. F., Furneaux, C. W., & Lewis, D. (2006). Characteristics of successful government/non-profit relations in Queensland, Australia. *Proceedings of the Tenth International Research Symposium on Public Management (IRSPM X).* Glasgow Caledonian University, Scotland.

Salamon, L. M. (1987). Of market failure, voluntary failure, and third-party government: Toward a theory of government-nonprofit relations in the modern welfare state. In S. A. Ostrander (Ed.), *Shifting the debate: Public/private sector relations in the modern welfare state.* New Haven, CT: Transaction Books.

Salamon, L. M. (1989). *Beyond privatization: The tools of government action.* Washington, DC: Urban Institute Press.

Salamon, L. M. (Ed.). (2002). *The tools of government: A guide to the new governance.* New York, NY: Oxford University Press.

Savas, E. S. (1987). *Privatization: The key to better government.* Chatham, NJ: Chatham House.

Schmid, H. (2000). Agency–environment relations: Understanding task environments. In R. J. Patti (Ed.), *The handbook of social welfare management* (pp. 133–154). Thousand Oaks, CA: Sage.

Schmid, H. (2004). Organization-environment relationships: Theory for management practice in human service organizations. *Administration in Social Work, 28*(1), 97–113.

Scott, W. R. (1995). *Institutions and organizations.* Thousand Oaks, CA: Sage.

Simon, H. A. (1946). The proverbs of administration. *Public Administration Review, 6*(1), 53–67.

Swanstrom, T. (1997). *The nonprofitization of housing policy: Slipping between the horns of policy dilemmas.* Paper presented at the Annual Meeting of the Urban Affairs Association, Toronto, Canada.

Taylor, F. W. (1911). *Principles of scientific management.* New York, NY: Harper & Row.

Turner, J. H. (1986). *The structure of sociological theory.* Chicago, IL: Dorsey Press.

Wamsley, G. L., & Wolf, J. E. (1996). *Refounding democratic public administration: Modern paradoxes, postmodern challenges.* Thousand Oaks, CA: Sage.

Wamsley, G. L., & Zald, M. N. (1976). *The institutional ecology of human service organizations.* Bloomington: Indiana University Press.

Watson, L. D. (2007). *Factors influencing the relationship between nonprofit child care providers and the Texas Department of Family and Protective Services as a predictor of policy outcomes.* (Unpublished doctoral dissertation). University of Texas at Arlington, Texas.

Watson, L. D. (2012). Factors influencing the relationship between contract providers and a state funding agency. *Administration in Social Work, 36*(4), 343–358.

Watson, L. D., & Hegar, R. (2013). The tri-sector environment of social work administration: Applying theoretical orientations. *Administration in Social Work, 37*(3), 215–226.

Watson, L. D., Rycraft, J., & Hernandez, S. (2006). Public administration and the role of the nonprofit sector. *The International Journal of Knowledge, Culture, and Change, 5*(3), 117–128.

Weber, M., Gerth, H. H., & Wright, M. C. (1946). *From Max Weber: Essays in sociology.* Oxford: Oxford University Press.

Weick, K. E. (1995). *Sensemaking in organizations.* Thousand Oaks, CA: Sage.

Yelaja, S. A. (1965), The concept of authority and its uses in child protective services. *Child Welfare, 44*(9), 514–522.

Young, D. R. (1998). Complementary, supplementary, or adversarial? A theoretical and historical examination of nonprofit-government relations in the United States. In E. T. Boris & C. E. Steuerle (Eds.), *Nonprofits and government: Collaboration and conflict* (pp. 31–67). Washington, DC: The Urban Institute Press.

Additional Resources

"Classical management theory" [Video file]. Retrieved from https://www.youtube.com/watch?v=d1jOwD-CTLI

Frederickson, H. G., Smith, K. B., Larimer, C. W., & Licari, M. J. (2015). *The public administration theory primer* (3rd ed.). Boulder, CO: Westview Press.

Waldo, D. (2017). *The administrative state: A study of the political theory of American public administration.* London, UK: Routledge.

HELPFUL TERMS

Contingency Theory—moves toward an open-system perspective as opposed to the closed-system view of the Rational Approach. In this theory, the structure of an organization is variable and contingent on the characteristics of the organization's environment, including environmental heterogeneity and stability, technological certainty, organizational size, and power (Mintzberg, 1979).

Critical Theory—similar to Postmodernism in that it views organizations as repressive systems. All Critical Theory is historical in the sense that it tries to analyze the long-term development of oppressive arrangements in society (Turner, 1986).

Human Relations Perspectives—an approach based on the Hawthorne experiments that illuminated the importance of the human element in organizational life. Dimensions of worker motivation beyond economic incentives and fear were introduced as valid areas of study (Lewis, Lewis, Packard, & Souflee 2001).

Hybrid Organizations—organizations not classified as subsidiaries or partnerships but instead new organizational types that function at the intersection of the traditional nonprofit and for-profit sectors.

Institutional Perspective—the idea that survival depends on the degree that structure reflects and reinforces the institutional rules shared by the community of organizations; the more the organization adheres to rules, the greater its legitimacy and chances of survival.

New Public Management (NPM)—reform initiatives that have resulted in numerous traditional government functions being shifted to the private and nonprofit sectors.

Organizational Culture and Sense Making—enables members of the organization to make sense of their work and construct common understanding of their internal and external environment. Sense making is the process that ties together the beliefs and actions of the organization and the individuals in the organization.

Political Economy Perspective—the idea that for organizations to survive and produce services, they must secure legitimacy and power, as well as production or economic resources. The Political Economy Perspective views the organization as a collectivity that has multiple and complex goals, paramount among them, survival and adaptation to the environment (Hasenfeld, 2000).

Population Ecology—views the organization within the context of the community of organizations and services. In this view, the dynamics of founding and survival of organizations—that is, the founding and failure of organizations—are explained by population dynamics and density dependence. Population dynamics is seen as a factor in stimulating the founding of new organizations.

Postmodernism—the term *postmodern*, put simply, implies a reaction against the modern condition. There is, however, a deeper meaning that attempts to move to a higher level of social thought. The common denominator to the many meanings of Postmodernism is the idea that individuals and societies today have lost the capacity to represent the "real" (Denhardt, 2004).

Rational Approach Theories—classical theories of organization from the 19th century. Max Weber's ideal bureaucracy, Frederick Taylor's scientific management, and Henri Fayol's management principles are still influential today (Lewis, Packard, & Lewis, 2011).

EXERCISES

1. In-Basket Exercise

Directions

Work with a group of three or four of your classmates and consider the following memo from the supervisor of refugee services to you, the administrator of the organization. Develop a memo in response to this memo. Use Institutional Theory to frame your response memo and then read your response to the class.

Memo

Date: February 13, 20XX

To: Administrator

From: Refugee Services Supervisor

Subject: Television Spots for Refugee Services

Our new public service spots began running on all the local TV stations this week. As you know, the spots are intended to find employers willing to hire our newly arrived refugees. I think the spots are very well done. They open with a shot of the Statue of Liberty, with the voiceover saying, "Give us your tired, your poor, and your huddled masses longing to breathe free." We have received a few calls from potential employers (two or three calls), but my phone has been ringing off the hook with "hate" calls. The most common complaint is the perception that we are taking away jobs from Americans and giving them to these foreigners. As you know, our program is not very popular in this community. I'm proposing that we pull the spots from the air as soon as possible. Your thoughts?

2. In-Basket Exercise

Directions

Work with a group of three or four of your classmates and consider the following memo from the parenting services coordinator to you, the administrator of the organization. Develop a memo in response to this memo. Use Population Ecology Theory to frame your response memo and then read your response to the class.

Memo

Date: June 29, 20XX

To: Administrator

From: Parenting Services Coordinator

Subject: Request for Letter of Support

I have recently learned that there is a move under way in the community to develop a new parenting services agency. In fact, I received a call today asking if our agency will provide a letter of support that they can use as part of their grant proposal to the local community foundation. I am worried that this will be in direct competition with our service and that they will compete for funds from our funding sources and donors. There is always a need for additional services, but I think we would be in a better position to provide more services rather than have this group start a new agency. They are asking for a letter of support by the end of this week. What shall I do?

3. In-Basket Exercise

Congratulations! You have been appointed as executive director of Acme Social Services Agency. The agency has 50 employees and a budget of $3.2 million. The agency provides a variety of services, including emergency assistance, refugee resettlement, residential youth services, and counseling services. The agency is facing a $50,000 deficit by year's end if things do not change. Some of the staff are very unhappy that the former executive director was forced to resign after 20 years with the agency.

Based on each theoretical perspective, what are the three most important things you will want to do in your first 100 days in office? Why are these three tasks the most important?

Rational Approach Theories

1.

2.

3.

Human Relations Perspectives

1.

2.

3.

Contingency Theory

1.

2.

3.

Political Economy Perspective

1.

2.

3.

Population Ecology

1.

2.

3.

Institutional Perspective

1.

2.

3.

Organizational Culture and Sense Making

1.

2.

3.

Postmodernism

1.

2.

3.

Critical Theory

1.

2.

3.

ASSIGNMENTS

1. Write a brief statement called "My Theory of Administration." Which of the theories presented in this chapter best fit with your beliefs and approaches to administration?

2. Write a five-to-seven-page paper on the work of Max Weber and how you see the influence of his work on the administration of human service organizations today.

3. Pick one area of human services, such as domestic violence programs, hospice, youth services, or any other service area. Using the concepts of Population Ecology Theory, explain the founding of organizations providing this service.

Image Credits

PART II

Leadership and Communication

Now that you have a firm grounding in the "big picture" elements of the field (context, ethics, and theory) we turn to what we think of as prerequisite leadership knowledge: understanding what leadership is and how leaders communicate. Being a leader entails keeping many activities going at once and being able to switch tasks many times a day. You also want to be as effective in communicating as possible, both in working with others and in writing.

We know that many (if not most) social work leaders have received little or no training in management, either in school or after starting their management career. Therefore, their knowledge of how to manage relies only on what they have been exposed to in the past. Some people's only experience is with managers who are also untrained, which compounds the problem of unskilled management. Therefore, we provide two chapters to give you a solid grounding in leadership and personal communication skills. The topics in this section are what we think of as "precursor leadership skills" or the personal assets that anyone should bring to their management job in the organization.

In Chapter 4 (Leadership), you will learn what the term means in a social work (not business or military) context. You will discover different approaches to being a leader and what your efforts should focus on. You will understand why you need to acquire a large set of skills so that you can match the skill to the situation. You may be surprised by the information you read in the section on diversity, women, and diverse populations in leadership, as well as other topics. Near the end, we present more detail on the four-quadrant model of social work management skills, which will be expanded throughout the rest of the book.

Personal communication is such an important topic for leaders (at all levels) that it merits a chapter on its own (Chapter 5). Research indicates that the ability to communicate effectively is always ranked near the top of desired management skills, no matter who the raters are. The basics of communication are also not well taught to most social workers, other than in some direct practice courses. While it is true that working with clients requires good oral and written communication skills, it is a mistake to believe that you can use the skills in the same ways when you are a supervisor or manager. Leaders need to use their communication skills to create a sense of shared identity with staff members and other stakeholders and to sharpen their storytelling abilities to be able to create deeper and more lasting impact on their listeners.

Leaders face different pressures than other workers in human service organizations. Emotional self-management takes on different forms to help you manage the pressures you face. The final section in chapter 5 reminds us that we live in a diverse society. Different populations speak differently, receive information differently, and respond to events differently. You, as a leader, need to be able to bridge these differences, inside and outside of your organization, to be effective.

After completing the readings and exercises in these chapters, you will find you have expanded your repertoire of leadership skills and have practiced them in real-life situations. You will have built your competencies in the core aspects of social work leadership. You will no longer be stuck inside the boundaries of your personal experiences with the potentially untrained leaders you have met.

Leadership

Being a leader in a nonprofit organization is challenging. You must acquire a host of skills and use them well to be successful. There are few "right" answers, and conditions change constantly, bringing new opportunities and issues each day (Hopkins & Hyde, 2002). Satisfaction and joy are part of the job, as well (Watson & Hoefer, 2016). These rewards most often come from doing your best to fulfill your organization's mission and working with staff to help them progress in their careers and improve clients' lives. Part of the genius of successful nonprofit leaders is in knowing which skills are called for in which situations. This chapter provides guidance for nonprofit leaders to be more successful in their jobs by discussing what leadership is, what it is used for in a nonprofit setting, what skills nonprofit leaders should possess, and other topics.

What Is Leadership?

The term *leadership* is bandied about so frequently that it is easy to think that strong agreement exists on what it means. Shelves at libraries are filled with books on the subject, some written by business leaders, some by officers in the military, and others by elected officials. Leadership is usually seen as a generic skill—that is, leadership is leadership, whether in the commercial sector, military, or government arenas. Most of this reading material is not academically rigorous—in fact, it is little more than entertaining storytelling, with a few kernels of wisdom amid the large amount of chaff that readers have to sift through. Still, leadership is important, and learning more about it is good for

BOX 4.1 EPAS Competencies Covered

The material in this chapter relates to all of CSWE's competencies but is most closely linked to Competency 6: Engage with Individuals, Families, Groups, Organizations, and Communities; Competency 7: Assess Individuals, Families, Groups, Organizations, and Communities; and Competency 8: Intervene with Individuals, Families, Groups, Organizations, and Communities. Leading and managing well is basic for the survival and health of an organization and thus affects the ability of all working there to achieve success for their stakeholders, including clients.

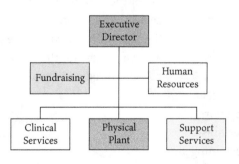

organizations and society. Poertner (2006) shows that client outcomes vary in connection with the leadership ability of agency managers. Warren Bennis (2009), a business leadership guru, indicates that leaders shape the effectiveness of organizations, provide inspiration, restore hope in troubled situations, and recognize problems. In essence, they rise above the current context of society (and their organizations) to see a better tomorrow. Successful social work leaders do the same.

A classic definition of leadership is from organizational theorist Richard Cyert (1990): "Leadership is the ability to get participants in an organization to focus their attention on the problems that the leader considers significant" (p. 29). In a similar vein, Shenkman (2007) argues, "The leader's real work is to create followers" (p. 13).

In social work, however, the aim of leadership is not merely to create followers, but rather to create followers to accomplish something useful, such as quality services for clients. The centrality of values in the nonprofit sector is widely recognized and supported (Rothschild & Milofsky, 2006). Thus, being a social work leader in the human services sector requires a personal commitment to the core values inherent in the field and those of the particular organization employing you.

A definition of leadership that emphasizes the idea that leaders themselves are the most important element of a successful organization lends itself well to the most common sort of organizational chart, wherein the executive director is at the top of a pyramid, with others in the organization reporting directly or indirectly up the "chain of command" (see Figure 4.1 for a simple example of an hierarchical organizational chart). This hierarchical visualization communicates that the director at the apex of the organization is the primary decision-maker, with little need to consult with or take into account the views of others. After all, everyone else "reports to" the leader.

Recently, social work scholars such as Lawler and Bilson (2010) and Vito (2018) have expressed discontent with the existing definitions of leadership (Cyert, 1990; Shenkman, 2007) that are being applied to human services executives. Peters (2018), for example, states that the leadership theories most used in social work were originally based in the military, then transferred to the business world. Because of this, she believes they miss the mark when applied to social work organizations, which have different purposes and philosophies. Peters sets forth a new definition of social work leadership,

FIGURE 4.1. Hierarchical Model of Organizational Structure

which she argues is "a collection of organizational, relational, and individual behaviors that effect positive change in order to address client and societal challenges through emotional competence and the full acceptance, validation, and trust of all individuals as capable human beings" (p. 40). Thus, "positive change" is the key goal of social work leaders. This definition is much more amenable to a different visualization of the organization. This is the "hub" model of organizational structure, which shows a much more coordinating style of leadership within the organization while also taking into account influences from outside the organization (see Figure 4.2). Grant and Crutchfield (2008) describe the importance of leadership being shared. These authors studied 12 nonprofit organizations extensively for a number of years, developing lessons about what made these organizations so high-impact. One of the most important of these lessons is, "leaders of these organizations are able to *share power and inspire others to lead. Leadership doesn't stop at the top; rather, it extends throughout the organization and a larger network or movement*" (p. 46, italics in original). The analogy used by Grant and Crutchfield is important: They describe the nonprofit director not as the person on top of the hierarchy, but rather the person at the hub of many people, all working to accomplish the mission of the organization.

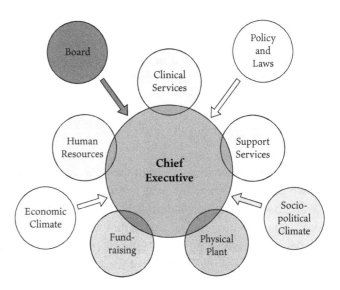

FIGURE 4.2. Hub Model of Organizational Structure

Leadership in a nonprofit often requires working closely with staff members, funders, and other stakeholders. A successful executive values their input for the additional insights they have and the opportunities they offer to come to better decisions. In addition, people who are involved in workplace discussions are more likely to go along with the final decision, even if it wasn't their preferred option. While made in a different context, President Dwight D. Eisenhower's observation is apt: "Leadership is the art of getting someone else to do something you want done because he wants to do it" (quoted in Hughes, Ginnet, & Curphy, 2006, p. 405). Leadership in social work is not fundamentally about commanding but rather relies on influencing others. At the same time that executives of nonprofit organizations are engaged with all the internal aspects of the job, such as client services, support services, physical plant, and fundraising (for example), they have multiple stakeholders to involve and external conditions to pay heed to, as well.

Are There Differences Between Social Work Leaders, Administrators, and Managers?

In this book, we do not make clear distinctions between the terms *leader, administrator,* and *manager,* although there are differences in meaning as described in the literature. Foremost among the differences discussed is the sense that leaders chart the overall direction of organizations, administrators lay out the plans for moving forward, and managers get the front-line workers to implement the plans. Naturally, there is less difference in practice than this glib typology suggests. We believe that the roles are interdependent and often interchangeable, depending on the exact situation. We also believe that putting too much emphasis on "leadership" compared to "administration" or "management" discourages people from taking on appropriate activities that may be outside of their job description. Leadership can take place from any position—it is not only the purview of the top executives in an organization. Figure 4.2 shows, for example, an executive leader working with several different aspects of the organization, each of which has a middle manager leader in charge of that function. Even if no one has an official title to lead in that area, someone will be handling that aspect of organizational life.

What are Social Work Leadership Skills Used For?

A question often overlooked in thinking about leadership in human service organizations is exactly what leaders should be trying to accomplish. While this may seem to be an easy question to answer, and hardly worth considering, the issues are not as simple as they may first appear.

The common-sense view of nonprofit organizations is that they can best be understood as single-goal-maximizing organizations. In the case of human service organizations, their goal would be to eliminate the problems of their clients. For sports nonprofits, the goal could be to maximize the number of youth playing the sport. For arts organizations, the goal might be to expose as many people as possible to theater, opera, or music productions or the visual arts.

A major problem with this approach is that organizations, as organizations, cannot have goals— only people can have goals (Mohr, 1982). Treating the organization as a single person all following one leader in lockstep fashion leads to a failure to understand the nuances of what leaders must do to get individuals to align their goals with the organization's mission and vision. Other problems with this organizational goal perspective are that goals often are not very specific, and unofficial or unstated goals are often as important to the nonprofit's staff as are the professed goals of the organization (Herman & Renz, 1997). For example, agency leaders may try to achieve certain outcomes in an organization, not for the good of the agency or clients but because it will put them in a good position to get a better job in another organization.

A second theoretical approach to understanding what goals a social work leader is pursuing is the system resources approach, which posits that the key metric for understanding organizational success is the level of resources extracted from the environment to support the organization. In other words, the larger the budget (or the larger the percentage increase in the budget), the more successful the organization (and thus its leader) is said to be (Herman & Renz, 2004). This approach

to what nonprofit leaders are trying to achieve would have to be an implicit, rather than an explicit, goal of the leader. Other things, such as the articulated mission or achieving client outcomes, are what provide a nonprofit with its legitimacy and, thus, its ability to obtain resources from the environment. Donors or other stakeholders would not look kindly on a nonprofit leader espousing the goal of accumulating a large amount of cash reserves. Funding would probably decrease if this were the leader's announced goal.

A third view of what leaders in the nonprofit sector are working for, the multiple constituency view, says that the different stakeholders of an organization (leader, staff, clients/patrons, funders, general public, and so on) may all have different ideas about what the organization is established for and how it should act. Because each group is important in the nonprofit's work, each of these stakeholders' views about what the organization is for is correct, even if the views are contradictory to other stakeholders' views (Herman & Renz, 2004). The task for the organization's leader is to balance the demands on the agency to accomplish these different goals.

Funders may value organizational effectiveness in solving client problems, clients may want to know that their assigned staff member cares about them as individuals, staff members may want a secure job, and the general public may want to have the agency be free from scandal. The nonprofit leader is thus required to pay attention to different stakeholders sequentially, attending first to one aspect of the organization, then another. This requires a tremendous repertoire of skills and a highly developed dose of political savvy. It also requires understanding theories about leadership.

Leadership Theories

Perhaps the oldest theory of leadership, sometimes known as the *great man (person)* or *trait theory*, is that there are "born leaders" who have the traits that are needed to be effective (Carlyle, 1907). Some of the traits associated with successful leaders are drive, leadership motivation, honesty, integrity, self-confidence, cognitive ability, and knowledge (Kirkpatrick & Locke, 1991), although many additional traits could be added to the list. If you believe in this theory of leadership and you wanted to develop leaders, you would first identify the traits of leadership you desire, screen the population for people who have these traits, and then provide training and opportunities for these traits to be used. This theory has practically no research support, but it does make for powerful storytelling.

Leadership research gives us many more options for understanding the role of leaders and how they can be developed. Lewin, Lippitt, and White (1970) proposed three styles of leadership: authoritarian, democratic, and laissez-faire. (Some authors refer to these styles of leadership as *directive*, *participative*, and *delegative*.) Authoritarian leaders tell others what to do without consulting with them much. Democratic leaders solicit others' opinions and seek to influence their ideas so that a general consensus emerges. Laissez-faire leaders do not put much effort into being leaders and allow others to do as they wish. The subjects in Lewin et al.'s studies generally preferred the democratic leaders, followed by laissez-faire leaders, with lowest levels of approval given to authoritarian leaders.

Despite the popularity of the democratic (or participative) style of leadership, later research indicates that each style of leadership can be effective, given the right circumstances (Vito, 2018). For example, when time is limited and the leader has all the facts needed to make a decision, the authoritarian approach can (and perhaps should) be used. In other circumstances, such as when staff members have some or all of the information needed to reach a decision and the leader does not have all the information necessary, a democratic leadership style brings about better results.

The key realization from this research is that there is not just one correct model of leadership; rather, the leadership style must match the situation. This basic idea, described in Chapter 3, is known as Contingency Theory, of which several different versions have emerged. Perhaps the most influential was developed by Fielder (1967).

Fielder (1967) argued that leadership could be understood as behavior undertaken to accomplish tasks. Two approaches (which exist on a continuum) for how to get tasks taken care of exist.

On the one hand, a leader can get tasks accomplished by developing positive relationships with people so they will work because they like or trust the leader. This style is called *relationship orientation*. The other end of the spectrum involves focusing on getting things done rather than worrying about relationships. This style is called *task orientation*. Neither of these styles works all the time. Fielder's critical insight was to try to determine when an effective leader uses one style and when the other.

According to Fielder (1967), when relations are good between leader and followers, the task is well structured, and the leader has high position power, then task orientation is effective. When the opposite is true (that is, relations are not very good, the task is poorly structured, and the leader does not have very high power from her position), task orientation can also be effective. For situations that are intermediate in relationship, structure, or position power, then relationship orientation is more effective. A recent restatement of contingency leadership declares that the best outcomes occur when the fit between leader and circumstances is "aligned" (Dym & Hutson, 2005).

Two additional recent leadership approaches include *transformational leadership* (Burns, 1978) and *servant leadership* (Greenleaf, 1991). Transformational leadership offers followers a chance to accomplish great things by making large changes in their organization and themselves. Transformational leaders create a vision, sell that vision to followers, and then move forward, along with their followers, to enacting the vision, always leading the charge. Transformational leaders are usually charismatic, inspirational, intellectually stimulating, and people-oriented, providing individualized attention to others.

Greenleaf (1991) describes servant leadership as a feeling and a choice that the leader makes to lead, but lead in a way that is in service to others. The goal for the "servant-leader" is to serve first and to acquire power or influence later, and then only to continue to serve others better.

People employing different theories and styles use different sets of skills. An authoritarian leader requires far fewer "people skills" than does a leader following a servant-leader model. Leaders who want to be successful over the long term must be flexible in how they approach their job based on the needs of the organization. As Rothschild and Milofsky (2006) remind us, the needs of the organization (which can vary according to where it is in its life cycle, the state of its distinctive technologies, and what the demands of its external constituencies are) determine how the leader must act to be effective, and the personal desires of the leader are secondary. For example, a person not normally seen as charismatic may need to use such abilities to develop a following for a large-scale and difficult project. At other times, a visionary leader may need to focus on detailed "running of the

ship" to achieve the vision that has come together. (Of course, another option for when a leader's skills do not match the organization's situation is to find a different leader.) Vito (2018) presents her analysis of three organizations, all professing to believe in transformational/participatory leadership approaches. Yet when stress from the environment was encountered (in terms of potential loss of funding), two of the three leaders quickly moved away from participatory approach to a much more directive leadership style.

Putting Together the Pieces: Understanding Social Work Leadership

Contingency Theory argues that different leadership styles are more effective or less effective depending on the situation facing an organization. Schmid (2006) has assembled an excellent empirically based approach to linking an organizational situation to the leadership duties required.

As noted earlier, leaders can locate themselves and their organization's needs on a two-axis plane (Schmid, 2006; see Figure 4.3). One axis is labeled task vs. people orientation, while the other axis is labeled internal vs. external orientation. This creates four quadrants, which we will examine in more depth in later chapters. Social work leaders do not "live" in any one quadrant but shift from one area to another as the need arises. The administrator may plan to work on the budget (Quadrant I) but is interrupted by an urgent call from the agency's fundraiser regarding an upcoming special event (Quadrant II). Immediately thereafter, the director of client services sends an email detailing the reason why front-line staff need additional training on their recently adopted evidence-based program (Quadrant III). When trying to return to budgeting, the administrator receives a phone call from the chair of the board asking how the agency should respond to quickly developing political moves to eliminate the organization's funding from the county (Quadrant IV). This series of situations is why social work leaders need to have a large repertoire of skills and a flexible mindset.

Quadrant I represents skills that are "task-oriented with an internal focus." The leader using such skills will focus on achieving organizational goals using standard work processes. Centralization of decision-making will be needed most of the time, with few opportunities for others to be involved. The leader will need to keep subordinates on a short leash, with strict attention to meeting organizational goals and objectives and demand that staff members strictly follow organizational rules and processes. This type of leader is likely to use Theory X (McGregor, 1957), which was discussed in Chapter 3.

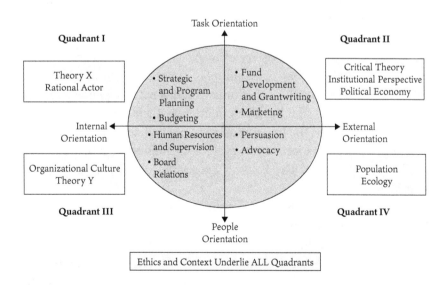

FIGURE 4.3. The Four-Quadrant View of Leadership, Needed Skills, and Linked Leadership Theory

While this type of leader does not sound very much in tune with the social work values of democracy and openness, Schmid (2006) argues that such a set of behaviors in a leader has its place. Residential boarding institutions, for example, require strict following of rules to protect residents' rights, maintain legitimacy, and assure an adequate flow of resources into the organization. Reports of abuses by staff of dependent clients (such as in prisons, state schools, or nursing homes) are far too common and reflect a breakdown in the control of the organization, leading to lawsuits, governmental inquiries, and possible demise of the organization.

Quadrant II sets aside the internal focus of Quadrant I to look outside the organization while remaining task-oriented, as in Quadrant I. Quadrant II can be seen as the leader "conquering" the world outside of the organization—the push is to acquire legitimacy and resources from external sources so as to institutionalize the nonprofit. Leaders in this situation tend to be very directive and authoritative and rely on their formal authority much more than their ability to influence indirectly or through the use of inducements. Because the task of organizational institutionalization is so important, staff members and volunteers are frequently seen narrowly as resources to be used to achieve the goal, rather than as important actors in the process. This is squarely in line with the Institutional Perspective (Scott, 1995) mentioned in Chapter 3.

Quadrant III also has an internal orientation, but the leader in this case is people-oriented, not task-oriented. Leadership behaviors in this quadrant are used to motivate, involve, and empower staff to do the work of the organization. The leader acts as coach and mentor, seeking to develop staff members to achieve more and to be committed to improving themselves as they accomplish the goals of the organization. This type of leader seems closely aligned with the Human Relations Perspectives model of leadership, or Theory Y (McGregor, 1957), both discussed in the previous chapter.

Schmid (2006) argues that the most appropriate time for Quadrant III leadership is during the early years of a nonprofit organization's existence. This is when rules have not yet been written, patterns are not yet fully established, and the founders of the organization have the most direct influence on the organization and its members, clients, and staff. An internal focus for leadership is necessary to stabilize the organization and to create job processes and procedures that can lead to routines being established at the organization.

Quadrant IV represents the convergence of an external orientation with a people focus. Leaders in this area of the model seek to control the future of their organization by reducing its dependence on others for resources while making other organizations more dependent on them. Considerable attention is paid to developing staff members to improve their ability to handle the external environment's constraints. Because the leader is using so much time and energy to build coalitions and alliances outside of the organization, lower-level staff members must be trained to handle as many issues as possible by themselves. The Political Economy Perspective (discussed in Chapter 3) fits well in this quadrant.

It is important to remember that none of the quadrants is inherently "better" than another. None of the sets of skills described is inferior to another. Working in each quadrant is vital, even though each presents a different set of challenges and requires a different set of skills to be successful. Just as a carpenter uses many different tools, depending on the job to be done, nonprofit managers must have a basic set of skills at their disposal to be able to match the ones that best work in the situation.

Diversity and Social Work Leadership

Almost all the research and theorizing on leadership until recently has accepted white males as the standard leader. This section provides a look at what we know about women and other populations in management and leadership positions.

Women

For decades, the number of women in the nonprofit sector's ranks has been much greater than that of men. Yet the vast majority of these women find themselves and their careers inhibited by the same glass ceiling that is so pervasive in the corporate world. Just as in the for-profit sector, women are dramatically underrepresented in leadership roles, especially within larger organizations where ingrained pathways to upper management and executive positions both favor and are dominated by men. Patz (2018) indicates that women comprise 73% of the nonprofit workforce but only 45% of CEOs. Moreover, where women do find upper-level executive work in the nonprofit sector, they can expect to earn significantly less—only about 66% of what male CEOs earn (Patz, 2018). Furthermore, despite some progress in the for-profit sector in this area, the nonprofit income gap appears to be growing. According to data from 2014, this income gap is especially pronounced in organizations with operating budgets of less than $500,000. Among these agencies, the annual wage gap ranged from around $2,500 to more than $30,000, depending on the type of position and the agency's financial situation (Stiffman, 2015). All of this happens in a sector in which there already exists a lower overall salary for entry-level and nonmanagement positions and an uncertain level of job security because funding for small and mid-level organizations diminishes under economic and political pressures (Stiffman, 2015).

These facts are more than a little disturbing, given that the nonprofit sector is itself designed to serve disenfranchised populations such as women, children, racial and ethnic minorities, impoverished peoples, oppressed religious groups, and any number of other groups who struggle under the weight of innumerable institutions from which they find themselves alienated. The status quo is also quite frustrating considering that nonprofit organizations with larger proportions of women in leadership roles are more effective in their missions, have higher employee satisfaction and lower employee turnover, are more effective in fundraising, and employ a more democratic and participatory style of leadership. Research has further shown that organizations with more female board members are more likely to report satisfaction with board performance. They are also better equipped to reach out to and establish a reliable female donor and volunteer base (Williams, 2015).

Despite all of these issues, women continue to be drawn to the nonprofit sector for many reasons. Nonprofits tend to be more willing to provide flexible schedules, thus allowing workers to more easily balance family and work. There is also an abundance of opportunity for women in nonprofit organizations. Due to lower entry-level salaries and an existing wealth of women in the field, men are less likely to begin their careers at a nonprofit. This leaves the lion's share of these positions to women (Williams 2015).

Women are also drawn to work at a nonprofit for value-related reasons. Decision-making in the nonprofit world tends to be more collaborative than competitive, and thus egos and posturing are less likely to be on display as a valued professional trait. Finally, the lower pay of nonprofit work is less discouraging to many women entering the industry, who are willing to trade lower earnings for a greater sense of accomplishment, philanthropy, or social consciousness (Williams, 2015).

Racial (and Other) Diversities

Though a scarcity of research on women and nonprofit leadership exists, it is relatively well studied compared to the topic of racial and other diversities in nonprofit leadership. An important exception is the work of Vakalahi and Peebles-Wilkins (2009), who provide an edited volume of essays by 49 women of color who have become nonprofit directors and academic leaders in the San Francisco area.

Crawford (2018) notes that African American collegiate women attributed an important role to their spirituality in developing their leadership identity. Spirituality helped them know themselves, giving them confidence, which in turn gave them the desire to be leaders on their campus. Barkdull (2009) reports her research on Native American female leaders in social work. She notes five major themes her respondents discuss: (1) knowing "who I am," (2) turning points, (3) walking in two worlds (biculturalism), (4) call to service, and (5) women are the backbone (gender and matrilineality).

We believe that social work and nonprofit organizations need to approach the issue of leadership in a structural, holistic, and intersectional way. People of color have different issues in their careers than do whites. Women have different situations than do men. Women of color have still additional life experiences in their intersection of identities. We see other identities as well: gender, sexual orientation, age, difference in physical and mental abilities, class, different approaches to learning, and so on. We thus encourage everyone to see the need for equitable opportunities to be leaders as a structural issue, not just an individual one.

For decades, the majority of what were considered legitimate employment opportunities worked with the same, albeit unwritten, rule. Leadership, management, and the rigor of the corporate world were the sole realms of white men. They wrote the rules and therefore were really the only ones capable of playing the game as it was meant to be played. Thankfully, time and social struggle (including the recent #metoo movement) have done much to change this state of affairs. Structural-level change still needs to occur, however, if everyone is ever going to have an equal chance at success.

We must foster a culture that empowers people from marginalized populations in their search for leadership positions in the same way it does white men. The first step in this complicated process is to actively support the training and advancement of all qualified people into leadership roles. It must be established as a goal of organizations to not only find the best and brightest to fill open positions but to provide everyone with the same kind of mentoring and professional advancement programs that have primarily been available to white men. We must also ensure that these processes are formalized, in an attempt to overcome the informal networks and pathways to advancement that we have already discussed. It is essential to create an environment where healthy communication and relationships are allowed to grow and feed the culture and success of each organization without excluding, whether on purpose or not, any one group of employees (Outen, 2015). Additional concrete suggestions for changes to make in nonprofit organizations are found in Box 4.2.

BOX 4.2 Suggestions for Improving Pay Equity in Nonprofits

- Incorporate equity into your nonprofit's operations.
- Analyze job descriptions to ensure no gender bias exists.
- Confer raises transparently enough across programs/departments to keep compensation even across the organization.
- Offer parental/family leave rather than "maternity leave."
- Provide flexible leave arrangements throughout employment so that employees with family care responsibilities maintain access to quality work opportunities and benefits.
- Do not allow what people earned in the past to determine what salary you offer new hires.

Source:Adapted from Chandler, J. (2017).

What Do Social Work Leaders Do?

Nonprofit organizations come in a variety of sizes, fields, and purposes. Obviously, some are small local organizations, aiming to affect one neighborhood or community by providing services to a marginalized group. Contrast this with international organizations whose purposes are worldwide in scope, such as trying to reverse the process of global climate change. While the exact skills of being a leader may be somewhat different in different types of nonprofits, the literature has some clear guidelines regarding what skills are necessary. Chief among these are being able to work with a Board of Directors (Herman & Heimovics, 2005). This topic is so important for nonprofit administrators that it has an entire chapter devoted to it (Chapter 12).

Besides being adept with board relations, Herman and Heimovics (2005) make additional suggestions for successful leadership at the executive director level in the nonprofit world:

- Spend time on external relations.
- Develop an informal information network, particularly regarding future events.
- Know your agenda.
- Improvise and accept multiple partial solutions.
- Use a political framework to understand issues.

In summary, Herman and Heimovics (2005) declare that "board-centered, external, and political skills are what distinguish particularly effective nonprofit chief executives" (p. 169). However, lest one believe that nonprofits should operate under a "great leader" model, wherein all the responsibility for success or failure rests on the shoulders of one person, it is possible to recruit and train most people in these skills.

In addition to these normative research results, the mid-1990s saw considerable research to answer basic questions in the field of nonprofit administration. Hoefer (1993, with a follow-up article in 2003) addresses the question of what should be taught to prepare students to be effective nonprofit leaders. Hoefer (2003) develops three primary conclusions based on the ratings of the skills:

- "Strong agreement exists regarding which skills are most important at the three different levels of administration across disciplines and types of administrators" (p. 41).
- The desired knowledge, skill sets, and attitudes of human service administrators do not change very much as they move from lower levels of administration to higher levels. But it is important to become more accomplished in each of the areas as one reaches a higher level of administration.
- "For all respondents, at all levels, 'people skills' are the most important, and 'management' skills are the least important" (p. 38).

Another conceptualization of what social work managers should know was developed by the National Network for Social Work Managers (NSWM) and discussed in Wimpfheimer (2004). It was then updated by the NSWM (2018). Developed through a lengthy process of consultations with practitioners and academics, it discusses 14 competency areas that are considered vital for social work managers. To receive the "Certified Social Work Manager" credential from the NSWM, applicants must demonstrate their abilities in these areas. The standards of the NSWM are not minimum standards but are the competencies that are expected for experienced and academically trained managers. These standards have solid face validity, given the process used to develop and refine the list.

Leadership Skills at Different Levels of an Organization

Most people do not move directly from graduating college or graduate school to becoming the executive director of a nonprofit organization. They move up the ranks, just as in the corporate and government worlds. Still, leadership skills are necessary at all levels of nonprofits.

Research indicates that the types of skills needed in social work leadership positions are the same regardless of the level of administration (Hoefer, 1993). What changes, however, is that the leader is expected to have higher levels of all of the same skills as a manager and administrator than at lower levels in the organization. Even first-level supervisors should have good people skills, but executive directors should have *excellent* people skills (Hoefer, 1993, Hoefer, 2003). Thus, it is vital to remember that your leadership skills should be improved throughout your career and throughout your life.

Future Directions

Leadership is a fascinating topic for those in the nonprofit field. Given the difficult-to-define nature of nonprofits and the multiplicity of theories about how to be a good leader, continued research is imperative. Besides better defining which skills might be most important in what type of situations, other areas for research are needed. One of the important topics is assessing efforts for students and current leaders to learn new skills and improve on current basic levels of leadership skills. Some research has been done in this area (Austin, Regan, Samples, Schwartz, & Carnochan, 2013; Hoefer & Sliva, 2014). One

area of additional needed research is perhaps the most difficult of all: How does improved leadership link to improved outcomes for clients, students, or the public at large? Because nonprofits are legally chartered to enhance the public good, we must always keep sight of the connection between what leaders do and how the public benefits from those actions.

Conclusion

In the end, we must echo Tschirhart's (1997) words as she ends her book on leadership in nonprofit arts organizations: "There are no simple formulas to adopt" (p. 84). Despite this warning, we have identified what leadership is and what it can be used for and described a four-quadrant system (and associated leadership theories) to show how different skills can be categorized and used in nonprofit leadership. We have also identified basic leadership skills that are needed across the spectrum of nonprofit organizations (particularly human service agencies) and the situations in which they are most useful. With this as a guide, organization leaders may find it easier to have a positive impact, despite daunting challenges in their everyday work.

Reference List

Austin, M. J., Regan, K., Samples, M. W., Schwartz, S. L. & Carnochan, S. (2013). Building managerial and organizational capacity in nonprofit human service organizations through a leadership development program. *Administration in Social Work, 35*(3), 258–281.

Barkdull, C. (2009). Exploring intersections of identity with Native American women leaders. *Affilia, 24*(2), 120–136.

Bennis, W. (2009). *On becoming a leader* (4th ed.). New York, NY: Basic Books.

Burns, J. M. (1978). *Leadership.* New York, NY: Harper & Row.

Carlyle, T. (1907). *On heroes, hero-worship, and the heroic in history.* Boston, MA: Houghton Mifflin.

Chandler, J. (2017, March 15). The gender pay gap is a sleeper threat to nonprofit effectiveness and sustainability. Retrieved from National Council of Nonprofits website: https://www.councilofnonprofits.org/thought-leadership/the-gender-pay-gap-sleeper-threat-nonprofit-effectiveness-and-sustainability

Crawford, K. (2018). I am, therefore I lead: Exploring the intersection of spirituality, authenticity, and leadership identity in African American women leaders at a predominantly white institution. Doctoral dissertation, Texas A & M University. Retrieved from http://hdl.handle.net/1969.1/173638

Cyert, R. (1990). Defining leadership and explicating the process. *Nonprofit Management & Leadership, 1*(1), 29–38.

Dym, B., & Hutson, H. (2005). *Leadership in nonprofit organizations.* Thousand Oaks, CA: Sage.

Fielder, F. (1967). *A theory of leadership effectiveness.* New York, NY: McGraw-Hill.

Grant, H. M., & Crutchfield, L. (2008). The hub of leadership: Lessons from the social sector. *Leader to Leader, 2008*(48), 45–52.

Greenleaf, R. (1991). *The servant as leader* (Rev. ed.). Indianapolis, IN: Robert K. Greenleaf Center.

Herman, R., & Heimovics, R. (2004). Executive leadership. In R. Herman (Ed.), *The Jossey-Bass handbook of nonprofit leadership and management* (2nd ed., pp. 153–170). San Francisco, CA: Jossey-Bass.

Herman, R. D., & Renz, D. O. (1997). Multiple constituencies and the social construction of nonprofit organization effectiveness. *Nonprofit and Voluntary Sector Quarterly, 26*(2), 185–206.

Herman, R., & Renz, D. (2004). Doing things right: Effectiveness in local nonprofit organizations, a panel study. *Public Administration Review, 64*(6), 694–704.

Hoefer, R. (1993). A matter of degree: Job skills for human service administration. *Administration in Social Work, 17*(3), 1–20.

Hoefer, R. (2003). Administrative skills and degrees: The "best place" debate rages on. *Administration in Social Work, 27*(1), 25–46.

Hoefer, R., & Sliva, S. (2014). Assessing and augmenting administration skills in nonprofits: An exploratory mixed methods study. *Human Service Organizations: Management, Leadership & Governance, 38*(3), 246–257.

Hopkins, K. M., & Hyde, C. (2002). The human service managerial dilemma: New expectations, chronic challenges and old solutions. *Administration in Social Work, 26*(3), 1–15.

Hughes, R., Ginnet R., & Curphy G. (2006), *Leadership: Enhancing the lessons of experience.* New York, NY: McGraw-Hill.

Kirkpatrick, S., & Locke, E. (1991). Leadership: Do traits matter? *Academy of Management Perspectives, 5*(2), 48–60.

Lawler, J., & Bilson, A. (2010). *Social work management and leadership: Managing complexity with creativity.* New York, NY: Routledge.

Lewin, K., Lippitt, R., & White, R. (1970). Patterns of aggressive behavior in experimentally created "social climates". In P. Harriman (Ed.), *Twentieth century psychology* (pp. 200–230). Manchester, NH: Ayer.

McGregor, D. (1957). *The human side of enterprise.* New York, NY: McGraw Hill.

Mohr, L. (1982). *Explaining organizational behavior.* San Francisco, CA: Jossey-Bass.

Network for Social Work Management (NSWM). (2018). Competencies. Retrieved from https://social-workmanager.org/competencies/

Outen, P. (2015, November 20). Women in nonprofits: Then and now [Web log post]. Retrieved from https://trust.guidestar.org/blog/2015/11/20/women-in-nonprofits-then-now/

Patz, E. (2018, March 8). Where are all the women in nonprofit leadership? [Web log post]. Retrieved from https://topnonprofits.com/women-nonprofit-leadership/

Peters, S. C. (2018). Defining social work leadership: A theoretical and conceptual review and analysis. *Journal of Social Work Practice, 32*(1), 31–44. doi:10.1080/02650533.2017.1300877

Pfeffer, J., & Salancik, G. R. (1978). *The external control of organizations: A resource dependence perspective.* New York, NY: Harper and Row.

Poertner, J. (2006). Social administration and outcomes for consumers: What do we know? *Administration in Social Work, 30*(2), 11–24.

Rothschild, J., & Milofsky, C. (2006). The centrality of values, passions, and ethics in the nonprofit sector. *Nonprofit Management & Leadership, 17*(2), 137–143.

Schmid, H. (2006). Leadership styles and leadership change in human and community service organizations. *Nonprofit Management & Leadership, 17*(2), 179–194.

Scott, W. R. (1995). *Institutions and organizations.* Thousand Oaks, CA: Sage.

Shenkman, M. (2007, March–April). Defining your leader brand. *Nonprofit World,* 13–14.

Stiffman, E. (2015, September 15). Women nonprofit leaders still make less than men, survey finds. *The Chronicle of Philanthropy.* Retrieved from https://www.philanthropy.com/article/Women-Nonprofit-Leaders-Still/233129

Tschirhart, M. (1997). *Artful leadership: Managing stakeholder problems in nonprofit arts organizations.* Bloomington: Indiana University Press.

Vakalahi, H., & Peebles-Wilkins, W. (Eds.) (2009). *Women of color on the rise: Leadership and administration in social work education and the academy.* New York, NY: Columbia University Press.

Vito, R. (2018). Social work leadership revisited: Participatory versus directive approaches during service system transformation. *Journal of Social Work Practice.* doi:10.1080/02650533.2018.1529026

Watson, L. D., & Hoefer, R. A. (2016). The joy of social work administration: An exploratory qualitative study of human service administrators' positive perceptions of their work. *Journal of Social Work Education, 52*(2), 178–185.

Williams, K. (2015, April 24). Why female CEOS thrive in nonprofits. *Forbes.* Retrieved from https://www.forbes.com/sites/work-in-progress/2015/04/24/why-female-ceos-thrive-in-nonprofits/#338d068e5335

Wimpfheimer, S. (2004). Leadership and management competencies defined by practicing social work managers: An overview of standards developed by the National Network for Social Work Managers. *Administration in Social Work, 28*(1), 45–56.

Additional Resources

Dudley, D. (2010). Leading with lollipops [Video file]. TEDxToronto. Retrieved from https://youtu.be/hVCBrkrFrBE

Institute for Women's Policy Research (n.d.). Pay equity and discrimination. Retrieved from https://iwpr.org/issue/employment-education-economic-change/pay-equity-discrimination/

The National Child Welfare Workforce Institute

The National Child Welfare Workforce Institute has free interactive online training materials for supervisors and leaders that you can use on your own or in a group to learn many skills (https://ncwwi.org/index.php/special-collections/curricula-and-training-materials). While geared toward people working in the child welfare arena, most of the material is about supervision and middle management, which is useful no matter what type of organization you work in. Their exercises allow you to practice as you learn.

The Network for Social Work Management

This organization provides a wealth of information for social work managers and leaders. Here are just two:

Network for Social Work Management. (2018). *Human services management competencies: A guide for non-profit and for-profit agencies, foundations, and academic institutions.* Retrieved from https://social-workmanager.org/wp-content/uploads/2018/12/HSMC-Guidebook-December-2018.pdf

Network for Social Work Management. (2018). Managing oneself: tools to take one's development to the next level [Video file]. https://socialworkmanager.org/nswm-event/14443/ (This is a pre-recorded webinar you can watch.)

HELPFUL TERMS

Authoritative leadership style—a leadership style marked by telling people what to do without providing many opportunities for feedback or suggestions from those being affected, also called directive style.

Contingency leadership theory—a theory regarding leadership that says the effectiveness or appropriateness of a leader's behaviors is determined to some degree by the leader's environment.

Democratic leadership style—a style of leadership in which the leader seeks out others' opinions and attempts to influence others so that a general consensus around a decision emerges, also called participative style.

Directive leadership style—see "authoritative leadership style."

"Great man/great person" leadership theory—a theory regarding leadership that posits that "leaders are born, not made," also called trait theory. In other words, people have the innate ability to be a "great leader" or not.

Laissez-faire leadership style—a style of leadership in which the leader puts little effort into being the leader or making decisions, allowing others to do as they wish.

Multiple constituency theory—a theory of leadership that indicates that leaders must attend to the needs and desires of a number of stakeholders (constituencies) rather than having only one constituency to satisfy.

Organizational effectiveness—a concept that is usually linked to the ability of an organization to accomplish its stated goals. Sometimes the concept is operationalized differently, however, such as, "an effective organization is one that has survived" or "an effective organization is one that is growing."

Participative leadership style—see "democratic leadership style."

Servant leadership—an approach to leadership in which the leader chooses to lead in a way that is in service to others. The goal for the servant-leader is to serve first and to acquire power or influence later, and then only to continue to serve others better.

Single goal/maximizing organization theory—the idea that an organization can be thought of as a unitary entity pursuing one goal to the utmost.

Stakeholder—any individual or outside organization with a vested interest in what occurs within an organization. Typical stakeholders in a nonprofit include service recipients, funders, employees, board members, and the public at large.

System resources theory—a theory of organizations that indicates that the key measure of organizational success is the amount of resources extracted from the environment, with a larger budget indicating a more successful organization.

Trait leadership theory—a theory of leadership characterized by lists of individual traits that are said to be associated with being a good leader, also called "great man/great person" theory.

Transformational leadership style—a style of leadership in which the leader creates a vision, sells that vision to followers, and then moves forward to enact the vision with the followers.

EXERCISES

1. Personal Goal-Setting Exercise

Before we begin this section, we want you to write your career goal. We encourage you to dream big, but be honest about your ambition. Use these few lines (or write a draft elsewhere) to write down your current professional goal.

_____

_____

_____

_____

Naturally, as a student and ambitious individual, you are no stranger to setting goals. Professional life is all about working toward your goals, whether long-term or immediate. However, when it comes to the larger context of our lives, our life's work, and our careers, we often create goals that, while noble and poetic, are unrealistic, impractical, or unattainable. It's one thing to want to "change the world." But this goal is not that practical by itself.

Where do you start? How do you know you're on the right track? How will you know when you've succeeded? In order to avoid these pitfalls, numerous methods of goal setting have been proposed for a myriad of settings and personal styles. For our purposes, and based simply on personal preferences and experiences, we focus on creating SMART goals. This particular method emphasizes forming your personal or professional goals by asking, are your goals Specific, Measurable, Achievable, Realistic, and Time-bound? Since you've already established the overarching goal for your career in the space above, use the following table to examine this goal more closely.

SMART	Ask yourself:	Your Goal: How is it SMART?
Specific	What do you want to accomplish? Why is the goal important? Who is involved in achieving the goal? Where can the goal be attained? Which requirements or restrictions are involved?	
Measurable	How will you know when you've accomplished your goal? How much? How many? Focus on quantifiable measures and checkpoints.	
Achievable	Can YOU achieve the goal? Is it in line with your other priorities? Do you have an accurate picture of what it takes to succeed?	
Realistic	Are there any unavoidable barriers to success? Will your personal background or external factors hurt your efforts?	
Time-bound	When do you want to succeed? What can you do to-day? What can you do in six weeks? Six months?	

Now that you've had a chance to adjust your goal through the SMART process, write your revised goal below:

_____

_____

_____

_____

The purpose of this exercise is twofold. First, while it may seem obvious that anyone who would read this book would be at least marginally driven to advance to a leadership position, the process of laying out your goals and then making them more real by going through some analytical process will often temper the grandeur of your ambition. When faced with some stark realities, many people realize that their true goals are dramatically different from their idealized ambitions. In this case, the suggestions within this exercise can be taken in parts and with varying levels of intensity based on your newly refined goals. The second purpose, for those who are truly driven to management and leadership positions in their current fields, is to lay out a goal in a way that provides a roadmap for success. By ensuring that your goal not only is SMART but also readily answers the questions that make up each component of a SMART goal, you have in essence laid out the basic steps that must be taken to succeed.

2. In-Basket Exercise

Directions

Pretend you are Rebecca Mayes the recently appointed Chief Executive Officer of Bound for Success, Inc., (BfS), a youth-serving agency specializing in assisting teen foster children in successfully transitioning to independent adulthood by the time they are 22 years of age. Read the following memo from Jim Kreslin, a consultant you have hired to help you get your bearings straight in your new position. Your agency faces many challenges, and it is up to you to provide guidance to the consultant so he can provide information on possible paths for agency sustainability. You will, of course, need to work closely with the Board of Directors of BfS, but you would like to have some concrete ideas to start the conversation with them.

Your assignment is to write a memo to your consultant that indicates your top three priorities (in rank order) and the specific actions you believe should be taken to implement these priorities. Provide clear rationales for your decisions so that the consultant can be most helpful to you in his next report. As you write your memo to the consultant, be clear in your mind which stakeholder group(s) you have in mind as your primary reference point. Are you looking more to satisfy the Board of Directors of BfS, donors and other funders (current and potential), clients, staff members, or some combination of these? You will find that knowing who you are trying to satisfy most will have a large impact on the clarity of your thinking.

Memo

Date: September 21, 20XX

To: Rebecca Mayes, CEO, Bound for Success, Inc.

From: Jim Kreslin, Consultant

Subject: Strategic Planning Ideas

As requested, I have completed a preliminary analysis of Bound for Success's (BfS's) current situation. Before moving forward, I need direction from you regarding your priorities and the options you feel are most in line with your desired strategy.

There are several important trends impacting BfS. The first is the anticipated decrease in opportunities for federal and state grants. As you know, government sources of funding are becoming fewer and fewer as elected officials promise to reduce taxes, "get back to basics," and let private donors and foundations take more of the funding role for social services. At the same time, many foundations are still unable to provide as much funding as they have in the past due to difficult times in the stock market, where much of their assets are invested. Private donors are also barely keeping their levels of funding even, as the economic situation is unsettled for so many. Even BfS's own board's giving has dwindled.

To address these factors, BfS could choose from among the following options:

- Increase its spending on marketing to the general public so that our name recognition and good work is more widely known

- Hire an external grantwriter (at a significant fee) to supplement current fundraising efforts

- Improve and expand current communication channels with important stakeholders and potential donors (we have not used social media outlets such as Facebook and Twitter to any extent, and our web page has not been updated for six months)

- Join coalitions of human service agencies to advocate more funding for human services in general and agencies serving our client population in particular

- Engage the BfS board more actively to donate at previous or even expanded levels

- Recruit more donors by training board members to fundraise among their peers more effectively

At the same time that BfS must understand and deal with these external issues, a number of other issues are important within the organization. As you are aware, no raises have been given to staff for the past three years. Not only has this impacted morale among the agency's workers, but it is also leading to higher levels of staff turnover and increased costs in recruiting new staff members. The high-quality applicants we would like to hire are not attracted by our starting salaries, yet the persons willing to work for what we currently offer do not have the skills we need. If we were somehow able to increase our starting salaries for the type of employee we have had, their salaries would be higher than those of loyal workers who have been on the job for many years. I am afraid this would lead to a loss of our more senior workers. Another important issue is that proper building maintenance has been deferred for several years. The building's age shows, and both residents and staff see this general deterioration as a negative.

Additionally, it has been at least six years since BfS took a serious look at its programming. A great deal of research has been conducted in this time, and our programs are no longer using the evidence-based information that made them so attractive to funders only a few years ago. The programs we use are not necessarily culturally relevant to the many youth of color we serve, and funding for training to improve staff members' ability to be culturally competent has not kept up with the needs we face, particularly with the high turnover noted earlier.

We should be implementing what are seen to be the most effective services available at the current time, but we have no one assigned to the task of staying abreast of the research literature on this topic. Regaining the reputation for being at the forefront of effective service delivery is an important task.

Some steps that BfS could take to handle these (mainly internal) issues include the following:

- Work with a salary and benefits consultant to come into line with local averages for employee compensation

- Hire a researcher from Southeastern University's School of Social Work (or other university) to determine what are currently the most effective, evidence-based services for our clients

- Revamp our service delivery system to be more efficient and to require fewer front-line employees. Savings from having fewer staff could be used to fill a rainy day fund or increase salaries for current and future employees

- Restructure our entire agency to reduce the need for (relatively) expensive admin- istrative positions such as separate directors of "Clinical Services" and "External Relations and Development"

- Engage trainers to assist staff with issues of cultural and racial diversity

Also at your request, I interviewed representatives of some of the important stakeholder groups at BfS. Board members are most concerned with financial stability and organizational sustain- ability. Staff members would like to see a stronger focus on pay and working conditions, as well as on being able to assist clients more effectively. Current donors express no negative feelings, but many of them have been surprised at a lack of outreach to them, whether to communicate future plans or even to give thanks for past contributions. Current clients are so focused on their problems that they have few opinions regarding the direction of the agency, as long as their existing needs are met.

I would appreciate it if you would provide guidance as to which issues are your most important priorities and which options I should explore further to address those priorities. If you would also explain the reasons for your decisions, that will greatly benefit me as I work to provide you and the board with a viable plan for agency sustainability.

3. Follow the Leader

Purpose: to experience the difficulty of directing other people to perform specific tasks. One aspect of leadership is being able to communicate clearly and directly. This exercise shows how challenging a task this can be!

Preparation: You will need an open area (as in the middle of a room) to conduct this exercise. Have participants get in pairs, standing together to one side of the open area. One person from each pair should be blindfolded or must promise to keep his or her eyes closed during the exercise. The other person is the "leader." On the floor in the open area, scatter a number of sheets of paper.

Task: The leader in each pair must direct the follower to walk across the open space without the follower touching any of the scattered sheets of paper. The follower must not be able to see the paper. The leader may not use any guidance techniques except for telling the follower what to do. No touching or guiding with props is allowed. Of course, the leader may not touch the sheets of paper either!

Variations

a. The task can be made more or less challenging depending on the number of sheets of paper used. Hav- ing to navigate a few sheets of paper can be thought of as the "front-line supervisor level," a moderate number can be the "department or program leader level," and a large number would be the "CEO level" of leadership. This exercise works best if both members of the pair take turns being leader and follower and if everyone experiences at least two levels of leadership to show how the process gets more com- plicated with increasing responsibility.

b. The leader may be allowed to stay beside the follower or may be forced to stay 5–10 feet away from the follower.

c. Add a time dimension by allowing only a certain amount of time for the task to be completed.

d. The leader may become responsible for more than one follower simultaneously. If any of the followers touch the paper on the floor, all are out.

e. Add a competitive element by timing each pair. The pair that completes the task most quickly without touching the paper wins a small prize.

f. The leader may choose a leadership or management theory to implement during this process. Thinking about the ways different theories would try to elicit particular follower behaviors can bring home differences in how management and leadership theories work "in real life." The instructor can start with discussing the differences between how an authoritarian leader and a laissez-faire leader would approach leading a follower from one side of the room to the other and allow students to try out these approaches or use other leadership theories and perspectives in their efforts.

4. Discuss Your Passion for Nonprofit Leadership

Purpose: to facilitate students' thinking about and ability to express why they would like to be a nonprofit leader. Understanding your own motivation and passion to be a nonprofit leader can be challenging. Discussing such topics in front of a group can be embarrassing. To succeed in a nonprofit leadership position (or to be hired in the first place), it is important to be able to speak fluidly and with ease about these topics. With practice, discussing these topics becomes easier.

Preparation: Students form into pairs. One is the interviewer, and one the interviewee. (Note: A person can practice answering questions on his or her own, if desired or needed.) Develop a set of two or three questions as a class or small group. The following are some suggested questions:

- What makes you excited to be a nonprofit leader?

- What motivates you to work in a nonprofit rather than a for-profit organization?

- If you were interviewing for a leadership position in a nonprofit agency, what would you say makes you a good fit for such a job?

- Fill in the blanks: "My preferred style of leadership is _____ because _____."

Task: The two students in each pair practice asking and answering the chosen questions. When they are comfortable with their ability to answer the questions, have the students do this in front of the class (or have only volunteers do this).

Variations

a. Have students make videos of themselves answering the questions in class (using their cell phones if available). Have them critique their own performance with their partner. Have students discuss what they would do to improve their performance.

b. Students can be assigned to make a video outside of class of themselves answering the questions. This would then be posted to a class wiki or other area to be viewed by the instructor and/or other students. This variation works well for online courses.

5. Being the "Dancing Guy"

Purpose: One definition of being a leader is having one or more followers. Leadership occurs at all levels of organizations, not just at the top of the organizational chart. Leadership skills need to be developed throughout your career, as many of them are similar in nature no matter where in an organization your current position is. This exercise shows the way leadership can emerge anywhere and at any time.

Preparation: Go to YouTube and search for the term "Leadership Lessons from the Dancing Guy." Select any one of the versions of the video available. (They are all copies of the original one by Derek Sivers at https://www.youtube.com/watch?v=fW8amMCVAJQ.) Cue up the video for your class or group. Announce that you are going to demonstrate that anyone can be a leader.

Task: First, watch the video without sound. Lead a discussion with students about what they saw. Then discuss the sorts of things that they can do in the spirit of being the "dancing guy" at their job or in their volunteer time. Discuss the differences between formal leadership positions and informal leadership. Then show the video again, with sound, to listen to the commentary by Derek Sivers.

Variations

a. Have students try being "the dancing guy" in some part of their lives (for extra credit), perhaps by starting a dancing mob or engaging in some other non-dangerous behavior, even just looking up at the top of a building. Have them debrief for the class what occurred and how it felt.

b. Have students take the exercise one step further by preorganizing the "spontaneous" first and second followers to join in. What other ways can they think of to improve their perceived leadership abilities by using theory and knowledge in their work?

ASSIGNMENTS

1. A huge number of sources exist regarding leadership, and more become available constantly. This assignment asks you to "curate" information for yourself and others in your class or group. Be willing to post the results of these assignments to a class or group wiki or other method of dissemination.

    a. Find two to three books on leadership or by leaders you'd be willing to read. What makes them attractive to you? What can they tell you about how to be a better leader?

    b. Find four to five videos on leadership in nonprofits, searching YouTube, Vimeo, or other free sources. Write a synopsis of what each video is about. Rate each video from 1 (not good at all) to 5 (excellent source of information) and explain your rating.

    c. Search for a nonprofit leadership training or seminar you could attend, live or virtually. Try to find participant reviews of it. Describe the training and reviews for others in your class or group.

2. Think about leaders you are aware of, whether you have known them or only read or seen information about them. These people may be as varied as a Scout leader, an historical leader such as Jane Addams or Abraham Lincoln, an instructor or teacher, or a boss in one of your jobs. Make a list of the qualities you see that are good leadership traits, skills, or behaviors. Have at least 15 different entries. Look over this list and group the individual items into a smaller number of overarching behaviors or skills. Label these groups. Write or find a definition that matches your idea of what YOU mean by each term. Be prepared to discuss your list and definitions in class or other group setting.

3. Select a person who is in a leadership position in the nonprofit world. (This position may be paid or volunteer.) Arrange to interview him or her. Find out about that person's journey to the current leadership position. What led to starting in this position? What training does your interviewee have (formal or informal)? Does this person follow any "theories" of leadership, such as being directive, participative, or delegative? Did the person you talked with have a mentor? (Note: This assignment works best if several or all students or group members ask similar questions so that, after sharing what was discussed in the interview, generalizations can be made about the processes of becoming a leader in the nonprofit world.)

Image Credits

Personal Communication

Accoording to research, oral and written communication skills are among the most important skills for leaders to have, regardless of type of organization (Hoefer, 2003). In fact, it is safe to say that if people cannot communicate well, they cannot be effective leaders, regardless of their job title. This chapter provides information about understanding *what* you want to communicate and *how* to communicate well. Communication is such a vital skill for nonprofit leaders that we also have Chapter 13 (Persuasion) and Chapter 14 (Advocacy), which also deal with communication. Those chapters are geared toward communication with the purpose of moving others to agree with you and to take certain actions. The skills in this chapter are important for being able to be persuasive, as well, so these interpersonal skills really form the foundation for communication of all types.

Before moving forward, it is important to remember that the techniques of communication are rarely important for their own sake. The most well-written and well-delivered speech, for example, even if it is a wonderful application of communication theory, will fall flat if personal connection is not made with the intended audience. Communication, at its core, is sending and receiving messages—messages of transformation, direction, praise, correction, affirmation, hope, affection, or belonging, for example. Leaders must know the techniques of effective communication to make connections with others within and outside their organization and to provide a means of accomplishing organizational goals through the work of those others.

Just as with the topic of leadership (Chapter 4), the amount of material about personal communication in the research literature can be overwhelming. Thus, we must choose a selection of everything that could be covered. Resources are

BOX 5.1 EPAS Competencies Covered

The CSWE Competencies we connect with most in this chapter are Competency 2: Engage Diversity and Difference in Practice; Competency 3: Advance Human Rights and Social, Economic, and Environmental Justice; Competency 6: Engage with Individuals, Families, Groups, Organizations, and Communities; and Competency 8: Intervene with Individuals, Families, Groups, Organizations, and Communities.

listed at the end to guide you to additional material to delve into specific topics. In this chapter, we have six topics. First, we discuss how to create a shared identity, which is linked to more effective communication in general. Second, explore active listening techniques to improve your ability to understand what others want to communicate to you. Third, we show how managers must manage their emotions so that they communicate what they want to communicate and not something else. Fourth, we look at storytelling as a method of making your message resonate. Fifth, we examine the topic of written communication. Finally, we touch on communicating with diverse audiences. All of these are important in developing your leadership capacity.

Create a Shared Identity

Molenberghs, Prochilo, Steffens, Zacher, and Haslam (2015) describe the importance of connecting with the people you wish to communicate with. They show that the messages leaders intend to be inspirational are much more likely to be perceived that way when the recipients feel a shared identity with the leader. Leaders wanting to inspire should understand that they can change how much their followers identify with them. The level of feelings of shared identity can be changed, are different in different settings, and exist on a continuum (Molenberghs et al. 2015). Additional research shows that leaders need to work on clearly indicating what it means to be a member of the group by clarifying group norms, identifying elements of group norms, and structuring the organization to promote a reality of group identity in line with aspirational statements (Molenberghs et al. 2015). When members of an organization feel estranged from leaders and managers, effective personal communication will be difficult.

One of the most important researchers in communication and persuasion studies is Robert Cialdini (we'll see more of him in Chapter 13). Cialdini (2016) argues that easy similarities help, but the true level of relationship for effective, persuasive communication is a shared identity: "It's about the categories that individuals use to define themselves and their groups, such as race, ethnicity, nationality, and family, as well as political and religious affiliations" (p. 175). It is an enormous struggle to persuade anyone who does not see you as a member of their "in-group." Managers who do not identify with their workers and leaders who are not seen as being part of the organization face significant challenges.

What can you do to increase your image as part of the group you're communicating with rather than an out-of-touch or autocratic leader who doesn't understand the life of those under you? Research indicates that you can increase your perceived level of "identity" in various ways. Are you from the same town, know the same people, share the same values? Did you graduate from the same school? Are your clothes the same brand? What can you do to point out that "you" and "me" are actually "we," even in minor ways? Any way that you can create the sense of being "of the same group" will make your job as a leader easier, even if finding this connection may be difficult. Box 5.2 contains tips for creating a greater sense of group identity between yourself and your audience, no matter the form of communication. We need to emphasize that authenticity is essential in using these tips. Your message will be doomed if you are perceived as faking a connection when you want to show that you and others share an identity.

BOX 5.2 **Tips for Increasing the Sense of Group Identity in Communication**

1. Look for indications of common interests and speak about them.
2. Wear clothing or emblems similar to those of the audience.
3. Use vivid imagery to link your words to concepts you want to implant in the audience's mind. Photos or other images can be very effective.
4. Connect your ideas with "family" metaphors and references whenever possible. Show images of happy people working together.
5. Develop a motto, chant, tagline, or slogan that is unique to your organization or team within the larger agency. Even something as simple as, "We serve people," can be enough to focus on what is important for the agency and acts as a clear guide to everyday decisions.

Source: Adapted from Cialdini, 2016.

Listen Actively

Arguably the most important skill for effective personal communication (as a manager or otherwise) is to use active listening. Based on the work of Carl Rogers, this process is seen as part of a manager's job (Rogers & Farson, 2015). An effective manager will "appreciate both the meaning and the feeling" (Rogers & Farson, p. 1) behind what the speaker is saying. According to Rogers and Farson the purpose of active listening is to "help employees gain a clearer understanding of their situations, take responsibility, and cooperate with each other" (p. 1).

Active listening is not easy. Rogers and Farson caution that leaders must not rely on the everyday approach often used in conversation, thinking more about what *they* are going to say, rather than what the speaker is saying.

Active listening, according to Rogers and Farson (2015), brings about better self-understanding for the speaker, who becomes "more emotionally mature, more open to their experiences, less defensive, more democratic and less authoritarian" (p. 3). The listener also benefits by obtaining more information from the speaker, developing deep positive relationships, and constructively improving attitudes.

To achieve these results, the active listener must use the following techniques:

- **Listen for meaning, not just content.** Messages and conversations have content, but content can be surrounded by additional contextual information. For example, a colleague could tell you, "I just completed the quarterly report for the new project we're starting," and you would be likely to give a positive response.

Suppose that colleague told you instead, "I finally got done with the quarterly report for the director's pet project—now I can do some real work!" You would probably understand that a significantly different set of meanings was intended by your colleague. Even if you gave the same content response, such as "Congratulations!" it might be construed differently in the two situations by your colleague. In the first situation, you might find the meaning given to your word is that of a straightforward and supportive acknowledgment. In the second situation, however, your coworker might assume you are being ironic, which could still be seen as supportive but might be interpreted as disrespectful by the director if you were overheard.

- **Respond to feelings.** For active listening to take place, you must let the speaker know that you have comprehended both the content of the statement and the feelings that emerge with the content. In the same example, you could be a better listener if you replied, in the first instance, "Congratulations! That must feel good to have that finished!" and, in the second, "You sound like you're not too happy with having to do that job. It must be a relief to move on to something else." Neither of these responses takes much longer to say, but both indicate that you are trying to understand how your coworker feels about what has just been said.
- **Note nonverbal cues.** Communication happens through many channels, including tone of voice, speed of talking, volume level, vocal hesitations, facial expressions, hand gestures, and other body language. To completely understand someone else's meaning, you must decode what all these nonverbal signals mean.

While the benefits of active listening are many, there are at least three reasons why people do not listen actively. Multitasking is a common behavior, wherein we try to do something else while the speaker is talking. This frequently results in miscommunication, because important nonverbal and emotional cues are not noticed. It is best to lay aside other things and focus on the speaker when you wish to listen carefully. Some people are unable to actively listen to a speaker because they are formulating their own responses to the previous statement the speaker said. They may even be lining up the reasons why the speaker is wrong instead of following along with what is being said. Remember that you are not engaging in a debate but rather attempting to understand the other person's viewpoint.

Another barrier to active listening that frequently occurs at work is that the person speaking is of lower status than the listener. While we would all like to believe that we pay attention to everyone regardless of status, the facts show otherwise. Our supervisors and leaders usually receive our attention because what they say can affect our job situation positively or negatively. It is more difficult to listen attentively to someone who reports to you, particularly when you have a lot of other work to complete. It can be even worse if the person speaking is in a different department or is unknown to you. Unfortunately, we may respond to communications from clients with a lack of attention as well. Despite our best intentions, we may also harbor biases and prejudices about certain populations that get in the way of listening to them. The best way to guard against these tendencies is to stay aware of our own biases and to feel deeply that each person has inherent worth, just as Carl Rogers taught.

Schwartz (2017) provides questions to ask yourself as you are listening, which we adapt here for social work managers and leaders (see

Box 5.3). We believe active listeners should be able to answer them before a conversation ends. In fact, as you end conversations dealing with important topics or when you have delegated tasks, you may wish to ensure that the person you've communicated with can provide a good answer to these questions, too.

BOX 5.3 Schwartz's Four Questions for Active Listening (Adapted to Social Work Management)

---

1. Why am I being given this information?
2. Do I need additional information to understand the full importance of what I've been told?
3. To what degree is this information and decision relevant to my organization's mission?
4. If this is a request for action, do we have the time and resources to move forward now?

Source: Schwartz, 2017

The first question is, "Why am I being given this information?" Without knowing the purpose of a communication, the listener will find it difficult to pay attention and thus take appropriate action. Scaffolding is an important adult education approach that links new information to information that a person already has. In this way, the listener can more easily retain and grasp the importance of the new information. Also, when you are trying to send a clear message, you will want to have your listener be able to figure out why they are being given the information. Keeping this in mind, you can create your own message to ensure understanding of the purpose behind it. You can use this question as a way to provide feedback to people communicating with you, as well. This thought process will help them craft their messages for maximum impact and minimum time used.

The second question is vital before making a decision or planning action: "Do I need additional information to understand the full importance of what I've been told?" Sometimes this can be phrased as a question to the person you are working with: "What questions should I ask that haven't been covered yet? If you were in my shoes, what else would you want to know?" By being open to revealing your own gaps in knowledge, you overcome one of the most important cognitive biases to effective leadership—not knowing what you don't know.

The third question relates to the action that you may want or need to take based on the information you now have: "To what degree is this information and decision relevant to my organization's mission?" If the answer is that there is little or no relevance, you may want to ask more questions of the person you are speaking with to ensure you understand their view about its relevance. If you have been a good active listener, the speaker will have covered the answer, because this question overlaps with the first question. If you see that the information is quite relevant to your nonprofit's mission, you will understand its importance. You may want to take immediate action, or it may be important but not urgent, something to add to the list of things to take care of at a specified time or to delegate to someone else.

The final question related to active listening is, "If this is a request for action, do we have the time and resources to move forward now? If not, how would we acquire them?" Of course, this question may need to wait for additional information and thinking about larger planning issues, but when a new idea is presented is a good moment to ask about needed resources.

Becoming skilled in active listening techniques will not solve every problem you encounter as a manager. You will still need to work with employees who are not performing well. Some employees may expect you to understand them using ESP, so they don't need to explain to you what they are thinking. This is a challenge. Over time, however, using active listening will make your job easier because you will at least understand what your coworkers want to tell you. This will go a long way toward making every day smoother because your colleagues will learn to trust that you will listen to them before you make decisions that affect them. Your colleagues will have seen you seeking to understand their views first before you take action. Even if they don't agree with your final decision, they will be more likely to follow your lead because their ideas have been heard.

Manage Your Emotional Self

Related to the need to be a skilled active listener, and thus to understand what other people want to communicate, is the need to manage your own emotional self. While the idea of emotional intelligence is currently heatedly debated on both conceptual (Eysenck, 2000; Locke, 2005) and methodological (Brody, 2004) grounds, managers need to understand their own emotions (as they occur) and be able to handle them appropriately. Managers and leaders are frequently put into positions where conflict is either raging or bubbling under the surface. Frequently, tough decisions must be made. The outcomes of these decisions can have severely negative repercussions for some people—staff members might be laid off or fired, client services may be reduced, or programs might be eliminated entirely.

Even if you have used active listening to its fullest, sometimes people are going to be very distraught and angry. They may yell at you, threaten you, or start other unpleasant or even dangerous situations. It is at times such as this that your ability to notice how you are feeling (angry, frightened, irritated, afraid, withdrawn, and so on) is vital. Strong emotions can result in an "emotional hijacking" (Goleman, 2006), wherein your feelings literally avoid the rational parts of your brain and affect your "primitive brain" directly. Such a hijacking can cause you to invoke the "flight or fight" response, which motivates you to run away or to lash out. Hormones and adrenaline are immediately released by your body, which then stimulate action without thought. While this type of reaction is important if one is about to be attacked by a predator, it has less use in a nonprofit office. Being unable to take back control after an emotional hijacking can be quite damaging to your career and have negative effects for your organization.

In this type of situation, being able to note and classify your emotional state allows you to reroute your hijacked brain so that your thoughts go through the rational parts of the cortex and allows you to regain the ability to think logically about how to respond to the perceived danger you face. It may be that you are not threatened nearly as much as you first thought. Taking the time to calm down enough to think again will usually save considerable amounts of time later on, as you will not need to retrace your steps or attempt to undo hasty actions.

Once the emotions are noted, they have less power to control you. You can also take four additional steps when confronted with an emotionally difficult situation at work. First, take control of yourself. If you are not under control, you won't be able to assist others. One way to manage yourself is to breathe deeply and slowly, forcing oxygen into your system (which is good for thinking) and preventing you from rashly taking action. In situations like this, it is better to take slow steps, even take a step back mentally, than to jump ahead quickly without thinking things through. Second, you can also take a few moments to think about how you would like the situation to end and the steps you can take to achieve that preferred end. Third, by engaging your active listening skills, you can determine what your colleague wants from the situation. This action will take time and also help pacify the other person to some extent. Finally, you can try to interject some humor into the situation. This must be genuine humor, and preferably self-deprecating, rather than a sarcastic or snide sort of joking about the other person. While not always an easy thing to do, finding a way to comment on something funny about yourself or the situation relieves tension and creates a path for a peaceful resolution. Many times, a mild disagreement can escalate into something much worse, a situation that causes lasting damage to relationships and job performance. These few simple steps on your part can help you keep communication open.

As a leader, you will at times need to manage your team and their feelings in group (rather than one-on-one) situations. You must be clear about your own feelings, as noted earlier, and you can use similar techniques to bring about good results in meetings. One of the more important elements of communicating during group sessions is to be clear about what others in the group are thinking and feeling. Often when there is conflict within a group, or as options are being discussed, frustrations arise if participants do not feel they are being heard. You need to ask for clarification and use your active listening skills in these situations. You should also ask questions and be willing to challenge ideas that are put forth so that pros and cons can be brought out ahead of any decisions. In addition, it is wise to have the group discuss issues such as what are "best case" solutions and what alternative solutions are acceptable. By separating out these two levels of results, solutions meeting different needs or views can often be found. By modeling what you expect from others, you will help create a higher functioning group. In the end, your final decision probably will not make everyone happy. Still, if the process is open and people have a chance for meaningful participation, you can usually retain good working relationships.

A final way to keep emotional hijacking from occurring is to take the surprise element out of the situation. It may not be that your fight-or-flight response is related to the actual topic (as conflictual as it might be) but rather that your emotions are aroused because of the suddenness or unexpectedness of the issue arising in that moment. It is often appropriate to take a step back and request a short break or to schedule a separate meeting time for topics with high emotional loads. You will have time to consider what you want to accomplish with the discussion, as will everyone else involved. By lowering the stress levels for yourself and others, you will ensure that better decisions are made.

If you have introduced the concept of emotional hijacking to your coworkers and explained how our emotions can bypass our logical thinking processes, leading to unnecessary escalation of responses to issues, everyone on the team can be on guard to keep the whole group or a member of the group from succumbing to this common problem. It can even turn into a group practice that a certain phrase be used to signal to people that they may need to check and monitor their emotional situation. When used in this way, the power of the group is enhanced, and individuals within it can be nudged by colleagues to become more self-aware and productive.

Tell Stories

Humans have told stories since we developed the ability to communicate. It continues to be a primary means for helping people listen to and remember important messages (Heath & Heath, 2007). Listening to carefully crafted stories has been shown to create changes in the listener's brain chemistry, increasing both cortisol, which focuses attention, and oxytocin, which improves the ability to empathize and create feelings of care (Zak, 2011).

Excellent stories have an advantage in communicating ideas because they have a clear narrative and so are easy to follow; they are concrete; they are credible; they contain a surprising element; and they pack an emotional jolt. Even mediocre stories that have just some of these elements help people retain key, simple points that help them act in desired ways (Heath & Heath, 2007). Stories are seen to be more captivating, conversational, outwardly focused on the audience, entertaining, compelling, textured, and real than typical organizational communications (Hoffman, 2011).

Different types of stories exist for different purposes. Simmons (2007) describes many types of stories that are useful to achieve different types of goals. We look at four here. The first, "Who I am," is useful when you want to get across your values and the kind of leader or person you are. You open yourself up a bit to allow those around you to see who you are. This type of story is important in job interviews, for example, when interviewers might ask you to describe a time when you overcame an obstacle or approached a new situation. Political candidates have a well-rehearsed story of "Who I am" so they can connect with the electorate, particularly as they start wooing new sets of voters.

A second type of story is called the "Why I am here" story and can be related to the first type. When you are a leader, people working with and for you want to know not only who you are but also why you are in your current position. You've chosen to be part of an organization, in fact, to be a leader within it. People rightly want to have insight into what you want to accomplish.

Teaching stories are the third type Simmons (2007) discusses. For millennia, the parables of Jesus, such as the Good Samaritan, or the fables of Aesop, such as the Boy Who Cried Wolf, have become shorthand ways of communicating the right way or the wrong way to live. If you can encapsulate "best practices" for your organization in a teaching story, you can be sure that the message will get through.

The fourth type of story communicates a vision. Martin Luther King, Jr.'s "I Have a Dream" speech is such a story, and so is John Kennedy's speech about sending a man to the moon and returning him safely. When you and your organization can develop a story of where you want to go, such inspiration will help you keep going through even massive difficulties. In Chapter 6, you will read about the value of an organizational vision. Remember that your vision is only a set of words unless you can get people to act to achieve it. A vision story provides the means to make the vision "sticky"—easily remembered and thus capable of being worked toward (Heath & Heath, 2007).

Roam (2016) describes four story arcs: the *report*, which seeks to change the audience's level of knowledge; the *explanation*, which increases the audience's abilities; the *pitch*, which shows the audience how to overcome an obstacle and thus changes the audience's actions; and finally, the *drama*, which impacts the audience's beliefs. You can use many of the types of stories mentioned by Simmons (2007) in any of the four story arcs Roam discusses.

When you have an important message to deliver to your coworkers, a story might be the best way to begin. When using storytelling in this way, you need to prepare—few of us are able to speak extemporaneously in an effective way (although we can get better with practice). Good stories, even very short ones, often have the following features in common:

1. A protagonist in a situation: usually this should be someone like the audience members, not you)
2. A challenge (internal and/or external): this could be your beliefs or attitude or a blockage such as a natural force or a person who is an antagonist or villain
3. A resolution to the challenge: how did the protagonists or situation change for the better, for example, and achieve their goal?
4. Moral or application: what should the audience do based on the story's challenges and resolution?

The first three features together are called the *dramatic arc*. Longer stories have more challenges that need to be dealt with and have smaller resolutions and setbacks along the way, leading eventually to the ultimate showdown and climax to the story. In the end, something has changed, whether it is the situation, the protagonist, or both. When stated plainly, this becomes the moral of the story. Sometimes it is left up to the listeners to determine the moral for themselves, especially if the story is left unfinished as part of a current situation or as a way of stimulating engagement in the decision-making process.

Naturally, you will need to speak and write in other ways as well, for example, when communicating a set of facts or options that are being considered. Even here, however, you can incorporate a look at challenges, emotions, and successes in narrative forms that will hold your audience's attention and stick in their heads. Once you begin communicating with stories, you will find that people remember what you have to say and you have more of an impact (Simmons, 2007).

One of the beneficial aspects of storytelling is that you are forced to determine what point you wish to make before you can effectively communicate it. We have all been in conversations with people who want to tell a story that is lacking a dramatic arc, rambles endlessly, and has no point.

As you begin to use stories in your work life, remember to describe a person or situation, the challenges to be faced, the difficulties in overcoming obstacles, and the benefits that ensue when the deeds are successfully accomplished.

Written Communication

Written and oral communication skills share some similarities, because they both use words to communicate. Written communication, however, may actually be easier for some because you have more time to draft and revise your work before it is sent to the audience. You also do not have to worry about the nonverbal messages you are sending, often without knowing it. Still, written communications do take time to prepare so that you make the best impression. Expectations are high for managers and leaders to write well, so do not disappoint your readers. Here are a few ideas to keep in mind with every written communication.

Work to improve your writing. If you are not comfortable writing, you must learn and practice. Even if you were a straight-A student, your writing can still be improved for a nonacademic environment. Much of organizational life is dependent on written communication, whether it is an annual report, a memo, an email, material for your organization's webpages and social media posts, or elsewhere. Each of these applications of written work needs to be clear, concise, and correct.

Consider your audience before you begin writing. Who you are writing to shapes the words and the format you use. Writing an email to your department leaders may be less formal than writing to board members, for example.

Focus on the purpose of communication. Just as with oral communication, understand the purpose and goals of the document. What do you want to be different after your audience reads it? If you are not sure what you want, your readers won't be either, leading to wasted time, frustration, and stalled progress.

Select your writing's approach. Recall the four types of presentations we mentioned earlier in the chapter (Roam 2016): the report, the explanation, the pitch, and the drama. Consciously decide which approach you want to use and have a rationale for your choice. Each is useful in some circumstances but not others. Choose deliberatively and wisely.

Use direct, active sentences. An active sentence emphasizes the subject taking action. Instead of writing "These changes need to be made by all staff members," you should consider "All staff members need to implement these changes."

Structure your writing for easy comprehension. Help your audience follow the flow of your written communication. People often tend to skim written work, looking for the few sentences they believe are important for *them*. A short summary at the start of a long document can counteract the tendency to not read a document at all because it seems overwhelming. Write the summary so that the reader understands the value of tackling the entire work.

Another technique to structure your longer written work is to include headings and subheadings. Write these so that readers can follow your story arc even without reading the actual paragraphs in between. Long advertisements in newspapers and magazines do this well, because the authors know readers will not read every detail. For another example, look at well-written textbooks (such as this one). Readers use the headings and subheadings in chapters or long documents to orient themselves to the flow of the work and to focus on what may be most important to them at that time.

Provide a call to action. To ensure readers understand what you want them to do, have a clear "call to action." Do you want an acknowledgment of receipt? Say that. Do you want a report sent to you within a week? Make it clear. Far too many communications leave the reader unsure what to do next and by when. Make sure yours are not that way.

Avoid grammatical errors. When you are pressed for time, errors creep in (for example, misusing "they're," "their," and "there"). Not all your readers may notice your mistakes, but those who do will question your competence.

Proofread before publishing or sending. Proofreading can be difficult because you tend to skip through the writing—it is so familiar that your mind wanders and does not note details. One key to effective proofreading is to slow your eyes down. You can do this by reading sentence by sentence from the end or by reading it aloud. It is true that proofreading your work takes time (even in short emails or other writing that may not need to be perfect), but the added value to your reputation for effective communication will be worth it.

Communication with a Diverse Society and Workforce

It is now a truism to say that the American society, and thus its workforce, is more diverse than ever (Chappell, 2017). Diversity exists in terms of gender, race, sexual orientation, age, physical capacity, country of origin, language, and many other characteristics. As a social work manager and leader, your stakeholders have high expectations that you will be able to communicate effectively with everyone within your organization and also to people who are outside of your agency. You may find yourself unsure how to proceed, no matter what your characteristics are or how well-intentioned you feel yourself to be. The question is, then, what to do? Researchers have at least some answers available to improve intercultural communication, using the intergroup communication perspective.

Oetzel (2017) explains that effective communication within workgroups is affected by the larger situation they are in, such as the level of homogeneity or heterogeneity they experience. Individual characteristics of the people in the workgroup also influence ease of communication. A higher level of homogeneity enables easier communication but Oetzel shows that diversity in communication patterns and styles can be overcome.

Gallois, Watson, and Giles (2018) admit that the field of intergroup communication (IGC) is filled with "complexity and messiness" and needs "more diversity in theory and method" (p. 309), but they provide useful tips based on their review of the research literature. Of particular interest is their position that "miscommunication" is not just a mistake but is a key feature of communication. It should be no surprise, then, that we all often seem to stick our feet in our mouths and make situations worse, rather than better, when we communicate. Proponents of the IGC perspective argue that everyone has a tendency to attribute miscommunication to the personality of the other person(s) involved, or

their cultural rules, instead of reflecting on differing goals or structures of communication.

Adherents of IGC ideas (such as Gallois, et al., 2018) remind us that we all have multiple "identities" or groups we belong to and that intersectionality is something that applies to everyone. You may be a straight, white female manager with two children and a caretaker for an ill parent. You may switch from feeling any of these roles to another in an instant—for example, if you receive a text that your mother has fallen *and* an email that your child forgot her lunch, it is possible that you may not pay attention to the managerial work you should be doing with the employee in front of you. That employee, who has multiple group identities, as well, and a history of interacting with you (and other managers), may feel sympathy or feel anger at being ignored in that moment. Which identity you link to has an impact on the identity the employee connects with, as well, in a potentially affirming or negative spiral.

Gallois et al. (2018) argue that communication skills, such as active listening, are important, but they "must be understood in context, taking full account of intergroup and interpersonal histories, along with motivations, intentions, and reactions to the behavior of others" (p. 314). Despite the messiness of the situation, Gallois et al. remind us that communication does take place, and things do get accomplished because of it.

The major takeaways from the IGC perspective are:

1. People (including managers) have many identities, and it is not always possible to know which one you are communicating with or to.
2. Miscommunication is actually an almost constant situation, so it is better to take the attitude that if you and others do communicate successfully, it is something to cherish rather than expect.
3. Communications training can be helpful, but it doesn't have all the answers.

Intercultural and intergroup communication may be one of the most difficult aspects of being a social work leader, but it is an unavoidable task. You must do your best, striving to listen and to present your authentic self. Be prepared for miscommunication, yet keep trying to make progress. Effective communication in a diverse environment is beneficial to the workplace but the impact may go beyond the workplace to promote higher-quality communication outside of the workplace for individuals adept at bridging seemingly wide divides (Oetzel, 2017).

Conclusion

This chapter describes six areas of interpersonal communication skills that leaders need to master. These are (1) creating a shared identify with your audience, (2) using active listening, (3) managing your emotions, (4) telling stories, (5) improving written techniques, and (6) communicating with diverse audiences. When you implement these skills well, you will improve the level of trust between you and your audience, learn what others want to communicate to you, show only the emotions you believe are helpful, grab and sustain attention for your messages, and communicate effectively through writing. You will use these skills every day as a social work leader. It is worth the effort to focus on improving all of them to improve your ability to communicate about yourself, your organization, and the future you are working for.

Reference List

Brody, N. (2004). What cognitive intelligence is and what emotional intelligence is not. *Psychological Inquiry, 15*(3), 234–238.

Chappell, B. (2017, June 22). Census finds a more diverse America as whites lag growth. *National Public Radio.* Retrieved from https://www.npr.org/sections/thetwo-way/2017/06/22/533926978/census-finds-a-more-diverse-america-as-whites-lag-growth

Cialdini, R. (2016). *Pre-suasion.* New York, NY: Simon & Schuster.

Eysenck, H. (2000). *Intelligence: A new look.* Piscataway, NJ: Transaction Publishers.

Gallois, C., Watson, B. M., & Giles, H. (2018). Intergroup communication: Identities and effective interactions. *Journal of Communication, 68*(2), 309–317. doi:10.1093/joc/jqx016

Goleman, D. (2006). *Emotional intelligence: Why it can matter more than IQ* (10th anniversary ed.). New York, NY: Random House.

Heath, C., & Heath, D. (2007). *Made to stick: Why some ideas survive and others die.* New York, NY: Random House.

Hoefer, R. (2003). Administrative skills and degrees: The "best place" debate rages on. *Administration in Social Work, 27*(1), 25–46.

Hoffman, L. (2011, September 22). Infographic: Storytelling vs. corporate speak [Web log post]. Retrieved from https://www.ishmaelscorner.com/infographic-storytelling-vs-corporate-speak/

Locke, E. A. (2005). Why emotional intelligence is an invalid concept. *Journal of Organizational Behavior, 26*(4), 425–431. doi:10.1002/job.318

Molenberghs, P., Prochilo, G., Steffens, N. K., Zacher, H., & Haslam, S. A. (2015). The neuroscience of inspirational leadership: The importance of collective-oriented language and shared-group membership. *Journal of Management, 43*(7), 2168–2194. doi:10.1177/0149206314565242

Oetzel, J. (2017). Effective intercultural workgroup communication theory. In *The International Encyclopedia of Intercultural Communication.* New York, NY: Wiley & Sons.

Roam, D. (2016). *Show and tell: How everybody can make extraordinary presentations.* New York, NY: Penguin.

Rogers, C., & Farson, R. (2015). *Active listening.* Mansfield Centre, CT: Martino Publishing.

Schwartz, K. (2017, October 10). 5 important communication skills for leaders [Web log post]. Retrieved from https://trainingindustry.com/blog/leadership/5-important-communication-skills-for-leaders/

Simmons, A. (2007). *Whoever tells the best story wins: How to use your own stories to communicate with power and impact.* New York, NY: American Management Association.

Zak, P. (2011). Trust, morality—and oxytocin [Video file]. Retrieved from http://www.youtube.com/watch?v=rFAdlU2ETjU

Additional Resources

Brown, B. (2018). *Dare to lead: Brave work. Tough conversations. Whole hearts.* New York, NY: Random House.

Neuliep, J. W. (2018). *Intercultural communication: A contextual approach* (7th ed.). Thousand Oaks, CA: Sage.

Phillips, D. (2010). The 110 techniques of communication and public speaking [Video file]. TEDxZagreb. Retrieved from https://youtu.be/K0pxo-dS9Hc

HELPFUL TERMS

Active listening—a type of listening that seeks to understand the meaning behind words rather than just the words themselves.

Emotional hijacking—a situation in which your feelings are strong enough to overcome your rational thought process.

Emotional intelligence—the concept that there exists a set of skills that allow people to understand their own and others' emotions, help them regulate their emotions, and help them plan and achieve goals in their life.

Scaffolding—an important adult education approach that links new information to information that a person already has. In this way, the listener can more easily retain and grasp the importance of the new information.

Teaching story—a type of story that has an explicit moral or lesson that will help listeners behave in the desired manner after hearing it.

TL;DR or **tl;dr**—an abbreviation for "too long; didn't read," indicating that the reader is unlikely to read what you have written.

Unconditional positive regard—a term associated with the work of psychologist Carl Rogers, meaning acceptance of a person as a person, even when you may not agree with his or her behavior. It is a way for the manager to point out and seek to correct employee mistakes or errors without the employee feeling less worthy as a person.

Vision story—a type of story that communicates the preferred future that you or your organization is working to achieve.

Why I am here story—a type of story that communicates your reason for being in the position you are in and what you hope to accomplish.

Who I am story—a type of story that communicates who the storyteller is by revealing personal values, beliefs, and history. It is very useful in allowing others to become comfortable with you as a person because they feel they know you and can perhaps more easily trust you.

EXERCISES

1. In-Basket Exercise

Directions

For this exercise, pretend you are Becky Jones, communications director for Youth Services of Eastern Oklahoma. Your boss, the CEO of the entire agency, needs your help. Using the ideas presented in this chapter, craft a three-minute presentation with PowerPoint slides (or other visual aids) or a speech (without visual aids) that will give the CEO something "compelling, entertaining, and (hopefully) lucrative," as he requests.

Memo

Date: September 1, 20XX

To: Becky Jones, Communications Director

From: Shawn O'Malley, CEO, Youth Services of Eastern Oklahoma

Subject: Message for End-of-Year Fundraising Kickoff

In two weeks, I will provide the closing talk to the End-of-Year Fundraising Kickoff dinner with some of our best donors. Usually, I list off the goals and objectives we set at the start of the year and how we've done in accomplishing them so far. In the past few years, I have found that we are not getting the financial benefits from these events that are expected by members of the board and what our agency needs. I've looked in the mirror and found what I think is the reason for this lack of success. Frankly, I have given boring speeches, but I don't know how to make them better.

This year, I am asking for your help to take the usual list of goals, objectives, and results and turn it into a compelling, entertaining, and (hopefully) lucrative communication with our best donors. Here are the facts—I would like to hear back from you with your draft by next week.

I know people like to hear how their money is spent, so I have gotten this information for you. So far this year, we have served 147 youth (85 boys and 62 girls). We have served over 132,000 meals, washed sheets nearly 7,000 times, administered 219 prescriptions, and bought 46 pairs of glasses, 93 dresses, 151 pairs of pants, 289 shirts/tops, 308 pairs of shoes, and many dozens of socks and pieces of underclothing. Our cleaning supplies budget is $12,000. Office supply purchases have topped $14,000, due mainly to the need to upgrade the computers we have in the residences and offices. Luckily, we were able to get a good price on those from the local Best Buy store. Groundskeeping, with all this snow we had last winter, has run over budget and stands at $7,450. Utilities have also been high this year, costing about $21,000 so far. We are hoping for a milder winter next year.

The economy of the state has been poor this year, with the economic downturn lingering in its effects. Unemployment is at 12%, job losses are in the thousands in our area, and natural disasters are sucking potential donors dry. Our foundation supporters have reduced funding by 15% over the past three years, and government reimbursements are running six months behind. Our total income for the year is down 4%, after previous dips of 1% and 6%.

We anticipate that we will exhaust our cash reserves within six months and be forced to do something drastic to continue serving the same number of clients. We are not likely to be forced to close our doors next year, but the future after that is rather grim.

Here is our mission, and a snapshot of some of our typical clients, for your easy reference: "We protect children and youth from abuse and neglect by providing a safe, caring residential alternative when needed."

Typical client 1: Sally, a 12-year-old girl who has been abused for a period of 10–12 months by a family member. Parents have relinquished rights. Adoption for this type of client is rare. She is under our care and protection for perhaps the next six years.

Typical client 2: Nicodemus, a 16-year-old boy who is looking at the end of his time with us in less than two years. He came to our facility after being orphaned a year ago and attempting to live on the streets. He wants to be independent but doesn't have strong social or living skills.

As the largest provider of services to youth in the eastern Oklahoma area, we strive to ensure that no child is left in an unsafe situation for more than 24 hours. We do this through three emergency shelters, one residential facility, and 43 staff members. We also provide parent-training programs to prevent problems before they begin. We don't turn children away, calling on an extensive network of emergency foster care parents when other resources are full or otherwise unavailable to meet the needs of impacted children.

See what you can do with this information, will you?

2. Creating a Shared Identity

Part A. Reflect on organizations you have volunteered for, been a member of, or worked at. These can be as diverse in nature as a club, sorority or fraternity, Boys and Girls Clubs, a religious institution, the Department of Child Protective Services, or a branch of the military. In what ways were shared identities formed? Were uniforms involved? Have you learned special knowledge related to your role or participated in initiation rites? When questions about proper behavior arise, what stories are told? Discuss this in groups of 3–5 people. Note the many ways leaders and organizations can try to achieve this goal that the people in your small group have experienced.

Part B. With Part A as a bank of possibilities, discuss in your group how you might try to increase a sense of shared identity in your class, your school, your work team, or your organization as a whole (choose an example you all share). Which would be the most successful? What would it take for it to "stick"?

Part C. Before leaving this topic, reflect on any possible pitfalls to increasing your sense of shared identity in the example you chose in Part B. Is it possible that you could make your sense of shared identity "too strong" and have it lead to something negative? What would that be, and how could you mitigate the downside?

3. Emotional Self-Management

Think of a situation at work or school in which you were quite irritated or angry and you let it show. Discuss with a colleague or two what happened and what you did. If you were to find yourself in a similar situation, how could you apply some of the tools for emotional self-management discussed in the chapter? Do you think they would be effective in this situation?

4. Active Listening

Active listening is very helpful in many workplace situations. Working with the same person you talked with in Exercise 3, pretend that you are that person's instructor or supervisor who witnessed the situation. Role-play how you would work with your colleague to resolve the situation.

5. How Was Your Day?

Sitting with a partner, tell the story of what you did this morning to get to school or work on time. Don't make anything up, just stick to the facts. Complete this task in two minutes or less. This is the sort of typical "How was your day?" approach to conversation and communication. This is similar to Roam's (2016) report style of telling a story. Listen to your partner's story. Now, take a 10-minute break and revise your story, keeping in mind the following questions: What obstacles did you face to get to school or work (internal or external)? How did you address each issue? What lessons can you draw from this experience? Retell the story of your morning. Which approach do you think will be remembered longer by your audience?

ASSIGNMENTS

1. A number of communication self-assessment tools can be found online. Assess yourself and write an overview of what the assessment indicates, both positive and negative. Here are a few tools you might use:

    *   http://htc-consult.com/new/wp-content/uploads/Communication-Skills-Self-Assessment-Inventory.pdf

    *   http://fogartyfellows.org/wp-content/uploads/2015/01/5DCase.pdf

    *   https://www.mindtools.com/pages/article/newCS_99.htm.

2. The concept and measurement of emotional intelligence is controversial. Some authors say that it doesn't really exist as an "intelligence." Write a four- to five-page paper discussing the main arguments about the validity of emotional intelligence as a concept. Which side of the argument do you believe is correct? What are the implications of your position as a nonprofit manager?

3. The idea of active listening is derived from the work of psychologist Carl Rogers. Unconditional positive regard is another concept he developed and embraced. Write a short paper (four to five pages) on the pros and cons of Rogers' work as it applies to being a manager or leader in a nonprofit organization. Which techniques, if any, would you like to incorporate into your management and leadership style?

4. Storytelling is an art and a profession. There are storytelling events and workshops across the country. If possible, attend one to gain a deeper understanding of this ancient craft. If you cannot attend one live, locate a book or other training aid about storytelling. Search through YouTube for examples of professional storytelling. Write a review of what you saw, heard, or read and how you can apply the principles to your own life, particularly your life as a social work leader and manager.

5. Write about an incident that happened between you and someone else that you believe may have been made worse due to intergroup miscommunication. Relying on the information in this chapter, which "identity" were you feeling at the time? How about the other person? How did your history get involved in the situation? Can you think of anything that you could do differently using an IGC perspective that might have improved the situation then, or moving forward?

Image Credits

Skills

Quadrant I: Internal and Task Orientation

The information in this section looks at three of the skills social work leaders and managers need to have that fall into Quadrant I of the four-quadrant model. These are skills on the task and internal orientation sides of our two continua. We have chapters on strategic planning, program planning, and budgeting and financial management. These topics have been chosen due to the central role they play in achieving the organization's mission and vision.

Strategic planning (Chapter 6) includes laying the foundation for any work done by the organization, and thus every employee and volunteer (including yourself!). By knowing how to successfully create or renew an agency's mission, vision, and goals at the strategic level, the leader can ensure the organization's relevance to the community and funders. *Program planning* (Chapter 7) is tightly linked to strategic planning but requires thinking and operating at a level closer to the front lines of the agency. Program planning uses tools such as logic models and program evaluation to provide frameworks for later program success. *Budgeting and financial management* (Chapter 8) is the last major skill in Quadrant I that we cover. Budgeting is really another tool of planning—it turns more or less ethereal plans into the dollars that are needed to make those plans come to fruition. Once the dollars are budgeted, you must also keep track of where they are spent and if actual spending is in line with planned spending.

By the time you complete this part of the book, you will know a great deal about how leaders can work within their organizational context to shape the future for their agency and their clients. All social work leaders must know how to plan and budget to be successful. The exercises and assignments will bring what might be abstract ideas into tangible competencies.

CHAPTER

6 Strategic Planning

BOX 6.1 **EPAS Competencies Covered**

The material in this chapter links to CSWE's Competency 3: Advance Human Rights and Social, Economic, and Environmental Justice; Competency 4: Engage in Practice-Informed Research and Research-Informed Practice; Competency 7: Assess Individuals, Families, Groups, Organizations, and Communities; and Competency 8: Intervene with Individuals, Families, Groups, Organizations, and Communities. Planning requires using research skills to unlock information from many sources and to put that information into a form useful to making appropriate decisions about the future. The purpose of planning is to understand how to intervene with organizations and communities to impact problem areas and develop the best programs to assist organization clients.

Think back five years ago. What were the key issues in the world and your community? Come back to the present. Has anything important changed? Are funding patterns, social service needs, or political debates different now from just a few years ago? If you are honest, you will admit that a great number of things are quite different compared to just a half decade ago. Many of these changes have a significant impact on social work leaders and the organizations they manage. Given that the pace of change in society seems to be accelerating, we see the need to ensure that administrators can conduct planning well, while keeping their eyes open for shifts that were not anticipated even a couple of years previously. Plans may become out of date in whole or in part, but having no plan is a recipe for problems.

Planning, as we will discuss, can be used in human service organizations to chart the general direction of the agency (strategic planning), as well as smaller-scale decisions about the specific actions and programs to implement within the organization (program planning, which we cover in Chapter 7). We show seven important differences between these two different types of planning efforts in Box 6.3.

These important differences show that the time horizon, the goal focus, and the focus of decision-makers are different in strategic as opposed to operational, or program, planning. Strategic planning, because it focuses on understanding both external and internal elements that influence the organization's future, requires top level and board involvement. It involves making decisions about what the organization's reason to exist is (the mission), what it hopes to achieve (the vision), and what values will guide it. Decisions will

TABLE 6.1   **Differences Between Strategic and Program Planning**

Planning Element	Strategic Planning	Program Planning
Time Period	Looks at goals for next 3 to 5 years.	Looks at a shorter time period, typically one year.
Goal Focus	Shows how organization will work toward its long-term vision and mission.	Shows how organization's programs achieve part of the strategic plan and the steps to take within the program to be successful.
Focus of Decision-Makers	External and internal elements impacting organization.	Primarily internal elements related to resources, process, and outcomes.
Plan Generation	The highest-level decision-makers make final decisions.	Department or program leaders have responsibility for making program decisions on a frequent basis to ensure successful implementation.
Locus of Monitoring and Adjusting Plans	Top-level decision-makers in organization examine received high-level data quarterly or annually.	Mid-level administrators and managers create and disseminate reports to guide immediate actions on a weekly or monthly basis.
Budget	Funding comes from a special part of the budget to create and monitor the impact of strategic initiatives.	Funding comes from annual budgets and is part of the day-to-day activities of departmental or program managers.
Reporting	Updates occur at a high level of abstraction to examine how well overall goals are being achieved.	Frequent detailed updates on progress of implementation and achievement of outcomes.

Source: Adapted from Foley, A. (n.d.), with additions.

be made regarding which sources of funding and other resources will be in line with the organization's mission, vision, and values; available in sufficient amounts; and most desirable to pursue. Monitoring of results is done quarterly or annually. Program planning is almost wholly restricted to elements internal to the organization. Decisions at the program level are primarily regarding the best ways to use the resources (funds and personnel) allocated to the program or department as a result of strategic planning. Department directors and program managers monitor program processes and outcomes.

In strategic planning, human service administrators provide leadership in developing tools that move the organization in the right direction. From time to time, we need to ask our key stakeholders, "What direction do we want to take?" Many times, this question comes during the process of strategic planning. Program planning is done at a different,

more operational, level. Once a general strategic direction is decided, the particular programs that will be continued or developed to reach the agency's strategic goals are implemented. This requires a more specific set of planning details.

Strategic Planning

We should understand how strategic planning is defined and the purposes it fulfills before discussing the steps in doing it. Bryson, Edwards, & Van Slyke (2018) define strategic planning as a "deliberative, disciplined effort to produce fundamental decisions and actions that shape and guide what an organization (or other entity) is, what it does, and why" (p. 317). The key takeaway from this definition is that strategic planning should produce "decisions and actions," not just a nicely bound document or attractive web pages. If decisions have not been made and actions not taken within a relatively short amount of time, the planning has been a waste of time and effort.

Poister and Streib (1999, pp. 309–310) list what at least some of the decisions should be due to strategic planning:

- Determine what the most important issues facing the organization are and what should be done to respond to those issues.
- Clarify the organization's purpose and values, settling on a mission statement that provides guidance when facing important decisions.
- Decide which external trends and movements are most important in impacting the organization's mission and strategies.
- As much as possible, balance different internal and external stakeholder groups' views on all matters.
- Lead to the development of implementation plans.
- Focus on positioning the organization well for the future when the identified issues come to pass.

A strategic planning process that achieves these things is a strong one that provides immeasurable assistance to the organization that has undertaken the effort.

While there are variations in the approach to strategic planning, we believe the following steps are helpful:

1. Determining the organization's governing ideas: vision, mission, and values
2. Conducting a SWOT Analysis or other analytical assessment (the SWOT process is explained later in this chapter)
3. Setting strategic goals to accomplish the mission, taking into account what was learned in the SWOT analysis
4. Developing ideas to meet strategic goals
5. Evaluating performance of strategic goals
6. Thinking about and making necessary corrections (which may involve changing goals and associated programs or conducting another round of strategic planning)

Strategic planning allows an organization to evaluate the vision, mission, and all that the organization does to accomplish its goals and objectives. Without a clear and up-to-date vision and mission for the organization, there is the danger that a great deal of activity will happen but very little of importance will be accomplished. If we don't a have good idea about our ultimate destination, it doesn't make a lot of difference what direction we take to get there. Lewis Carroll's Alice learned this lesson from the wise cat in *Alice's Adventures in Wonderland*:

"Would you tell me, please, which way I ought to go from here?"
"That depends a good deal on where you want to get to," said the Cat.
"I don't much care where—," said Alice.
"Then it doesn't matter which way you go," said the Cat.
"—so long as I get SOMEWHERE," Alice added as an explanation.
"Oh, you're sure to do that," said the Cat, "if you only walk long enough." (Carroll, 1865)

As a social work leader, you don't want to get "somewhere"—you want to get to a clearly defined future state. Strategic planning involves formulating a course of action that will move the organization from its present state to some desirable future state. Such planning is important for the agency being able to get things done, because it allows the board, administration, and staff to have an "end-in-mind" perspective that helps to orchestrate the day-to-day decisions that are made throughout the agency and to minimize the possibility of activity without purpose. Such planning involves creating and articulating a vision of a desirable and attainable future

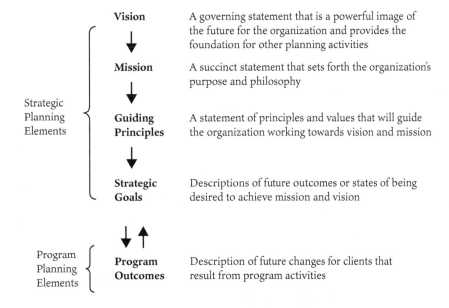

FIGURE 6.1. Strategic and Program Planning Elements

state, having a clear and concise mission, and articulating the guiding values of the organization. Once these are developed in the form of a vision statement, mission statement, and a statement of guiding principles, the organization can move on to identify appropriate goals at both strategic and program levels. At the program level of planning, managers derive outcomes, processes, and activities to accomplish these goals (see Figure 6.1). An important subtlety of Figure 6.1 is how program outcomes derive from and feed back into the strategic goals. In other words, programming is done with the intent to achieve strategic goals, but the program outcomes are not necessarily exactly the same as the strategic goals. (We go into much more detail about program planning in the next chapter.)

Governing Ideas

Peter Senge (1990) presents the concept of "governing ideas" for an organization in his work *The Fifth Discipline*. He states that the mission should answer the question, "Why do we exist?" and the core values should answer, "How do we want to act?" He presents vision as the way to describe the ideal future for the organization and as the foundation of the planning process, including strategic planning, setting goals and objectives, and designing programs (as cited in Lewis, Packard, & Lewis, 2011). Let us more closely examine the concepts of vision, mission, and values and their associated documents: the vision statement, the mission statement, and the values statement. These elements are the cluster of planning elements that we consider to be part of "strategic planning" rather than "program planning."

Vision Statement

Helen Keller, a widely recognized blind person from the United States, is supposed to have said, "What would be worse than being born blind? To have sight without vision." With guidance from Helen Keller and Alice's Cheshire Cat, we must conclude that having a clear mission is an important thing!

Developing a vision statement is a powerful way to frame the agency's mission, goals and objectives, and activities; provide a powerful image of the future for the organization; and provide the foundation for planning activities (Lewis, Packard, & Lewis, 2011). A key component of developing a vision statement is that it is developed from throughout the organization. It is not something that

you can write in isolation sitting in your office. The vision statement is really the "shared vision" of the organization. The vision is what you and your stakeholders believe or dream that your organization can be in the future. It answers the question, "What do we want the organization to be?" What would the organization look like in the next 10 to 15 years if there were no resource constraints? What would you want your organization to mean in the lives of your clients? An organization is more likely to succeed when as many stakeholders as possible share the same vision of the future. The process of developing a vision statement to describe that shared vision can be an important event in the life of the organization (Worth, 2009). The purpose of a vision statement is to give the organization a vision of the future. The real value in developing a vision statement is to engage the board, staff, and other stakeholders in the process to develop a shared vision of their future. Those participating in the process should not be constrained in their creativity by thinking about the resources available at the present time. The assumption needs to be made that the agency will have all it needs in money, staff, and other resources to reach the agreed-on vision (Austin & Solomon, 2009). The following are examples of vision statements from some leading human services organizations:

- **Amnesty International:** "Our vision is for every person to enjoy all the rights enshrined in the Universal Declaration of Human Rights and other international human rights standards" (Amnesty International, 2018).
- **Goodwill:** "Every person has the opportunity to achieve his/her fullest potential and participate in and contribute to all aspects of life" (Goodwill, Inc., n.d.).
- **World Association of Girl Guides and Girl Scouts:** "All girls are valued and take action to change the world" (World Association of Girl Guides and Girl Scouts, n.d.).

These vision statements are as unique as each organization. The reader has little doubt after reading them what the organization is working to achieve. Specific vision statements help bring volunteers and donations to the nonprofit to help with the work and funding needed to make the vision a reality.

Mission Statement

Simply put, the mission statement explains why your organization exists. Drucker (1992) has stated that one of the most common mistakes in developing a mission statement is to make it into a "kind of hero sandwich of good intentions" (p. 5). He cautions that the statement needs to be simple and clear. A mission statement, according to Smith, Bucklin & Associates, Inc. (2000), is "[a] succinct statement that sets forth the organization's purpose and philosophy. Although brief, the mission statement will specify the fundamental reasons for the organization's existence; establish the scope of the organization; and identify the organization's unique characteristics" (p. 13). A good mission statement should be inspiring but, at the same time, be concise and easily understood and remembered (Brody & Nair, 2013). It is sometimes said that the mission statement should be short enough to fit on the back of a business card. It is the mission statement that gives the organization a sense of direction.

The ongoing and constant question for all other elements of organizational life and decisions should be, "Does this fit within our mission?" This question often arises in organizations when new funding opportunities arise. The alternative to evaluating funding opportunities in light of the agency mission is to be involved in "chasing dollars." Just because funding is available or a new service opportunity emerges does not mean that it is right for the agency. All such opportunities need to be evaluated within the context of the mission of the organization. The mission statement gives direction and continuity (Kettner, Moroney, & Martin, 2017).

A key component of the mission statement is that it focuses on the future state of the clients if the agency is successful in addressing their problems or meeting their needs (Kettner et al., 2017). For anyone reading the mission statement, it should be clear to them why the organization exists and what difference it makes to the clients it serves. Take a look at the following examples of mission statements. Do they meet the requirements of a good mission statement?

- **American Red Cross:** "Prevents and alleviates human suffering in the face of emergencies by mobilizing the power of volunteers and the generosity of donors" (American Red Cross, n.d.).
- **Catholic Charities USA:** "The mission of Catholic Charities is to provide service to people in need, to advocate for justice in social structures, and to call the entire church and other people of good will to do the same" (Catholic Charities USA, n.d.).
- **March of Dimes:** "Prematurity is the #1 killer of babies in the United States. We are working to change that and help more moms have full-term pregnancies and healthy babies. From polio to prematurity the March of Dimes has focused on researching the problems that threaten our children and finding ways to prevent them." (March of Dimes, n.d.).

It is important to know that it is the Board of Trustees (or, in the case of public agencies, the legislative body) that determines the mission of the organization. The development of the mission statement is and should be a collaborative effort between the human service administrator, the board, and the staff. However, the reality is that the mission statement is a policy statement and, therefore, is within the responsibility of the board. Mission statements are not static documents; they can and do change over time, but those changes must be made in a systematic and thoughtful way as part of a planning process. The board should constantly ask, "Is this within the mission of our agency?" If the answer is "No," then the activity should not be undertaken or the mission should be modified. Likewise, the board must always ask, "Is our mission still relevant?" If the original purpose of the organization is no longer relevant, the board must decide whether the agency has a reason to continue to exist.

BOX 6.2 A Case Study in Changing Missions

The Methodist Mission Home in San Antonio, Texas, was established in 1895. For most of its history, the agency served as an unwed mothers' home. It had started out in a small house and by the mid-1960s was serving over 300 young women each year with residential services. In 1968, the agency moved from the small facility to a beautiful new 30-acre campus with six buildings. However, by the time the new facility opened, there were only six women in residence. Many things had changed: birth control, abortion, single parenthood, and changing societal views. The need for which the facility was built was no longer valid. After a long period of planning, the board made the decision to continue the original mission of serving unwed mothers (but on a smaller scale) and to expand their mission to serving deaf adults in need of independent living and job skills training. The agency continues to serve both populations today and has expanded to serve other people with disabilities.

Values (Guiding Principles)

A statement of principles describes the values that will guide the organization. These are the things that will not be compromised and are often based on deeply held convictions and traditions. Many times, agencies will find themselves caught between the policies, needs, and desires of funders or their contract agencies and their own agency principles. Human service administrators need to be clear in knowing the guiding principles of their organization and carrying out their responsibility to uphold them. For that reason, it is very important to be sure that your personal values are in sync with the agency where you work. Can you support the principles of the organization even if they are not exactly the same values that you hold? If you are working for an organization that is religiously affiliated and you are not a member of that religious group, can you support and uphold the guiding principles of the organization? These are important questions to ask yourself when considering where you want to work.

In addition to the guiding principles of an organization, we each have professional values and ethics that come into consideration (recall the material from Chapter 2). As a social work administrator, you will work with professionals from many different disciplines that come with different codes of ethics and work from different guiding principles.

Example of One Organization's Governing Ideas

In order to help you understand how all of the governing ideas documents fit together, Box 6.3 shows many of the governing ideas from one organization. ACH (formerly All Children's Home) is an agency serving children in Fort Worth, Texas. It has been selected as an example because it is a local nonprofit that has done an excellent job in developing all of the core elements of strategic planning and posting them prominently on its website for easy access. You can see how the vision, mission, guiding principles, and goals link to one another. Additional items (such as self-description

---

BOX 6.3 ACH's Strategic Governing Ideas

Self Description: ACH is a nonprofit organization dedicated to helping children, youth and families in our community overcome life's challenges.

ACH utilizes a solution-focused, competency-based care approach to working with our clients. All ACH services are child-centered and family-focused to best address the needs of children while closely involving families. We partner with our clients to provide the right services and right level of assistance that will help our clients overcome life's challenges and achieve their own goals. ACH operates its programs and services from a variety of locations in the 19 counties we serve. Our central mailing address and administrative location is our Wichita Street Campus.

Tagline: Protecting Children. Preserving Families. Since 1915.

Vision: Through leadership, research and training, ACH will set a recognized example for replicable programs in child welfare that dramatically strengthen families and reduce child abuse. Our vision

---

is to be the foremost service provider in the communities we serve, so families thrive and children experience safety, hope and love.

Mission: We protect children from abuse, neglect and family separation and help children overcome these things when they do happen. Abuse and neglect are significant problems in the communities we serve, and without help, the long-term impact on children can prevent them from living healthy, productive lives. Some of our programs keep children and families together, and others provide a healing home for children who can't live with their families.

Guiding Principles: Through strength-based partnerships, ACH brings resources and skills to children and families struggling with life's challenges. Together we develop solutions that create safety, hope, love and the capacity to thrive.

We know that the best way to accomplish our mission is to work with families, whenever possible, to strengthen their ability to care for their children. Through strength-based partnerships, ACH brings resources and skills to children and families struggling with life's challenges. Together we develop solutions that create safety, hope, love and the capacity to thrive.

Values

Childhood. We believe all children deserve a childhood that provides safety, love, nurturing, fun, and opportunities to learn skills needed to reach their maximum potential.

Families. We understand that a child's needs are best met in a family environment. We believe that all families have strengths and that focusing on these strengths can create new possibilities for change. We strive to partner with families and support their efforts to provide environments for children to thrive. We work to secure a family setting when one is unavailable to children.

Effective services. We will provide services that are built upon clearly defined intervention models, research and best practices. Characteristics of effective services include well trained staff, comprehensive program descriptions, effective supervision, culturally sensitive approaches, and measurable outcomes that indicate program success. Effective programs respond to an identified need and impact it positively.

Stewardship. We will use our financial and human resources to address the needs of those we serve using cost effective and transparent practices. We will utilize and develop resources to address the needs of both current and future consumers and look for creative ways to leverage our resources with those of other organizations.

Spirituality. We build upon our Christian foundation in our belief that unconditional love and hope are essential for healing. We strive to convey love and hope to all our clients and to our staff. We recognize and respect the individualized spiritual backgrounds of those we serve and support family efforts to continue in their faith traditions.

Advocacy. In addition to helping the children and families directly participating in our programs, ACH will strive to leverage our skills and knowledge to shape public policy, opinion and response to children and families in need. We will work collaboratively with other entities with similar goals to maximize resources for overcoming abuse, neglect and family separation.

Learning. We strive to learn from our work through thoughtful analysis of our results and methods. We will utilize innovative approaches and maintain awareness of work being done in other communities. We aim to develop knowledge that is helpful to children and families and to share this knowledge with others.

Strategic Goals Connected to Program Areas

Hope (Homeless Outreach Project Experience) Street Outreach Program. HOPE provides outreach and case management services to runaway, homeless youth and sexually exploited and/or trafficked youth and youth at risk for sexual exploitation and/or trafficking. HOPE's services increase youths' safety, well-being and self-sufficiency through permanent connection to caring adults, family reunification, transition to shelter or safe and stable housing, assessment, and safety and resource planning.

The LIFE (Learning Independence from Experience) Project. The LIFE (Learning Independence from Experience) Project promotes self-confidence and self-sufficiency for eligible young adults by providing a variety of housing options for young adults. These different settings allow young adults to experience independent living while continuing to receive support, guidance and assistance with skills development.

Families Together. Families Together provides transitional housing for single mothers and their children who are experiencing homelessness due to domestic violence. The program offers a safe and stable living environment while they work to overcome the trauma that led to their homelessness and return to independent living. Families receive intensive case management and therapeutic services designed to help them heal from the trauma and victimization they've experienced, while gaining the skills they need to promote long-term self-sufficiency and obtain stable housing.

Summit Program. This is an innovative crisis stabilization and respite program designed to serve youth, ages 10–17. This program provides youth who are experiencing crisis with acute mental health assessment and stabilization within a pleasant and home-like residential environment. The goal of the program is to prevent further deterioration or the need for hospitalization or out-of-home placement for youth that do not meet the criteria for inpatient hospitalization. In addition, the program works to promote family stability by providing a variety of services to meet individualized needs of each family and youth. Each family is provided with referral or connection to aftercare services that will support their ongoing progress.

Source: ACH Child and Family Services, n.d.

and tagline, are also provided to give you a clear look at what can (and should) be developed and communicated to anyone looking at the organization.

Every organization needs to be able to describe itself on its website and elsewhere. In the case of ACH, the reader learns quickly what the organization is (a nonprofit), who it sees as its major client population (children, youth, and families) and what its major purpose is (helping clients overcome life's challenges). Readers can quickly determine what this organization is "about." When situations arise, staff members have clear guidelines on these matters. The tagline, "Protecting Children. Preserving Families. Since 1915." is easy to remember, and is a way to brand the organization in a very positive light, as well as proving it has staying power.

SWOT Analysis

In the beginning of this chapter, we outlined the steps of the strategic planning process. Step 2 is to conduct a SWOT Analysis (examining the organization's **S**trengths, **W**eaknesses, **O**pportunities, and **T**hreats) or other assessment tool. Typically, the SWOT Analysis will be conducted in a group setting (see Figure 6.2). For example, a board retreat could be devoted to a strategic planning process that includes a SWOT Analysis. The executive team or the entire staff can be valuable in the SWOT process. After listing the many strengths of the organization, it is then time to turn to the weaknesses. While this can be a painful process, it is critical to take a hard and realistic look at the organization. Weaknesses could be such things as the lack of visibility of the organization in the community or inadequate fundraising plans. This type of information may need to be collected using research techniques such as listening sessions, comprised of

various stakeholders, and formal surveys. Clients, employees, board members, community members with no direct connection to the organization, and even members on your organization's email list are important stakeholder groups from which to gather this type of information.

After examining the internal strengths and weaknesses, it is then time to examine the environment in which the organization exists to identify opportunities and threats. Is there a newly identified need in the community that the agency can address? In the "strengths" section, does the agency have resources to bring to bear on this identified need? Are there new funding opportunities on the horizon? Do opportunities for mergers or collaborations with other organizations exist? After reviewing the opportunities, it is important to look at threats in the environment. Are there political trends that are a threat to the organization? Is the agency vulnerable to economic downturns? Are there issues with any of the major funding sources? These types of questions require research efforts to provide solid information for decision-making.

The purpose of the SWOT analysis is to assess how internal strengths and weaknesses relate to external opportunities and threats (Bryson, 2018; Lewis, Packard, & Lewis, 2011). You undertake

Internal	
Strengths	**Weaknesses**

External	
Opportunities	**Threats**

SWOT Analysis Summary

FIGURE 6.2. SWOT Analysis Template
Source: "SWOT Analysis," (2009).

the planning process to maximize the strengths and opportunities and address the weaknesses and threats realistically. SWOT analysis requires a considerable amount of time in order to be accurate and helpful. If done well, however, the results are a useful roadmap to organizational planning. Because a nonprofit organization's environment is constantly shifting in positive and threatening ways, SWOT analysis is an integral aspect of strategic planning by social work leaders.

Developing Ideas to Meet Strategic Goals

Having a lofty goal is wonderful, but it is not enough. Building on everything your organization has accomplished so far (creating a vision, mission, guiding principles, and strategic goals), it is now time to think about and agree on how to move forward with action steps. This step requires a considerable amount of thoughtfulness and creativity. Let's return to the example of ACH. Its mission is, "We protect children from abuse, neglect and family separation and help children overcome these things when they do happen" (ACH Child and Family Services, n.d.). What are some action items to do that? In ACH's case, they have developed programs in many different areas (for example, homeless outreach, housing programs, and crisis stabilization). The strategic goals are providing services in specified areas. All of these link to the belief that the selected program areas are key to achieving transformations for clients.

The strategic goals chosen depend a great deal on the organization's internal characteristics and external environment. Another agency going through a strategic planning process, even with similar guiding documents, could decide on strategic goals that were much different. For example, goals regarding rehabilitation of parents with opioid addictions or promotion of kinship care reasonably connect to protecting children from abuse and family separation. Mission statements are often broad enough that a variety of goals can be appropriate.

At the strategic level of planning, goals describe future outcomes or states of being and, typically, are not focused on being measurable or achievable. Instead, goal statements focus on general outcomes and are ambitious and idealistic. Strategic goals must support the vision and mission statements and be consistent with the guiding principles of the organization. Goal statements are the overarching framework for the program goals, which are operational in nature (we delve into this topic more deeply in Chapter 7). Goals address the problems and needs of the agency's target population and articulate an ideal outcome (Coley & Sheinberg, 2016). If you formulate strategic goals well and they flow from the governing ideas, then the specific program goals will flow naturally from the goals and will assist in achieving the strategic goals.

An aspect of strategic goals is that, unlike program goals, they can be less "nailed down." They often are developed to indicate that the agency is providing some type of services, but not in a specific way. Strategic goals do not state the exact number of services offered or the precise methods or programs to be implemented. That material is part of program planning, which we will look at closely in Chapter 7.

Evaluating the Existing Strategic Goals

Because strategic goals are rarely specific in nature, evaluating them is not always considered possible. We believe that they should be assessed anyway. As noted previously, mission and vision can be approached in a variety of ways, producing different goals. Given the nature of changing strengths, weaknesses, opportunities, and threats, goals may need to change. If, for example, foundations supporting your organization want to stop some programs but give you funding for a different sort of program (that is still within your mission), it is vital to think through what to do. Or you may discover that other organizations in your community are better able to provide a service that you have provided. Is it time to reallocate your resources and pursue different goals? In this sense, the evaluation of the goals is a question of whether this is the best way for your organization, at this time, to move toward achieving some part of your mission. If not, it is time to create new goals.

Thinking About and Making Necessary Corrections

Any organization has a set of routines and activities. If changes are proposed through the strategic planning process due to changes seen by conducting a SWOT analysis, then changes will need to be made that have repercussions for the people working in the current situation. Grantwriters may need to begin to focus on new sources of funding. Eliminating or shifting the focus of current programs may mean staff members must learn new skills. Sometimes employees will be laid off, even if they

BOX 6.4 A Personal Experience with Strategic Change

by Richard Hoefer

For many years I have been a contract evaluator, being paid by agencies that received Federal government grants that required an evaluation expert. One organization providing social services to people with HIV/AIDS had received a string of grants and hired me over the course of several years.

At one point, I was asked to meet with the administrator overseeing my work. She indicated that the organization was seeing two changes taking place in the field. First, because of the success of drug protocols for stopping the AIDS disease and the lower mortality rates from AIDS, fewer supportive social services were needed, and grants were becoming fewer and more competitive. Second, medical professionals were increasingly being hired to oversee the work of HIV/AIDS professionals planning and conducting prevention and support services. The new CEO of this agency, for example, was an MD and PhD and had replaced a longtime director with an MSW.

Because of these changes, the decision had been made to reduce the organization's reliance on service grants, shift resources to medical programs in alliance with a local medical research institute, and hire an internal evaluator with a biomedical background. It was at that point I learned that my contract would not be renewed after it ran out the next month.

While I was affected negatively from a financial perspective, I was able to understand and agree with the decisions being made by the organization's leaders. Their foresight into the shifting financial winds and needs of their clients stabilized the agency and set them up for a renewed ability to compete for funding.

were good in their jobs. As part of the strategic planning process, these changes need to be considered before changes are finalized (see Box 6.4 for a personal story about being caught up in strategic change).

Conclusion

Knowing how to conduct strategic planning for an organization is a critical skill for you as a social work administrator. Without careful planning, the organization can be like a vessel adrift at sea without a clear destination. Your job is to provide leadership to the board and staff in assuring that the organization is moving forward in a direction to best serve the clients of the organization.

Reference List

ACH Child and Family Services. (n.d.). Retrieved from http://www.achservices.org

American Red Cross. (n.d.). Mission statement. Retrieved from https://www.redcross.org/about-us/who-we-are/mission-and-values.html

Amnesty International. (2018). *Amnesty International report 2017/2018: The state of the world's human rights*. London, UK: Author. Retrieved from https://www.amnesty.org/download/Documents/POL1067002018ENGLISH.PDF

Austin, M. J., & Solomon, J. R. (2009). Managing the planning process. In R. Patti (Ed.), *The handbook of human services management* (2nd ed., pp. 321–338). Thousand Oaks, CA: Sage.

Brody, R., & Nair, M. (2013). *Effectively managing and leading human service organizations* (4th ed.). Thousand Oaks, CA: Sage.

Bryson, J. M. (2018). *Strategic planning for public and nonprofit organizations: A guide to strengthening and sustaining organizational achievement.* San Francisco, CA: Jossey-Bass.

Bryson, J. M., Edwards, L. H., & Van Slyke, D. M. (2018). Getting strategic about strategic planning research. *Public Management Review, 20*(3), 317–339. doi:10.1080/14719037.2017.1285111

Carroll, L. (1865). *Alice's adventures in wonderland.* London, UK: Macmillan.

Catholic Charities USA. (n.d.). Our mission, our vision, our ministry. Retrieved from https://www.catholiccharitiesusa.org/about-us/mission-vision/

Coley, S. M., & Scheinberg, C. A. (2016). *Proposal writing: Effective grantsmanship for funding* (5th ed.). Thousand Oaks, CA: Sage.

Drucker, P. F. (1992). *Managing the non-profit organization: Principles and practices.* New York, NY: HarperCollins.

Foley, A. (n.d.). Strategic planning vs. operational planning: The 5 main differences. ClearPoint Strategy. Retrieved from https://www.clearpointstrategy.com/strategic-planning-vs-operational-planning/

Goodwill, Inc. (n.d.). Goodwill's heritage, mission, vision and values. Retrieved from http://www.goodwill.org/about-us/goodwills-heritage-mission-vision-and-values/

Kettner, P. M., Moroney, R. M., & Martin, L. L. (2017). *Designing and managing programs: An effectiveness-based approach* (5th ed.). Thousand Oaks, CA: Sage.

Lewis, J. A., Packard, T., & Lewis, M. D. (2011). *Management of human service programs* (5th ed.). Belmont, CA: Brooks/Cole.

March of Dimes. (n.d.). Mission. Retrieved from https://www.marchofdimes.org/mission/mission.aspx

Poister, T. H., & Streib, G. D. (1999). Strategic management in the public sector: Concepts, models, and processes. *Public Productivity & Management Review, 22*(3), 308–325. doi:10.2307/3380706

Senge, P. M. (1990). *The fifth discipline: The art & practice of the learning organization.* New York, NY: Doubleday/Currency.

Smith, Bucklin & Associates, Inc. (2000). *The complete guide to nonprofit management* (2nd ed.). New York: John Wiley & Sons.

SWOT Analysis. (2009). Retrieved from http://www.whatmakesagoodleader.com/swot_analysis_template.html#SimpleSWOTAnalysisTemplate

World Association of Girl Guides and Girl Scouts. (n.d.). Mission & vision. Retrieved from https://www.wagggs.org/en/about-us/who-we-are/mission-vision/

Worth, M. J. (2009). *Nonprofit management: Principles and practice.* Thousand Oaks, CA: Sage.

Additional Resources

Allison, M., & Kaye, J. (2015). *Strategic planning for nonprofit organizations: A practical guide for dynamic times.* Hoboken, NJ: John Wiley & Sons.

Gowdy, H. (2015). Revolutionizing strategic planning for non-profits [Video file]. Retrieved from https://youtu.be/Rgomo5S59-k

McNamara, C. (n.d.) Free nonprofit micro-eMBA Module 6: Developing your strategic plan. *Free Management Library.* https://managementhelp.org/freenonprofittraining/strategic-planning.htm[1]

---

1   This Free Management Library module for strategic planning provides a considerable amount of information and additional resources. It can be used as an online resource for others on the strategic planning team to agree on a process and appropriate steps.

HELPFUL TERMS

Goals—descriptions of future outcomes or states of being that typically are not measurable or achievable. Instead, goal statements are focused on outcomes and are ambitious and idealistic.

Governing ideas—the vision statement, the mission statement, and the statement of guiding principles (Senge, 1990).

Guiding principles—a statement of principles that describes the values that will guide the organization; the things that will not be compromised, based on deeply held convictions and traditions.

Mission statement—a "succinct statement that sets forth the organization's purpose and philosophy" (Smith, Bucklin & Associates, Inc., 2000. p. 13).

Objectives—the results that are expected as the organization works toward its stated goals. Objectives are the steps that will be taken to reach the stated goals.

Outcome objectives—answers the question, "So what? What difference did it make in the lives of the people served?" Outcome objectives are stated as improved behavior, increased skills, changed attitudes, increased knowledge, or improved conditions.

Process objectives—quantify the usage of the services and identify how much service will be provided. Process objectives are designed to determine whether the program is doing what it says it will do. It describes the services that are to be provided, in what quantities, and in what time frames.

Program Activities—what will be done by program staff and volunteers with, and on behalf of, service recipients.

SMART—a useful acronym to remember when developing objectives. Objectives need to be specific (S), measurable (M), achievable (A), realistic (R), and timely (T).

Strategic Planning—a "deliberative, disciplined effort to produce fundamental decisions and actions that shape and guide what an organization (or other entity) is, what it does, and why" (Bryson, 2018, p. 317).

SWOT Analysis—a process for examining the organizations strengths (S), weaknesses (W), opportunities (O), and threats (T), usually in the context of a strategic planning process.

Vision statement—a governing statement that is a powerful image of the future for the organization and provides the foundation for other planning activities.

EXERCISES

1. SWOT Analysis

Work with a group of three or four students in your class to develop a SWOT Analysis of this class. What are the strengths and weaknesses internally, and what are the opportunities and threats in the external environment? Use the SWOT template and report your findings to the class.

2. In-Basket Exercise

Directions

You are Jerome Harris, the CEO of LIFT (Lifelong Independence for Texans), a nonprofit that works with people in Texas who have multiple challenges with non-typical physical and mental characteristics. Read the following memo from your board chair, Marianne Nunnelly. She believes that the current mission statement is inadequate and wants you to draft a new, and better, one. Work with a group of three or four of your classmates and frame a response memo based on the material in this chapter. Be sure to explain in your response why the new mission statement is better than the current one.

> **Memo**
>
> Date: August 4, 20XX
>
> To: Jerome Harris, CEO, Lifelong Independence For Texans (LIFT)
>
> From: Marianne Nunnelly, LIFT Board Chair
>
> Subject: Our Mission Statement
>
> As we are preparing for our strategic planning retreat, I have been thinking that the current mission statement leaves much to be desired. It is important that you and I are on the same page about a new mission statement. I know that we have not revised the mission statement in several years. It now seems far too generic and lackluster. As you recall, it states "LIFT's mission is to help people realize their full potential." This does not seem to capture precisely what we do in helping people with multiple disabilities to live and work independently. It certainly is not being an effective way to draw new volunteers and donors to support LIFT. I'm advocating that we change the mission statement as we move forward to develop new goals and objectives. Please get with your executive team and afterwards share your thoughts with me what your new and improved mission statement is.

3. Guiding Principles

If you were starting a new agency, what values would guide you in your administration of the agency? Write a guiding principles statement for your new agency, and read your statement to the class.

ASSIGNMENTS

1. Examine the websites of three human service organizations in your community. Analyze the mission statements of the three organizations by comparing and contrasting them. What are the strengths and weaknesses of each? What recommendations would you make for improving each of the mission statements?

2. Make an appointment to interview a human services administrator about a recent strategic planning process. Write a five-page paper that describes the process. Pay special attention to the role of the administrator in the planning process.

3. Find an agency that has changed its mission statement in the past five years. Compare the old and the new statements. How are they different? How are they similar? Write a three-page paper that describes the possible reasons behind the change in the mission statement. If possible, talk with a human service administrator who was involved in the process to understand the change process more fully..

Image Credits

7

Program Planning, Logic Models, and Program Evaluation

Social work leaders and managers must be skilled in both planning and evaluating programs. A logic model is useful for both these tasks, even though planning happens before the program begins and evaluation happens after it has been in operation. A good evaluation, however, is planned at the same time that the program is designed so that a clear process is in place to collect necessary data along the way, rather than after the program finishes. This chapter discusses program planning (as opposed to strategic planning, which is covered in Chapter 6), describes the process of logic modeling, and then shows how to use the logic model to plan an evaluation. You will use research skills to select and improve programs as you manage them and as you plan evaluations. The programs chosen, as well as the evaluation methods you choose, are elements of intervening. Finally, the material on evaluation clearly relates to evaluating practice.

Program Planning

In your career as a social work administrator, you will have opportunities to be responsible for running programs or entire agencies that existed before you came on board. These will be part of the territory you need to understand and, if possible, improve. You may also need to create a logic model or design a program evaluation for it. Managing a current program or conducting a program evaluation without a logic model is possible, but it is much more difficult than if you have one.

In addition, you may be responsible to plan a new program, particularly when writing a grant proposal but also at other times, such as when your organization's strategic planning process leads to changing priorities. While you may do this totally from scratch, we suggest you search for an evidence-based program that has already been shown to be effective in addressing the problems your clients are experiencing. You will need to create a logic model and evaluation plan for this new program as you present it to others, such as funders. This chapter presents the information you need and shows the usefulness of understanding the benefits of logic models for planning and evaluation purposes, whether you are running a program already in existence or planning a new one.

Planning a program means making a set of connections between strategic goals and program goals, as noted in Chapter 6. At the program level, however, you must think on a very practical and measurable level. You also need to differentiate between program processes and impact.

As demonstrated in Figure 7.1, program planning is a continuation of the strategic planning process. The strategic goals decided upon by the board of the organization lead to a string of steps: deciding what long-term outcomes you want to achieve with a particular program, then the medium-term and short-term outcomes that must be achieved as prerequisites to achieve longer-term outcomes. The planning process must also include planning for the processes that must occur and planning what the activities completed by staff members and clients are. It can be easier to follow

the logical process of program planning by starting at the bottom of Figure 7.1 and working your way up the chart. (That is, in essence, what a logic model does. We cover that material in a few pages.) Starting at the top of the figure, however, emphasizes the connection to the larger purposes of the organization.

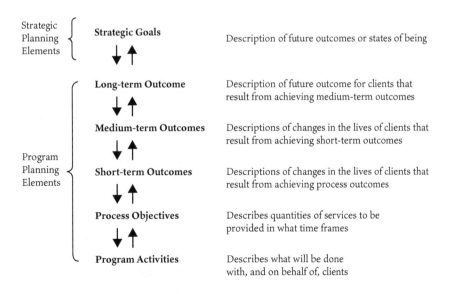

FIGURE 7.1. Program Planning

What are Evidence-Based Programs?

The term *evidence-based program* refers to a program that has been designed to solve a particular problem and has been proven through research to reduce the problem in the desired way. As one arm of the United States federal government has stated, "An evidence-based program (EBP) is a program proven through rigorous evaluation to be effective" (Family and Youth Services Bureau, n.d., p. 1).

This concept emerges from evidence-based practice and derives from the term used in the field of medicine to denote practices that are effective in decreasing particular medical issues. In medicine, of course, double-blind tests of new drugs and procedures are standard practice, and the efficacy and safety of anything new needs to be proven through clinical trials before being released to the public. While the same level of proof is not usually available for social program interventions, this is the model on which evidence-based practices in social work, and human services in general, is based.

All programs are made up of various components that come together to try to improve lives. In programs that are not evidence-based, aspects or parts of the program are included because the designer "feels" or "believes" that they are important. Evidence-based programs must meet a higher standard, with all of the parts of the program being tested to determine if they help achieve program outcomes. Evidence-based programs usually have two types of components: *core* and *adaptable*. Core components are based on theory and need to be implemented according to the program developer's guidelines if you wish to achieve the results that have been shown to result from the program. According to the Family and Youth Services Bureau (n.d.), "Core components of an evidence-based program are the characteristics that must be kept intact when the program is being replicated or adapted, in order for it to produce program outcomes similar to those demonstrated in the original evaluation research (i.e., the essential ingredients of an evidence-based program)" (p. 2). Core components are made up of the following:

- Staff selection
- Pre-service and in-service training
- Ongoing consultation and coaching
- Staff and program evaluation
- Facilitative administrative support
- Systems interventions

The Family and Youth Services Bureau (n.d.) indicates that core components (for educational programs) fit into three categories: content, pedagogy, and implementation. Thus, important core components always include *what* is taught, *how* it is taught, and the *logistics* that go into making for a productive learning environment (Family and Youth Services Bureau, n.d., p. 2–3).

While core components are those that may not be changed, lest the efficacy of the intervention be lost, other aspects of the planned program may be considered adaptable, because they can be changed to meet the needs of another locale, population, or culture. Adaptable components are ones that have been tested but are not necessarily vital to achieving positive results. Choosing a program based on the evidence that it is effective but then changing the core components of the program is quite unsound and can result in a waste of considerable time, energy, and other resources. Altering "non-core" or adaptable components constitutes a reasonable effort to increase the fit of the evidence-based program to a new environment and situation. Program planners must be careful when they change elements of any evidence-based program and should carefully plan how to monitor these changes (see Box 7.2). Developing a fidelity monitoring plan before you start the program is needed to document that you will include all required appropriate content and activities, deliver content as specified, and use the right type of staff (Banikya-Leaseburg & Chilcoat, 2013). (As discussed later in this chapter, using a logic model assists in developing a fidelity monitoring plan.)

BOX 7.2 How to Plan and Implement an Adaptation to a Selected EBP

Not all adaptations are acceptable [to a] program, especially if they are not informed by the EBP's core components. There are several theoretical approaches on how to make adaptations to EBPs in a planned and thoughtful way ... Most include the following steps:

1. **Assess:** Analyze the results of assessments of the target population(s) and the organization's capacity. These will highlight the important factors to include in the program.
2. **Know the selected program(s):** Identify and review the goals, objectives, logic model, curriculum activities and cultural appropriateness of the selected EBP(s) and compare the factors addressed in the program (i.e. increasing negotiation skills) to the determinants most relevant to the target population (i.e. self-efficacy in negotiating with sexual partners). ...
3. **Identify adaptation challenges:** Assess fidelity concerns or adaptation challenges that emerge from considering how the curriculum activities may conflict with the target population needs and/or agency capacity and logistical constraints. Assess acceptability of the motives for these changes as well.

   In addition to having the appropriate motives for adaptations, there are only certain things that can be changed in an EBP in order to maintain fidelity to the core components and maintain the program's effectiveness in achieving identified behavior change and/or sexual health outcomes. ...
4. **Select and plan adaptations:** Using information about the EBP (i.e. curriculum, core components, logic model) and adaptation resources (i.e. adaptation guidelines, fidelity monitoring tools), determine whether or not each proposed adaptation is an acceptable change and maintains program fidelity.
5. **Pilot and monitor adaptations:** Before full implementation, pilot the entire curriculum and/or pilot test the proposed adaptations with a subgroup of participants. This will serve as an opportunity to correct glitches and to test assumptions (e.g., how long an activity might take, whether the audience reacts as intended, whether concepts are clear, etc.). Then, gather feedback and make changes as needed. Use a fidelity monitoring tool to monitor and assess the success of the adaptations, and to provide feedback and continuous quality improvement for implementation, as well as evaluate the overall EBP implementation.

Source: Family and Youth Services Bureau, (n.d.).

Family and Youth Services Bureau, "How to Plan and Implement an Adaptation to a Selected EBP," Making Adaptations Tip Sheet, U.S. Department of Health and Human Services. https://www.acf.hhs.gov/sites/default/files/fysb/prep-making-adaptations-ts.pdf

An example of the difference may be useful. According to Reconnecting Youth (n.d.) one of their program offerings is CAST (Coping and Support Training). It consists of

twelve, 55-minute sessions facilitated by an adult who works well with at-risk youth and who is trained to implement the CAST program. The 12 CAST sessions are usually offered twice per week in a (middle or high) school setting as a pull-out program, or outside of the school setting by youth-oriented agencies, mental health professionals, and community centers (Reconnecting Youth, n.d.).

A core component of the CAST program is that twelve 55-minute sessions are held over a 6-week period, covering specific topics in a specific way, as shown in the course curriculum notebooks (Reconnecting Youth, n.d.). If an organization changes the number, length, timing, or content of the sessions, it will be altering at least one core component, and this should be avoided. On the other hand, the age of the students may be adaptable. Currently, the information about the program indicates that positive effects are found when using the curriculum and program with adolescents and young adults from the ages of 13 to 25. Would this approach be as effective with "emerging adults" up to the age of 30? No information is currently available, but a case might be made that this is a reasonable extension of the initial research and so the age of the student could be seen as an adaptable component.

Certain government agencies have lists of programs that they believe have evidence to support their efficacy when implemented according to guidelines. These lists do change as new programs are added that have gained research support and old, "promising" programs are dropped as new evidence determines that the programs are not effective, after all. A number of these directories are provided at the end of the chapter under Additional Resources.

Before you definitively choose a new program to begin or include in a grant proposal, you will want to ensure that program manuals, guides, training, and evaluation tools are available so you can implement the program as intended. You should determine if the EBP is a fit for your organization and community in other ways, as well. Nine things to consider when you are in the process of selecting a program are the fit with

- Your population
- Your setting
- Your target population's culture
- Availability of training
- Values of the community
- Values of the local power structure
- Organizational mission, vision, and culture
- Administrative feasibility
- Capacity of staff
- Availability of sufficient financial, time, and other resources

What If No EBP Is Available?

Sometimes you will want to start a program to address a particular need, but you cannot find an EBP listed in government directories that fills your organization's needs. In this case, you need to become creative and put together the best program you can that has yet to be tested. Two sources of information that you can use are the Campbell Collaboration and Cochrane Collaboration websites.

The Campbell Collaboration (campbellcollaboration.org) showcases comprehensive literature reviews of program impact relating to social welfare and international development issues. The

vision of the Campbell Collaboration is "better evidence for a better world" (Campbell Collaboration, n.d.), and the mission statement is, "The Campbell Collaboration promotes positive social and economic change through the production and use of systematic reviews and other evidence synthesis for evidence-based policy and practice" (Campbell Collaboration, n.d.).

Another source of evidence for programs comes from the Cochrane Collaboration (cochrane.org). It is very similar to the Campbell Collaboration, although it has a different focus area. The Cochrane Collaboration focuses on health and mental health issues. Its vison is "a world of improved health where decisions about health and health care are informed by high-quality, relevant and up-to-date synthesized research evidence," and its mission is "to promote evidence-informed health decision-making by producing high-quality, relevant, accessible systematic reviews and other synthesized research evidence" (Cochrane Collaboration, n.d.).

Once you have selected a model program to use as your starting point, it is time to create a logic model for it. Having a one-page illustration of the program in this way eases communication about what the program's purpose is and all the elements that are needed to make it effective. It also links processes and impacts clearly.

Logic Models

The idea of logic models as an adjunct to program evaluation extends back at least as far as 2000, when the Kellogg Foundation published a guide to developing logic models for program design and evaluation. According to Frechtling (2007), a logic model is "a tool that describes the *theory of change* underlying an intervention, product or policy" (p. 1). You can find many explanations describing how to construct a logic model, but not all demonstrate how it is a versatile tool to design programs, assist in their implementation, and guide their evaluation. This section describes one basic approach to logic modeling for program design and evaluation. We thus link the planning and evaluation aspects of human service administration.

You should understand that not all current programs have been designed with the aid of a logic model, although that is becoming less common every year. Federal grants, for example, often require applicants to submit a logic model, and their use throughout the human services sector is growing through academic education and in-service training. If there is no logic model for a program you are working with, it is possible to create one *after* a program's implementation. You can thus bring the power of the tool to bear when changing a program or creating an evaluation plan. You may find this leads to staff and clients' better understanding the program's purposes and results in a higher level of effectiveness.

Logic model creation uses system theory terminology. Because logic models describe the program's "theory of change," it is possible to believe that this refers to something such as social learning theory, cognitive-behavioral theory, or any one of a number of psychological or sociological theories. In general, though, logic models have a much less grand view of theory. We begin with the assumption that any human services program is created to solve a problem. The problem should be clearly stated in a way that does not predetermine how the problem will be solved. The usefulness of a logic model is to show how the resources used (inputs) are changed into a program (activities) with closely linked products (outputs) that then lead to changes (outcomes) in the short, medium, and long terms. The net effect of these changes is that the original problem is solved or at least made better. An example of a logic model is shown in Figure 7.2.

The problem being addressed by the example program is, "School-aged youth have anger management problems, leading to verbal and physical fights at school and home." This problem statement is specific about who has a problem (school-aged youth), what the problem is (anger management problems leading to verbal and physical fights), and where it is a problem (school and home). It also does not prejudge what the solution is, allowing for many possible programs to address the problem. An example problem statement that is not as good because it states the problem in a way that allows only one solution is, "There is a lack of anger management classes in schools for school-aged youth."

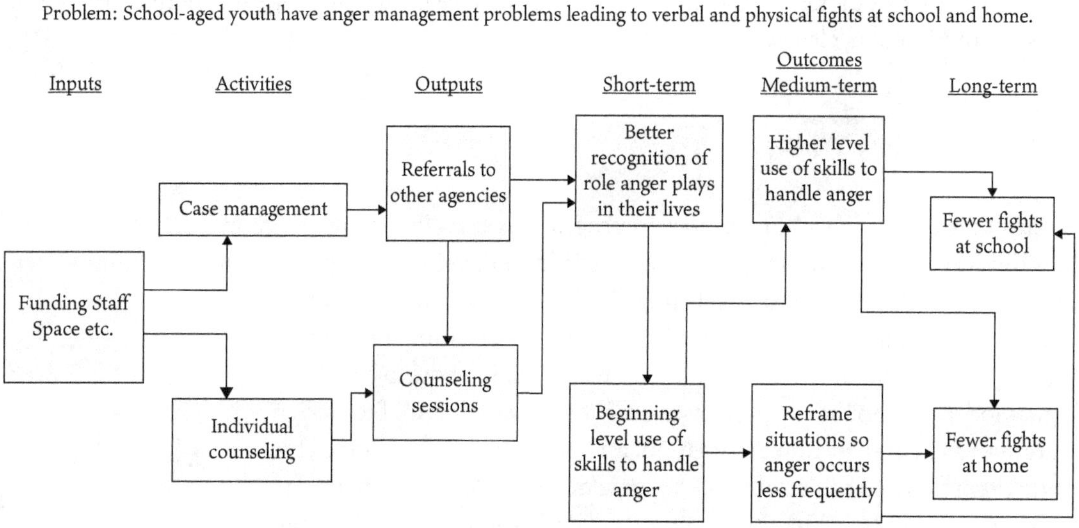

Problem: School-aged youth have anger management problems leading to verbal and physical fights at school and home.

FIGURE 7.2. Example Logic Model

Another way to make the problem statement strong is to phrase the statement in such a way that almost anyone can agree that it is actually a problem. The example problem statement might make this point more clearly by saying, "There are too many verbal and physical fights at school and home among school-aged youth." Phrased this way, there would be little doubt that this is a problem, even though the statement is not specific about the number of such fights or the cause of the fights. Note that if the program personnel want to focus on anger management problems, this way of stating the problem might lead to a host of other issues that might be leading to fights being addressed instead—such as overcrowding in the halls, gang membership, conflict over curfews at home, or anything else that might conceivably cause youth to fight at school or home. Be prepared to revisit your first effort at the problem statement and seek input from interested stakeholders to be sure that you are tackling what is really considered the reason for the program. The problem statement is vital to the rest of the logic model and evaluation, so take the time to make several drafts to get full agreement.

After the problem statement, the logic model has six columns. Arrows connect what is written in one column to something else, in the next column to the right or even within the same column. These arrows are the "logic" of the program. If the column to the left is achieved, then we believe that the element at the end of the arrow will be achieved. Each arrow can be considered to show a hypothesis that the two elements are linked. (The example presented in Figure 7.2 is intentionally not "perfect" so that you can see some of the nuances and challenges of using this tool.)

The first column is labeled "Inputs." In this column, you write the major resources that will be needed or used in the program. Generically, these tend to be funds, staff, and space, but they can include other elements, such as type of funds, educational level of the staff, and location of the space (on a bus line, for example), if they apply to your program. The resource of "staff," for example, might mean MSW-level licensed counselors. In the end, if only staff members with bachelors degrees in psychology are hired, this would indicate that the staff input was inadequate.

The second column is "Activities." In this area, you write what the staff members of the program will be doing—what behaviors you would see them engage in if you sat and watched them. Here, as elsewhere in the logic model, there are decisions about the level of detail to include. It would be too detailed, for example, to have the following bullet points for the "case management" activity:

- Answer phone calls about clients
- Make phone calls about clients
- Learn about other agencies' services
- Write out referral forms for clients to other agencies

This is what you would see, literally, but the phrase "case management" is probably enough. Somewhere in program documents, there should be a more detailed description of the duties of a case manager (such as a job description), so that this level of detail is not necessary in the logic model, which is, after all, a graphical depiction of the program's theory of change, not a daily to-do list.

The other danger when developing your logic model is being too general. In this case, a phrase such as "provide social work services" wouldn't be enough to help the viewer know what the employee is doing, as there are many activities involved in social work services. Getting the correct level of specificity is important in helping develop your evaluation plan here and throughout the logic model.

As you can see from the arrows leading from the inputs to the activities, the program theory indicates that, given the proper funds, staff, and space, the activities of case management and individual counseling will occur. This may or may not happen, however, which is why a process evaluation is needed and will be discussed later in this chapter.

The third column lists "Outputs." An output is a measurable result of an activity. In this example, the activity of "case management" results in client youth being referred to other agencies for services. The output of the activity "individual counseling" is counseling sessions. It is important to note that outputs are not changes in clients—outputs are the results of agency activities that may or may not then result in changes to clients. The connection between agency activity and outputs is perhaps the most difficult part of putting together a logic model, because many people mistakenly assume that if a service is given and documented, then client changes are automatic. This is simply not true.

The next three columns are collectively known as "Outcomes." An outcome is a *change in the client*. These changes occur in a client's knowledge, attitude, belief, status, or behavior. Outcomes

are why programs are developed and run—to change clients' lives or decrease community problems. You can develop outcomes for any level of intervention—individual, couple or family, group, organization, or community of any size. This example uses a program designed to make a change at an individual youth level, but it could also target changes at the school or district level, if desired.

Outcomes are usually written to show a time dimension with short-, medium-, and long-term outcomes. The long-term outcome is the opposite of the problem stated at the top of the logic model and thus ties the entire intervention back to its purpose—to solve a particular problem. The division of outcomes into three distinct time periods is obviously a helpful fiction, not a tight description of reality. Still, some outcomes are expected to come sooner than others. These short-term outcomes are usually considered the direct result of outputs being developed. On the example logic model, the arrows indicate that referrals and individual counseling are both supposed to result in client youth better recognizing the role that anger plays in their life. After that is achieved, the program theory hypothesizes that clients will use skills at a beginning level to handle their anger. This is a case where one short-term outcome ("change in self-knowledge") leads the way for a change in behavior ("using skills").

BOX 7.3 Outcomes vs. Goals and Objectives: What's the Difference?

People sometimes have difficulty understanding the difference between the terms "Outcome" and "Goals and Objectives." Logic models use the term *outcome* to signify desired changes in clients, but many people use the terms *goals and objectives* to talk about what a program is trying to achieve. What's the difference?

In reality, there is not much difference. Goals and objectives are one way of talking about the purpose of a program. This terminology is older than the logic model terminology and perhaps is more widespread. But it can be confusing, too, because an objective at one level of an organization may be considered a goal at another level or at a different time.

Outcomes are easier to fit into the logic model approach by their relating to resources, activities, and outputs. This terminology avoids some of the conceptual pitfalls of "goals and objectives" thinking, particularly when thinking about the time dimensions involved. It is easier to think of which outcomes occur first, then second, and so on in your logic model than to worry about what is a goal and what is an objective and how they are related over time to other goals and objectives.

No matter which terms are used in your organization or by your funders, you need to feel comfortable with the concepts. Most importantly, you should realize that both sets of words are ultimately talking about the same thing: the actual changes an organization is working for to make people's lives better.

The element of "beginning-level use of skills to handle anger" in Figure 7.2 has two arrows leading to medium-term outcomes. The first arrow leads to "higher level use of skills to handle anger." In this theory of change, there is still anger at this point, but the youth recognizes what is occurring and takes measures to handle it in a skillful way that does not lead to negative consequences. The second arrow, leading to "reframe situations so anger occurs less frequently," indicates that the program designers believe that the skills youth learn will assist them in reframing situations they are in so that they feel angry less frequently. This is a separate behavior than applying skills to handle anger, so it receives its own arrow and box.

The final column represents the long-term outcomes. Often, there is only one element shown in this column, one indicating the opposite of the problem. In this logic model, since the problem is seen to occur both at school and at home, each is looked at separately. A youth may reduce fights at home but not at school, or vice versa, so it is important to leave open the possibility of only partial success.

This example logic model shows a relatively simple program theory, with two separate tracks for intervention but with overlapping outcomes expected from the two intervention methods. It indicates how one element can lead to more than one "next step" and how different elements can lead to the same outcome. Finally, while it is not necessarily obvious just yet, this example shows some weak points in the program's logic that will emerge when we use it as a guide to evaluating the program.

Many people use the goal-setting acronym SMART to help them develop their outcome statements, particularly at the short- and medium-term levels (see Table 7.1). (The example logic model in Figure 7.2 does not show a SMART format because of space limitations, but it can be used in the full program materials.) Outcomes need to be specific (S), measurable (M), achievable (A), realistic (R), and time-bound (T). Table 7.1 helps explain each of these attributes. An example of

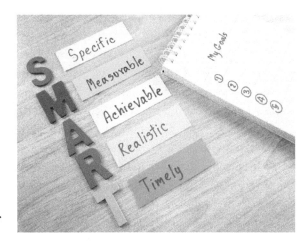

TABLE 7.1 **Attributes of SMART Objectives**

Attribute	Description
Specific	Clear and concrete
Measurable	How many, how much
Achievable	Can be achieved with appropriate program activity and resources
Realistic	High enough that there is a possibility that the objective won't be reached, and not so low that achieving the stated objective would be meaningless
Time-bound	Provides a time span within which the objective will be achieved

Adapted from Lewis, Packard, & Lewis (2011).

using the SMART format for the short-term outcome of "beginning level use of skills to handle anger" is "95% of program participants will successfully demonstrate one anger management technique in a role-play situation after 2 weeks in the program." The use of the SMART approach is clearly more specific and measurable than the more general statement. It is also longer and more difficult to fit into a small box in the logic model format. Remember also that the purpose of the logic model is to show the overall rationale for the program elements and how they relate to each other, not to describe the details of the program. The SMART format can be used in expanding the description of program activities and outputs, as well. An example is "During the first year of operations, program staff will provide a total of 100 individual counseling sessions to students in the program."

Conceptually, the logic model can be divided into two parts. The three columns on the left (Resources, Activities, and Outputs) are about the *process* of running the program. What is shown in these columns represents what you have to do to reach your program outcomes, or to impact your clients. Although it can be confusing, the term *process objectives* is sometimes used to label statements about the quantity of services provided. Process objectives are designed to determine whether the program is doing what it says it will do. They describe the services that are to be provided and in what quantities in what time frames. For example, the process objective might be to deliver 250 counseling hours to 75 clients within a six-month period of time.

The three columns on the right relating to how clients will be different after being in the program (short-, medium-, and long-term outcomes) indicate the impact of the program. Outcome statements answer the "so what?" question. If you deliver the 250 counseling hours to 75 clients, the questions you want to answer are, "What difference will it make in the lives of the people served? How are they different afterward?" The outcome objectives become the basis of the outcome evaluation for your program. Outcome objectives indicate what will be different after the service is delivered. These may be stated as improved behavior, increased skills, changed attitudes, increased knowledge, or improved conditions. The well-developed, complete outcome objective will follow the SMART formula and include the target group, the number of program recipients, the expected results, and the geographic location (Coley & Scheinberg, 2016). We stress that this complete objective is difficult to fit in the logic model, so use a shortened version there and have the complete version in the full program description materials for reference.

Program Evaluation

As you can see from this discussion, we have used a logic model to represent what we believe will happen when the proper inputs are applied to the correct client population. In the end, if all goes well, clients will no longer have the problem the program addresses, or at least the degree or extent of the problem will be less.

Evaluation is a way to determine the worth or value of a program (Rossi, Lipsey, & Henry, 2019). There are two primary types of evaluation: *process* and *outcome*. The first, process evaluation, examines the way a program runs. In essence, a process evaluation examines the first three columns of a logic model to determine whether required inputs were available, the extent to which activities were conducted, and the degree of output accomplishment. Another aspect of a process evaluation, called *fidelity assessment*, examines whether the program being evaluated was conducted in accordance with the way the program was *supposed* to be conducted. If all components of a program are completed, fidelity is said to be high. Particularly with evidence-based and manualized programs, if changes are made to the program model during implementation, the program's effectiveness is likely to be diminished.

The value of the logic model for evaluation is that most of the conceptual information needed to design the evaluation of a program is in the logic model. The required inputs are listed, and the evaluator can check to determine which resources actually came into the program. Activities are similarly delineated, and an evaluator can usually find a way to count the number of activities that the program completed. Similarly, the logic model describes the outputs that are expected, and the evaluator merely has to determine how to count the number of completed outputs that result from the program's activities.

Looking at the example logic model shows us that we want to have in our evaluation plan at least one way to measure whether funding, staff, and space (the inputs) are adequate; how much case management occurred and individual counseling was conducted (the activities); and the extent to which referrals were made (and followed up on) and the number of individual counseling sessions that happened (the outputs). This information should be in program documents to compare what was planned for with what was actually provided. Having a logic model from the beginning allows the evaluator to ensure that proper data are being collected from the program's start, rather than scrambling later to answer some of these basic questions.

As noted earlier, this is not a perfect logic model. The question in the process evaluation at this stage might be to determine how to actually measure "case management." The output is supposed to be "referrals to other agencies," but there is much else that could be considered beneficial from a case management approach. This element may need careful delineation and discussion with stakeholders to ascertain exactly what is important about case management that should be measured.

The second primary type of evaluation examines program outcomes. Called an *outcome evaluation*, it focuses on the right half of the logic model, where the designated short-, medium-, and long-term outcomes are listed. The evaluator chooses which outcomes to assess from among the various outcomes in the logic model. Decisions need to be made about *how* to measure the outcomes, but the logic model provides a quick list of *what* to measure. In the example logic model, the short-term outcome "better recognition of the role anger plays in their lives" must be measured, and this could be accomplished using a set of questions asked at intake into the program and after some time has passed after receiving services. One standardized anger management instrument is called the "Anger Management Scale" (Stith & Hamby, 2002). A standardized instrument, if it is appropriate for the clients and program, is a good choice because it can help you find norms, or expected responses to the items on the instrument. It is helpful to you, as the evaluator, to know what "average" responses are so you can compare your clients' responses to the norms. Sometimes, however, it can be difficult to find a standardized instrument that is fully appropriate and relevant to your program.

Another way of measuring is to use an instrument you make up yourself. This has the advantage of simplicity and of being directly connected to your evaluation. In this case, for example, you could approach this outcome in at least two ways. First, you could request a statement from the caseworker or counselor indicating that the client has "recognized the role that anger plays" in his or her life, without going into any detail. A second approach would be to have the client write a statement about the role anger plays in his or her life. Neither of these measurements will have a lot of practical utility. Going through the logic model in this way in the design stage can show that this link in program logic is difficult to measure and may not be necessary.

While it may seem startling to have an example in a text that shows a less-than-perfect approach, it is included here to show that a logic model is very useful in showing weak spots in the program logic. This link to "better recognition" is not a fatal problem, and it may indeed be an important cognitive change for the client. The issue for evaluation is how to measure it and whether it really needs to be measured at all.

Of more importance is the next link, which leads to "learn skills to handle anger." The evaluation must ensure that clients understand skills to help them handle anger and so document these skills. It is not enough to indicate that skills were taught, as in a group or individual session. Teaching a class is an activity, and so would be documented in the process evaluation portion of the overall evaluation, but being in a class does not guarantee a change in the client. In this evaluation, we would like to have a measure that can show a client's change in the ability to perform the anger management skill. This attribute of the measure is important because we expect the clients to get better in their use over time and have included more skillful use of the techniques as a medium-term outcome in the logic model.

The other medium-term outcome shown is that clients will be able to reframe situations so that they actually get angry less frequently. The program logic shows this outcome occurring as a result of both beginning- and higher-level use of skills. Because this element is broken out from the "use of skills to handle anger," it will need a separate measure. As an evaluator, you can hope that an established, normed instrument is available or that this is a skill that is measured by a separate item on a longer scale. If not, you will need to find a way to pull this information from staff members' reports or client self-assessments.

The final links in the logic model connect the medium-term outcomes to the long-term outcomes of fewer fights at school and fewer fights at home. Because youth having too many fights was identified as the problem this program is addressing, we want to know to what degree fights have decreased. The measure here could be client self-reports, school records, or reports from people living in the home.

Implicit in the discussion of the use of this logic model for evaluation purposes is that measurements at the end will be compared to an earlier measure of the same outcome. This is called a *single group pretest–posttest evaluation* (or research) design. It is not considered a strong design, due to the ability of other forces (threats to internal validity) to affect the results. The design could be stronger if a comparison group of similar youth (perhaps at a different school) were chosen and tracked with the same measures. The design could be *much* stronger if youth at the same school were randomly assigned to either a group that received the program or a different group that did not receive the program. It is beyond the scope of this book to cover in detail all the intricacies of measurement and evaluation design, but we hope this brief overview whets your appetite to learn more.

Accurately measuring outcomes is an important part of any evaluation effort. If measures are not appropriate or have low validity and reliability, the value of the evaluation will be seriously compromised. We suggest that anyone designing an evaluation consult a book on evaluation (such as Rossi, Lipsey, & Henry, 2019) or other research methods (such as Rubin and Babbie, 2017) and also have access to books about measures (such as Corcoran & Fischer, 2013). You may desire to access evaluation training exercises (such as Preskill & Russ-Eft, 2015), as well. (The cost of new books on these topics may be high, but recent used editions contain much the same information and usually cost considerably less.) You should also consider hiring a program evaluation consultant who can assist you with the process.

Sometimes program evaluations find evidence of outcomes occurring that are not "expected" to happen. These are called *unanticipated outcomes* (see Box 7.4).

BOX 7.4 **What is an Unanticipated Outcome?**

Outcome evaluations also sometimes include a search for unanticipated outcomes. An unanticipated outcome is a change in clients or the environment (positive or negative) that occurs because of the program, intervention, or policy but that was not thought would result and so is not included in the logic model. Unanticipated outcomes are often missed because they are not being looked for or measured. Be open to the possibility that clients or others are reporting things that were not part of your original thinking. They can be very important to notice and report.

Conclusion

This chapter covers a large amount of information regarding the three topics presented: program planning, logic models, and program evaluation. Each topic is the subject of entire books you can read, but this chapter lays out the key elements. Working through the exercises at the end of the chapter will help you solidify your competency in this material. The mutually reinforcing interconnections among these three topics will help you move forward quickly in your understanding and assist you in applying your knowledge.

Reference List

Banikya-Leaseburg, M., & Chilcoat, D. (2013). How much change is too much change? Preserving fidelity while making informed adaptations. US Department of Health and Human Services, Administration for Children, Youth, and Families. Retrieved from https://www.hhs.gov/ash/oah/sites/default/files/fidelity_and_adaptation_20130216.pdf

Campbell Collaboration. (n.d.). Our vision, mission and key principles. Retrieved from https://www.campbellcollaboration.org/about-campbell/vision-mission-and-principle.html/

Cochrane Collaboration. (n.d.). About us. Retrieved from https://www.cochrane.org/about-us

Coley, S. M., & Scheinberg, C. A. (2016). *Proposal writing: Effective grantsmanship for funding* (5th ed.). Thousand Oaks, CA: Sage.

Family and Youth Services Bureau. (n.d.). *Making adaptations tip sheet*. Retrieved from https://www.acf.hhs.gov/sites/default/files/fysb/prep-making-adaptations-ts.pdf

Corcoran, K., & Fischer, J. (2013). *Measures for clinical practice and research: A sourcebook* (5th ed.). New York, NY: Oxford University Press.

Frechtling, J. (2007). *Logic modeling methods in program evaluation*. San Francisco, CA: Jossey-Bass.

Lewis, J. A., Packard, T., & Lewis, M. D. (2011). *Management of human service programs* (5th ed.). Belmont, CA: Brooks/Cole.

Preskill, H., & Russ-Eft, D. (2015). *Building evaluation capacity: Activities for teaching and training* (2nd ed.) Thousand Oaks, CA: Sage.

Reconnecting Youth. (n.d.). CAST: Coping and support training. Retrieved from http://wp.reconnectingyouth.com/cast/

Rossi, P. H., Lipsey, M. W., & Henry, G. T. (2019). *Evaluation: A systematic approach* (8th ed.). Thousand Oaks, CA: Sage.

Rubin, A., & Babbie, E. R. (2017). *Empowerment series: Research methods for social work* (9th ed.) Boston, MA: Cengage.

Stith, S. M., & Hamby, S. L. (2002). The anger management scale: Development and preliminary psychometric properties. *Violence and Victims, 17*(4), 383–402.

Additional Resources

Hoefer, R. (2012). Hiring an evaluator: 5 steps on how to hire an evaluator [Video file]. Retrieved from https://www.youtube.com/watch?v=hMEEBZJT4uE

Hoefer, R. (2015). Creating a logic model in Microsoft Word [Video file]. Retrieved from https://youtu.be/Ph2jtBaVKMM

Learning for Action. (n.d.). Define the outcomes. Retrieved from http://learningforaction.com/define-the-outcomes

SAMHSA's The Evidence-Based Practices Resources Center (https://www.samhsa.gov/ebp-resource-center). Formerly the National Registry of Evidence-based Programs and Practices (NREPP), this new website was created to provide guidance regarding programs that have evidence to support their use.

The Office of Justice Programs' CrimeSolutions (crimesolutions.gov) and Model Programs Guide (www.ojjdp.gov/MPG) websites are resources to find information about evidence-based programs in criminal justice, juvenile justice, and crime victim services.

HELPFUL TERMS

Activities—element of a logic model that describes what is done in the program, intervention, or policy with the inputs allocated.

Fidelity evaluation or fidelity assessment—a type of process evaluation specifically designed to determine the fidelity with which a program, intervention, or policy was implemented. In other words, a fidelity evaluation (or fidelity assessment) determines the degree to which the program was conducted in the way it was supposed to be conducted. It is thus a final assessment determined after the program ends. (See also Fidelity monitoring.)

Fidelity monitoring—a process to ensure that the implementation of and evidence-based program conforms to the core elements of the program, even when adaptations are made. This planning occurs before the program begins and is ongoing throughout the program's existence. (See also Fidelity evaluation.)

Fidelity monitoring tool—a tool, such as a checklist of core evidence-based program elements, used to track how well an EBP is being implemented. Appropriate tools are typically developed by the evidence-based program's developers to assist program implementers.

Goals—descriptions of future outcomes or states of being that typically are not measurable or achievable. Instead, goal statements are focused on outcomes and are ambitious and idealistic (see Chapter 6).

Inputs—element of a logic model that describes the resources that will be used to address the problem described in the problem statement. Inputs typically include funding, staff, and space.

Logic model—a "tool that describes the *theory of change* underlying an intervention, product or policy" (Frechtling, 2007, p. 1). A logic model displays the relationships between program resources, activities, and desired outcomes.

Measurement—the act of operationalizing concepts (such as a particular change in clients) and assigning a score or value to the level of that concept.

Objectives—the results that are expected as the organization works toward its stated goals. Objectives are the steps that will be taken to reach the stated goals (see Chapter 6).

Outcome evaluation—a type of evaluation in which the focus is on answering questions about the achievement of the program's stated desired outcomes. Sometimes, efforts are included to measure unanticipated outcomes, that is, effects of the program that were not included in the logic model.

Outcomes—elements in logic models that describe changes in recipients' knowledge, attitudes, beliefs, status, or behavior. These are often divided into short-, medium-, and long-term outcomes to show that some outcomes come before others.

Outputs—element of a logic model that describes the measurable results of program, intervention, or policy activities.

Problem statement—element of a logic model that describes the problem that the program, intervention, or policy is trying to improve on.

Process evaluation—a type or part of a larger evaluation that examines the way a program, intervention, or policy is run or is implemented.

Program evaluation—using a set of research-based methods to determine the worth or value of a program.

EXERCISES

1. In-Basket Exercise

Directions

For this exercise, you are Roberta McIntosh, a social work intern at Urban AIDS Services, Inc., who has received a memo from Jonas Sigurdson, a grantwriter. He requests for you to develop a logic model using the information from the chapter and in the memo. He is a novice and self-taught grantwriter and may not present his ideas as clearly as you may like. Do the best you can with his memo, but note in a separate memo to yourself what you would do differently in designing the Serve More Project program.

> **Memo**
>
> Date: October 30, 20XX
>
> To: Roberta McIntosh, Social Work Intern
>
> From: Jonas Sigurdson, Grantwriter
>
> Subject: Logic Model Needed
>
> As you know, we are working on a grant application for the Serve More Project program. The funder wants to see a logic model as part of the application. Since I know you have studied how to do a logic model in your classes, and I am a bit unsure what is required, I would like you to read over the draft program description and develop a logic model by Thursday. Be sure to include all the required elements of a logic model, and use only outcomes that we can measure without too much trouble. I should warn you that this is a fairly complicated program, so developing a logic model will likely take you a pretty good chunk of time and several drafts before you get one that really captures what we're trying to do.

Serve More Project Program Description

The Serve More Project of Urban AIDS Services, Inc. (UAS), the largest nonprofit provider of HIV/AIDS case management services in the northwestern United States, is designed to reduce the incidence of HIV infection and increase the engagement of at-risk King County, Washington, Blacks and Latinos, including subpopulations of women and children, returning prisoners, injection drug users, and men having sex with men (MSM) who are not injection drug users, in preventive, substance abuse treatment, and medical services.

The Serve More Project expands and enhances UAS's Integrated HIV/AIDS Substance Abuse Treatment (IHASAT) program, funded by the Substance Abuse and Mental Health Services Administration (SAMHSA), with special focus on the burgeoning Hispanic population. UAS's robust HIV/AIDS services are linked with dual disorders treatment providers.

Serve More's **objectives** are to (1) apply evidence-based practices; (2) enhance cultural competency of services; (3) create new bilingual outreach and case management positions located strategically in collaborating agencies; (4) create a bilingual community resource specialist position; (5) create a community action council to plan collaborative response to the focus population's needs; (6) improve services to returning prisoners; (7) increase outreach to women and engagement services; and (8) increase and enhance collaborative partnerships.

Serve More's **project goals** include both *process* and *client* outcomes. **The process** outcomes are to (1) expand outreach efforts, with emphasis on Latinos, Blacks, and women, to reach an additional 3,060 of the focus populations each grant year; (2) increase the number of individuals receiving HIV testing by UAS's staff by 220 annually; (3) provide case management to at least 160 project clients annually; (4) provide substance abuse treatment to at least 60 project clients annually; (5) track for evaluation follow-up 75 individuals each year of the grant period, focusing on Latinos and Latinas; (6) refer 100% of outreach contacts requesting substance abuse and/or mental health treatment; (7) link 95% of all clients with positive HIV case findings from testing to HIV care and services; (8) achieve at least 50% medical adherence; and (9) achieve at least 80% substance abuse treatment adherence.

Project **client outcomes** are to **increase** the percentage of clients who (1) do not use alcohol or illegal drugs; (2) are currently employed or attending school; (3) have a permanent place to live in the community; (4) experience no alcohol or illegal drug-related health, behavioral, or social consequences; and (5) have no involvement with the criminal justice system and to **decrease** the percentage of clients who (1) inject illegal drugs; (2) engage in unprotected sexual contact or engage in unprotected sexual contact with (a) a person high on drugs; (b) an injected drug user; or (c) a person who is HIV+ or has AIDS.

Target Population and Geographic Area Served—The focus populations to be served by the Serve More Project are Hispanics/Latinos and Blacks/African Americans. Subpopulations include (1) men who inject drugs, including non–Intravenous Drug Using (non-IDU) men who have sex with men (MSM); (2) women, including women and children; and (3) the recently incarcerated. The geographic area for the project is King County, Washington.

2. The Chocolate Chip Cookie Evaluation Exercise

[This idea is adapted from Preskill and Russ-Eft (2015). It is one of my students' favorite exercises, and they now use it with their students.]

Have participants get into small groups of no more than four people. This works well in work settings as well as in classes. The task of each group is to develop an evaluation system to determine the "ideal" chocolate chip cookie. The only caveat is that all members of the group must agree to the process developed. Each group should develop a set of criteria that individual members will be able to use to rate how closely any individual chocolate chip cookie nears "perfection." This means the criteria must be understood similarly by all, with an agreed-on benchmark. (For example, one student group I gave this exercise to indicated that "shape" was an important attribute of the perfect cookie. I challenged them on this because the group did not indicate what shape was preferred, and I correctly pointed out that all cookies have a shape.) After all group members have agreed to a set of criteria, the leader gives each group a cookie from several different varieties of store-bought or homemade cookies. Group members must then individually go through all of the criteria for each cookie and, based on the criteria chosen, choose the "best" cookie from among those they were given.

Often, groups come up with very different criteria, and individuals using the same criteria rate the same cookie very differently. This variation in criteria and ratings provides a very good basis for understanding the underlying principles of criterion-based evaluation and measurement issues.

3. Design Your Own Logic Model

Choose a program or intervention with which you are very familiar. With one or two other people who share your knowledge, develop a logic model (if you are a student, you might choose your educational program; if you are employed, use the program you are employed with). Be sure to construct a problem statement—what problem is being addressed? (Knowing the purpose is sometimes a difficult question to answer, but it is essential.) When you are done, show your work to another group or talk about it in class. What were the easier parts of the process, and which parts were the more challenging?

4. Using a Logic Model to Plan an Evaluation

Using the logic model that you created in Exercise 3, discuss how you would ideally evaluate this intervention. What are the most important process and client outcomes to measure? What measures will you use? Who will collect the information? How will it be analyzed to determine whether the recipients of the intervention changed? Which were the easier parts of the process, and which were the more challenging parts?

ASSIGNMENTS

1. Select a problem area that a social welfare agency might be involved in, such as substance abuse, teen pregnancy, reintegration of service members into the civilian population, or another topic of interest to you. Using the resources in this chapter or others you find, compare two different evidence-based programs that address this problem. Using a memo format, discuss the relative strengths and weaknesses of both approaches as they would be used in your community. Make a recommendation for which one is preferable, supported by the information you have uncovered.

2. Do an online search for "logic model" (you'll find millions of results, including YouTube videos). Find three different sources (not including Wikipedia) describing what a logic model is and how to develop one. Compare and contrast these with the information in this chapter. Make two different logic models of a simple program you're familiar with, following the guidelines from two different sources. Which variation(s) makes the most sense to you?

3. Conduct an online search for a program evaluation of a program that you are either familiar with or that you would like to know more about. Write a paper about the evaluation, answering these questions: What is the program being evaluated? What are the results of the evaluation, both process and outcome? How strong do you think the evaluation research design was? What measures were used, and what are their strengths and weaknesses? How much credence do you place in the results? Finally, how does this evaluation affect your willingness to try the program with the clients in your (possibly hypothetical) agency?

4. Find a set of three to four program objectives or outcomes for a program you're familiar with and briefly describe them. Look for standardized instruments to be able to accurately measure these objectives or outcomes. Describe the source of the instruments and what makes them good measures for the objectives or outcomes you have found. Write up the information as a memo recommending these instruments to the lead researcher of the program evaluation team.

Image Credits

Budgeting and Finance

Most social work administrators start their careers as direct service providers and come to human services with a desire to make a difference in people's lives through service, advocacy, and policy reform. Very few begin with the goal of becoming financial managers, and therefore, most have little formal education or training in financial management. However, new social work administrators learn very quickly, and sometimes painfully, that financial management is a major part of their job.

Social work administrators do not have to give up their natural inclination toward client services to adopt a financial management perspective. Financial management is a skill critical to assuring quality services for clients and is just as important as policy analysis, social planning, casework, and program evaluation (Martin, 2016). The phrase, "Put your money where your mouth is," applies to a great extent to budgeting and financial management. If we, as social workers, say that we believe in diversity and that we believe in social and economic justice, we must be willing to apply our organization's financial resources to back up these words. In fact, our code of ethics (National Association of Social Workers, 2017) includes important standards for social work administrators related to budgeting. The code requires social work administrators to advocate within and outside their agencies for adequate resources to meet clients' needs. This chapter provides you with information on how to apply resources to run programs in a responsible way. Without skillful application of such knowledge, an agency will not exist for long.

Human services administrators do not need to be accountants, but they must be able to prepare a budget and to read and understand financial reports. Budgets and financial reports are important management tools in assuring the financial health of the organization. Financial management is a critical skill needed to provide quality services for the clients of the organization.

This chapter will present the basic accounting terms you will need as a social work administrator and give you the tools you need to read and understand the key elements of a budget and financial statement. You will also learn the basic steps in preparing a budget, including identifying multiple funding sources, projecting income and expenses, and understanding concepts of program accounting. After reading the chapter, you will work with a balance sheet and a financial statement to complete the exercises.

The Financial Health of the Nonprofit Sector

The health of the nonprofit sector is vital to our society. Nonprofits play a critical social role in almost all areas of our lives. When nonprofits suffer financially, so do some of the most vulnerable in our society. The nonprofit sector is also the place of employment for many of our citizens, and the loss of a nonprofit means the loss of income or pensions for hardworking families.

A recent analysis by Guidestar and Oliver Wyman (2018) shows just how fragile the nation's nonprofits really are:

- 7–8% are technically insolvent, with liabilities exceeding assets.
- 30% face potential liquidity issues, with minimal cash reserves and/or short-term assets less than short-term liabilities.
- 30% have lost money over the last three years.
- 50% have less than one month of operating reserves.

The state of the nonprofit sector is a major problem, and restoring currently insolvent nonprofits to solvency would require an investment of $40 billion to $50 billion. The possibility of losing charitable donation deductions in the tax code and further cuts to human services in the federal budget will only increase the crisis (Wyman, 2018). (Recall information from Chapter 1 regarding current difficulties in sustaining organizations.)

The financial stress in the nonprofit sector requires that administrators be skillful financial managers. While the picture presented above is somewhat bleak, the reality is that there are many nonprofits that are financially sound, and a part of your job may be to help manage the major assets of such an organization. Whether your organization is one that is prosperous and flourishing or one that is struggling, you will need skills to navigate the financial waters of your particular situation.

Understanding Financial Statements

The Generally Accepted Accounting Principles (GAAP) are a basic set of rules governing how the financial books and records of an organization are to be maintained, including how revenues, expenditures, and expenses are to be accounted for and how financial statements are to be prepared. The Financial Accounting Standards Board (FASB) establishes the GAAP for nonprofit and for-profit organizations. The FASB rules require all private nonprofit organizations to prepare "general

purpose external financial statements" at least once each fiscal year and must be reflective of the overall financial activities in their entirety during that fiscal year (American Institute of Certified Public Accountants, 1998).

The FASB requires that four types of financial statements be prepared annually by nonprofit human service organizations. The required reports are (1) a statement of activities, (2) a statement of financial position, (3) a statement of cash flows, and (4) a statement of functional expenses by functional and natural classifications. In most cases, these reports are prepared by an independent auditor hired by the organization to examine the financial records of the organization each year. These reports are based on the monthly statements prepared by the organization throughout the fiscal year.

Statement of Activities

In simple terms, the statement of activities is the profit and loss statement for the organization. It is essentially the same report that a business would use to report its profits and losses for the year. The report tells the reader that, for example, there was "excess of revenues over expenses" (a profit) or that the expenses exceeded the revenues (loss) during the fiscal year.

Can a nonprofit organization make a profit? Absolutely! They can and should. There is much confusion about this point, given the term "nonprofit." Many believe that a nonprofit human service agency is prohibited from making a profit; on the contrary, it is acceptable and desirable for the organization to bring in more revenue than it spends. The issue is what the organization does with the excess income. The revenues must be used to promote the mission of the organization. For example, the profits cannot be paid to the board members as dividends, but it is perfectly all right to develop a reserve fund, buy equipment, or establish an endowment—anything that furthers the mission of the organization.

To understand financial reports, it is necessary to understand the following terms.

Statement of Financial Position

A *balance sheet* is the term for a statement of the financial position of an organization that states the assets and liabilities at a particular point in time. The balance sheet illustrates the financial "worth" of the organization. Statements can be prepared as often as the administrator or the Board of Trustees wants but must be prepared at least annually, on the last day of the fiscal year. The annual audit will include a balance sheet and will, in most cases, compare the current year to the year before to see if there has been a change in the financial position of the organization. The sum of an organization's assets minus liabilities gives a picture of the organization's net assets or the "net worth" of the organization.

Statement of Cash Flows

The cash flow statement is used to analyze the cash inflows and outflows (i.e., where the money came from and where it went) during a designated time period. This is especially important for nonprofit agencies where donated funds come at specific times of the year rather than throughout (Women's Economic Self-Sufficiency Team, 2001). From the monthly statement of activities report, you will find there are certain items that may not affect your statement of activities for some time, such as the following:

- Substantial increase in inventory purchases
- Increase in accounts receivable (money owed to you)
- Purchase of equipment
- Lump sum payment of debt

A cash flow statement will highlight these activities in a way that an income statement will not. Without the cash flow statement, you will have an incomplete picture of your organization.

Statement of Functional Expenses

All voluntary health and welfare organizations must provide a statement of functional expenses. FASB requires that the statement include the organization's total expenses for the fiscal year and that the expenses be separated out by functional categories, such as program, management, general, and fundraising, and by natural categories, such as salaries, and fringe and usual operating expenses. This report also presents revenue and expenses for each program of the organization.

The Independent Audit

The independent audit is an important part of the financial management of an organization. As a part of this process, the independent auditor examines the financial records for the fiscal year and makes a report to the board of trustees. If the report does not find any significant problems in the financial reporting of the organization, it is said to be a "clean" audit. Auditors will often make recommendations for changes in the financial procedures of an organization to strengthen the "internal control" processes. These recommendations assure checks and balances in the financial system of the organization. The report is made not to the administrator, but to the Board

of Trustees. It is the board that has the ultimate responsibility to protect the financial health of the organization.

As mentioned earlier, the financial reports and the independent audit are based on the organization's fiscal year. A *fiscal year* is usually a 12-month period of time for which the financial records of the organization are maintained. The organization can decide on the fiscal year in which it will operate. Some organizations choose to use the calendar year, from January through December, as their fiscal year. Others choose to use the fiscal year of their primary funders. For example, the federal government's fiscal year is October through September. Some states operate on a July to June fiscal year, and others on a September to August fiscal year.

Cash and Accrual Accounting

Two major types of accounting are cash accounting and accrual accounting. For our purposes, we will be dealing with accrual accounting, since this is the method used by most human service organizations and most businesses. In cash accounting, transactions are recognized (recorded) only when cash is received and only when cash is paid out. This is an acceptable but simplistic method and has serious limitations as a planning tool for human services administrators.

Accrual accounting means that transactions are recognized (recorded) when revenues are earned and when expenses are incurred. Accrual accounting provides a more complete financial picture through the use of accounts receivable and accounts payable. Accrual is the preferred method of accounting in human services administration.

Examples of Cash and Accrual Accounting

Think of cash accounting as keeping the money in a shoebox. When the money comes in, you put it in the shoebox, and when you spend money, you take it out of the shoebox. In accrual accounting, you recognize the income when you earn it. So, for example, if you have a contract to provide counseling services, you recognize the income in the month you provide the services. For example, during the month of June, you provide 100 hours of counseling services and send a bill to the contract agency. Since you have provided the services, you record the income in June, not in August when the check finally comes. The same is true of expenses. If you receive $1,000 worth of office supplies in June, you recognize the $1,000 expense in June, not when you pay the bill in July.

BOX 8.2 **Be Patient**

You will often hear people say, "I am just not mechanical," meaning that they are not good at making repairs or working on equipment. What they should say is, "I don't have the patience or take the time to see how things work." It is much the same when dealing with financial statements. Saying, "I can't understand financial statements," is really saying, "I don't have the patience or take the time to study financial statements." As you work on the exercises and assignments at the end of this chapter, make a commitment to be patient and invest the time in understanding the financial statements.

Financial Statement Examples

The following financial statements are examples of the monthly statements prepared by organizations. These are the basis of the financial reports prepared by the independent auditor. Take a few minutes to examine the following financial statements. Look at the heading of each column and the line items in each statement. Don't be intimidated by the numbers. Just look at each row and number and think about the purpose of the report and what information the report is giving you.

To understand the report, you will need to know the meaning of several terms used in the report. Here are a few you will need now. There is a more extensive list of terms at the end of this chapter.

Assets—anything owned by an organization that has economic value. Assets may include cash, bank accounts, accounts receivable (see definition below), equipment, buildings, property, and automobiles.

Liabilities—obligations to pay somebody something. All debts or amounts owed by an organization in the form of accounts payable (see below), loans, mortgages, and long-term debts are liabilities.

Net assets—what is left over when liabilities are subtracted from total assets.

Revenues—usually in the form of cash and checks and may come from many sources, such as fees for service, contracts, grants, donations, third-party payments, insurance, managed-care firms, or investment income.

Revenue classifications—there are three classifications of revenues to human services:

1. *Permanently Restricted Funds*—Some funds may be permanently restricted to a specific use. Endowment funds are usually in this category. A donor may give a gift to the organization but requires that only the earnings from those funds be used by the organization. For example, a donor gives a $100,000 gift to the organization's endowment fund. Let's assume that the interest rates or earnings rate on the $100,000 is 5%. This means that the organization can use $5,000 each year and still have the original $100,000 intact.

2. *Temporarily Restricted Funds*—These funds are given for a specific project. For example, a donor might give $50,000 to the organization to renovate a building owned by the organization. The donor might choose to give the entire $50,000 at one time and then the organization would pay the contractors for the work as the project progressed. The $50,000 would be temporarily restricted and could be used only to renovate the building.

3. *Unrestricted Funds*—These are funds on which the donor has placed no restrictions. An example of these funds is operating funds raised in an annual campaign. A donor may respond to a direct mail solicitation by sending a $500 check. Unless the donor specifies that the gift is to be used by a specific program or for a specific purpose, the $500 is unrestricted and can be used by the organization as needed.

Expenses/expenditures—There is a difference in the meaning of the terms *expenditures* and *expenses*. Expenditures are cash that goes out of the agency. For example, the salaries paid for staff are an expenditure to the organization. Expenses are resources consumed by an agency (insurance, computer equipment, etc.). To understand this concept, think about buying a new computer for the organization. You will pay for the computer with cash, but you will use the computer over several years. You have traded one asset (cash) for another asset (the computer). Assume the life of the new computer will be three years. If you paid $3,000 for the computer, you will have an "expense" of $1,000 per year for each of the three years.

While there is a difference between expenditures and expenses, you often hear the terms used interchangeably. The important concept to grasp from this discussion is the concept of depreciation (see next).

Depreciation—an estimate of the decrease in the value of an asset. Depreciation takes into account the reality that equipment, buildings, automobiles, and so on, become obsolete or simply wear out over time. It is a method to show how much of the value of an asset remains.

Accounts receivable—revenues earned by a human service agency but not yet received. For example, if services have been provided and a contract has been billed for that service, the amount of the bill is an account receivable. It remains as an account receivable until the cash is received by the organization.

Accounts payable—money owed by the organization to someone else but not yet paid. For example, if office supplies are received but have not yet been paid for, that amount is an account payable for the organization. Employee vacation time that has accumulated but not been taken is carried on the financial statements as an account payable.

Spend some time looking at the balance sheet. The two columns of numbers are a "snapshot" of the current year's financial picture compared to the prior year. Look at each of the line items in the report. The first section lists all of the assets. The second section lists all of the liabilities and the fund balances (also called the *equity*). The formula for the balance sheet is Assets = Liabilities + Fund Balances.

TABLE 8.1 Sample Balance Sheet

ABC NONPROFIT CORPORATION
COMPARATIVE BALANCE SHEET
AUGUST 31, 20XX

ASSETS	YEAR TO DATE	
	ACTUAL	PRIOR YEAR
CURRENT ASSETS		
Cash	507,058	156,314
Accounts receivable	329,561	342,035
Prepaid expenses	51,462	67,015
TOTAL CURRENT ASSETS	888,081	565,364
INVESTMENTS		
Permanent endowment assets	1,748,432	1,618,953
Investments	227,657	243,963
TOTAL INVESTMENTS	1,976,089	1,862,916
FIXED ASSETS		
Land & buildings	3,809,845	3,708,297
Equipment, vehicles, furniture	796,436	846,205
Less: accumulated depreciation	(1,966,301)	(1,822,562)
TOTAL FIXED ASSETS	2,639,980	2,731,940
TOTAL ASSETS	5,504,150	5,160,220
LIABILITIES AND FUND BALANCES		
CURRENT LIABILITIES		
Accounts payable	55,801	55,293
Accrued expenses & payroll	110,773	106,471
Notes payable	1,095,531	
Interagency transfers	70,000	821,540
Designated funds	117,412	74,517
TOTAL CURRENT LIABILITIES	1,449,517	1,057,821
FUND BALANCES		
Unrestricted	2,242,049	2,723,851
Retained earnings—current year	57	(317,345)
Temporarily restricted	73,293	81,659
Permanently restricted endow	1,739,234	1,614,234
TOTAL FUND BALANCES	4,054,633	4,102,399
TOTAL LIABILITIES AND FUND BALANCES	5,504,150	5,160,220

UNAUDITED FINANCIAL STATEMENTS FOR INTERNAL USE ONLY

What assets does this organization have (own), and in what form? What are the liabilities of the agency? How does the financial picture for the current year compare to the previous fiscal year?

Now look at the monthly statement of revenue and expenses reports (Table 8.2, All Departments; Table 8.3, Administration; Table 8.4 Department A; and Table 8.5, Department B). This imaginary organization has two major program components, plus the administrative structure. The first report (Table 8.2) is the combined report of the two programs and the administration. The columns give information about the current period (last month) and then compare the actual figures to the budgeted amounts. For now, look only at the current period. Which of the income categories exceed the budgeted amount? Which income items are falling short of the budgeted amounts? Next look at the "year to date" columns. Are the same items that were under or over budget for the month also over or under for the year? We will use these financial reports in the exercises at the end of this chapter.

TABLE 8.2 **Sample Monthly Statement of Revenue and Expenses: All Departments**

ABC NONPROFIT CORPORATION
MONTHLY STATEMENT OF REVENUE AND EXPENSES—ALL DEPARTMENTS COMBINED
FOR THE EIGHT PERIODS ENDING AUGUST 31, 20XX

	PERIOD TO DATE		YEAR TO DATE	
	ACTUAL	CURR BUDGET	ACTUAL	CURR BUDGET
INCOME				
Fees for services—Dept. A	98,343	81,000	808,068	648,000
Fees for services—Dept. B	30,965	48,508	422,075	388,067
Church contributions	3,155	6,390	126,958	120,065
Individual contributions	13,501	3,690	124,589	74,936
Foundation/corp./board	7,900	8,333	197,018	216,667
Wills & estates—unrestricted	3,750		48,950	
Grants & contracts	7,452	6,417	58,526	51,333
Rental income	2,935	8,333	71,260	66,667
Investment income	2,816	3,500	31,437	28,000
TOTAL INCOME	170,817	166,171	1,888,881	1,593,735
OPERATING EXPENSES				
Salaries	132,005	118,691	1,021,329	949,526
Benefits	20,366	21,988	167,367	179,908
Advert./promo/printing/postage	7,713	17,657	62,966	90,072
Auto exp.	2,158	1,231	16,189	9,853
Computer exp.	30		13,435	
Contract services	11,021	5,998	90,941	48,539
Dues/memberships	382	1,156	4,752	10,882
Food	9,499	6,250	99,110	50,550
Insurance	3,937	4,025	31,061	32,199
Interest exp.	6,121	7,554	57,491	60,430

Legal & professional	780	871	7,399	8,966
Maintenance & repair	6,125	2,849	35,472	24,400
Office/other supplies	3,991	3,781	37,305	30,958
Recruiting exp.		106	12,057	1,496
Rent exp.	2,894	1,694	15,154	13,352
Staff development	80	1,133	8,380	10,367
Travel	2,546	7,023	30,641	56,180
Telephone/communications	3,654	5,180	35,588	41,836
Utilities	8,475	9,500	73,525	62,200
Other	322	1,533	46,003	17,716
TOTAL OPERATING EXPENSES	222,099	218,220	1,866,165	1,699,430
NET INCOME (LOSS)	(51,282)	(52,049)	22,716	(105,695)

UNAUDITED FINANCIAL STATEMENTS FOR INTERNAL USE ONLY

TABLE 8.3   Sample Monthly Statement of Revenue and Expenses: Administration

ABC NONPROFIT CORPORATION
MONTHLY STATEMENT OF REVENUE AND EXPENSES—ADMINISTRATION
FOR THE EIGHT PERIODS ENDING AUGUST 31, 20XX

	PERIOD TO DATE		YEAR TO DATE	
	ACTUAL	CURR BUDGET	ACTUAL	CURR BUDGET
INCOME				
Fees for services—Dept A				
Fees for services—Dept B				
Church contributions	3,155	6,390	126,958	120,065
Individual contributions	8,186	3,690	118,574	74,936
Foundation/corp./board			173,318	95,000
Wills & estates—unrestricted	3,750		48,951	
Grants & contracts	7,452	6,417	58,526	51,333
Rental income	2,935	8,333	70,960	66,667
Investment income	2,815	3,500	31,336	28,000
TOTAL INCOME	28,293	28,330	628,623	436,001
OPERATING EXPENSES				
Salaries	41,830	49,065	356,901	392,519
Benefits	6,693	9,333	63,306	75,665
Advert./promo/printing/postage	2,480	11,342	19,652	39,690
Auto exp.	2,158	1,190	16,189	9,520

(Continued)

	PERIOD TO DATE		YEAR TO DATE	
	ACTUAL	CURR BUDGET	ACTUAL	CURR BUDGET
Computer exp.			12,134	
Contract services	5,103	4,517	44,890	36,133
Dues/memberships	175	346	1,875	3,117
Food	9,451	6,250	98,270	50,000
Insurance	3,137	3,258	24,617	26,067
Interest exp.	6,085	7,554	57,137	60,429
Legal & professional	780	700	6,910	7,600
Maintenance & repair	6,125	2,083	34,918	18,267
Office/other supplies	3,786	2,592	31,943	20,733
Recruiting exp.		10	11,115	330
Rent exp.	1,561	1,089	14,378	8,512
Staff development	80	263	3,767	4,500
Travel	784	2,188	5,386	17,500
Telephone/communications	2,206	2,005	20,958	16,439
Utilities	8,475	9,500	73,526	62,200
Other	(79)	397	30,490	8,523
Allocation of indirect o/h	63,937	(18,214)	(300,173)	(145,709)
TOTAL OPERATING EXPENSES	164,767	95,468	628,189	712,035
NET INCOME (LOSS)	(136,474)	(67,138)	434	(276,034)

UNAUDITED FINANCIAL STATEMENTS FOR INTERNAL USE ONLY

TABLE 8-4   **Sample Monthly Statement of Revenue and Expenses: Department A**

ABC NONPROFIT CORPORATION
MONTHLY STATEMENT OF REVENUE AND EXPENSES—DEPT A
FOR THE EIGHT PERIODS ENDING AUGUST 31, 20XX

	PERIOD TO DATE		YEAR TO DATE	
	ACTUAL	CURR BUDGET	ACTUAL	CURR BUDGET
INCOME				
Fees for services—Dept A	98,343	81,000	808,068	648,000
Fees for services—Dept B				
Church contributions				
Individual contributions	5,290		5,290	
Foundation/corp./board	7,900	8,333	23,700	121,667
Wills & estates—unrestricted				
Grants & contracts				
Rental income				
Investment income				
TOTAL INCOME	111,533	89,333	837,058	769,667

OPERATING EXPENSES				
Salaries	64,563	42,494	439,360	339,951
Benefits	9,090	8,139	65,176	65,116
Advert./promo/printing/postage	520	1,114	4,203	8,675
Auto exp				
Computer exp	30		1,070	
Contract services	4,065	1,122	39,240	9,539
Dues/memberships	167	120	925	1,645
Food	10		565	350
Insurance	400	384	3,222	3,066
Interest exp	36		354	
Legal & professional		25		200
Maintenance & repair		666	516	5,334
Office/other supplies	66	530	3,728	4,350
Recruiting exp		63	82	500
Rent exp		605	(2,206)	4,840
Staff development		450	3,657	3,250
Travel	409	1,735	7,313	13,880
Telephone/communications	573	1,015	5,156	8,118
Utilities				
Other	103	176	4,039	1,413
Allocation of indirect o/h	51,517	13,733	239,671	109,861
TOTAL OPERATING EXPENSES	131,549	72,371	816,071	580,088
NET INCOME (LOSS)	(20,016)	16,962	20,987	189,579

UNAUDITED FINANCIAL STATEMENTS FOR INTERNAL USE ONLY

TABLE 8.5   Sample Monthly Statement of Revenue and Expenses: Department B

ABC NONPROFIT CORPORATION
MONTHLY STATEMENT OF REVENUE AND EXPENSES—DEPT B
FOR THE EIGHT PERIODS ENDING AUGUST 31, 20XX

	PERIOD TO DATE		YEAR TO DATE	
	ACTUAL	CURR BUDGET	ACTUAL	CURR BUDGET
INCOME				
Fees for services—Dept A				
Fees for services—Dept B	30,965	48,508	422,075	388,067
Church contributions				

(Continued)

	PERIOD TO DATE		YEAR TO DATE	
	ACTUAL	CURR BUDGET	ACTUAL	CURR BUDGET
Individual contributions	25		725	
Foundation/corp./board				
Wills & estates—unrestricted				
Grants & contracts				
Rental income			300	
Investment income			100	
TOTAL INCOME	30,990	48,508	423,200	388,067
OPERATING EXPENSES				
Salaries	25,612	27,132	225,069	217,056
Benefits	4,583	4,516	38,885	39,127
Advert./promo/printing/postage	4,713	5,201	39,111	41,707
Auto exp.		41		333
Computer exp.			231	
Contract services	1,853	359	6,811	2,867
Dues/memberships	40	690	1,953	6,120
Food	38		275	200
Insurance	400	383	3,222	3,067
Interest exp.				
Legal & professional		146	489	1,166
Maintenance & repair		100	38	800
Office/other supplies	139	659	1,634	5,874
Recruiting exp.		33	860	666
Rent exp.	1,333		2,982	
Staff development		421	957	2,617
Travel	1,353	3,100	17,942	24,800
Telephone/communications	875	2,160	9,473	17,280
Utilities				
Other	298	960	11,474	7,780
Allocation of indirect o/h	<u>12,421</u>	<u>4,481</u>	<u>60,502</u>	<u>35,847</u>
TOTAL OPERATING EXPENSES	53,658	50,382	421,908	407,307
NET INCOME (LOSS)	(22,668)	(1,874)	1,292	(19,240)

UNAUDITED FINANCIAL STATEMENTS FOR INTERNAL USE ONLY

Budgeting

A *budget* is a plan for anticipating income and expenses to achieve specific objectives within a certain time frame (Brody & Nair, 2013). Some view budgeting as a planning process, while others see budgeting more as a political process. As a planning process, budgeting can be seen as a process to make rational decisions about the allocation of resources. Those who view budgeting more as a political process see competition between different factions for scarce financial resources. In this chapter, we will focus on the mechanics and planning aspects of budgeting, but it is important to always remember that there is a political element to the process.

Budgeting Systems

There are many different types of budget systems, but there are three major types that you will need to understand.

Line-item budget. The line-item budget is the simplest and most common form of budgeting and the form used by most human service organizations. This budget type is concerned with expenditures and revenues related to commodities. The question is, "How much do things cost, and how much of each thing do we need?" This question relates to everything from number of employees to amounts of office supplies. The major purpose of this approach is economy and control of costs. A major purpose of the line-item budget is to identify all sources of anticipated funding and then allocate that funding to the different units of the agency for the next fiscal year.

Performance budget. Performance budgeting is based on the output of each department of the agency. The typical measure is based on a "unit of service." Unit of service can be defined in many ways. Some examples are counseling hours, foster placements, housing units developed, or however the product of the agency is defined. To develop a performance budget, it is necessary to determine the total program costs for a fiscal year and divide the total cost by the units of service to be provided for the fiscal year. If a department's total budget is $1,000,000 and they provide 10,000 counseling hours, the unit cost for this service is $100. Performance budgeting helps evaluate the productivity of an agency. In our example, if the department provided only 2,500 counseling sessions for the year and the budget remained at $1,000,000, then the unit cost would be $400 per counseling hour. As the administrator, this would likely raise concerns for you, which would lead you to reduce expenses or increase productivity. The counseling hour example is a simple and straightforward unit of service. Unfortunately, most units of service are not as easily defined. Even if an agency does not adopt a true performance budget, it is essential that the administrator have a method to monitor the unit costs for each department of the agency.

Program budget. A program system budget is built by examining the expenses of each program in the organization, defining the measures of program outcomes, and calculating the cost to the program to achieve the desired outcomes. The program budget computes the total program cost for the fiscal year and divides that cost by the number of outcomes to establish a cost per outcome. Much like performance budgeting, program budgeting is effectiveness budgeting. The primary difference is that performance budgeting is based on outputs, whereas program budgeting in based on outcomes (Martin, 2016).

A Comprehensive Budgeting System

Line-item budgeting, performance budgeting, and program budgeting are all important tools for the human services administrator. Each provides important information essential to the management of a human service organization. Each provides data and information from a different perspective. The line-item budget emphasizes financial control, whereas the performance budget focuses on productivity, and the program budget stresses effectiveness. The competent administrator will use elements from all three of the major budgeting systems (Martin, 2016).

The Budgeting Process

As stated earlier, budgeting has both a planning and a political component. When we think of the politics of budgeting, we often think of the budget battles in Congress or in the state legislatures, but we should also remember that there is a political component to the decisions made about how much one unit of an organization will get compared to another unit. The complex interplay between budget planning and budget politics makes it difficult to reduce the budgeting process to a few simple steps, but it is important to have a framework when engaging the process of developing a budget.

In this section, we will concentrate on developing a line-item budget, since it is the most common budget system in human service organizations and is the base from which you as an administrator can build measures of performance using program and performance budgeting techniques. There are several steps in the budget process. For our purposes, we will use the steps outlined by Brody and Nair in *Effectively Managing and Leading Human Service Organizations* (2013).

Step 1: Set Organizational Objectives

The budget is one of the tools used to help an organization carry out its mission and achieve its objectives. Building the budget is a process of setting priorities and defining what is important to the organization. The old saying, "Follow the money," is good advice when developing a budget. To allocate resources of one activity over another is to declare that activity to be a higher priority than the other. For example, leasing an additional van for client transportation rather than buying new computers for staff members prioritizes one stakeholder group over another, and good arguments can be made for both. The selection of one over the other, which is a budgeting decision, clearly also has value elements embedded in it. It is critical to be clear on the mission, goals, and objectives of the organization before engaging in the budget-building process.

Step 2: Establish Budget Policies and Procedures

Budget building is a complex task and requires the same level of organization and planning as other major projects. As the administrator, you should develop a budget timeline so that all the parties involved in the process can coordinate their efforts. You, the program directors, the finance committee, and the Board of Trustees all have a role in the budget process. As the leader of the budget-building process, you will assign responsibilities for gathering the needed information. There will be many questions to be answered: What are the staffing needs for the next year? Will the cost of medical insurance be going up? How accurate were our predictions in the last budget year? In which line items did we overspend or underspend? Were our income projections realistic, and what is the outlook for the coming year?

Finally, you will need to develop the budget format to be used by each person involved in the process. In most cases, you will provide each person working on the budget with a report that compares the actual income and expenses to date in the current year to the current year's budgets. From this information, program directors are asked to project their needs for the next fiscal year. You may also set guidelines for preparing the budget. For example, you may set a guideline that budget increases may not exceed 3% (or whatever is appropriate).

Step 3: Set Annual Income and Expense Targets

The arithmetic of developing a budget is very simple:

Projected income – projected operation expenses = projected operating surplus or deficit.

Remember that it is perfectly acceptable for nonprofit organizations to have a surplus at the end of the year. In most cases, the budget presented to the board is a balanced budget, in which the projected income and projected expenses are equal, but there are times when an agency may adopt a deficit budget. It is also very common for organizations to budget a surplus to build cash reserves for the organization.

The first section of the budget deals with the projected income for the coming fiscal year. Sources of income can include donations, corporate gifts, foundation grants, government contracts or grants, fees for service, and third-party payments. Any money anticipated to come into the agency should be included in the income budget. Remember that the expenses you budget are dependent on meeting the income goals in the budget. You can budget all the expenses you want, but if the income is not available, you will be forced to cut budget expenses to be within the projected net income.

The next section of the budget is the expense side, which includes all of the cash operation expenses of the organization. Salaries, fringe benefits, office supplies, rent, utilities, advertising, liability insurance, and any other expenses are to be categorized and included in the expense side of the budget.

Once the administrator has examined the income and expenses to date and made preliminary projections about the following year, the individual departments or units are given the information so they can propose their departmental budget. Your work will be the basis on which they will make their recommendations for their departmental budgets.

Step 4: Each Unit Proposes Its Budget

Each unit head will go through the same process in projecting income and expenses for the department and must justify increases in expenses. If new expenses are proposed, the program director must specify what new income will be generated to support the expenses. When this process is completed, the management team meets to develop the final draft of the overall budget document.

Step 5: Management Team Proposes Budget to Board

It is the responsibility of the administrator to develop the final budget proposal for the board. While there is a great deal of work from many parts of the organization to develop the budget, it is ultimately the responsibility of the administrator to present a budget to the board. The administrator will also be held accountable for carrying out the budget plan.

In this step, the administrator presents the budget proposal to the finance committee of the board. This is the place for the representatives of the board to take a hard look at the budget proposal. The finance committee should be asking certain questions: Are the income projections realistic? Are the expenses reasonable? Does this budget advance the mission of the organization? Any adjustments required by the finance committee are made, and then the finance committee presents the budget to the full board with a recommendation. Finally, the board adopts the budget for the next fiscal year.

Conclusion

This chapter examined one of the most challenging tasks for administrators of human service organizations. There are great needs to be addressed by a human service organization, but there are always limited resources. Budgeting and financial management are the tools used to plan and use the resources of the organization in the most effective way. The administrator must manage many tasks at the same time, but financial management must be a priority, or the organization will have little chance to live up to the challenges of its mission.

This chapter will surely not make you an accountant, but it will give you the basic tools to learn the art of financial management. As the administrator, you will depend on the expertise of the chief financial officer of the organization, who is an important member of the management team. In addition to a strong in-house financial person, every organization should have a contract agreement with a certified public accountant (CPA).

Reference List

American Institute of Certified Public Accountants. (1998). *AICPA audit and accounting guide: Not-for-profit organizations*. New York, NY: Author.

Brody, R., & Nair, M. (2013). *Effectively managing and leading human service organizations*. Thousand Oaks, CA: Sage.

Martin, L. L. (2016). *Financial management for human service administrators*. Long Grove, IL: Waveland Press.

National Association of Social Workers. (2017*). Code of ethics of the National Association of Social Workers*. Washington, DC: Author.

Women's Economic Self-Sufficiency Team. (2001, October 10). *Preparing your cash flow statement*. Albuquerque, NM: Author. Retrieved from http://www.onlinewbc.gov/docs/finance/cashflow.html

Wyman, O. (2018). The financial health of the United States nonprofit sector: Facts and observations. *Guidestar*. Retrieved from https://learn.guidestar.org/products/us-nonprofits-financial-health

Additional Resources

Capital Business Solutions. (2018, September 3). 3 Major Differences Between Government & Nonprofit Accounting. Retrieved from https://www.capitalbusiness.net/resources/3-major-differences-government-nonprofit-accounting/

McCarthy, J. H., Shelmon, N. E., & Mattie, J. A. (2012). *Financial and accounting guide for not-for-profit organizations* (8th ed., Vol. 6). Hoboken, NJ: John Wiley & Sons.

Mitchell, G. E., & Calabrese, T. D. (2018). Proverbs of nonprofit financial management. *The American Review of Public Administration, 49*(6), 649–661. doi:10.1177/0275074018770458

Wallace Foundation. (2015). 5 step guide to budget development: Resources for nonprofit financial management [Video file]. Retrieved from: https://www.youtube.com/watch?v=edC7v81Fmj8

Zietlow, J., Hankin, J. A., Seidner, A., & O'Brien, T. (2018). *Financial management for nonprofit organizations: Policies and practices*. Hoboken, NJ: John Wiley & Sons.

HELPFUL TERMS

Accounts—classifications of transactions into one category. Accounts can be for income or expenses, such as fees collected, salaries paid, or equipment purchased.

Accounts payable—money owed by the organization to someone else but not yet paid. For example, if office supplies are received but have not yet been paid for, that amount is an account payable for the organization. Employee vacation time that has accumulated but not been taken is carried on the financial statements as an account payable.

Accounts receivable—revenues earned but not yet received. For example, if services have been provided and a contract has been billed for that service, the amount of the bill is an account receivable. It remains as an account receivable until the cash is received by the organization.

Accrual accounting—transactions are recognized (recorded) when revenues are earned and when expenses are incurred. Accrual accounting provides a more complete financial picture through the use of accounts receivable and accounts payable.

Assets—anything owned by an organization that has economic value. Assets may include cash, bank accounts, accounts receivable (see definition above), equipment, buildings, property, and automobiles.

Balance sheets—a snapshot in time of an organization's assets and liabilities, produced monthly, quarterly, or annually. These reports subtract liabilities from assets to show the organization's worth.

Budget—a plan for anticipating income and expenses to achieve specific objectives within a certain time.

Depreciation—an estimate of the decrease in the value of an asset. Depreciation takes into account the reality that equipment, buildings, automobiles, and so on, become obsolete or simply worn out over time. It is a method to show how much of the value of an asset remains.

Financial projections—reports that forecast or estimate future income and expenses.

Financial reports/Financial statements—reports on historical financial transactions. Examples include budget reports, activity reports, and balance sheets.

Generally Accepted Accounting Principles (GAAP)—basic sets of rules governing how the financial books and records of an organization are to be maintained, including how revenues, expenditures, and expenses are to be accounted for and how financial statements are to be prepared.

Liabilities—obligations to pay somebody something. All debts or amounts owed by an organization in the form of accounts payable (see above), loans, mortgages, and long-term debts are liabilities.

Net assets—what is left over when liabilities are subtracted from assets.

Permanently restricted funds—funds permanently restricted to a specific use. Endowment funds are usually in this category. For example, a donor may give a gift to the organization but require that only the earnings from those funds be used by the organization.

Revenues—usually in the form of cash and checks and may come from many sources, such as fees for service, contracts, grants, donations, third-party payments, insurance, managed-care firms, or investment income.

Temporarily restricted funds—funds given for a specific project.

Unrestricted funds—funds on which the donor has placed no restrictions.

EXERCISES

1. In-Basket Exercise

Directions

Read the following memos from your in-basket. For each memo, draft a reply outlining your decision or the action you plan to take. Use the ABC Monthly Statement of Revenue and Expenses—All Departments in Table 8.2 as the basis for your answers.

> **Memo**
>
> Date: June 25, 20XX
>
> To: Karen Wilson, Administrator Blue Skies Family Services
>
> From: Janice Sides, Finance Committee Chair
>
> Subject: Financial Report to the Board of Directors

I will be presenting the financial report to the full board at our next meeting. I have received the financial statements (the monthly statement of activities and the balance sheet), but I need your help in preparing my report. Please prepare a narrative report that explains the financial statements. I need an overall statement about the financial condition of the agency so far this fiscal year and how we are doing compared to last year. Also, please explain any variances in the budget in both income and expenses, and give me your recommendations for any adjustments that will be needed for the remainder of the fiscal year.

Memo

Date: August 31, 20XX

To: Karen Wilson, Administrator Blue Skies Family Services

From: Santos Terrazas, Board Chair

Subject: Budget for Next Fiscal Year

In reviewing the income statements for August, I noticed there are some rather large variances between the budget-to-date amounts and the actual amounts. I know we will be starting the formal budgeting process next month, but it would be helpful if you could give me some advance information on our financial picture. Please look at the administration statement, the Department A statement, and the Department B statement and project what you think our income and expenses are likely to be next fiscal year. I don't need a lot of detail. Just give me a one-page projected budget by using the actual income and expenses for the first eight months of this year and projecting next year's 12-month budget.

(Hint): Remember the year-to-date actual and the current budget are only for the first eight months of the year. Your task is to examine the eight months' actual income and actual expenses and project what next year's budget might look like.

2. Strengths and Weaknesses in Financial Management

Working in a small group in class, discuss your personal strengths and weaknesses related to financial management and budgeting. Report to the class how you plan to better prepare yourself for the financial functions you will need to perform as a social work administrator.

ASSIGNMENTS

1. Go online to Guidestar.org and search for a local nonprofit agency. Examine the agency's IRS Form 990 and write a two-page summary that describes the financial position of the organization.

2. Prepare a line-item budget for a fictitious agency with a budget of $2 million per year. Assume the $2 million in income comes from the United Way, fees for service, and donations. Develop an income and expense budget that reflects the most common expenses for a human service organization.

3. Call the finance director of a local organization and ask him or her for a telephone interview concerning the organization's budgeting process. Ask the director to describe his or her role in the process and the role of the administrator and the board of directors. Write a three-page summary explaining what you learn from the interview.

Image Credits

Skills

Quadrant II: External and Task Orientation

As we move to Quadrant II, we remain in the task-oriented side of our model but shift to the external environment. It is not a completely foreign place at this point, because understanding the world outside of your organization is needed when developing a strategic plan and looking at trends that will affect the agency. Still, the emphasis here is not on what that information will do for the agency in its planning, but rather how the environment can be used more effectively to support the agency in its plans.

Chapter 9 (Fund Development and Grantwriting) centers on the resources from the environment that can be moved into the organization's coffers. These resources are vital to keep the agency alive and to provide services to clients. Thus, it is vital that we know how to bring funding into the organization in ethical ways. In this chapter, we see again how the strategic plan and the associated documents produced in that process bring clarity to what occurs in the organization. You will learn about several different ways to bring resources into your agency, such as annual campaigns, special events, direct mail, and various types of direct donations, tapping into donor motivations to accept opportunities to give.

Marketing (Chapter 10) is really just another way to bring resources to the organization. In for-profit organizations, marketing is sometimes seen as a way to lure customers to part with their money for shady deals and products—anything to make a buck! In the nonprofit world, though, marketing must maintain an ethical stance of providing information about and opportunities to support a worthy endeavor. For nonprofits, marketing can be used to inform the outside world of the work they do, the people they work with, the results they achieve, and the opportunities that exist to aid that work in order to achieve more for clients. Opportunities can be donating cash or other resources, volunteering time and skills, and spreading the word about the organization further. Especially with social media, where viewers "like" and "share" information, the nonprofit can receive great benefits at little cost.

When you complete these chapters, you will think differently about how to connect the external world to the internal aspects of your organization's resource requirements. In a seemingly contradictory way, you must use your "people skills" to provide task-oriented solutions for obtaining resources. The subtle aspects of linking the tasks of fund development and marketing to the strategic elements of planning are fascinating and provide a well-paid career for many.

Fund Development and Grantwriting

Without funds, there are no programs," is a mantra of all fundraisers. This chapter presents the basics of a fundraising program and the competencies you will need in this area of practice (see Box 9.1).

Hoefer (2017) describes the three main legs of nonprofit fundraising as *individual giving, foundation giving,* and *government grants and contracts.* We will explore each of these areas and will present several approaches to securing individual gifts, including the annual campaign, direct mail, special events, major gifts, and planned gifts. There is a lot of charitable gift money out there. American individuals, estates, foundations, and corporations gave an estimated $410 billion to charitable causes in 2017, according to Giving USA Foundation (2017). You will need skills in each of these areas to be effective in your role as an administrator. Of course, fundraising is not the only source of income for nonprofits or human services. Fees for service are a large part of the budget for many human services organizations. Figure 9.1 shows the mix of income streams for the nonprofit sector as a whole. The human services sector relies more heavily on government grants, fees, and contracts and private contributions but less on fees for services income from private sources. In this chapter, we focus on the skills that support fundraising to secure private contributions (individual and foundation) and government grants.

BOX 9.1 EPAS Competencies Covered

The information in this chapter is directly connected to CSWE's Competency 8: Intervene with Individuals, Families, Groups, Organizations, and Communities..

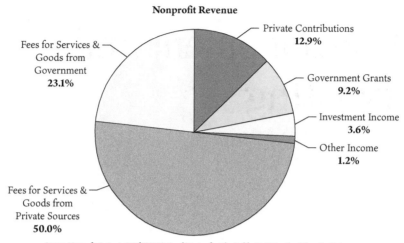

Source: *Nonprofit Sector in Brief 2014* National Center for Charitable Statistics, the Urban Institute

FIGURE 9.1. Sources of Nonprofit Revenue

The Three Main Legs of Fund Development

Individual Giving

For a few years during the Great Recession of 2008, individual giving decreased considerably across the nonprofit world. Fortunately, in 2013, the tide turned and overall charitable giving increased by 4.9% (MacLaughlin, 2014). The Blackbaud Institute for Philanthropic Impact reports that in 2018 the trend continued, with the longest sustained period of charitable giving growth since the recession (MacLaughlin, 2019). The problem for nonprofits is that no one can be sure just how well the economy is going to do in the next few years. Some economists argue that there will be a stock market correction, with a resulting loss of stock portfolio value, causing individuals to again lose significant ground financially. If this occurs, they will be less likely to give, just as they gave less during the other economic downturns, including the Great Recession that lasted from December 2007 to June 2009. In addition, income inequality is continuing to grow, with the percentage of Americans in the middle class declining. According to the Pew Research Center, "U.S. income inequality has been increasing steadily since the 1970s, and now has reached levels not seen since 1928" (Kochhar & Fry, 2014). This assessment is backed up by the figures from the Bureau of Labor Statistics (Karageorge, 2015). Thus, it is not clear what will happen with individual donor giving. Blackbaud (MacLaughlin, 2019) reports that the average age for a donor is 62 and that for those giving over $1,000, the median gift is $2,049. For those giving less than $1,000, the median gift is $20. The average online donation was $147. Online giving and social media fundraising are important emerging areas of fund development strategies.

Foundation Funding

According to the Foundation Center (Lawrence, 2014), there were over 84,000 foundations in the United States in 2014. They are responsible for 15% of all private giving in the United States

(MacLaughlin, 2016) and gave approximately $66.9 billion in 2017—an increase of 6% from 2016 (Giving USA Foundation, 2017). Human service organizations received about 16% of total foundation giving. Giving by foundations increased in the past few years after falling to a recent low in 2010.

Government Grants and Contracts

When government grants and contracts decline, the nonprofit sector feels the pinch quickly because of the extent of government funding for nonprofits. For example, in 2011, government grants and contracts provided one-third of revenue for public charities (Pettijohn & Boris, 2013). Results from their survey of human service nonprofits showed that, in 2012, "almost 30,000 nonprofits reported close to $81 billion in government contracts and grants" (Pettijohn & Boris, p. 35). In 2013, nearly 50 percent of organizations surveyed indicated that they experienced a decrease in local, state, or federal funds (Pettijohn & Boris, p.35).

The national government still provides tens of billions of dollars of funding per year, but as with other sources of income, competition is greater, and the need to have an excellent grantwriter is heightened if a nonprofit is relying on the national government for support.

Developing Gifts from Individuals

There are several different approaches to soliciting donations from individuals. These include the annual campaign, direct mail, special events, major gifts, online campaigns, and planned gifts. The concept of moving donors from annual giving to major gifts and planned gifts will be presented. This chapter will also explore donor motivation and present a fundraising strategy based on the concept of providing donors with opportunities rather than approaching fundraising as a "begging" activity.

Begging is not an effective strategy to raise funds. The alternative to begging for funds is to have a well-developed fundraising program. Even if the organization employs a professional fundraiser, the administrator is still the chief fundraising officer and, as such, will develop professional fundraising skills or risk becoming the chief beggar for the organization. Securing resources for the organization is ultimately the responsibility of the board of directors, but it is the administrator's responsibility to develop and oversee a well-developed fundraising program.

There are many "truisms" in fundraising, but the one most important to remember is that "people give to people, not to organizations." This is another way to say that fundraising is really "friend-raising." The people that will give money to your organization are those who share a passion for the mission of the organization and who trust that their money will be used wisely. It is the responsibility of the administrator to develop and nurture relationships that will financially sustain the organization.

Another truism is that people will not give anything to meet your agency needs, but they will give when presented with the opportunity to invest in an organization that will make a difference in the lives of others. People will give when they think they can make a positive difference in something they care about. At whatever level of fundraising activity, your approach should be to present opportunities that will make a positive impact in the lives of the people your organization serves and not to present the "needs" of the agency. You may need funds to hire a new counselor, but the fundraising approach should be to secure funds to serve more clients. You must tell the potential donor why the clients need this service and what difference it will make in their lives if the services are provided. The approach should NOT be that your organization "needs a new counselor."

Remember that people want to give to successful causes. You want to give the donor not only the opportunity to give but also a reason to contribute to a cause that will support success. Your appeal is not that your organization has great needs but that it is successful in meeting the needs of your clients.

Before we explore the many levels of activities in a fundraising program, we will look at the factors that motivate people to give.

Donor Motivation

Why do people give? Often, you will hear that most people give a donation because they will get a tax break. It is very seldom that tax donations are the major reason for making a donation.

BOX 9.2 I Don't Want to be Rich

A new executive director was excited to learn that an elderly couple had decided to leave their 1,000-acre ranch to the organization in their will. The executive went to visit the couple and raised the possibility that they could use a planned giving vehicle to go ahead and make their gift to the agency and at the same time enjoy a tremendous tax advantage, plus increase their income for the rest of their lives. In fact, through this gift, the couple could become rich. After listening politely, the elderly woman said, "Young man, I don't want to be rich. I want to go to our ranch and hunt birds!" It is important to know what motivates a donor. In this case, it was certainly not a tax break or more income.

People will give only when they are interested and involved in your cause. Of course, there are different levels of giving. The new donor, responding to a direct mail piece, will be very different from a board member donor with years of experience with the organization. People will respond to different kinds of appeals, because they have different reasons for giving. So, why do they give? Different authors provide varying answers to this question. Giving behavior is just as complex as any other.

In a review of over 500 articles on charitable giving, Bekkers and Wiepking (2011) found eight mechanisms to be the most important forces that determine a person's decision to give.

These are (1) awareness of need, (2) solicitation, (3) costs and benefits, (4) altruism, (5) reputation, (6) psychological benefits, (7) values, and (8) efficacy.

In his book *Tested Ways to Successful Fund Raising*, George A. Brakeley, Jr. (as cited in "8 Rules of Thumb," 2012) wrote that virtually every fundraising campaign and development program depends on the following eight factors in motivating donors to support their organization:

1. The right person or persons ask them, at the right time, and in the right circumstances.
2. People have a sincere desire to help other people.
3. People wish to belong to or be identified with a group or organization they admire.
4. Recognition of how vital their gifts can be satisfies a need for a sense of personal power in many people.
5. People have received benefits—often, personal enjoyment—from the services of the organization and wish to support it.
6. They "get something" out of giving.
7. People receive income and estate tax benefits from giving.
8. People may need to give; that is, altruism might not be an option but a "love or perish" necessity for many people.

Donor motivation research by Tsipursky (2017) found that most donors give to receive a feeling of self-satisfaction or social prestige. Some researchers disagree, but most of the research exploring why donors give concludes that they do so because it makes them feel good. For donors, how they feel about making a contribution is even more important that what can be accomplished by the donation. The feeling of self-satisfaction is most powerful when the donation is based on a deeply held personal value. A contribution to any worthy cause may produce a feeling of enhanced self-value, but a donation to an organization that is dear to the donor's heart and represents their deeply held values will produce an enhanced feeling of self-value. The donors who have a strong interest in your organization based on their value system are the donors who have the greatest potential to be the major donors to your organization.

The donor who sends in a few dollars from a direct mail appeal is very different from the donor who strongly believes in what your organization represents. Wright and Bocarnea (2007) found that the level of connection to an organization is a key factor in determining if the potential donor has a positive or negative attitude toward the organization. The way that the organization interacts with the donor will shape the attitudes toward the organization, and the more a donor is connected to an organization, the more likely it is that they will view the organization positively (Gorczyca, & Hartman, 2017). Whatever their other motivations, people will give only when they are interested and involved and when they are asked. To determine how to ask for a gift, we must know where our donors fit on the "donor pyramid."

The Donor Pyramid

Fundraising professionals often use the donor pyramid to conceptualize the fundraising program (see Figure 9.2). Each level in the pyramid builds on the level beneath it. For example, direct mail solicitation is appropriate to attract new donors to your organization, but once they have responded with even a small gift, your goal is to move them up to the next level of the pyramid. You want your new direct mail donors to become major givers. Of course, some donors will always be small givers or even stop giving to your organization, but most of your future major gift donors of tomorrow are your small gift givers today. Also, remember that all those small gifts add up and are very important to your overall fundraising plan.

The Association of Fundraising Professionals (AFP) *Fundraising Dictionary* ("Donor pyramid," 2004) describes the donor pyramid as:

> A diagrammatic description of the hierarchy of donors by size of gifts. The diagram reflects that: as the size of donations increases, the number of donations decreases; as the number of years a donor is asked to renew increases, the number of donors decreases; as campaign sophistication progresses from annual giving to planned giving, the number of donors decreases; as donor involvement increases, the size of the donor's contribution increases and the response to campaign sophistication increases.

As you work through this chapter, refer back to the donor pyramid. In a sophisticated fundraising program, donors will be treated differently depending on where they are on the donor pyramid. Donors will move up the donor pyramid through involvement with the organization and through receiving personal attention from the board and staff of the organization. Notice that, as you move up in the pyramid, the fundraising techniques become increasingly more personalized.

What seems to be a simple and obvious truism is, "No one gives at any level unless they are asked!" As uncomfortable as it may be at times, eventually someone has to ask for the gift, but if you and your board believe in your mission and truly believe you are giving others the opportunity to participate in your important work, then the "ask" will be less difficult.

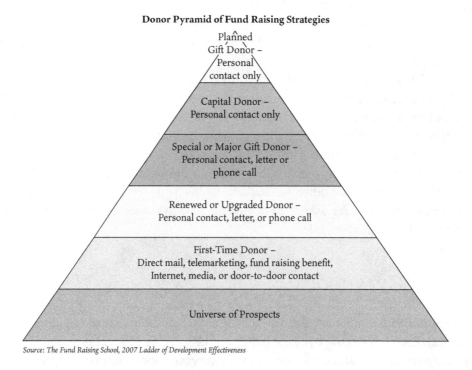

Donor Pyramid of Fund Raising Strategies

Planned Gift Donor – Personal contact only

Capital Donor – Personal contact only

Special or Major Gift Donor – Personal contact, letter or phone call

Renewed or Upgraded Donor – Personal contact, letter, or phone call

First-Time Donor – Direct mail, telemarketing, fund raising benefit, Internet, media, or door-to-door contact

Universe of Prospects

Source: The Fund Raising School, 2007 Ladder of Development Effectiveness

FIGURE 9-2. Sample Donor Pyramid

While the donor pyramid is a simple way to conceptualize a fundraising program, many professional fundraisers say that the pyramid is dead. Others describe the pyramid as a dinosaur that has had a good long run but is now extinct. Some of the objection to the old paradigm is that it is based on forcing donors to climb the pyramid to higher levels. The alternative is presented as "meeting people where they are." This should be an easy concept for social work administrators to grasp. We are all about meeting our clients where they are, and so it should make perfect sense that we would meet donors where they are.

Claire Axelrad (2014) says that the digital age has changed how people connect to and interact with organizations and that this offers new opportunities to connect and build relationships. She asks a legitimate question, "Are folks finding out about you through a letter you sent in the mail, or through something they saw on the internet? Are they reading your email appeals at their desks or on a smart phone just before bed?" She suggests that the current conceptual model is more like a vortex into which donors enter and exit at different levels. For example, someone you have never heard of might make a major gift as their first gift to your organization. It is not unusual that an organization receives a major gift through a will from a person they have never encountered before. The pyramid is useful to think about categories of donors and to provide a road map for increased engagement and increased support, but the reality is that donors may come in at any level of support. The digital environment provides us with great new challenges and opportunities (Axelrad, 2014).

Where's the Money?

American individuals, estates, foundations, and corporations gave an estimated $410 billion to charitable causes in 2017, according to Giving USA Foundation (2017). Why do individuals, foundations, and corporations give so much? What motivates a person to give?

"People are motivated to give because they value the cause, whether it is religion, education, health care, or international relief," said Henry (Hank) Goldstein, chair of Giving USA Foundation. "Charitable giving above 2 percent of gross domestic product is one demonstration of our nation's renewed commitment to the good works done by charities and congregations" (cited in Hoffman, 2011).

Notice in Figures 9.3 and 9.4 that 70% of donations come from individual donors. While corporate, foundation, and planned giving are all important elements of a fundraising program, individual donors give the most every year. It is critical to bring new individual donors into your organization.

Now look at Figure 9.4, which shows types of recipient organizations. Only

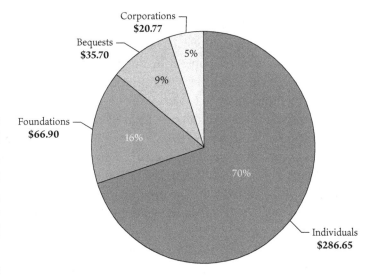

FIGURE 9.3. 2011 Contributions: $410 Billion by Source of Contributions

about 12% of the funds donated go to human services activities. It is important for you to know what other types of organizations are competing for the charitable dollars available.

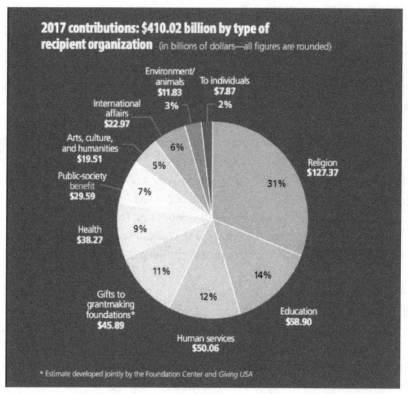

FIGURE 9.4. 2011 Contributions: $410 Billion by Type of Recipient Organization
The Basics of Fundraising

Annual Campaign

The annual campaign consists of the fundraising activities that are conducted to support the organization's annual operating budget. Even though these funds will be used for the organization's operating budget, your approach will focus on the services to be provided, not on the need for things like staff raises or paying the electric bill. The operating expenses support the services your organization provides. Ask your donors to help serve your clients. Generally, the largest number of donors will be giving to the annual campaign. Some organizations may not think of their many and diverse fundraising activities as an "annual campaign," but whether it is thought of in these terms or not, mailings, special events and similar activities are in effect the annual campaign for the organization. The approaches used in the annual campaign may include direct mail, social media appeals, phone-a-thons, or special events such as golf tournaments or galas.

The defining feature of annual funding activities is that they are activities intended to raise gift income *every year*. It is expected that you will approach the same donors every year and, sometimes, several times within the same year. Funds donated to the annual campaign are intended to support operational costs such as salaries, supplies, utilities, and client needs. The purpose is to support any part of the organization's operation that requires continuous and regular support.

Most donors will come into your organization through the annual campaign. It is possible but rare that a person's first gift to the organization will be a major gift. More likely, those who become major donors are those who have been consistent annual campaign donors.

Direct Mail

You probably know about direct mail fundraising from your personal experience. Direct bulk mail is used to ask millions of people for money, and most people receive solicitations in their mail on a regular basis. What rate of return should you expect from your direct mail campaign? Typically, the response is somewhere in the range of 1%. Even though the return is small, it is an economical way to get your message in front of thousands of potential donors. It is a key strategy in bringing new people into the bottom of your pyramid. The typical direct mail package includes the carrier (outside envelope), the letter, a reply device, and a return envelope.

The carrier or outside envelope should be designed with one objective in mind: to get the recipient to open it. If the piece goes into the trash, your chance of getting a donation is zero. The goal is to make the pieces look as much as possible like a personal letter and to make it look different from other solicitations in the mail box that day. Ideally, the envelope could be hand addressed, but since direct mail is a strategy of large numbers, this is rarely possible. Precanceled bulk mail stamps give a more personal look than the standard postal indicia used on most bulk mail. The other strategy is to use an envelope other than the standard "number 10" business envelope that many fundraisers refer to as "the number 10 ugly." Choose an envelope that is smaller, larger, or a different shape. You may also want to consider using color or a see-through window to pique your potential donors' interest.

Once you get the potential donors to open the letter, your task is to capture their attention long enough to have them consider making a gift to your cause. The task here is not to write a scholarly piece or to impress anyone with your vocabulary. The letter should strike an informal tone and be easy to read and understand. Kim Klein (2000) proposes a set of principles to remember as you develop your letter:

1. People have a very short attention span. Sentences should be short and take no more than six to 15 seconds to read.
2. People love to read about themselves. The letter should refer to the reader at least twice as often and up to four times as often as it refers to the organization sending it. For example, "You may have read ..." or "If you are like me, you care deeply about ..."
3. People must find the letter easy to look at. The page should contain a lot of white space and wide margins and be in a clear and simple font. Paragraphs should be short, no more

than two or three sentences. You should feel free to use contractions (*won't, you're, can't, we're*) as this will add a more informal tone to your letter.

4.   People read the letter in a certain order. First, they read the salutation and the opening paragraph, but then, no matter how long the letter is, they read the closing paragraph, and then the postscript. Only a small number of people will read the entire letter.

The opening paragraph of your letter is critical. It must capture the attention of your readers and make them want to read on. Remember the truism that people will not give anything to meet your agency needs, but they will give when they have an opportunity to invest in a service that is of interest to them. Your letter must be about the people you serve, not the needs of your organization. Also, people do not relate well when you talk about the thousands of people you serve. Your letter should tell the story of one person helped by your organization and how this potential donor can make a difference in the life of someone else.

How long the letter should be is always a debate. Our natural instincts tell us that the letter should be short and to the point, but many fundraising consultants counsel that long letters are better, claiming that a two-page letter will get a better response than a one-page letter and that even three- and four-page letters will often outperform a shorter letter. There are many theories about why you should consider writing a longer letter. Some will say that it gives the impression that your organization has a lot to say, while others believe that more pieces of paper and longer letters give an opportunity for the potential donor to feel more involved with your organization.

In the closing paragraph, you ask for the money. Tell the reader what you want them to do. They have read your letter, now what do you want them to do about it? For example, say, "Send your gift of $25, $50, or $100 today." It needs to be direct and specific. No one gives unless they are asked.

The postscript is that small P.S. at the end of the letter. The reader will read the P.S. if they do not read anything else in the letter. This is your final opportunity to ask for the gift. Examples of an effective postscript are, "Send your check today," or, "Johnny needs your help."

Finally, the reply device is a small card that gives the potential donor the opportunity to respond. It will typically have a box to check that says something like, "Yes! I'll help," and then gives several options of giving—$10, $25, $50, $100, or more. The donor completes the card, encloses the check, and returns it in the enclosed return envelope. With that, your campaign is a success—at least with this donor.

Social Media

Social networking applications such as Facebook, Twitter, and Instagram offer new ways for non-profits to engage the community in fundraising efforts. Today, these three are the most commonly used, but the landscape changes rapidly. Linkedin, YouTube, and Pinterest are other platforms used in fundraising campaigns. Blackbaud Institute's Charitable Giving Report (MacLaughlin, 2019) shows that since 2016, online giving has grown 17%, and average online gift amounts have continued to increase. The percentage of total fundraising that came from online giving reached a record high in 2018. Approximately 8.5% of overall fundraising revenue, excluding grants, was raised online, and 24% of online transactions were made using a mobile device (MacLaughlin, 2019). Developing and maintaining a social media presence for your organization will be an important function for you as an administrator.

Special Events

Special events are limited only by your imagination. The events may be galas, golf tournaments, walk-a-thons, performances—the possibilities are endless. Many times, special events do not raise large sums of money for the first few years but grow over time into major events that raise large amounts of money. When planning a special event, there are considerations other than the amount of money to be raised. The special event may be the activity that will raise the visibility of your organization in the community and an opportunity to involve more volunteers in your work.

Special events are by their nature very labor intensive and can take a great deal of your time and staff time. Before deciding on a special event, it is important to consider the volunteer and staff resources necessary for a successful event. Any special event will require a major investment of time in planning, marketing, and execution.

Major Gifts

Major gifts are the larger gifts that you will solicit for your cause. These gifts will typically come from those individuals, foundations, and corporations with whom you have developed a long-term, ongoing relationship. Many times, major gifts are solicited within the framework of a "capital campaign," fundraising for the purpose of capital improvement, such as building a new building or, in some cases, to develop or strengthen the endowment of an organization. An organization will often contract with a consulting firm to conduct a capital campaign. You, your board, and your staff will still have to solicit the gifts, but a good consultant can help structure and focus a successful campaign.

Major gifts require personal solicitation and the preparation of a proposal. A foundation may require a fully developed proposal, but an individual donor may prefer a short, well-developed statement of the purpose of the proposed donation. These donors are higher on the "pyramid" and, in most cases, know about your organization, believe in your work, and are willing to make a major contribution. When seeking a foundation or corporate gift, it is important to research the previous gifts and areas of interest of the foundation or corporation. As in all fundraising, finding a personal connection between your organization and the foundation or corporation is a great asset in your attempt to secure a gift. See the section below on foundations for a fuller discussion of foundation proposals.

Planned Gifts

Planned giving is a complex area. The bequest is the simplest form of planned giving. This means that someone has named your organization in a will and that, on their death, a portion or sometimes all of that person's estate will come to your organization. As the administrator, you have an awesome responsibility to see that a person's life work is used for the intended purposes.

Other planned giving arrangements include charitable gift annuities, revocable and non-revocable trusts, and other financial vehicles to transfer funds from the donor to the organization. These gifts have tax implications for the donor and are in many cases a part of the estate planning process. Any gift of this type will involve an attorney or certified public accountant. The role of the administrator is to see that the organization has the structure and the advisors necessary to accept gifts of this nature.

Say Thank You!

It is important to say "thank you" to any person or entity that donates to your organization, but it is especially important in dealing with individual gifts. It is impossible to say thank you too much

to your donors. The acknowledgment or "thank you" is a vital part of your fundraising system. Donors should be thanked in writing as quickly as possible for their gift, and whenever possible, donors should be thanked with a telephone call. For large donations, you as the administrator or your board chairman should make a phone call or a visit to thank donors for their gifts. Since successful fundraising is based on relationships, it is important to nurture and sustain relationships by showing gratitude to those who invest in the mission of your organization.

Developing Gifts from Foundations

What are foundations? According to the Minnesota Council on Foundations (MCF), "A foundation is a nonprofit organization that supports charitable activities in order to serve the common good" (Minnesota Council on Foundations, 2014). According to the Foundation Center (Lawrence, 2014), in 2012 there were 86,192 foundations in the United States. They held $715 billion in assets and gave away $52 billion. There are several different types of foundations that exist under the law. The first, independent foundations, are the most common and typically are created by individuals or families that want to promote attention to a certain problem or approach to a problem. Independent foundations can be either family foundations or other independent foundations, although there is no precise legal definition of the term "family foundation," as they are part of the larger category of independent foundation (Minnesota Council on Foundations, 2014). The Blackbaud Charitable Giving Report (MacLaughlin, 2019) finds that giving to foundations and donor-advised funds (DAFs) continues to grow in response to supporter preferences and changes in incentives.

The second type of foundation is the corporate foundation. These are set up by corporations as legally separate entities and are overseen by a Board of Directors, often made up of corporate directors and employees. Funding for corporate foundations varies but can include an endowment, contributions from current corporate profits, or even donations from employees. Some corporate foundations provide grants only to locales or states where the parent company has a strong presence; others have broader eligibility criteria. Corporate foundations are not the same as corporate giving programs, which often donate goods and services rather than cash or provide only small amounts of direct funding for nonprofit projects. Another difference is that corporate foundations are governed by Internal Revenue Service rulings and law, while corporate giving programs are entirely in the hands of the corporation.

Community foundations are the third major type of foundation. These are tied very closely to a particular geographic area and are usually funded by pooling smaller amounts of donations from people in the community. Donation decisions are made by a Board of Directors that is supposed to be representative of the community at large.

All private foundations are required to follow at least three very important regulations in order to maintain their standing as foundations, according to the Minnesota Council on Foundations (2014). First, they must pay out (donate) no less than 5% of the value of their investment assets. Second, they pay taxes of 1% or 2% of their earnings. Third, with rare exceptions, they can only donate to other organizations that are 501c3 (charitable) organizations. Not all organizations with the word "foundation" in their name provide grants to applicants. The Henry J. Kaiser Family Foundation, for example, uses its resources to develop nonpartisan information on health care issues (Henry J. Kaiser Family Foundation, n.d.), so it is important when searching for foundation funding to carefully look up information on each prospective foundation.

Researching Foundations

It is critical that you conduct a thorough search to find a foundation that has interest in your area of service. As stated above, some foundations are restricted to a particular geographic area, and almost all foundations have a preference of the kinds of services they wish to fund. The number one source of information regarding foundation grants is undoubtedly the Foundation Center. According to its website, the Foundation Center has access to over three million funding records and opportunities from 90,000 grant makers. The Foundation Center (http://foundationcenter.org) and GuideStar (https://www.guidestar.org/) have recently joined forces to become Candid, a 501c3 nonprofit organization (Guidestar, 2019). In their announcement, they state that, "Candid connects people who want to change the world to the resources they need to do it."

While this service can be extremely useful, the cost of access to Foundation Center information is outside the price range of some nonprofits that have only an occasional need to actually use this vast array of data. Fortunately, many public libraries carry a subscription at some level, and grant-writers can receive training from the library staff to use the Foundation Directory Online (FDO) on the premises. Sometimes access to the FDO is available through other entities, such as a nonprofit consortium, university, or government agency (Foundation Center, 2019).

While the trouble with using the Foundation Center's information is cost, the trouble with searching on your own is that, according to the Foundation Center, only 10–15% of foundations have websites. Thus, you are not necessarily going to get as many results on your own as you may think you will. You are also not going to gain access to as much information as the FDO can give you if you use a search engine approach.

Writing the Proposal

Once you determine that your organization is within the guidelines of a foundation and that you meet all their eligibility requirements, it is time to write the proposal. So what should go in the proposal? The answer is, whatever they want. Most foundations will give you the guidelines for what they want included in their proposals. Some small foundations may want a one-page summary of your request. Other more developed foundations may ask for a detailed proposal including your goal and objectives, your outcome data, and a detailed budget. Make sure that when they receive your proposal, they know that you have read and understood their guidelines for proposals.

Relationships

Just like in individual giving, it is important to establish and nurture relationships to be successful in raising funds from foundations. You have the best chance of success if you have some personal connection with the foundation board members or staff. You should know if any of your board members have personal relationships with families who have family foundations or if they know people who serve on foundation boards. The same is true for corporate foundations. Do you have board members who are executives or employees of corporations that make corporate or corporate foundation gifts?

Takeaways of Foundation Funding

You should take away the following key lessons from this discussion regarding foundation funding. First, the Foundation Center's Online Directory (FDO) is most likely your best source for information on foundation grants. They have collected vast amounts of information that can be beneficial to your efforts. Because it is too costly for many nonprofits to order on their own, grantwriters should try to find a free way to use it through a public library or other source, such as a nonprofit resource center.

Second, whether using the FDO or your own online searches, constantly search for foundations that are active in areas you would like to apply for. Remember, applications may only be allowed for a short period once each year, so you must keep notes of when recurring deadlines are. Set up a "tickler" file or notices that will remind you to look up current proposal deadlines and requirements.

Third, knowing that foundations are more and more interested in working with a smaller number of nonprofits they already are aware of, you'll need to be more proactive than ever before. Foundations can, and do, alter their own rules about allocating their funds. Be sure to publicize your organization's efforts year-round, targeting people and finding connections to those who make foundation funding decisions.

Fourth, your organization should be conducting and publicizing rigorous program evaluation results, overseen by outside evaluators. Foundations are looking for successful nonprofits to partner with and soliciting applications only from them. You need to have evidence of effectiveness when you contact (or are contacted by) potential funders.

Fifth, keep an easily referenced set of notes on as many foundations as you can manage. Subscribe to any RSS or email lists from those foundations to keep up to date on what they are doing and the grants they are making.

Government Grants and Contracts

How do you find a government grant? This section discusses the primary ways of finding government funding sources, particularly at the federal level. While national government grants are perhaps the easiest to research, they are also therefore much more competitive to receive. Nonprofits looking for government funding need to be able to research and find ways to locate state and local government grant opportunities, as well. The principles described in this chapter will work at the state and local levels, although the details will vary from location to location.

What Is the Difference Between a Government Grant and a Contract?

Nonprofit leaders may talk about receiving a government grant or a government contract as if they are the same thing. While both bring funding to an organization, they are different in many important ways. This section looks at the main ways they differ (see Table 9.1).

TABLE 9.1   Differences Between Federal Government Grants and Contracts

Characteristic	Grant	Contract
Purpose	Transferring money, property, services, or anything of value to a recipient (31 U.S.C. Section 6304)	Obtaining (purchase, lease, or barter) goods or services (31 U.S.C. Section 6303)
Goal	Accomplishing a public purpose	Achieving something for the direct benefit of the U.S. Government
Amount of Government Involvement Once Awarded	Minor	Major
Who Sets Scope of Work?	Nonprofit	Government
How Regulated?	Through OMB Circulars A-21 (2 CFR 220) and A-110 (2 CFR 215)	Through Federal Acquisition Regulations (FAR) and Federal Agencies FAR Supplements

Source: Adapted from Woodward (2011).

First, the purposes and goals of a grant and a contract are not the same. A grant has the purpose of transferring "money, property, services or anything of value to a recipient (31 U.S.C. section 6304)," whereas the purpose of a contract is to "obtain (purchase, lease or barter) goods (property) or services (31 U.S.C. section 6303)." A grant's goal is to "accomplish a public purpose," while the goal of a contract is to achieve something "for the direct benefit of the U.S. Government" (Woodward, 2011).

Once a grant is awarded, there is only minor involvement with the operations of the grantee, and the grantee is given fairly free rein to accomplish the public purpose, although grantees must provide required reports and respond to performance issues. These are the main ways the government maintains contact with the grantee. When a contract is awarded, the government still has major involvement in the terms of the contract and how it achieves its purposes. Definite tasks, milestones, and deliverables expected are part of the contract between government and agency.

With grants, nonprofits generally set their scope of work in responding to the government agency's request for proposals (RFP). While the RFP lays out the general parameters of the applications, each responding nonprofit may define its own response. With a contract, on the other hand, the government is explicit in what it wants, and nonprofits have limited scope in determining what to offer other than the stated goods or services. Finally, grants are regulated through OMB Circulars A-21 (2 CFR 220) and A-110 (2 CFR 215), whereas contracts are regulated by the Federal Acquisition Regulations (FAR) and Federal Agencies FAR Supplements (Woodward, 2011). Examples of the two funding mechanisms can help clarify the situation.

Grant Example

A grant mechanism was used by a federal government agency, the Administration for Children and Families, Office of Community Services (OCS), to "address food deserts; improve access to healthy, affordable foods; and address the economic needs of low-income individuals and families through the creation of business and employment opportunities." This does not have a fixed price; agencies can decide how much to request, up to the maximum amount allowed ($800,000), for up to five years. More specifically, OCS seeks to fund projects that will implement innovative strategies for increasing healthy food access while achieving sustainable employment and business opportunities for recipients of Temporary Assistance for Needy Families (TANF) and other low-income individuals whose income level does not exceed 125% of the federal poverty level. When talking about a grant, the government agency states the general purpose, but the way to achieve the stated purpose is left up to the organization making the application. Thus, a considerable amount of creativity is required within the grant application.

Contract Example

An example of a contract is the Centers for Medicare and Medicaid Services signing an agreement for "Administrative Management and General Management Consulting Services" with the Health Research and Educational Trust for almost $76 million. Again, a contract specifies definite tasks, milestones, and deliverables expected as part of the contract between government and agency. Another funding stream for many human service organizations is the "fee for service." For example, a state agency may contract with a nonprofit agency to provide foster care and adoption placement or to provide vocational rehabilitation for citizens with disabilities. These arrangements are also a type of government contract and are a major funding source for many nonprofit organizations. State agencies will most often issue a request for proposals and will direct such requests to organizations already providing such services.

Finding Government Grants

The primary research tool to find grants (not contracts) at the federal government level is grants.gov (www.grants.gov). Some states have similar portals for state-level funding. If you live in a state that has a similar system, the information will be applicable there as well. An example is Texas eGrants Search (https://www.texasonline.state.tx.us/tolapp/egrants/search.htm).

The fact that all federal government grants can be accessed through one portal is a great boon to grant seekers. It does, however, place a premium on your ability to conduct an effective search there. Dr. Hoefer has developed a quick step-by-step video that's posted on YouTube called "How to Use Grants.gov to Find Federal Grants" which is available at (http://youtu.be/yDbGerr5Oek). Other videos with helpful information are available on the grants.gov website and on YouTube if you search for "how to use grants.gov."

Astute grantwriters will not only look at the current grant opportunities but will also take the time to do a careful longitudinal analysis of several years' worth of the funding opportunity statements. These statements contain all the requirements, goals, and other information you must have in order to write your proposal. While these opportunities are closed, it will give you insight into what will be required when the next funding cycle is announced. The information available from such research will provide you with information about:

- Who is eligible to apply
- Deadlines for submission
- Whether pre-application conference calls will be held for questions to be asked, and when
- Contact information
- Overview of the funding opportunity
- Award information
- Program scope, including purpose areas, priority areas, out-of-scope activities, and unallowable activities
- How to apply
- Application contents, including formatting and technical requirements, application requirements, project narrative, budget detail worksheet and narrative, and more
- Additional required information
- Selection criteria, including review process, past performance review, compliance with financial requirements, and more
- Post award information requirements

While it sometimes happens that the contents of the funding opportunities change drastically from one year to the next, this is relatively rare. If you look at several years of the same funding announcement and the information is very similar, you have found a way to anticipate what is likely to be requested for the next round of applications. This way, instead of having about six weeks to get your 30–50 pages of application written, you have a year or more, with only small changes to be made based on minor changes in what is being asked.

Takeaways of Government Grants and Contracts

Here are key points to recall regarding Government Grants and Contracts:

- Differences exist between federal government grants and contracts, with grants providing the applicant with considerable latitude to propose their solutions to the pressing problem to be addressed, as described in the Funding Opportunity Announcement or Request for Proposals.
- Grantwriters must learn how to use the advanced search features in grants.gov, the main portal to all federal grants and contracts. Using this process allows you to know which grant

opportunities are currently open for applications and which are forecasted to be open in the near future.

• Beyond knowing which opportunities are forecasted and currently open, perusing "closed" and "archived" funding opportunities on the grants.gov site allows you to compare several years of grant announcements. Having access to this information lets you do two important tasks: The first is to improve your planning by putting approximate dates on your calendar for when the next year's announcement will be posted and when the application will be due. If you do this for all the federal grant opportunities you are interested in, you can more effectively make long-range plans. The second task is to compare multiple years of grant application requirements so that you can determine what the likely requirements will be in the next round. Priorities often do not change much from one year to the next. Because one year's change in priority may be the next year's change in requirements, knowing what has stayed the same and what has been altered gives you a fantastic opportunity to get a peek into what may be coming around the bend before it gets here. If you can be 80–90% sure of what the application is going to call for next year, you can already be putting together a coherent grant proposal now, giving yourself far more than six weeks to write a strong grant application.

Conclusion

Effective fundraisers work from a strategic fundraising plan that is long term, has specific goals, and uses a variety of fundraising methods and techniques. The organization's financial strength can be developed and maintained only through a fundraising strategy that is diversified by using many different fundraising approaches appropriate for their various categories of donors. Fundraising must be approached like any other major project, in that it requires the administrator to set goals, allocate resources, develop action steps and timelines, and then evaluate the process. As the administrator, you are the chief fundraising official for the organization. You may have others that perform these daily functions but it is your responsibility to understand what motivates the donors to your organization and to coordinate the efforts of everyone involved in the fund development task. A comprehensive development program will include *individual giving, foundation giving,* and *government grants and contracts* (Hoefer, 2017). You will need skills in each of these three areas.

Reference List

8 rules of thumb when soliciting prospects. (2012, May 23). *The NonProfit Times.* Retrieved from http://www.thenonprofittimes.com/management-tips/8-rules-of-thumb-when-soliciting-prospects

Donor pyramid. (n.d.). In *Association of Fundraising Professionals (AFP) Fundraising Dictionary*. Retrieved from https://afpglobal.org/fundraising-dictionary

Axelrad, C. (2014, July 8). Yes, the donor pyramid is really dead: An open response to Andrea Kihlstedt [Web log post]. Retrieved from https://trust.guidestar.org/blog/2014/07/08/yes-the-donor-pyramid-is-really-dead-an-open-response-to-andrea-kihlstedt/

Bekkers, R., & Wiepking, P. (2011). A literature review of empirical studies of philanthropy: Eight mechanisms that drive charitable giving. *Nonprofit and Voluntary Sector Quarterly, 40*(5), 924–973.

Foundation Center (2019). Retrieved from https://foundationcenter.org/

Giving USA Foundation. (2017). *Total charitable donations rise to new high of $390.05 billion*. Retrieved from https://givingusa.org/giving-usa-2017-total-charitable-donations-rise-to-new-high-of-390-05-billion/

Gorczyca, M., & Hartman, R. L. (2017). The new face of philanthropy: The role of intrinsic motivation in millennials' attitudes and intent to donate to charitable organizations. *Journal of Nonprofit & Public Sector Marketing, 29*(4), 415–433.

GuideStar. (2019). *Foundation Center and GuideStar join forces to become a new nonprofit entity named Candid*. Retrieved from https://learn.guidestar.org/news/news-releases/foundation-center-and-guidestar-join-forces-to-become-a-new-nonprofit-entity-named-candid

Henry J. Kaiser Family Foundation. (n.d.). About us. Retrieved from http://kff.org/about-us/

Hoefer, R. (2017). *Funded!: Successful grantwriting for your nonprofit*. New York, NY: Oxford University Press.

Hoffman, M. (2011). Americans give $241 billion to charity in 2003. *Foundation for the Carolinas*. Retrieved from https://www.pgdc.com/pgdc/americans-give-241-billion-charity-2003

Karageorge, E. (2015). The growth of income inequality in the United States. *Monthly Labor Review, 138*.

Klein, K. (2000). *Fundraising for social change* (4th ed.). Oakland, CA: Chardon Press.

Kochhar, R., & Fry, R. (2014). Wealth inequality has widened along racial, ethnic lines since end of Great Recession. *Pew Research Center, 12*(104), 121–145.

Lawrence, S. (2014, June 9). Have foundations recovered from the great recession? [Web log post]. Retrieved from http://pndblog.typepad.com/pndblog/2014/06/have-foundations-recovered-from-the-great-recession.html

MacLaughlin, S. (2014). *Charitable giving report: How nonprofit fundraising performed in 2014*. Blackbaud Institute for Philanthropic Impact. Retrieved from https://www.blackbaud.com/files/resources/downloads/2014/2013.CharitableGivingReport.pdf

MacLaughlin, S. (2016). *Charitable giving report: How nonprofit fundraising performed in 2016*. Blackbaud Institute for Philanthropic Impact. Retrieved from https://institute.blackbaud.com/asset/2016-charitable-giving-report/

MacLaughlin, S. (2019) *Charitable giving report: How fundraising performed in 2018*. Retrieved from https://institute.blackbaud.com/wp-content/uploads/2019/02/2018CharitableGivingReport.pdf

Minnesota Council on Foundations. (2014). What's a foundation or grantmaker? Retrieved from https://mcf.org/whats-foundation-or-grantmaker

Pettijohn, S. L., & Boris, E. T. (with De Vita, C. J., & Fyffe, S. D.). (2013). *Nonprofit-government contracts and grants: Findings from the 2013 national survey*. Washington, DC: The Urban Institute.

Tsipursky, G. (2017, April 29). The psychology of effective fundraising. Retrieved from https://www.psychologytoday.com/us/blog/intentional-insights/201704/the-psychology-effective-fundraising

Woodward, D. (2011). *Grants and contracts: How they differ*. Retrieved from https://www.cga.msu.edu/PL/Portal/DocumentViewer.aspx?cga=aQBkAD0AMgAxADQA

Wright, M. H., & Bocarnea, M. C. (2007). Contributions of unrestricted funds: The donor organization–public relationship and alumni attitudes and behaviors. *Nonprofit Management & Leadership, 18*(2), 215–235.

Additional Resources

Association of Fundraising Professionals (AFP, http://www.afpnet.org).

Bill & Melinda Gates Foundation. (2014). Who we are: Foundation fact sheet. Retrieved from http://www.gatesfoundation.org/Who-We-Are/General-Information/Foundation-Factsheet

Denver Public Library. (2019). Foundation Center Directory Tutorial [Video file]. Retrieved from http://youtu.be/tKlb8iurAK4

HELPFUL TERMS

Annual campaign—the fundraising activities that are conducted for the purpose of supporting the organization's annual operating budget.

Direct mail—a fundraising approach using bulk mail to reach potential donors. The typical direct mail package includes the carrier (outside envelope), the letter, a reply device, and a return envelope.

Donor pyramid—a diagrammatic description of the hierarchy of donors by size of gift. The diagram reflects that as the size of donations increases, the number of donations decreases; as the number of years a donor is asked to renew increases, the number of donors decreases; as campaign sophistication progresses from annual giving to planned giving, the number of donors decreases; as donor involvement increases, the size of the donor's contribution increases, and the response to campaign sophistication increases.

Major gifts—the larger gifts that typically come from individuals, foundations, and corporations with whom the organization has developed a long-term, ongoing relationship. Some major gifts are solicited within the framework of a "capital campaign," for the purpose of capital improvement, such as building a new building or, in some cases, to develop or strengthen the endowment of an organization.

Planned gifts—The bequest is the simplest form of planned giving. Other planned giving arrangements include charitable gift annuities, revocable and nonrevocable trusts, and other financial vehicles to transfer funds from the donor to the organization. These gifts have tax implications for the donor and are in many cases a part of their estate planning process.

Special events—very labor-intensive activities that have the advantage of increased volunteer participation and the opportunity to increase the visibility of the sponsoring organization; events such as galas, golf tournaments, walk-a-thons, performances, and so on.

EXERCISES

1. In-Basket Exercise

Directions

You are Bruce Lloyd, the CEO of Agape Children's Home, After being out of town on vacation, you return to find three emails relating to fundraising in your inbox. For each email, draft a reply outlining your decision or the action you plan to take, explaining your reasoning to the recipient.

Memo

Date: May 3, 20XX

To: Bruce Lloyd, CEO, Agape Children's Home

From: Phillip Johnson, Director of Development

Subject: Phone Call ref. Possible Bequest

I received a phone call today from Mr. Jim Wilson, one of our longtime supporters. Mr. Wilson stated that he is revising his will and is considering leaving his ranch to our agency. I was planning to send him our new brochure. Is there anything else I need to do? Please advise.

Memo

Date: May 4, 20XX

To: Bruce Lloyd, CEO, Agape Children's Home

From: Carla Wayne, Program Service Supervisor

Subject: Golf Tournament for the Agency

My husband played in a golf tournament for the ABC Children's Home last weekend. He was told that they raised over $10,000 in just one day! I've been talking with the social workers and secretaries in my unit, and we would like to organize a golf tournament for the agency to benefit our unit. We think it would be great fun and raise a lot of money. Do we have your permission to proceed? Please advise.

Memo

Date: May 4, 20XX

To: Bruce Lloyd, CEO, Agape Children's Home

From: Phillip Johnson, Director of Development

Subject: Fundraising Letter

You mentioned to me that you would like to personally write the fundraising letter for our "Christmas in July" appeal. I will need this to be to the printers in the next few weeks. Please send me your letter as soon as you can, and I will start working on the printing and production. Thank you.

2. Exercise – Develop a fundraising letter and response card

Directions

Use the following "fact sheet" to develop a direct mail fundraising letter and response card for Cornerstone Community Services.

FACT SHEET

Cornerstone Community Services (CCS)

Our Mission—To assist youth in becoming independent, self-sufficient adults who make a contribution to our society.

History—Cornerstone Community Services was established in 1895 by Rev. Joseph P. Wilson, a Protestant minister. At the turn of the century, Rev. Wilson became very concerned about the number of orphan boys who were unsupervised and becoming juvenile delinquents. In response to this, he worked with other ministers and established the Cornerstone Home and Training School for Boys. Rev. Wilson became the first superintendent of the school and served faithfully for over 25 years. The Home for Boys started in a small frame house near downtown. The Boys Home continued to grow, and in 1942 a beautiful 30-acre location was donated to the institution for a new campus. In 1968, a major fundraising campaign was conducted to build most of the buildings as they exist today. Through the years, the need for "orphanages" decreased, and the CCS Board of Trustees developed new programs to meet the changing needs of society.

Today, CCS has evolved to a multiservice organization with four major programs, including residential treatment services, therapeutic foster care, maternity and adoption services, and independent living services for youth with physical disabilities. Both residential and community-based services are provided. CCS has a $4 million annual budget and 85 employees. Funding sources include the Department of Protective Services, the Rehabilitation Commission, United Way, foundation grants, and fundraising.

ASSIGNMENTS

1. Find direct mail fundraising letters from three organizations. Evaluate the strengths and weaknesses of each of the letters in a five-page paper.

2. Find three peer-reviewed journal articles on fund development that have been written in the past three years. Give a brief summary of each article.

3. Go to www.grants.gov on your computer. Follow the steps in Dr. Hoefer's video (http://youtu.be/yDbGerr5Oek) (or other instructional video) and come up with at least three potential grant opportunities. Print off the information or save it electronically.

4. Look at forecasted and current grant opportunities in your area of interest, as well as RFPs that have expired and been archived. Create a calendar for yourself with the RFPs that are not now available but have a record of having been put forth for the past year or two.

Image Credits

Fig. 9.1: National Center for Charitable Statistics and the Urban Institute, "Sources of Nonprofit Revenue," The Nonprofit Sector in Brief 2014.

Img. 9.1: Copyright © 2018 Depositphotos/Liudmilachernetska@gmail.com.

Fig. 9.2: Source: https://www.pinterest.com/pin/365354588502212701/.

Fig. 9.3: Giving USA Foundation, "2011 Contributions: $410 Billion by Source of Contributions," The Data on Donor-Advised Funds. Copyright © 2017.

Fig. 9.4: Giving USA Foundation, "2011 Contributions: $410 Billion by Type of Recipient Organization," The Data on Donor-Advised Funds. Copyright © 2017.

Img. 9.2: Copyright © 2011 Depositphotos/Kelpfish.

Img. 9.3: Copyright © 2018 Depositphotos/Designer491.

Img. 9.4: Copyright © 2013 Depositphotos/Karenr.

Img. 9.5: Copyright © 2012 Depositphotos/Rrraum.

10 Marketing

BOX 10.1 **EPAS Competencies Covered**

The information in this chapter is directly connected to CSWE's Competency 8: Intervene with Individuals, Families, Groups, Organizations, and Communities.

The American Marketing Association defines marketing as "the activity, set of institutions and processes for creating, communicating, delivering and exchanging offerings that have value for customers, clients, partners, and society at large" (AMA, 2013). As the definition of marketing has evolved over time, it has become more applicable to the nonprofit and public sectors. In the past, marketing concepts were seen mainly as tools of the business sector, but they now apply equally well to public and nonprofit organizations. Seymour Fine (1992) notes that in 1985 the AMA adopted a definition of marketing that added "the exchange of ideas" to the traditional definition of marketing that had been exclusively focused on "goods and services." Fine views the change in definition as a milestone in the evolution of social marketing, as it reflects a new emphasis on the dissemination and exchange of ideas. According to Andreasen and Kotler, "Marketing is ... a means to achieve the organization's goal. It is a tool—really a process and set of tools wrapped in a philosophy—for helping the organization do what it wants to do. Using marketing and being customer-oriented should never be thought of as goals: they are ways to achieve goals (Andreasen & Kotler, 2003)".

The conversation in Box 10.2 illustrates the distaste that many human service organization employees have for the concept of marketing human services. The caseworker in the scenario reflects a *product mindset* that assumes if you "build a better mousetrap, customers will beat a pathway to your door." The CEO, however, comes from a *sales mindset* that an organization must persuade customers to choose their services rather than those of a competitor (Andreasen & Kotler, 2003). In some ways, both the caseworker and the CEO are wrong in their approach.

BOX 10.2 Isn't It Enough to Provide Excellent Services?

The monthly all-staff meeting included an agenda item called "marketing our services." The CEO talked about the need to increase the number of client referrals to the agency and the need to become better known in the community. She called on everyone to be a marketer for the organization and gave examples of how everyone could play a part in marketing the organization's services.

A hand went up in the back of the room. One of the caseworkers asked, "Isn't it enough that we provide excellent service? People will come to us if we provide excellent services, right?"

"No," answered the CEO. "Sadly, we will go broke providing excellent services if we are unwilling to market our organization."

Providing excellent services is not enough to assure organizational success, but neither is persuading potential clients and referral sources to use the organization's services. Both the product mindset and the sales mindset come from an inward-looking focus. More modern approaches to marketing begin by looking at the outside, from the perspective of the *customer mindset*, which "systematically studies customers' needs, wants, perceptions, preferences, and satisfaction, using surveys, focus groups, and other means ... and constantly acts on this information to improve its offerings and to meet its customers' needs better" (Andreasen & Kotler, 2003). That is why we place marketing in Quadrant II, with both task and external orientations. Of course, a human services administrator must view marketing activities within the context of the mission and goals of the organization. It is important to understand not only the preferences of the clients, funders, and donors, but also how these preferences fit within the mission of the organization.

The 5 Ps of Nonprofit Marketing

Marketing has become recognized as an important component of human service agency functioning (Lauffer, 2009; Lewis, Packard, & Lewis, 2011) and, therefore, an important task for human service administrators. Hardcastle and Powers (2004) review the business literature on marketing and find several sources that refer to the "Ps" of marketing (Andreasen & Kotler, 2003; Fine, 1992; Winston, 1986). While there are several versions of the Ps of marketing, the most common four are *products*, *price*, *place*, and *promotion*. Lauffer (2009) adds a fifth P for *publics* to represent the stakeholders in human service organizations.

Products

Products may be tangible goods such as food, or services such as counseling or case management. The product may be an idea, such as gun control or social justice. Regardless of the product offered by the organization, the expectation is that there will be an exchange of resources from the consumer (or a third party) to the organization for it to have the capacity to offer the products, services, or ideas (Hardcastle & Powers, 2004). Often, the product that is promised to the funder or to the community is a change in the conditions in the community. For example, if the desired impact is a reduction in childhood obesity or a reduction in teenage pregnancy, then it is an important marketing strategy to be able to demonstrate that the products provided are effective in producing the desired change. This is one reason why program evaluation is a critical component of agency functioning (see Chapter 7).

Price

Price has to do with the cost of providing the services in comparison to other providers of similar services. The human services administrator must have knowledge of the fees of other organizations providing similar services and of the unit costs (see Chapter 8). There is also the question of the reasonableness of the price of providing services. As government agencies and third-party insurance payers seek out contractors, they seek to find the best services they can find at the lowest cost. Part of a marketing plan is to make the case that the services provided are quality services at a reasonable and competitive price. There are also nonmonetary or intrinsic components when considering "price," sometimes referred to as "social price." These are other things that your stakeholders may pay. For example, there may be a cost in time and emotional energy. The idea of social price is often expressed as "spending time;" "paying respect" or "we paid dearly" (Fine, 1992).

Place

What is the geographic location of the agency and what is the geographic area served? There are several issues related to "place." Government contracts are restricted to the area of their governmental jurisdiction. Similarly, many corporations are interested in supporting organizations in the area where they have their headquarters or where their consumers are located. For example, think about utility companies that will provide grants in the states where they provide services. In some cases, foundations, donors, or even government agencies will restrict their gifts to an area that they perceive as having the greatest need.

There is also a practical and political dimension to where the human service organization is located (see Box 10.3). Is the agency or branch located in an area that is convenient for the population that it seeks to serve? Is there public transportation available so that the services are accessible? Think about "place" as aligning the needs of the clients served and the resources that can be attracted based on the geographic location of the agency and geographic area served by the agency. Think about the possibilities that exist within that common space.

BOX 10.3 **Location, Location, Location**

The administrator of a human service organization was being interviewed on local TV about the agency's new office location. The reporter made the point that the new office building was located in a very affluent part of town, but that its mission was to serve poor people. When the reporter asked the administrator why that location was selected, he said, "Because most of our employees live in this area"—not a good marketing strategy.

Promotion

Promotion is the communication between the agency and its various publics. Promotion takes many forms. It is the agency newsletter, the website, the fundraising letters, and the funding proposals. It is public speaking, participation in community activities, special events, and TV interviews. Promotion is about building relationships—with board members, with donors, with funding sources, and with the community. In the last chapter, we talked about the concept of "friend-raising." It is the same concept in marketing. Promotion is the art and the tools of persuasive communications to interpret the mission of your organization to others and to gain their support of your efforts. Promotion is about motivation and inspiration. As a human services administrator, it is the power of your conviction for the services that you provide and your commitment to those you serve that will inspire others to join you in your life's work.

Publics

Lauffer (2009) adds publics as the fifth P of marketing to recognize the unique character of nonprofit organizations. This characteristic applies equally well to all human service organizations regardless of their sector. While businesses are concerned with the consumers of their products, human services have other stakeholders that must be considered. Many times, it is not the client who is paying for the services provided, but the services are paid for by a third party through a contract; or, in the case of nonprofit organizations, the services may be paid for through donated funds. Therefore, it is not only the client (consumer) that must be considered in a marketing plan but other stakeholders as well, such as donors, funders, volunteers, and the community at large.

Content Marketing

An emphasis on *content marketing* should be an important part of a human service organization's marketing plan. The American Marketing Association offers the following definition:

CONTENT MARKETING

According to the Association of National Advertisers (ANA), *content marketing* involves various methods to tell the brand story. More and more marketers are evolving their advertising to content marketing/storytelling to create more stickiness and emotional bonding with the consumer (Association of National Advertisers -ANA, n.d.).

Content marketing is telling the story of your organization in order to strengthen the bond with your organization's stakeholders. In content marketing, the goal is not to solicit an immediate response, such as donating or volunteering, but rather to inform your publics about the organization and build a stronger connection. Of course, you also want to offer these opportunities, but the main focus is to inform and connect. See Chapter 4 (Leadership) and Chapter 13 (Persuasion) to learn powerful techniques of storytelling that will help you craft your content for this part of your marketing plan. An important part of your story can be presenting the results of your program evaluation. Few things are as powerful as proven results. Elizabeth Chung (n.d.) offers the following "takeaways" for content marketing:

- Take advantage of your website traffic and use your homepage to capture emails
- Update your blog consistently to create a steady flow of traffic to your website and landing pages
- Segment your email lists to create targeted, meaningful messages for different pools of supporters that set your organization apart
- Include calls to action in your emails to keep readers engaged, whether they lead people to your blog or donation checkout pages
- Stick to a diligent newsletter schedule to keep your organization, its mission, and its need for support visible throughout the year
- Use visual storytelling in your email and social media channels to create emotional connections and compel supporters to take further action

Content marketing can be a powerful tool for your nonprofit. It plays a huge role in building lasting relationships. Next, we will consider the rapidly changing environment of marketing channels for your message.

Marketing Channels

An important decision to make is how you will deliver your message (promotion) to your intended target audience. Marketing in the digital age gets more complex every day. The Buzzly Media Blog (Philanthropegie, 2016) shares "The Big Six Channels" for nonprofits:

- **Websites.** A nonprofit organization must have a website that is easy to navigate and mobile-friendly. If your website is hard to look through, users will get frustrated and leave. And if your site is not mobile-friendly, you could be losing a lot of traffic.

- **Email.** A survey by Adobe (Naragon, 2015) finds that email is still a key component in personal communications and that even millennials are addicted to email, checking it more frequently than any other age group. Email is a great way to directly reach your followers, but beware of fatiguing them with too much of it.
- **Traditional social media.** Facebook, Twitter, LinkedIn, Pinterest, and Instagram are valuable tools to an organization seeking to increase its public awareness. These channels will help make your organization more visible and promote engagement with followers.
- **In-person events.** The best form of communication is telling others about causes you care about. Nonprofits cannot afford to eliminate events from their marketing strategy. Take opportunities to present at civic clubs, and be present at community events.
- **Print marketing.** Printed materials are still an important part of marketing. The response may be skewed toward older stakeholders, but remember from Chapter 9 (Fund Development and Grantwriting) that the average age of donors is 62 and that board chairs are likely to be over 40. Print is expensive, but used wisely, it can still be an important channel for marketing.

- **Media relations and public relations.** Media relations is the agency's interactions with editors, reporters, and journalist in the community. Many media outlets have lists of experts as their "go to" people when they need comments or an expert on a topic. As a social work administrator, you have a great deal of expertise and could be a resource. Websites such as Media Helper (www.helpareporter) are good places to make yourself available as a content expert. As an administrator, you will want to have clear policies concerning who on the staff is authorized to contact or respond to the media. There should be designated staff (including yourself) who can talk with the media. It is important to have an emergency communication plan in place in case there is a negative incident in the agency that requires a response to the media.

Market Segmentation

To develop an effective marketing plan for an organization, it is first necessary to identify the *target markets*. Because of the many "publics" of a human service organization, this can be a complex task. Think first about the clients served by your organization. If you serve only one very specific population, then the task of segmenting the client market should not be that difficult, but many

organizations provide multiple program services for a variety of populations. The first task, then, is to identify each of the segments of the client market.

Clients are not the only public that requires you to think about market segmentation. What are the demographics of your donor population? Do you think it might require a different approach for your donors under 30 years old as opposed to your donors over 60? Is there a difference in your donors who have donated to your organization for many years and those who have made their first gift? Will you approach them any differently? Segmentation is required unless you can determine that all the people in the target market are likely to respond in the same way (Hardcastle & Powers, 2004). The first task is to identify each category in your target market and then to further refine these categories into subsets, as appropriate.

Components of Nonprofit Marketing Plans

Marketing plans for nonprofit organizations should specify how the organization plans to reach each target audience groups identified in the segmentation exercise. Mary Gormandy White (2013) outlines the typical components of a nonprofit marketing plan, which includes the following elements for each target population:

1. **Mission and Goal Statement:** This portion of your marketing plan should express what it is that your organization hopes to accomplish for the clients you serve. Your mission and goal statement should clearly define the overall purpose of your organization. The marketing plan should tie specifically to accomplishing the mission and goal.
2. **Outcome Objectives:** Define specific, measurable outcome objectives for each target audience (see Chapter 7). What do you want the results to be of your marketing activities? How many clients do you want to serve in the coming year? What kinds of results do you expect to see with the organization's stakeholders? How much money do you need to raise this year? How many volunteer hours do you hope to log?
3. **Develop Strategies Through Process Objectives:** What steps can you take to accomplish your outcome objectives? For example, if you want to increase the number of clients served by 250 next year, what will you need to do to accomplish this result? If you want to attract 50 new major donors, what steps will you take to reach this outcome objective?
4. **Action Plan:** How will your organization go about implementing the defined marketing strategies identified in the process objectives? Who is responsible for each component of the plan? What is the timeline for each activity to be implemented? The action plan should be written in a manner that makes it easy to determine who is to do what by when.

5. **Budget:** How is the marketing plan built into the organization's budget? What resources will be allocated to the marketing plan?
6. **Monitoring:** How will you evaluate your progress and make any necessary adjustments to the plan? What is the system for evaluation of both outcome and process objectives? Who is responsible to see that reporting and review procedures are followed? How will progress be measured? (White, 2013)

Marketing and Fund Development

In many ways, marketing and fund development are inseparable. They both share the responsibility for communicating with constituents and building relationships. Claire Axelrad (2015) states that development and marketing have the same two basic decisions to make: (1) which products to offer and (2) which channels to message in. The right product must be offered in the right way to the right customer. If marketing and development are targeting the same constituents (and in most cases they are), yet each chooses a different product or channel, this may cause confusion. Development and marketing efforts must have coherence. Often, no one has authority, or too many people share authority, for presenting the organization to the community. As the administrator, you will be responsible to ensure that the organizational structure and lines of authority create a consistent and appropriate message to present in your marketing program.

The Nonprofit Marketing Manifesto

Some marketing professionals and scholars believe that traditional definitions of marketing do not capture the reality of the nonprofit sector, and many administrators do not place a high priority on the marketing functions of their organization. Some administrators view marketing as nothing more than a tool for building awareness and raising funds. We join others in calling for a new expanded definition and commitment to marketing in the nonprofit sector.

Alyssa Conrardy & Lindsay Mullen (2018), cofounders of Prosper Strategies, contend that "for far too long, the nonprofit sector has thought far too small when it comes to marketing" (para. 1). They propose a new definition of nonprofit marketing:

Definition: Nonprofit marketing [noun]

Nonprofit marketing comprises the activities, touchpoints and messages that motivate stakeholders to take actions that advance a nonprofit's mission and create sustainable social change (Conrardy & Mullen, 2018).

They contend that marketing is much more than a tool for fundraising and awareness building and that marketing can support every goal a nonprofit sets, from recruiting volunteers to building partnerships to diversifying revenue streams, and that when this happens, marketing becomes a tool for advancing the mission and driving social change. In presenting their new definition on nonprofit marketing, they have offered a "nonprofit marketing manifesto" and ask those who support their concept to make ten commitments in their approach to nonprofit marketing:

Commitment #1: We will recognize marketing as a tool for driving social change. We will acknowledge that when leveraged properly by nonprofits like ours, marketing is capable of changing the world.

Commitment #2: We will develop a strong brand image and identity in alignment with our mission and values. We will recognize that our brands are the keys that unlock our mission and values for our stakeholders, and we will treat them accordingly.

Commitment #3: We will build cohesion internally and communicate with consistency externally. We will recognize that to advance our mission we must build trust, and that to build trust, there must be consistency between how we see ourselves internally, how we act, and how we represent ourselves externally.

Commitment #4: We will treat all of our stakeholders as brand ambassadors. We will recognize that every person our organizations interact with has the potential to amplify our brands, our missions and our impact.

Commitment #5: We will develop a marketing plan that aligns with our strategic plan and recognize that marketing can impact every single one of our strategic goals. We will stop developing our marketing and communications plans in a vacuum, and instead make marketing planning an integral part of strategic planning.

Commitment #6: We will invest properly in marketing and view it as core mission support, not overhead. We will stop short-changing marketing in favor of other "more important" functions at our organizations.

Commitment #7: We will ensure marketing is overseen at the highest level of our organizations and contributed to by everyone on our teams. We will give marketing and communications a seat at the leadership table and a spot on the board meeting agenda.

Commitment #8: We will use our brands and marketing to build partnerships and advance the broader causes we're focused on. We realize we're not an island, and we behave accordingly.

Commitment #9: We will avoid, at all costs, sacrificing the dignity of those we serve for the sake of our marketing and communications goals. We recognize that our marketing efforts are not a success if they marginalize, stereotype, or otherwise disempower the people we serve, no matter how well they perform by other metrics.

Commitment #10: We will measure the impact of marketing on our missions and continually optimize our efforts to drive more social change. We are unwilling to accept the notion that it is impossible to measure the impact marketing makes on our missions. (Conrardy & Mullen, 2018, headings)

Ethical Issues for Marketing Human Services

Murphy and Bloom (1992) outline generic ethical problems for marketers. We borrow heavily from their work to consider ethical issues you may face in marketing human services:

1. Is it fair? Are you presenting the story of your agency in a fair and truthful way? Are your proven "results" based on solid research methods, and do you present the true picture or only those findings that support your message? Does the story you tell about your clients reflect the reality of their lives?

2. Is your message manipulative? If your childcare institution has millions of dollars in endowments, is it ok to have a fundraising appeal to ask donors to buy a pair of shoes for a child in care? Campaigns that play on pity or guilt are sometimes referred to as *starving baby appeals* (Fine, 1992). Administrators must be careful not to engage in promotions that put their clients in a negative light or present them as the objects of pity.

3. Does your marketing play favorites? Is your message directed only toward those who can help your organization financially? Do you put equal emphasis on making your service accessible to those most in need? If your services are fee based, do you target only those with the financial resources to pay your fee?

4. Is your marketing seen as wasteful? It is always a balancing act for the administrator to produce marketing materials that are attractive and "eye-catching" but not to appear wasteful. Those who support your organization do not want to see program money spent on "slick" publications. The move toward social media and electronic marketing will help to alleviate this dilemma, since printed materials are often the target of this criticism. Other marketing strategies may also be criticized as wasteful. For example, you may want to give a parting gift to members rotating off the board, but you do not want these tokens of appreciation to be viewed as a waste of money (even by the recipient).

5. Is your approach intrusive? Are you gathering more information on your "publics" than you need? How are you protecting the information you gather? How do you keep your publics informed without becoming annoying and intrusive by having too many contacts with them?

As a social work administrator, you have an obligation to be fair, truthful, and open in presenting your organization to the public. You are also obligated not to be manipulative, wasteful, or intrusive in your marketing program.

Conclusion

Human services administrators must be aggressive marketers of their organizations. The organization is in competition for clients, funding, volunteers, staff, and the overall support of the community. Marketing is not advertising or sale. It is understanding the needs of clients and other stakeholders. It is integral to achieving the mission of the organization and, as such, can be a strategy to bring about social change. Like all functions of administration, there is a need to be systematic and to have a well-developed plan for marketing the organization. Understanding the interplay of products, price, place, promotion, and publics are keys to marketing the organization and its services. A clear understanding of the organization's market share and the segmentation of that market guide the administrator toward a well-developed and effective marketing program for the organization.

Reference List

American Marketing Association (AMA). (2013). About AMA: definition of marketing. *AMA*. Retrieved from https://www.ama.org/the-definition-of-marketing/

Andreasen, A. R., & Kotler, P. (2003). *Strategic marketing for nonprofit organizations* (6th ed.). Upper Saddle River, NJ: Prentice Hall.

Association of National Advertisers. Retrieved from https://www.ana.net/

Axelrad, C. (2015, January 14). The shocking truth about marketing and development for nonprofits [Web log post]. Retrieved from https://trust.guidestar.org/blog/2015/01/14/the-shocking-truth-about-marketing-and-development-for-nonprofit/

Chung, E. (n. d). Content marketing 101 for the modern nonprofit [Web log post]. Retrieved from https://www.classy.org/blog/content-marketing-101-modern-nonprofit/

Conrardy, A., & Mullen, L. (2018). *The nonprofit marketing manifesto*. Retrieved from Prosper Strategies website: https://prosper-strategies.com/nonprofit-marketing-manifesto/

Fine, S. H. (1992). *Marketing the public sector: Promoting the causes of public and nonprofit agencies*. New Brunswick, NJ: Transaction.

Hardcastle, D. A., & Powers, P. R. (with Wenocur, S.). (2004). *Community practice: Theories and skills for social workers* (2nd ed.). New York, NY: Oxford University Press.

Lauffer, A. (2009). Confronting fundraising challenges. In R. Patti (Ed.), *The handbook of human services management* (2nd ed., pp. 351–372). Thousand Oaks, CA: Sage.

Lewis, J. A., Packard, T., & Lewis, M. D. (2011). *Management of human service programs* (5th ed.). Belmont, CA: Brooks/Cole.

Murphy, P. E., & Bloom, P. N. (1992). Ethical issues in social marketing. *Marketing, 12,* 68–78.

Naragon, K. (2015, August 26). Subject: Email, we just can't get enough [Web log post]. Retrieved from https://theblog.adobe.com/email/

Philanthropegie, (2016) *6 essential marketing channels for nonprofits.* Retrieved from https://www.philanthropegie.org/6-essential-marketing-channels-nonprofits/

White, M. G. (2013). Nonprofit marketing plans [Web blog post]. Retrieved from https://charity.lovetoknow.com/charitable-organizations/nonprofit-marketing-plans

Winston, W. J. (1986). Basic marketing principles for mental health professionals. *Journal of Marketing for Mental Health, 1*(1), 9–20.

Worth, M. J. (2009). *Nonprofit management: Principles and practice.* Thousand Oaks, CA: Sage.

Additional Resources

American Marketing Association Website (https://www.ama.org).

Common Language Marketing Dictionary (https://marketing-dictionary.org/m/marketing).

Media Helper (www.helpareporter.com).

Miller, K. L. (2016). Nonprofit communications trends report [infographic]. Retrieved from http://www.nonprofitmarketingguide.com/blog/2016/01/05/the-2016-nonprofit-communications-trends-report-infographic/

Obrien, A. (2014, September 19). Public relations vs. media relations. *Everything-PR*. Retrieved from https://everything-pr.com/public-relations-media-relations/52598/

Pallota, D. (2016). Advertising & marketing in nonprofit organizations [Video file]. Retrieved from https://www.youtube.com/watch?v=6aRUSjGjE9o

Santo, A. (2019, March 27). 20 books every marketer should read in 2019 [Web log post]. Retrieved from https://www.brafton.com/blog/content-marketing/20-books-every-marketer-should-read-in-2019/

HELPFUL TERMS

Content marketing—involves various methods to tell the brand story. More and more marketers are evolving their advertising to content marketing/storytelling to create more stickiness and emotional bonding with the consumer (Association of National Advertisers -ANA, ND).

Market segmentation—the process of identifying each category of the organization's target market and then further refining the categories into subsets, as appropriate. For example, the clients and subsets of clients, as well as donors divided into subsets such as age, interest, or motivation.

Marketing—a means to achieve the organization's goal. It is a tool—really a process and set of tools wrapped in a philosophy—for helping the organization do what it wants to do. Using marketing and being customer-oriented should never be thought of as goals: They are ways to achieve goals (Andreasen & Kotler, 2013).

Product mindset—assumes if you "build a better mousetrap, customers will beat a pathway to your door."

Sales mindset—assumes that an organization must persuade customers to choose their services rather than those of a competitor.

Customer mindset—"systematically studies customers' needs, wants, perceptions, preferences, and satisfaction, using surveys, focus groups, and other means ... and constantly acts on this information to improve its offerings and to meet its customers' needs better" (Andreasen & Kotler, 2013).

Ps of marketing—Several authors refer to the Ps of marketing as *products*, *price*, *place*, and *promotion*. Lauffer (2009) adds a fifth P for *publics* to represent the stakeholders in human service organizations.

EXERCISES

1. In-Basket Exercise

Directions

Review the following memo and write a response explaining your decision on this matter.

> **Memo**
>
> Date: May 16, 20XX
>
> To: Eva Gonzalez, Administrator Sheltering Arms
>
> From: Karen Lyda, Board Chair
>
> Subject: Marketing Plan and Segmentation
>
> I am looking forward to the board retreat next month to develop our much-needed marketing plan for Sheltering Arms. I know from the meeting with our marketing consultant that one of our tasks will be to identify our target markets and to do a market segment analysis. Frankly, I'm a little stuck in trying to think about how to approach this issue. It seems to me that our only market is the homeless population in our community. I want to be prepared for the meeting and to provide appropriate leadership, but I need your help in thinking this through. I understand that we are to break the major market groups into subgroups. Please prepare a list of those groups and subgroups that you think of as our "markets." Thanks for your help.

2. Isn't It Enough ...?

Assume that you are the administrator leading an all-staff meeting for Sheltering Arms, and the topic is how to market the organization and its services. If an employee says, "Isn't it enough that we provide excellent service? People will come to us if we provide excellent services, right?" How would you respond? With your small groups, develop a response based on the content of this chapter. You will read your response to the class and ask for their feedback.

3. The Five Ps

Review the section of this chapter on the 5 Ps. Working within your group, think of an agency with which you are familiar. Define each of the Ps for that organization and report your work to the class.

4. Distaste for Marketing

This chapter starts with a statement that many human service organization employees have a distaste for the concepts of marketing human services. Do you think this is true? If so, why do you think it is true? If not, why not? Discuss this issue in your small group.

ASSIGNMENTS

1. *International Journal of Nonprofit and Voluntary Sector Marketing* provides an international forum for peer-reviewed papers and case studies on the latest techniques, thinking, and best practices in marketing for the not-for-profit sector. Find an article written in the journal within the past three years and write a two-page summary and review of the article.

2. Write a five-page executive summary of a marketing plan for a nonprofit organization. Cover each of the six components of a marketing plan as outlined in this chapter in the section on "Components of Nonprofit Marketing Plans."

3. You have been asked to be on a panel discussion concerning marketing of human service organizations. You are to make a five-minute introductory statement of the use of social media in marketing. Research this topic and write a two-page statement to be included in the handout materials for the panel presentation.

Image Credits

Skills

Quadrant III: Internal and People Orientation

Quadrant III is where the internal and people orientations meet. In this area, we acknowledge that tasks are completed by people and that the human side of the organization is as important as "getting things done." The danger of Quadrants I and II, with their task orientation, is that completing tasks can take precedence over the people doing the work. The potential danger of Quadrant III is that we focus so much on the people involved in the processes of running the organization that not much is accomplished. Fortunately, we are not stuck with an either/or situation. As noted before, the truly competent social work leader has skills in all areas and can switch from one to another as needed. The two chapters in this part of the book examine in detail Human Resources (HR) functions (Chapter 11) and working with the Board of Directors (Chapter 12).

For agency leaders, the HR aspects of the job can be challenging. It is not easy to know and follow all the laws and employment regulations about hiring, firing, and equal treatment of employees, or to ensure that the required information percolates throughout the organization. After all, it is not only your actions that can be the basis of low morale or even lawsuits, but the actions of everyone. Inappropriate sexual behavior and harassment is just one "equal-opportunity" career killer if it happens while you are in charge. Others include wrongful hiring and firing, financial improprieties, and other unethical behaviors. This material provides you a good starting point for your leadership roles in HR areas.

If working with your employees can be a minefield, working with the Board of Directors can be challenging as well. If you are not the top leader in the organization, it is likely that your interaction with board members will be limited, but that does not mean you can afford to be ignorant of their existence and their potential power to "shake things up." The board should be in control of the strategic direction of the organization, which of course affects everyone connected with the agency. Shifts in direction or desires to serve particular clientele can lead to resignations of key members of the leadership team. This can, in turn, lead to an exodus of talented employees at all levels. Our experience in working with students has been that boards are one of the most mysterious aspects of working in a nonprofit. Every nonprofit has a board, but they are seldom seen and even less frequently understood. As you move through your career, the closer you are to the executive director's chair, the more you will want to comprehend boards and how to work with them for the good of the agency and clients.

Human Resources and Supervision

Productive employees are truly the heart of any human service organization. One of the major functions of a human services administrator is to recruit, hire, and train productive employees. One of the less pleasant tasks of an administrator is to deal with unproductive employees through processes of discipline and termination. This is a difficult but necessary administrative function. Hiring and firing are tools that human services administrators use to either maintain existing norms in the organization or to change them (Wiener, 1988). Agency administrators often say that the most challenging part of their jobs is dealing with employee issues. As an administrator, you will be challenged not to get bogged down in staff issues that will take you away from the mission of your organization.

How do you find the right people for the jobs you have to fill? Remember that every vacancy that occurs is an opportunity for you to assess the vacated position and, if warranted, to restructure or reorganize in some fashion. Staff openings provide opportunities to bring in new perspectives, new energy, and diversity to the organization. You may want to look close to home to fill the vacancy. Are there people in the organization who would like to move up or to take on a different challenge? One of the advantages (and sometimes disadvantages) of this approach is that you and the employee know each other. You know their strengths and weaknesses, and they know the reality of working for the organization. If it's a good fit, then this kind of arrangement can strengthen the organization. This chapter will cover the essential functions of human resources management, including: talent acquisition, total rewards (compensation and benefits), learning and

BOX 11.1 EPAS Competencies Covered

The information in this chapter is directly connected to CSWE's Competency 2: Engage Diversity and Differences in Practice and Competency 7: Assess Individuals, Families, Groups, Organizations, and Communities.

development, performance management, and employment law. In addition to these elements, we will examine the issue of staff supervision. In many large organizations, there is a human resources department that has responsibility for the HR functions discussed in this chapter. More often, however, if you work in a small to medium-sized organization, these responsibilities will fall to you and your management team. Supervision is not a function of human resources departments, but for our purposes, we will consider supervision as a part of the human resources function. Being knowledgeable and competent in each of these areas is important to your success as an administrator. Making your organization an inclusive, challenging, and positive place to work will be the central theme throughout this chapter.

Hiring and Recruitment (Talent Acquisition)

Human services administrators must have the skills for hiring and recruiting new employees. The ability to identify, recruit, and hire high-performing employees is essential for the long-term success

of the human service agency. Your task as a human services administrator is to find the best people you can find to work in your organization. You can only achieve this task by making the organization an inclusive, challenging, and positive place to work. Your goal is for potential employees to *want* to work at your organization, and you want to retain the valuable employees you have. What are the elements that make an organization an inclusive, challenging, and positive place to work?

Montana and Charnov (1993) identified 25 factors that motivate employees and then examined a number of studies to determine perceptions about motivation and how these perceptions compared to the 25 factors. From this analysis, they identified the following nine factors as the most important motivating factors:

1. Respect for me as a person
2. Good pay
3. Chance to turn out quality work
4. Chance for promotion
5. Opportunity to do interesting work
6. Feeling my job is important
7. Being told when I do a good job
8. Opportunity for self-development
9. Large amount of freedom on the job (Montana & Charnov, 1993).

These nine factors represent the *perception* that employees have of what motivates them in their workplace. Psychological climate describes an employee's perception of the psychological impact of the work environment on her or his well-being. When employees in an organization agree in their positive perception of their work environment, their shared perceptions can then be said to form the organization's *climate* (Jones & James, 1979; Glisson, 2000; Glisson & Hemmelgarn, 1998). The organizational culture is the shared values, beliefs, and behavioral norms in an organization (Ouchi, 1981). The norms and values of the organization that influence the behavior of service provider employees create a social and psychological context that shapes tone, content, and objectives of the services provided (O'Reilly & Chatman, 1996). The organizational climate has a direct impact on how well the clients of the organization are served.

Are these nine factors important for you as you decide where you want to work? If they are important to you, then it makes sense that these are the same things that will be important to the people you hire and the people you wish to keep working for your organization.

Diversity and Inclusion in the Workplace

Having a diverse workforce is essential for the health and well-being of a human service organization. Diversity is not something that the human services administrator needs to "handle" or "manage" but rather is something that needs to be developed, celebrated, and cherished. The staffing

of the organization should, at a minimum, reflect the demographics of the community served by the organization. When clients come to the organization for services, they need to see people that look like them and that speak their preferred language. Diversity should be one of the "guiding principles" of a nonprofit organization (see Chapter 6). Mor Barak (as cited in Golensky, 2011) calls for an expanded definition of diversity that recognizes both the observable or readily detectable attributes, such as race, gender, or age, and less visible or invisible attributes, such as religion, education, tenure with the organization, or sexual orientation.

As we have come to understand the benefits of diversity in organizations, the study of diversity in organizations has shifted from diversity management to inclusion (Brimhall & Mor Barak, 2018). Diversity refers to the composition of differences among individuals in an organization (Homan & Greer, 2013), while inclusion refers to the extent to which employees feel valued, have a sense of belonging, and feel comfortable being their "true selves" within their work setting (Brimhall & Mor Barak, 2018; Mor Barak, 2015).

Recruiting staff, training, and mentoring are management activities used to develop a diverse staff (Roberson, 2006), and *inclusion management* refers to the extent to which an organization creates policies and practices that encourage employees to fully participate in the life of the organization (Mor Barak, 2015). A climate for inclusion exists when each member feels valued and appreciated as an important member of the organization (Mor Barak et al., 2016).

Leaders determine the climate of an organization by modeling their cultural perspective. The ability to model an inclusive cultural perspective and to articulate a value stance is a critical component of organization leadership. As a leader, your cultural awareness, cultural acceptance, accountability, and incorporation of staff differences will be on full display (Mustafa & Lines, 2013). In the *Specialized Practice Curricular Guide for Macro Social Work Practice* (CSWE 2018) the competency behaviors required to be an effective administrator are outlined as follows:

- formulate inclusive engagement strategies based on an intersectional analysis of systems of power, privilege, and oppression, both within and outside organizational, community, and policy contexts, including the political economy and, for example, areas of racism, sexism, and nativism
- demonstrate fluency in a variety of communication styles to effectively engage and work with people of different political ideologies, interests, religious and cultural backgrounds, and points of view
- engage with diverse stakeholders in promoting a deep self-awareness and cultural humility, with an understanding of how one's own personal biases, power, and privilege affect the engagement process and all aspects of macro practice
- create a climate of inclusion that builds on the strengths of diverse constituencies, integrates diverse points of view, and facilitates full engagement in ways that embrace the cultural and spiritual histories of people
- recognize the complexities and contradictions that may arise in adhering to the Universal Declaration of Human Rights while respecting cultural differences of clients and constituencies
- provide opportunities for open discussion about issues to promote sensitivity and use conflicts that arise in practice to forge new understanding and appreciation of one another
- develop leadership and staff teams in management, policy, and community practice that reflect the diversity of the communities in which they work
- mediate tensions and conflicts that arise from managing cultural, political, and social differences between and within diverse groups (Council on Social Work Education, 2018)

Compensation and Benefits (Total Rewards)

Human services administrators are responsible for the management of compensation and benefit plans. Pay and benefits are two critical factors that will determine how employees and potential employees feel about the organization. Administering an effective compensation system and determining the best benefits package for all of the agency employees are

vital administrative skills. The perception by employees that there is unfairness in the system has proved to be a powerful disincentive to optimum performance. Montana and Charnov (1993) say perceptions of fairness and equity are affected by two factors: (1) comparison of pay received to such factors as effort, job performance, education, experience, skill, and seniority and (2) comparison of the perceived equity of pay and rewards received to those received by other people. Money is not the primary reason one chooses to enter the field of social work, but Schweitzer, Chianello, and Kothari, (2013) find that compensation is still an important factor in predicting satisfaction once on the job.

As an administrator, it is important for you to have an understanding of the demographics related to the workforce in human services. Eighty-three percent of social workers are female, and women are likely to continue to dominate the profession, because 86% of the MSW graduates in 2015 were also female. According to McPhail (2004), social work is a female-majority profession, but it should be considered male-dominated, as men hold the majority of the positions of power and authority in the profession. A study by Lane and Flowers (2015) examined empirical evidence about salary and gender within the social work profession from the 1960s to present day. Almost every study of social workers in practice and social work faculty from the 1960s until the time of the 2015 study found salary disparities between men and women. Contributing factors from these studies were divided into three categories: (a) characteristics of the employing organizations, (b) characteristics of the position held, and (c) characteristics of the individual.

In terms of the settings, the greatest concentration of social workers (36.6%) is found in individual and family services, followed by 11.4% in administration of human resources programs, 10.6% in hospitals, and 8.3% in outpatient care centers. Federal, state, and local governments employ 41% of social workers. Private, nonprofit, or charitable organizations are the employers of 34.3% of all social workers. Private, for-profit companies and businesses employ 22.3% of social workers, leaving just 2.4% self-employed or working in a family business (Salsberg et al., 2017).

Compensation

There is considerable variation in compensation by type of education and setting. For individuals with a masters degree or higher, the highest median incomes are in national security and international affairs ($69,000), elementary and secondary education ($60,000), executive offices and legislative bodies ($57,500), insurance carriers ($57,000), hospitals ($56,000), and other health care settings ($56,000). The average salary in individual and family services, the largest single setting where MSWs work (31%), was $45,000 (Salsberg et al., 2017).

One of the underappreciated costs in administering a human service organization is the cost related to staff turnover. Staff turnover rates in mental health and human service organizations have been reported to range from 25% to 50% annually (Bliss, Gillespie, & Gongaware, 2010). A study by The Society for Human Resource Management (SHRM) predicts that every time a business replaces a salaried employee, it costs 6 to 9 months' salary, on average (Agovino, 2019), most of which is in "soft" costs such as reduced productivity, interview time, and lost knowledge (Work Institute, 2018; see Figure 11.1). Hard costs of staff turnover include the cost of employees involved in the recruiting and hiring process (other than interviewing), background checks, drug screenings, and temp workers (if used), among other expenses.

67%	33%
Soft Costs	**Hard Costs**
Such as reduced productivity, interview time and lost knowledge.	Such as recruiting, background checks, drug screens and temp workers.

FIGURE 11.1. Distribution of Costs of Staff Turnover

The demand for social workers has increased over the past 30 years and is expected to continue for the foreseeable future, but compensation has not significantly improved (Barth, 2003). The social work code of ethics requires social workers, including social work administrators, to "pursue social change ... primarily on issues of poverty, unemployment, discrimination, and other forms of social injustice" (National Association of Social Workers, 2017). As an administrator, you have an obligation to ensure that organizational practices are ethical, including practices that affect salary equity, such as hiring, promotion, and salary negotiation. Ethical issues can arise at both ends of the salary spectrum (Grobman, 2011). Does the organization pay a living wage to those at the lower end of the salary scale? Is the compensation just? Does the compensation live up to the social justice standards that the organization professes to promote? What about the salaries that will be paid to you and other top administrators? Are the salaries of the top administrators excessive, or are they fair based on the required skills, experience and education, along with the size and complexity of the organization? Human services administrators should be well paid, but compensation should not be excessive. Administrators must be mindful of being good stewards of money that comes to the agency, whether it comes from tax payers, donors, insurance companies, or clients.

Benefits

In addition to the base compensation, there are issues and financial considerations related to indirect compensation that employers are required to provide and the benefits they may want to provide in order to be competitive in recruiting talented people and providing compensation based on ideals of fairness and equity. In budgeting, it is common for benefits to be 25–30% or more of the compensation package for employees. Indirect compensation includes the following:

- Social Security—Employers are required to cover employees under a comprehensive program of retirement, survivor, disability, and health benefits (OASDHI).
- Workers' Compensation Laws—These require that employers finance a variety of benefits such as lost wages, medical benefits, survivor benefits, and rehabilitation services for employees with work-related illnesses or injuries.
- Federal Unemployment Tax—Employers must pay taxes to cover laid-off employees for up to 39 weeks, with additional extensions possible.
- Family Medical Leave Act of 1993—This requires employers to continue providing health care coverage to employees who are on leave for up to 12 weeks per year for a specified family emergency.

Optional employee benefits are those benefits that many employers choose to offer their employees that are not mandatory. Such benefits include health care insurance, disability insurance, life insurance, retirement plans, flexible compensation, and paid leave (vacation, sick leave, etc.). While these benefits are legally optional, in reality, most of these are considered the basic benefits expected by potential employees. With the passage of the Affordable Care Act, more employers have been required to provide health care insurance for their employees. For many employers, providing health care will not be an option but rather a required part of employment compensation.

Learning and Development

Training programs that improve employee performance and minimize performance problems can be a valuable asset for an organization. Well-designed and well-presented training can produce tangible results. Providing consistent employee feedback is necessary to meet the goal of continuous quality improvement in the organization. Van Wart (1998) suggests a seven-step organizational needs analysis as a means of determining the greatest need for training and development.

These seven elements are as follows:

1. Ethics assessments or audits to look for gaps between stated values and organizational performance.
2. Examining the organization's values, vision, mission, and planning statements to identify possible gaps in the needs.
3. Customer and citizen assessments to find emerging needs.
4. Employee assessments to reveal employee opinions and values.
5. Performance assessments to identify gaps between stated and actual performance.
6. Benchmarking to examine best practices (evidence based practices) elsewhere and using them as standards.
7. Quality assessment reviews.

After conducting the needs analysis using the elements above, the human services administrators and other appropriate top administrators will design the training program for the organization. The complexity and comprehensiveness of the training plan will depend on the size of the budget and the size of the organization. When budgets are tight, training and staff development are often the first place that administrators look to make budget cuts. While this approach is tempting, it can be very damaging to the organization. The following guidelines are presented by the World Health Organization (2005) and outline 10 steps for the development of a training program:

1. Define the target population for training.
2. List the tasks to be performed by the target population on the job.
3. List the skills and knowledge needed to do the tasks.
4. Select the skills and knowledge to be taught (these are the training objectives).
5. Organize the selected skills and knowledge into suitable teaching units (modules) and develop the training design, including brief outlines of modules content and planned training methods.
6. Draft expanded outlines of modules, including instructional objectives, main body of text, and descriptions of training methods, examples, and exercises.
7. Have experts provide realistic examples and information for use in exercises.
8. Draft the complete modules, facilitator guidelines, and course director guidelines.
9. Field-test the training materials.
10. Revise and finalize training material based on the field test (p. 3).

While training is most often the "in-house" method for improving staff functioning of specific tasks and functions within the organization, *professional development* is more typically offered by providers external to the organization (Gibelman & Furman, 2008). Providers may include universities or commercial and professional associations offering programs to help update professional skills. Professional development activities are a method thought to be beneficial to employee morale, productivity, and longevity on the job. Supporting employees to attend or present at their professional conferences is an example of professional development. Many employees who hold professional licenses or certifications will have annual requirements for continuing education credits (CEUs). Budgeting for conference tuition, allowing associated travel, and granting time away from work are ways to support employees in their professional development activities.

Many universities provide continuing education opportunities and professional development opportunities that can be invaluable to human services administrators in meeting their obligations for providing training and development activities for their organization and for themselves.

Performance Management

Many employees do not look forward to the dreaded "annual review." Even if the employee is confident she or he is doing a good job, there is something unpleasant about being put under the microscope. Part of it may be that it reminds someone that there is a power differential between the employee and supervisor, or it may raise old issues of being unfairly evaluated by others in the

past. The other side of the equation is that many people who do the annual evaluation don't like doing them any more than the employees like being subjected to them. However unpleasant, performance management is an important component of human services administration (Weinbach & Taylor, 2011). The ability to effectively manage the performance of employees is a major responsibility of human services managers, and establishing and implementing a complete performance improvement process is an essential skill. Designing your performance review process, maintaining it, and effectively monitoring its implementation are challenging tasks.

The purpose of employee appraisal is to determine to what extent employees are achieving the requirements of their jobs. For the evaluation to be effective, it must be based on realistic and measurable criteria that are clear, realistic, and achievable (Kadushin & Harkness, 2002; Pecora & Wagner, 2000). In regard to the use of performance assessments, the Council on Accreditation (2013) states:

> The performance review process assesses job performance, recognizes accomplishments, provides constructive feedback, and emphasizes self-development and professional growth, in relation to:
>
> a.   specific expectations defined in the job description;
> b.   organization-wide expectations for personnel;

   c. objectives established in the most recent review, accomplishments and challenges since the last review period, and objectives for future performance;

   d. developmental and professional objectives;

   e. recommendations for further training, skill building, and other resources that may contribute to improved job performance; and

   f. knowledge and competence related to the characteristics and needs of service recipients, if applicable. (para. 6.02)

Ideally, the performance evaluation allows you to tell employees that they are doing a great job and to support them in their work. From the strengths-based perspective, you want to highlight and build on the positive contributions being made by the organization's employees. Unfortunately, it will sometimes be your responsibility as a human services administrator to take corrective action because of the behavior of an employee or because he or she is not fulfilling the requirements of the job. This is a part of the job responsibility that you accept when you become a human services administrator, and, like with other skills, you must be able to perform the required function. Brody (2013) outlines several steps necessary when taking corrective action with an employee. First, you will need to document specific, concrete behaviors that reflect the unacceptable work performance or behavior. Once these have been well documented, you will need to discuss the unacceptable behavior as soon as possible after it occurs. This discussion should be conducted in private. The focus of the discussion is on changing behavior and is not about personalities or issues unrelated to the workplace. You should provide the employee with explicit expectations for behavior and performance. If the problem continues, you would begin a series of corrective actions, starting with a verbal warning. If there is not improvement, the next step is to issue a written warning indicating that if the employee does not correct the problem, it will result in suspension or termination. If the problem continues, follow through with the stated consequence of suspension or termination.

The effective human services administrator must have a working knowledge of the many laws that govern the administration of employee relationships. From the time you begin to recruit employees until the time employees leave the agency, there are laws and regulations that must be taken into account. Human services administrators need to know when they may need to consult an attorney or human resources professional. The best protection for you and your organization is to have clear policies that are followed consistently. The annual review process should be taken seriously. If there are performance problems but they are not documented in the review process, this can become a major problem for you and the organization. There is always the possibility of employment complaints or lawsuits related to employment practices. The way to minimize this risk is by operating fairly and communicating openly and candidly. Documentation is key in employment issues. Your motto should be, "Document, document, and document!"

Employment Laws

To be an effective administrator in the area of personnel management, you must have a basic understanding of employment law. Below are several of the major federal laws that govern employment practices and prohibit job discrimination. Review the applicable employment laws at the U.S. Equal Employment Opportunity Commission (EEOC) website (https://www.eeoc.gov/laws/statutes/index.cfm).

Title VII of the Civil Rights Act of 1964

This law makes it illegal to discriminate against someone on the basis of race, color, religion, national origin, or sex. The law also makes it illegal to retaliate against a person because the person complained about discrimination, filed a charge of discrimination, or participated in an employment discrimination investigation or lawsuit. The law also requires that employers reasonably accommodate applicants' and employees' sincerely held religious practices, unless doing so would impose an undue hardship on the operation of the employer's business.

Title VII of the Civil Rights Act does not speak directly to the issue of harassment. However, the Supreme Court recognized harassment as a form of discrimination in the 1986 decision of Meritor Savings Bank v. Vinson. This decision defined harassment as severe or pervasive conduct so offensive as to alter the terms or conditions of the plaintiff's employment. The Meritor case was about sexual harassment, but its ruling applied to harassment on the basis of other protected categories under Title VII, citing a lower court ruling recognizing harassment on the basis of race (Tippett, 2018).

The Pregnancy Discrimination Act

This law amended Title VII to make it illegal to discriminate against a woman because of pregnancy, childbirth, or a medical condition related to pregnancy or childbirth. The law also makes it illegal to retaliate against a person because the person complained about discrimination, filed a charge of discrimination, or participated in an employment discrimination investigation or lawsuit.

The Equal Pay Act of 1963 (EPA)

This law makes it illegal to pay different wages to men and women if they perform equal work in the same workplace. The law also makes it illegal to retaliate against a person because the person complained about discrimination, filed a charge of discrimination, or participated in an employment discrimination investigation or lawsuit.

The Age Discrimination in Employment Act of 1967 (ADEA)

This law protects people who are 40 or older from discrimination because of age. The law also makes it illegal to retaliate against a person because the person complained about discrimination, filed a charge of discrimination, or participated in an employment discrimination investigation or lawsuit.

Title I of the Americans with Disabilities Act of 1990 (ADA)

This law makes it illegal to discriminate against a qualified person with a disability in the private sector and in state and local governments. The law also makes it illegal to retaliate against a person because the person complained about discrimination, filed a charge of discrimination, or participated in an employment discrimination investigation or lawsuit.

The law also requires that employers reasonably accommodate the known physical or mental limitations of an otherwise qualified individual with a disability who is an applicant or employee, unless doing so would impose an undue hardship on the operation of the employer's business.

Sections 102 and 103 of the Civil Rights Act of 1991

Among other things, this law amends Title VII and the ADA to permit jury trials and compensatory and punitive damage awards in intentional discrimination cases.

Sections 501 and 505 of the Rehabilitation Act of 1973

This law makes it illegal to discriminate against a qualified person with a disability in the federal government. The law also makes it illegal to retaliate against a person because the person complained about discrimination, filed a charge of discrimination, or participated in an employment discrimination investigation or lawsuit.

The law also requires that employers reasonably accommodate the known physical or mental limitations of an otherwise qualified individual with a disability who is an applicant or employee, unless doing so would impose an undue hardship on the operation of the employer's business.

EEOC Enforcement

The EEOC enforces all of these laws and also provides oversight and coordination of all federal equal employment opportunity regulations, practices, and policies. Once you have a basic understanding of the law, you are in a better position to be sure that you do not discriminate in the interview process. Employment laws change over time, and it is not likely that you will become an expert in employment law. However, as a social work leader, you should be committed to value and promote diversity in the workplace and to strive for social justice in your employment practices. As a human services administrator, you should be committed to the spirit of the nondiscrimination laws and, therefore, committed to fairness and nondiscrimination in the workplace. Sometimes, this is not as easy as it sounds. Consider the following scenario:

A human services administrator was interviewing a candidate for the position of vice president for finance in the human services agency. Since this person would have a great deal of interface with the Board of Trustees, the administrator asked the board chair to join in an interview of the candidate. The interview was going well until the board chair asked the candidate, "By the way, Mr. X, how old are you?" Mr. X paused for a moment and then said, "Well, I've been around for a while." Not to be deterred, the board chair said, "No, really—how old are you?" More reluctantly, Mr. X said, "I'm 62." Fortunately, Mr. X was a great candidate and was hired for the job. However, if he had not been hired, the board chairman had given Mr. X a great opportunity to file a complaint against the agency based on age discrimination.

In conducting a job interview, you should focus only on what is essential to the job. In the example above, Mr. X's age had nothing to do with the essential job functions of the position. You should think through the way that you will ask questions in an interview. You cannot ask applicants about their child care arrangements or even if they have children. You can, however, legitimately ask if the candidate is available for working nights and weekends if those hours are a requirement of the job. In conducting an interview and in your hiring decisions, you must avoid discrimination based on race, gender, age, place of origin, sexual orientation, and disability.

Supervision

As an administrator, you have an ethical obligation to seek supervision of your own practice. In Chapter 2, we discussed the elements of supervision as they apply to the administrator of an organization. Go back to Chapter 2 and review this material and think of how it applies to you as a supervisor and the expectations you have of those in the organization who supervise others. In this context we will use the traditional definition of social work supervision as

> the relationship between supervisor and supervisee in which the responsibility and accountability for the development of competence, demeanor, and ethical practice take place. The supervisor is responsible for providing direction to the supervisee, who applies social work theory, standardized knowledge, skills, competency, and applicable ethical content in the practice setting. (National Association of Social Workers & Association of Social Work Boards, 2013)

Supervision of staff and volunteers is critical at all levels of the organization. In all but very small nonprofit organizations, the human services administrator will provide supervision of the executive team or the heads of the major components of the organization. Supervision tasks generally fall into three categories: administrative, educational, and supportive functions (Kadushi & Harkness, 2002). Administrative tasks include assigning employees to work units and developing procedures to increase productivity. The responsibility to complete performance evaluations and make recommendations for compensation, promotion, or discipline falls within the realm of administrative supervision. The educational tasks are teaching, orienting new employees, modeling professional behaviors, and helping employees access needed information. Supportive activities include providing emotional support, motivating, empowering, and mediating disputes (Kadushi & Harkness, 2002; Lauffer, 2011).

Variations on how to conduct supervision exist. One approach from a social work perspective is provided by Lewis, Packard, and Lewis (2011). It consists of six elements, which are not necessarily sequential; rather, an excellent supervisor will ensure that all six occur with their staff members on a regular and frequent basis:

1. Providing encouragement and support for the supervisee
2. Building motivation
3. Increasing the mutuality of individual and organizational goals
4. Enhancing the supervisee's competence in service delivery
5. Carrying out ongoing assessments on the supervisee's success in fulfilling his or her responsibilities
6. Providing prompt and objective feedback designed to enhance the supervisee's professional development

You must conduct all of these functions within the context of ethical practice. If our profession claims to stand for social justice and inclusion, we have an obligation to be ethical and culturally competent in our administrative practice. Lusk, Terrazas, and Salcido (2017) state that

> critical culturally competent supervision requires a keen understanding of the culture of the worker, a respect and appreciation for each supervisee's particular set of values, cultural humility, and an engaged social work practice that battles oppression, discrimination, and domination. But culturally competent leadership is also based on skills—learned aptitudes that are manifested in each communication and interaction with members of a diverse social work workforce. (p. 467)

Conclusion

This chapter has presented a brief overview of human resource management—one of the most challenging responsibilities of a human services administrator. We have discussed topics of hiring, employment law, compensation, training and development, performance management, supervision, and diversity. Human resources management can be one of the most difficult tasks of the administrator but can also be one of the greatest joys. To find employees who share your passion for the services you provide and see people grow and develop in their professional career is a rare opportunity.

Reference List

Agovino, T. (2019). *To have and to hold*. Retrieved from Society for Human Resource Management (SHRM) website: https://www.shrm.org/hr-today/news/all-things-work/pages/to-have-and-to-hold.aspx

Barth, M. C. (2003). Social work labor market: A first look. *Social Work, 48*(1), 9–19.

Brimhall, K. C., & Mor Barak, M. E. (2018). The critical role of workplace inclusion in fostering innovation, job satisfaction, and quality of care in a diverse human service organization. *Human Service Organizations: Management, Leadership & Governance, 42*(5), 474–492.

Brody, R. (2013). *Effectively managing and leading human service organizations* (4th ed.). Thousand Oaks, CA: Sage.

Council on Accreditation. (2013). *PA-HR 6:* Performance review. Retrieved from http://www.coanet.org/standard/pa-hr/6

Council on Social Work Education. (2018*). Specialized practice curricular guide for macro social work practice: 2015 EPAS curricular guide resource series.* Alexandria, VA: CSWE.

Gibelman, M., & Furman, R. (2008). *Navigating human service organizations* (2nd ed.). Chicago, IL: Lyceum Books.

Glisson, C. (2000). Organizational climate and culture. In R. Patti (Ed.), *The handbook of social welfare management* (pp. 195–218). Thousand Oaks, CA: Sage.

Glisson, C., & Hemmelgarn, A. (1998). The effects of organizational climate and interoganizational coordination on the quality and outcomes of children's service systems. *Child Abuse and Neglect, 22*(5), 401–421.

Golensky, M. (2011). *Strategic leadership and management in nonprofit organizations: Theory and practice.* Chicago, IL: Lyceum Books.

Grobman, G. M. (2011). *An introduction to the nonprofit sector: A practical approach for the 21st century* (3rd ed.). Harrisburg, PA: White Hat Communications.

Homan, A. C., & Greer, L. L. (2013). Considering diversity: The positive effects of considerate leadership in diverse teams. *Group Processes & Intergroup Relations, 16(1)*, 105–125.

Jones, A. P., & James, L. R. (with J. R. Bruni, C. W. Hornick, & S. B. Sells). (1979). Psychological climate: Dimensions and relationships of individual and aggregated work environment perceptions. *Organizational Behavior and Human Performance, 23(2)*, 201–250.

Kadushin, A., & Harkness, D. (2002). *Supervision in social work* (4th ed.). New York, NY: Columbia University Press.

Lane, S., & Flowers, T. (2015). Salary inequity in social work: A review of the knowledge and call to action. *Journal of Women and Social Work, 30*(3) 363–379.

Lauffer, A. (2011). *Understanding your social agency* (3rd ed.). Thousand Oaks, CA: Sage.

Lewis, J. A., Packard, T., & Lewis, M. D. (2011). *Management of human service programs* (5th ed.). Belmont, CA: Brooks/Cole.

Lusk M., Terrazas, S., & Salcido, R., (2017). Critical cultural competence in social work supervision. *Human Service Organizations: Management, Leadership & Governance, 41*(5), 464–476.

McPhail, B. A. (2004). Setting the record straight: Social work is not a female-dominated profession. *Social Work, 49(2)*, 323–326.

Meritor Sav. Bank v. Vinson, 477 U.S. 57, 66. (1986).

Montana, P. J., & Charnov, B. H. (1993). *Management.* Hauppauge, NY: Barrons Business Review Series.

Mor Barak, M. E. (2015). Inclusion is the key to diversity management, but what is inclusion? *Human Service Organizations: Management, Leadership & Governance, 39(2)*, 83–88.

Mor Barak, M. E., Lizano, E. L., Kim, A., Duan, L., Rhee, M. K., Hsiao, H. Y., & Brimhall, K. C. (2016). The promise of diversity management for climate of inclusion: A state-of-the-art review and meta-analysis. *Human Service Organizations: Management, Leadership & Governance, 40*(4), 305–333.

Mustafa, G., & Lines, R. (2013). The triple role of values in culturally adapted leadership styles. *International Journal of Cross Cultural Management, 13*(1), 23–46.

National Association of Social Workers. (2017*). Code of ethics of the National Association of Social Workers.* Washington, DC: Author.

National Association of Social Workers, & Association of Social Work Boards. (2013*). Best practice standards in social work supervision.* Washington, DC: NASW & ASWB.

O'Reilly, C. F., & Chatman, J. A. (1996). Culture as social control: Corporations, cults, and commitment. *Research in Organizational Behavior, 18,* 157–200.

Ouchi, W. G. (1981). *Theory Z.* Reading, MA: Addison-Wesley.

Pecora, P. J., & Wagner, M. (2000). Managing personnel. Handbook of Social Welfare Administration. Newbury Park, Calif.: Sage.

Roberson, Q. M. (2006). Disentangling the meanings of diversity and inclusion in organizations. *Group & Organization Management, 31*(2), 212–236.

Salsberg, E., Quigley, L., Mehfoud, N.,Acquaviva, K., Wyche, K., & Sliwa S. (2017). *Profile of Social Work Workforce. Washington, DC:* The George Washington University Health Workforce Institute and School of Nursing.

Schweitzer, D., Chianello, T., & Kothari, B. (2013). Compensation in social work: Critical for satisfaction and a sustainable profession. *Administration in Social Work, 37*(2), 147–157.

Tippett, E. C. (2018). The legal implications of the metoo movement. *Minnesota Law Review,103*(1), 229–302.

Van Wart, M. (1998). Organizational investment in employee development. In S. Condrey (Ed.), *Handbook of human resource management in government* (pp. 276–297). San Francisco, CA: Jossey-Bass.

Weinbach, R. W., & Taylor, L. M. (2011). *The social worker as manager: A practical guide to success.* Boston, MA: Allyn & Bacon.

Wiener, Y. (1988). Forms of value systems: A focus on organizational effectiveness and cultural change and maintenance. *Academy of Management Review, 13*(4), 534–545.

Work Institute. (2018). 2018 retention report: *Truths & trends in turnover.* Retrieved from http://info.workinstitute.com/retentionreport2018

World Health Organization. (2005). *Task analysis: The basis for development of training in management of tuberculosis.* Geneva: Author.

Additional Resources

Society for Human Resource Management (SHRM, https://www.shrm.org/).

SHRM. SHRM HR Comptency Model [Video file]. Retrieved from https://www.youtube.com/watch?v=985lM_Nzjgg

U.S. Department of Labor. (n.d.) Summary of the major laws of the Department of Labor. Retrieved from https://www.dol.gov/general/aboutdol/majorlaws

HELPFUL TERMS

Employee appraisal—an evaluation to determine to what extent employees are achieving the requirements of their jobs.

Organizational culture—the shared values, beliefs, and behavioral norms in an organization.

Professional development—activities beneficial to employee morale, productivity, and longevity on the job.

Psychological climate—an employee's perception of the psychological impact of the work environment on her or his well-being.

Staff training—most often the "in-house" method for improving staff functioning of specific tasks and functions within the organization.

EXERCISES

1. In-Basket Exercise

Directions

Review the following memo and write a response explaining your decision on this matter.

Memo

Date: September 1, 20XX

To: Anna Wilson, Administrator Our Kids

From: Jack Dawson, Director of Social Services

Subject: Request to offer employment

As you know, we have been interviewing candidates to fill the open caseworker position in our department. I have identified two finalists for the position. Here is a description of the two applicants:

Applicant 1. This applicant holds a masters degree in social work. She comes highly recommended to us. She has about one year of relevant experience.

Applicant 2. This applicant will complete her bachelor in social work next month. She has excellent references and has over seven years of experience working with the population we serve.

We advertised the position as requiring a bachelors degree, but in my opinion, Applicant 2's experience will be extremely valuable to us, and she will have the degree soon. In choosing between the two applicants, I think experience is more valuable to us than a masters degree. I would like to have your approval to move forward and offer the position to Applicant 2. Please advise.

2. Interview Questions

You have been recruiting to hire a new director of professional services for your organization. After screening the applicants, you are now ready for the interview. Because this is such an important position in the organization, you have asked other key administrators and a board member to help with the interview process. You want all of the candidates to be asked the same questions, so you have decided to write a list of questions that will be asked of each candidate. Keeping in mind the laws regarding what you can and cannot ask in an interview, develop 10 standard questions that you and the others will ask of the candidates during the interview process.

3. Nine Motivating Factors

Review Montana and Charnov's (1993) nine motivating factors. Assume that you are putting together a packet of information about your agency to send to potential employees. Write a one-page description of the working conditions at your organization that describe how your organization addresses these nine factors.

ASSIGNMENTS

1. As the manager of several human services units providing services to low-income families and seniors, you have received notification that one of the larger grants that has funded these services will not be renewed. This will most likely result in layoffs and termination of services to clients. Prepare a memo to announce this issue to the staff and develop an approach to plan for the changes that must be made.

2. One of your supervisors has approached you indicating a concern about possible substance abuse by an employee. The supervisor is requesting guidance on how to deal with the problem. Prepare written guidelines for the supervisor to follow in dealing with this issue.

3. Go online and look for employee evaluation forms that are available for public use. Find three different forms and compare them. How are they similar and different? Which of the forms, if any, would you want to use to evaluate the employees of your organization?

12 Boards

In this chapter, we examine the duties and responsibilities of the Board of Directors and how their duties relate to the duties of the administrator. We also review some of the techniques to build a strong and well-informed Board of Directors.

What is a Board of Directors? The Board of Directors is the governing body of a nonprofit organization. Board members are responsible for overseeing the organization's activities. They meet periodically to discuss and vote on the affairs of the organization. At a minimum, an annual meeting must occur with all board members present, and additional meetings are likely to take place throughout the year so board members can discuss and make other necessary decisions. Most organizations have terms for board members, which typically fall between two and five years, with a group of members rotating off the board as new members join the board (McRay, 2014).

One of the unique aspects of nonprofit organizations is that they are governed by volunteer Boards of Directors. The board does not own the nonprofit organization but has the responsibility to be caretakers of the public trust, and therefore, sometimes the Board of Directors is referred to as the *Board of Trustees*. In some ways, the term *trustees* more accurately describes the function of the board in protecting the organization, which belongs to the public. This chapter focuses on working with nonprofit Boards of Directors, but much of the material is applicable to working with advisory boards in public agencies or even boards in the private sector.

Board members and administrators have a responsibility to work together and to share the responsibility for the organization's success. The working relationship between the administrator and the Board of Directors is key to the effective operation of the organization. In fact, one of the key responsibilities of the board is to hire, and sometimes fire, the administrator. For this reason alone, it is important for the administrator to foster an effective working relationship with the Board of Directors.

BOX 12.2 Only One Agenda Item for Nonprofit Boards?

"There should be only one agenda item for a Board of Trustees: Should we fire the executive director or not? If the answer is 'no,' we should go home." This is a quote from the chairman of the board of a nonprofit organization. Few would agree totally with this assessment, but it does make the point that one of the most important roles for a Board of Trustees is to select and sometimes dismiss the executive director of an organization.

Because the Board of Trustees is responsible to hire the CEO of the organization, it is important to know what they value in a potential employee. It is particularly important to understand the preferences of board chairs in selecting a CEO. Hoefer, Watson, and Preble (2013) addressed two basic questions: (1) What skills do board chairs believe are most important for nonprofit human services executive directors to have? and (2) Which degree best prepares its holders to assume the responsibilities of the job in their agency? In the qualitative section of the study, board chairs were asked to expand on their answers and list the two or three most important skills that they require the executive director to have. Several themes emerged from their narrative answers. The most important skills listed were: communication, developing and managing many different kinds of relationships, financial management, dedication to the mission, vision and future orientation, leadership, management skills, and integrity and ethics.

One of the long-running debates in the field of nonprofit management concerns is which degree is best to have to be prepared to be a human services nonprofit executive director. When asked which degree they believed was the best, a large plurality of board chairs chose the Master of Business Administration (MBA). The second most selected option was the Master of Social Work (MSW), and the third choice was the Master of Public Administration (MPA). Board chairs were asked to explain the reasons for which degree they thought was the best educational background for an executive director. The common theme for those choosing the MBA as the best degree was that the organization is a business and must be managed as such. The common theme for those preferring the MSW degree was that the executive director would be better prepared to understand and serve the client population. The common theme for board chairs preferring the MPA degree was because of their agency's dealings with government entities in the political arena.

The study found that while it is important for social work administrators to have the management (business) skills necessary to compete and be technically able administrators, these management competencies are not a substitute for the core values of the social work profession. Watson's (2012) study of human services child care administrators found that human services managers embrace the need for management skills but still place a high priority on mutual respect and fairness. Board chairs that valued the MSW seemed to do so based on the core values of the social work profession. While it is important for social work administrators to develop the needed technical skills of administration, it should not be at the cost of minimizing the importance of the core values of social work.

Why Do Nonprofits Have Boards?

All U.S. nonprofits, regardless of their tax status, are required to have a governing board. Having a board is not a choice or a management strategy but a requirement of the law that authorizes the operation of a nonprofit organization. There are legal obligations that are externally imposed by the legal documents founding the organization, but there are other practices that are adopted by the board itself to ensure the board's duties of care, loyalty, and obedience are fulfilled (Gazley & Nicholson-Crotty, 2018).

Nonprofits are corporations, and as such, they are legal entities. Boards of Directors have legal and ethical responsibilities that cannot be delegated. According to Boardsource, the board's responsibilities fall into four major categories:

- **Legal and fiduciary**. The board is responsible for ensuring that the organization meets legal requirements and that it is operating in accordance with its mission and for the purpose for which it was granted tax exemption. As guardians of the public trust, board members are responsible for protecting the organization's assets.
- **Oversight.** The board is responsible for ensuring that the organization is well run. The board is responsible to hire and fire the administrator or chief executive.
- **Fundraising.** The board is responsible to see that the organization has the money it needs.
- **Representation of constituencies and viewpoints.** Often, board members are chosen so that they can bring to the board the experience or perspective of a particular group or segment of the organization's constituency (Ingram, 2015).

You can also think of the board's roles as: (1) strategic: setting organizational direction; (2) monitoring: monitoring actions and performance of the executive director, organization's assets, and programs; and (3) resource acquisition/networking/service: ensuring that an organization has adequate human and financial resources, representing the organization's interests in society, and advancing the reputation of the organization (Jaskyte, 2017; BoardSource, 2010; Zahra & Pearce, 1989).

Responsibilities of Nonprofit Boards

In *Ten Basic Responsibilities of Nonprofit Boards*, Richard T. Ingram (2015) outlines the 10 major responsibilities of nonprofit boards of directors:

1. Determine the organization's mission and purpose. It is the board's responsibility to create and review a Statement of Mission and Purpose that articulates the organization's goals, means, and primary constituents served.

2. Select the chief executive. Boards must reach consensus on the chief executive's responsibilities and undertake a careful search to find the most qualified individual for the position.

3. Provide proper financial oversight. The board must assist in developing the annual budget and ensuring that proper financial controls are in place.

4. Ensure adequate resources. One of the board's foremost responsibilities is to provide adequate resources for the organization to fulfill its mission.

5. Ensure legal and ethical integrity and maintain accountability. The board is ultimately responsible for ensuring adherence to legal standards and ethical norms.

6. Ensure effective organizational planning. Boards must actively participate in an overall planning process and assist in implementing and monitoring the plan's goals.

7. Recruit and orient new board members and assess board performance. All boards have a responsibility to articulate prerequisites for candidates, orient new members, and periodically and comprehensively evaluate its own performance.

8. Enhance the organization's public standing. The board should clearly articulate the organization's mission, accomplishments, and goals to the public and garner support from the community.

9. Determine, monitor, and strengthen the organization's programs and services. The board's responsibility is to determine which programs are consistent with the organization's mission and to monitor their effectiveness.

10. Support the chief executive and assess his or her performance. The board should ensure that the chief executive has the moral and professional support he or she needs to further the goals of the organization. (p. 9)

Look at this list again. As you can see, these functions describe the "trustee" functions of the Board of Trustees. BoardSource updated its "Ten Responsibilities" document in 2015, calling for a greater focus on advocacy. A key role for the administrator of an organization is to identify policy issues relevant to the organization and its clients and to engage the Board of Trustees in the advocacy process. In Chapter 14 you will learn about the advocacy process. As you study this material, think about your role in moving the board to advocate positions that protect and strengthen the organization. Next, we turn to the issue of structuring the board to carry out their important function as trustees.

Board Functioning

Van Puyvelde, Brown, Walker, & Tenuta, (2018) explored how perceived interactions in the boardroom are associated with perceptions of board effectiveness in nonprofit organizations. The study investigate the relationships between board chair leadership, board meeting practices, board group dynamics, and the perceived effectiveness of the board in several governance roles and responsibilities by surveying 443

executives of nonprofit organizations and their board chairs. The results found that interactions and functioning in board meetings are important to both board chairs' and chief executives' perceptions of board effectiveness. Based on their findings (Van Puyvelde et al., 2018) and our experiences with Boards of Trustees, we recommend the following suggestions for board functioning:

- Board chairs should be clear about their role and the roles of each member of the Board of Trustees. There should be clear expectations of board service, and there should be written job descriptions for each member of the board. These should include clear expectations of how the board will function and the responsibilities that members assume.
- When electing a board chair, the board should seek a candidate with good team-building and interpersonal skills. The chair should have the skills necessary to build a climate of trust, to lead strategic discussions, and to develop a constructive working relationship with the CEO.
- Good board meeting practice should require that board meetings are well run and start and end on time and that the meetings are focused on strategy and policy, not operational issues. The meetings should provide time for full participation by the board members and not be only an information dissemination exercise. There should be an expectation that board members will be well prepared for meetings and that they will be provided the information needed to make informed decisions.

How Should the Board Be Structured?

The size of the board, the officers of the board, how often they meet, and how members are elected are all defined in the legal documents of the nonprofit. The articles of incorporation outline the purpose of the organization, and the bylaws determine how the board will function. The bylaws also determine the size of the board and the committee structures. Still, considerable variation exists when it comes to some elements of nonprofit boards. Box 12.3 provides more information about "normal" board practices.

BOX 12.3 Is Your Board "Normal"?

According to the 2014 BoardSource Governance Index, is your board out of step with the norm? In some cases, these norms may reflect good standards of practice; in others, not so much.

Against the findings of the 2014 Governance Index, your board is in a very small minority if:

1. You pay board members an honorarium (98% do not)
2. Your CEO is a voting member of the board (88% are not)
3. You do not have director's and officers' insurance (96% do)
4. You do not get an annual financial audit (89% do)
5. You don't have a whistleblower policy (88% do)
6. You don't have a document retention and destruction policy (86% do)

7. You do not have a written conflict of interest policy (97% do)
8. You distribute the Form 990 to the board before filing (85% do)

These practices are generally recommended as components of good board governance, although when it comes to number 4, some groups are small enough to be able to replace the audit with financial statements—and, frankly, some still question the real need for D&O insurance. But you are *also* in a small minority if:

1. You do *not* have a white board chair (90% are white)
2. You do *not* have a white executive (89% are white)
3. You have a board chair who is 40 years old or under (91% are over 40)
4. You have an executive director who is 40 years old or under (94% are over 40)

Source: McCambridge (2015).

Size

Boards of Directors come in all sizes. Some are very small (five members or less), while others are very large (50 members or more). Many factors come into play in determining the size of the board. The size and complexity of the agency will often dictate the size of the board. It takes more than a few members to deal with a complex organization with many programs, a multi-program budget, and a large staff. The major determination is whether or not there are enough people involved to do the jobs necessary for the board to function productively. In most cases, the real work of the board is done in committees.

Officers

The officers of the nonprofit corporation are determined by the bylaws. The core offices are the board chair, secretary, and treasurer. Oftentimes, there is also a vice-chair or a chair-elect to provide continuity in board leadership when the chair's term is completed. Another variation on this theme is to have an immediate past chair. Sometimes, the chairs of each committee are considered officers of the board.

Typical Officers of the Board of Trustees

Board chair—responsible to conduct board meetings and work with the executive director to develop the board meeting agenda.

Vice-chair—conducts board meeting if the board chair is absent. Often the vice-chair will become the board chair after the term of the chair is expired.

Secretary—responsible to record the minutes of official actions of the Board of Trustees. Staff members often take minutes of the meeting, but it is the responsibility of the secretary of the board to verify the accuracy of the minutes and to present the minutes to the board for approval. Approval of the minutes is a standard agenda item on the board meeting agenda.

Treasurer—the treasurer is responsible to report the financial status of the organization to the full board. The monthly financial statements are typically prepared by staff or the organization's accountant, but it is the responsibility of the treasurer to present the financial reports to the board.

Board Committees

We have said that the work of the board is to perform a trustee function for the organization and to determine the policy. The committee structure of the board mirrors the many responsibilities of the administrator. Think about the major areas of responsibility for the administrator: program development and oversight, personnel management, budgeting and financial management, maintaining a positive work environment (physical plant), public relations, and fundraising. Each of these areas requires policy decisions by the Board of Trustees. There are many configurations of committees. The following list is only one possibility but will give you the idea of a typical structure. The committees we will consider here are standing committees of the board. These are the committees required in the bylaws.

Typical Board Committees

Executive committee—Many boards choose to have an executive committee that can act on behalf of the board between the times of regularly scheduled board meetings. A typical configuration is for the officers and, perhaps, standing committee chairs to act as the executive committee. While this arrangement can be very beneficial to smooth operations of the board, it can be problematic unless there are clear lines of responsibility between the full board and the executive committee.

Program committee—The program committee is responsible to study policy issues related to the organization's programs and to make recommendations to the full board. The program committee considers recommendations from the administrator when there is a proposal to begin a new program or to discontinue a program. The committee is also responsible to set program admission criteria, set fees, and determine the policies of each of the organization's programs. The program committee is also responsible to assess the effectiveness of the program services provided. It is the administrator's responsibility to have a program evaluation process in place, but it is the responsibility of the program committee to receive and evaluate this information.

Personnel committee—The organization's personnel policies are the responsibility of the personnel committee. Hiring and firing decisions are the prerogative of the administrator, but personnel actions must be taken within the structure of the organization's personnel policies. It is the responsibility of the committee to see that there is fairness in hiring, promotion, and firing decisions. The personnel committee is also responsible to assure equity in compensation for staff. Are employees treated equitably in their salaries, and are similar jobs compensated at the same rate? Defining the benefits package of the organization is a policy decision for the board. What will be the policy for vacation and sick leave? What insurance and pension benefits will be provided by the organization?

Finance committee—The finance committee is responsible to work with the administrator in developing the organization's annual budget. The preparation of the budget is, in most cases, a staff function, but the finance committee is responsible to review the budget, recommend changes, and, finally, recommend the budget to the full board for approval. The committee must examine the budget to see that it is realistic by comparing the proposed budget to the current year's operation. It is also the responsibility of the finance committee to review the monthly (or sometimes quarterly) financial statements. The finance committee must also fulfill its trustee responsibility by closely monitoring the financial performance of the organization. The finance committee must also monitor contract compliance. Is the organization performing to the levels required by the contracting agency's expectations, and is the contract financially advantageous to the organization? The finance committee must review the annual independent audit. This is the annual audit of the financial statement by a certified public accountant. The finance committee will typically meet with the independent auditor before the auditor presents the audit to the full board. It should be noted that the audit is presented to the board, not to the administrator. This is one of the checks and balances of the nonprofit board and administrator relationship.

Physical plant committee—This committee may go by other names, such as the work environment committee, but the function is to provide a safe and comfortable environment for staff and clients. At the most basic level, it must assure that health and safety standards are maintained. This committee deals with the issues of office space, program space, and the equipment needed by the organization to carry out its functions. The technology needs of the organization may be within the responsibility of this committee. If the organization maintains a large physical plant, this committee may have a major role to play in the functioning of the board. However, if the organization does not have or need a large space, then the functions of this committee may be handled by the finance committee.

Development committee—The development committee is concerned with the fundraising and public relations activities of the organization. Its members are first responsible to review and approve the communication vehicles used by the organization. The website, program brochures, and advertising are all items that the development committee should review and on which they should make recommendations to the administrator. This committee also makes recommendations to the board on the fundraising activities to be carried out by the organization. Proposed special events should be reviewed and approved by the committee. The committee should also be involved and help involve all the board in such activities. An overall fundraising plan is the responsibility of the administrator, and this plan should be approved by the committee and taken to the full board for approval. If there is the need for a major fundraising effort, such as a capital campaign to raise funds for a new building or other major undertaking, it is the responsibility of the development committee to bring this need to the board.

In addition to the standing committees, the board chairman may appoint ad hoc committees from time to time. For example, unless there is a standing committee for nominations, the board chair may appoint a committee to bring nominations for new board members. Another example of an ad hoc committee is a search committee. If the administrator's position becomes vacant, the board chair may choose to appoint a search committee to look for a new administrator and to bring candidates to the full board for their consideration.

Whose Job Is It?

If the administrator is responsible for all the functions out-lined above and the board also has responsibility in each of these areas, how is it determined who is responsible for which function? Board committees are supposed to help get the board's job done, not to help with the staff's job (Carver,

1990). It is often said that the job of the board of trustees is to set policy and the role of the administrator is to carry out those policies in the day-to-day operation of the organization. This concept dates back to the 1800s and comes from a theory known as the *politics–administration dichotomy* (Goodnow, 1900; Wilson, 1941). The idea is that elected officials define policy, and the administrator implements the policy. In this view, there is a clear division of responsibility between the officials (in our case, the elected Board of Directors) and the administrator. In the 1920s, charitable organizations that had been managed by boards began to hire professionals to serve as professional administrators. During this time, agency administrators promoted the idea that the function of the Board of Directors was to establish policy, and the administrator was to have full responsibility for day-to-day operations (Kirschner, 1986).

In general terms, it is true that boards establish policy and the administrator is responsible for day-to-day operations, but the reality is very different. Most Boards of Trustees rely heavily on the administrator to assist them in making policy decisions. It is the administrator who is intimately familiar with the day-to-day operations of the organization. It is ultimately the board's responsibility to set policy for the organization, but the administrator is in most cases a key player in the development and recommendations of those policies. It is critical for administrators and their Board of Directors to have excellent communication and a strong working relationship (see Box 12.4).

BOX 12.4 7 Questions to Ask in Developing Effective Board Information Materials

1. Concise—Is the information communicated as quickly or as briefly as possible?
2. Meaningful—Is the information presented in relationship to a significant factor, such as a goal set by the board, past performance, or comparative data?
3. Timely—Is the information relevant to the current agenda?
4. Relevant to responsibilities—Does the information help the board or board committee discharge its responsibilities?
5. Best available—Is the information the best available indicator of the situation or condition being described? Can better information be provided?
6. Context—Is it clear why this information is important?
7. Graphic presentation—Could the information be presented better graphically than in words?

It is not the board's responsibility to be involved in the day-to-day operations of the organization—that is the role of the administrator. When conflicts arise between board members and administrators, it can often be related to the question of, "Whose responsibility is it?" It is vitally important for the administrator to develop clear channels of communication with the board. We will now turn to some of the methods of communication.

Working with the Board

Working with boards has been described as doing the tango: You have to know when to lead and when to follow, all while keeping your balance (Robinson, 2001). To successfully dance this tango, there must be strong respect between the board and the administrator.

Remember that your board members are volunteers. While the agency consumes a large part of your time and attention, board members have jobs, business interests, and other nonprofits that put demands on their time. The effective administrator will respect the board members for their contribution of their time and talent to the organization and view the board as a valuable asset to help achieve the organization's goals. The administrator must respect the board members' time by providing clear and concise information to help them perform their board function. What are some of the methods used to provide such information?

Sharing Information

Your board should never be surprised. Anything they hear in the community about the organization, either positive or negative, should be news they have already heard from you. It has been said that if you don't like the news you need to share with the board, you will like it less later. In other words, the administrator needs to get information to the board as soon as possible. If there is a bad situation, it will only be worse if the board members hear it from another source. On the positive side, board members need to have the good news of the organization so they can help spread the good word and also so they will be knowledgeable when approached in the community about the organization. The following are some types of information you will have to share with your board.

Insider newsletter—Of course, your board members will receive your organization's newsletter, but your board members will need much more information. Administrators often find it helpful to develop an informational newsletter to go to insiders, such as board members and leadership staff, on a regular basis. The frequency of this communication device depends on the needs of the organization. It may need to be produced weekly, but in most cases, it is produced on a monthly basis. The frequency of board meetings will also influence your decision on how often to send the insider newsletter.

Board meeting materials—At least two weeks before the board meeting, you will mail or electronically transmit the board materials to be used at the board meeting. These materials will include the agenda, minutes of the previous meeting, committee reports, and financial reports. These materials, if done well, can take a great amount of your time and energy.

One of the most horrifying sounds to an administrator is the sound of board members opening their board packets (or searching online for their documents) at the beginning of the board meeting! The board chair can help avoid this situation by starting each meeting with a statement such as, "We will assume everyone has reviewed the board materials," and then move to the business at hand. This will set the expectation that the materials you developed will be read before the meeting begins.

The administrator and the board chair work together to develop the agenda for the board meeting. The administrator may also put out a call to the board membership and ask for any board agenda items they may have. The board meeting agenda will include reports, action items, and discussion items. It is important to identify action items on the agenda so board members can read the supporting materials, develop any questions they may have, and think about how they will vote on the issue. Each of the program areas may have action items. For instance, the finance committee may suggest a revision to the approved budget, or the program committee may recommend a change in the admission criteria for a program. These are policy issues that the board must decide. The board materials are provided to give the board members the information they need to make a decision.

Below is the skeleton of a board agenda. A real agenda would be much more detailed and would include the action items to be decided under each of the report items. The board agenda becomes the basis for the minutes of the Board of Trustees meeting and, therefore, the official document of the decisions of the Board of Trustees. The agenda and minutes of the board meetings are critical because they are the source of information when there is a question about the decisions of a board. The minutes also become an important part of the history of an organization. The minutes tell the story of the organization. The approval of the minutes is usually the first agenda item, when the board confirms, by their vote, that the minutes are a true and accurate representation of their actions at the last meeting.

Agenda

    I. Approval of the Minutes
   II. Review of the Agenda
 III. Reports
      a. Administrator's Report
      b. Program Committee Report
      c. Personnel Committee Report
      d. Finance Committee Report
      e. Development Committee Report
      f. Physical Plant/Work Environment Committee Report
   IV. Other
    V. Adjourn

In addition to the agenda, the board package should include the reports from the administrator and each of the committees. These reports will provide detailed information from each committee but, more importantly, will provide the information that board members will need to make decisions on the action items related to each committee report. Special attention should be paid to the materials related to the finance report. The finance committee should deal with the detailed financial report for the organization, but few members of the full board will want to study page after page of financial information. There should be a simplified, easy to understand summary

of the financial report for the entire board. Of course, the full financial report is made available to individual board members, if they wish, but a simplified version will be more useful to most board members and will help the board meeting go more smoothly.

Barry S. Bader (1985), a consultant and author specializing in hospital governance, identifies seven guidelines for developing effective board information that we recommend for whenever you are communicating with the board (see Box 12.5).

BOX 12.5 Who's in Charge?

The executive director of an agency was proposing a major change in the service delivery method of one of the agency's programs. The Board of Trustees was not convinced that this was the best move for the agency to make, and some board members were personally opposed to this method of service. During the board meeting, when the change was being debated, the executive director stated that this was really a program issue and was her decision to make. At that point, the board chair stated, "It may be your decision to make, but as a board it is our decision whether or not to raise money for the program." The executive director quickly saw the error of her thinking.

The Board Chair–CEO Relationship

One of the most important relationships in a nonprofit organization is the relationship between the board chair and the executive director (Olinske & Hellman, 2017). It is a relationship that you will need to cultivate and nurture as an administrator. One common reason that executive directors resign from their jobs is their relationship with the board or the chairman of the board (Peters & Wolfred, 2001). To work effectively, the board chair and the executive director must trust one another and work together harmoniously as the two members of the organization with the greatest amount of responsibility (Smith, Bucklin & Associates, Inc., 2000). It is understandable that there is the potential for conflict between the board chair and the executive director. These are the two most important positions in the organization, and they have complementary and overlapping responsibilities. The ideal board and executive director relationships are those in which the executive director does not dominate the board and the board does not micromanage the daily operations of the agency (Houle, 1989). Many administrators find they have very close and satisfying relationships with their board chairs. This is easy to understand, since the relationship starts with a shared interest in the organization and a shared goal of providing excellent services to the clients the agency serves.

Conclusion

Board members and human services administrators have a responsibility to work together and to share the responsibility for the organization's success. The working relationship between the administrator and the Board of Directors is key to the effective operation of the organization. Nonprofits are legal entities, and Boards of Directors have legal and ethical responsibilities that cannot be delegated. The board's responsibilities fall into four major categories: (1) legal and fiduciary, (2) oversight, (3) fundraising, and (4) representation

of constituencies and viewpoints. Working with Boards of Trustees is a critical administrative skill. Human services administrators must have excellent communication skills and develop strong working relationships with the members of the board. Remember your ethical responsibilities to promote diversity and social justice as you exercise your influence as a social work administrator in developing leadership in the organization you administer.

Look again at Box 12.3 (above). It seems we have a long way to go in bringing diversity to leadership of nonprofit boards and agencies. The BoardSource (2014) survey finds that board chairs and executive directors are almost always white (90% of chairs and 89% of executive directors). The survey also found very few chairs or executive directors under 40 years of age. We have work to do to improve the contribution of boards and their members to the social justice work we all want to accomplish.

Reference List

Bader, B. S. (1985). Keys to better hospital governance through better information. In R. D. Herman & Van Til, J. (Eds.), *Nonprofit boards of directors: Analyses and applications* (pp. 118–132). New Brunswick, NJ: Transaction.

BoardSource. (2010). *The handbook of nonprofit governance.* San Francisco, CA: Jossey-Bass.

Carver, J. (1990). *Boards that make a difference: A new design for leadership in nonprofit and public organizations.* San Francisco, CA: Jossey-Bass.

Gazley, B., & Nicholson-Crotty, J. (2018). What drives good governance? A structural equation model of nonprofit board performance. *Nonprofit and Voluntary Sector Quarterly, 47*(2), 262–285.

Goodnow, F. J. (1900). *Politics and administration: A study in government.* New York, NY: Russell & Russell.

Hoefer, R., Watson, L. & Preble, K. (2013). A mixed methods examination of nonprofit board chair preferences in hiring executive directors. *Administration in Social Work, 37*(5), 437–446.

Houle, C. O. (1989). *Governing boards: Their nature and nurture.* San Francisco, CA: Jossey-Bass.

Ingram, R. T. (2015). *Ten basic responsibilities of nonprofit boards* (2nd ed.). Washington, DC: BoardSource.

Jaskyte, K. (2017) Board effectiveness and innovation in nonprofit organizations. *Human Service Organizations: Management, Leadership & Governance, 41*(5), 453–463.

Kirschner, D. S. (1986). *The paradox of professionalism: Reform and public service in urban America 1900–1940.* New York, NY: Greenwood.

McCambridge, R. (2015, January 27). BoardSource's board governance index: Is your board "normal"? *Nonprofit Quarterly.* Retrieved from https://nonprofitquarterly.org/2015/01/27/nonprofit-board-governance-boardsource-index/

McRay, G. (2014, December 11). A nonprofit board of directors: What is a board? [Web log post]. Retrieved from https://www.501c3.org/nonprofits-board-directors/

Olinske, J. L., & Hellman, C. M. (2017). Leadership in the human service nonprofit organization: The influence of the board of directors on executive director well-being and burnout. *Human Service Organizations: Management, Leadership & Governance, 41*(2), 95–105.

Peters, J., & Wolfred, T. (2001). *Daring to lead: Nonprofit executive directors and their work experience.* San Francisco, CA: CompassPoint Nonprofit Services.

Robinson, M. K. (2001). *Nonprofit boards that work: The end of one-size-fits-all governance*. New York, NY: John Wiley & Sons.

Van Puyvelde, S., Brown, W. A., Walker, V., & Tenuta, R. (2018). Board effectiveness in nonprofit organizations: Do interactions in the boardroom matter? *Nonprofit and Voluntary Sector Quarterly, 47*(6), 1296–1310. doi:10.1177/0899764018762318

Watson, L. D. (2012). Factors influencing the relationship between contract providers and a state funding agency. *Administration in Social Work, 36*(4), 343–358.

Smith, Bucklin & Associates, Inc. (2000). *The complete guide to nonprofit management* (2nd ed.). New York, NY: John Wiley & Sons.

Wilson, W. (1941). The study of public administration. *Political Science Quarterly, 56*(4), 197–222.

Zahra, S. A., & Pearce, J. A., II. (1989). Boards of directors and corporate financial performance: A review and integrative model. *Journal of Management, 15*(2), 291–334.

Additional Resources

BoardSource website (https://boardsource.org/).

Dilenschneider, C. (2017). What is the most important role of nonprofit board members? (STUDY) [Video file]. Retrieved from https://www.youtube.com/watch?v=gED5rDA4ldE

Forti, M. (2018, February 13). Challenging conventional wisdom on nonprofit boards. *Stanford Social Innovation Review*. Retrieved from https://ssir.org/articles/entry/challenging_conventional_wisdom_on_nonprofit_boards

National Council of Nonprofits. (n.d.). Board roles and responsibilities. Retrieved from https://www.councilofnonprofits.org/tools-resources/board-roles-and-responsibilities

HELPFUL TERMS

Board agenda & minutes—the board agenda becomes the basis for the minutes of the Board of Trustees meeting and, therefore, the official document of the decisions of the Board of Trustees. The agenda and minutes of the board meetings are critical because they are the source of information when there is a question about the decisions of a board.

Board of Directors—the governing body of a nonprofit organization. Board members are responsible for overseeing the organization's activities. They meet periodically to discuss and vote on the affairs of the organization.

Board chair—responsible to conduct board meetings and work with the executive director to develop the board meeting agenda.

Board Vice-chair—conducts board meetings if the board chair is absent. Often the vice-chair will become the board chair after the term of the chair is expired.

Board Secretary—responsible to record the minutes of official actions of the Board of Trustees. Staff members often take minutes of the meeting, but it is the responsibility of the secretary of the board to verify the accuracy of the minutes and to present the minutes to the board for approval. Approval of the minutes is a standard agenda item on the board meeting agenda.

Board Treasurer—responsible to report the financial status of the organization to the full board. The monthly financial statements are typically prepared by staff or the organization's accountant, but it is the responsibility of the treasurer to present the financial reports to the board.

Board Size—Boards of Directors come in all sizes. Some are very small (five members or less), while others are very large (50 members or more).

Board of Trustees—term used interchangeably with Board of Directors, but in some ways, trustees more accurately describes the function of the board in protecting an organization that belongs to the public.

Legal and Fiduciary Responsibility—The board is responsible for ensuring that the organization meets legal requirements and that it is operating in accordance with its mission and for the purpose for which it was granted tax exemption. As guardians of the public trust, board members are responsible for protecting the organization's assets.

Oversight Responsibilities—The board is responsible for ensuring that the organization is well run. The board is responsible to hire and fire the administrator or chief executive.

EXERCISES

1. In-Basket Exercise

Directions

Read the following memos from your in-basket. For each memo, draft a reply outlining your decision or the action you plan to take.

Memo

Date: November 9, 20XX

To: Mildred Nisenbaum, Administrator—Food Bank of the Plains

From: Jeff Coleman, Board Chair

Subject: Committee Structure

As the new board chair, I have been giving some thought to our board structure. I do not really understand the need for a program committee. We have excellent program directors in each of our program areas. Since they are the experts, it seems redundant to have a program committee looking over their shoulders. Therefore, my recommendation to the board will be that we disband the program committee and reassign its members to more important committees. Please give me your thoughts on this.

Memo

Date: March 17, 20XX

To: Mildred Nisenbaum, Administrator—Food Bank of the Plains

From: Brenda Bolton—Program Director

Subject: Sick Leave

We continue to have problems with staff in my area abusing our sick leave policy. Some employees use their sick days as soon as they are accumulated. I would like to change our policy from a sick leave system to a well days system. We could lower our current number of sick leave days from 12 days per year to six days per year and simply add this number of days to our vacation days. Employees could use all of the days if they wished and would be entitled to the days whether or not they were sick. How can this change be made? Do I have your OK?

2. In-Basket Exercise

Directions

Respond to the memo below and structure your agenda using the committee structure outlined in this chapter.

Memo

Date: August 22, 20XX

To: Mildred Nisenbaum, Administrator—Food Bank of the Plains

From: Jeff Coleman, Board Chair

Subject: Board Meeting Agenda

As the new board chair, I want to be involved with you in developing the agenda for each board meeting. Please develop a draft agenda and send it to me. I want the agenda to include the items you think require the attention of each committee. Thank you.

ASSIGNMENTS

1. Attend a meeting of the Board of Trustees of a local nonprofit organization. Write a three- to four-page summary of your experience. Relate the material in this chapter to your experience in observing the board meeting.

2. Find a peer-reviewed journal article on the functioning of Boards of Directors. Write a review or critique of the article.

3. You have been assigned the task of developing a half-day orientation for new board members of your organization. Develop an outline of the major topics you will present to new board members. Choose the topics that you think are the most important for new board members to understand about their role and function as board members.

Image Credits

Img. 12.1: Copyright © 2018 Depositphotos/VitalikRadko.

Img. 12.2: Copyright © 2015 Depositphotos/Micicj.

Img. 12.3: Copyright © 2014 Depositphotos/Carmenbobo.

Img. 12.4: Copyright © 2011 Depositphotos/Forewer.

Img. 12.5: Copyright © 2016 Depositphotos/Kchungtw.

Img. 12.6: Copyright © 2015 Depositphotos/Kchungtw.

Img. 12.7: Copyright © 2019 Depositphotos/Depositedhar.

Skills

Quadrant IV: External and People Orientation

As a social work leader, your ultimate goal is to make positive change in the world. This has likely been a constant in your life from your beginning days in the field. There is no doubt that helping people find resources to improve their lives or training them to accomplish their dreams is a wonderful part of social work. But how would it be to be able to achieve that on a grander scale, wherein you influence policymakers and the creation of laws to do that for hundreds, thousands, or even millions of people? That is what we tackle in this final quadrant.

Some people, even those who are accomplished in all other aspects of their social work leadership positions, consider this quadrant the scariest. You must work beyond the comfort zone of your organization and often interact with people who have very different values and ideas than you do. Working with, and relying on, people who may not agree with you can ensure that this quadrant is the least predictable and most difficult to work in. At the same time, however, it can be among the most rewarding aspects of the leadership role, because you can extend your influence and impact far beyond your current horizons.

The key aspects of Quadrant IV that we cover are how to be persuasive (Chapter 13) and how to conduct effective advocacy (Chapter 14). This material extends far beyond the communications chapter earlier in the book (Chapter 5). It is more focused on not only letting people tell you what they want and know, but also how to get others to see your point of view and perhaps change theirs. When decision-makers consider choosing a position that you advocate, using your ability to persuade, you have done something important. Success is not only in getting *everything* you want, but also in getting *some* of what you deem essential or blocking an agreement that would be detrimental to many.

Getting involved in confrontational "politics" is not the only time you need skills in persuasion and advocacy. Sometimes coalition members do not see eye-to-eye with each other, and you want to help them reach agreement on how to help clients. You may see factions appearing among your board members, each wanting different (good) things from the organization. Using persuasion and advocacy skills may help you salvage a negative situation, even saving the organization from a terrible fight that goes public.

By the end of this material, you may have discovered a new aspect of your leadership journey, one that allows you to have an impact far beyond your current thinking. You may never become as famous as some of the social work heroes of the past, but you will be moving forward in their footsteps and encouraging others to do the same. That is the promise of Quadrant IV.

Persuasion

The ability to persuade others is a vital skill for managers and leaders. Persuasion involves getting people to do something because they want to, not because they must. With subordinates, you might believe you can just issue commands and people will obey. This seldom works well, however, as most people do not like to be ordered around. People may comply at one level, but they may also seek to undermine directives given in this manner. Being ordered to do things can decrease employees' engagement in their work. This is negative for them, your organization, and clients. Becoming a better persuader brings many beneficial results for everyone connected to the agency.

Another reason to become an effective persuader, not relying on command or coercion, is that nonprofit managers very often work with peers and people in the community, such as donors (or potential donors), elected officials, client group representatives, and other stakeholders, who have their own viewpoints and positions. These people are not your subordinates, and they must be persuaded to follow your lead of their own will. In addition, there are many opportunities within nonprofit organizations to be influential before you assume the organization's top spot, and it is important to practice your persuasion skills long before you apply for such positions. You will find that being able to persuade others is essential to being a successful social work manager and leader.

Research on persuasion usually treats it as a goal-oriented behavior (Wilson, 2002). Persuasion is in many ways more powerful than coercion or negotiation. If you command someone to do something and you have the power needed to ensure compliance, you may very well lose the willingness of your subordinate

BOX 31.1 EPAS Competencies Covered

The information in this chapter is directly connected to CSWE's Competency 3: Advance Human Rights and Social, Economic, and Environmental Justice; Competency 5: Engage in Policy Practice; Competency 6: Engage with Individuals, Families, Groups, Organizations, and Communities; Competency 7: Assess Individuals, Families, Groups, Organizations, and Communities; and Competency 8: Intervene with Individuals, Families, Groups, Organizations, and Communities.

to implement the order well or in the spirit of making the organization operate optimally. With negotiation, you and the other party make a series of concessions. This implies that neither side gets what it really wants. In persuasion, however, you are able to get the other party to accept what you want. In persuasion, one party gets all or nearly all of what it wants, and the other side, by now agreeing to a new view, also receives what it wants.

The big question you're probably wondering now is how you can become more persuasive. Fortunately, research provides a great deal of information about how to be more persuasive. In every persuasion attempt, four variables are important: the context, the message, the sender, and the receiver.

The Context

The context of the persuasion attempt determines most of the content used. How the situation is viewed by the actors establishes, to a large extent, their reaction to it. *Framing* is the process of getting a particular viewpoint accepted as the "right" way to see a situation. According to Rhoads (1997), "A frame is a psychological device that offers a perspective and manipulates salience in order to influence subsequent judgment" (para. 2). A frame thus provides a certain standpoint on how the facts should be seen, emphasizing some facts and minimizing others, to get the target to act a certain way. Framing is a skill often used by direct practice social workers and occurs in many other situations, as well. The ability to frame an issue advantageously is often enough to make you very persuasive.

Some frames hurt an idea's chances of being adopted, while other frames make an idea more likely to be chosen. When you are persuading someone, you will want to connect a particular frame with the idea in question. Here are some typical frames used to guide the way a situation is viewed (Hoefer, 2019; Rosenthal, 1993). The first five are useful when you want to work against an idea. The last four can be used to persuade people in favor of a proposal.

- *It isn't fair.* Proposals are often tagged "unfair" to one group or another. Almost any proposal an advocate comes up with, from helping one client more than others, to economic policy that affects global trading, can be called unfair. Because people like to be "fair," this frame can keep an idea from being adopted.

- *It won't work.* An alternative frame to argue against a proposal is that whatever goal is set won't be reached. If a proposal is seen as unworkable, it is easy to keep it from being tried.
- *It can be done in other ways.* This is similar to the previous frame, although it presents an alternative to what it attacks. The persuader substitutes a new idea in place of the one initially under discussion.
- *It costs too much.* An idea that is seen as too expensive is unlikely to be adopted.
- *It will hurt clients.* This frame can be used at any level, but it is often used in intra-agency debates by arguing that a new idea will do harm to the organization's clients. It is difficult for people in human service organizations to adopt ideas that they see will hurt clients.

- *It will help consumers/clients.* At the agency level, many advocates focus on the benefits of their suggestions for clients. If a plan is seen as being beneficial to clients, it is often difficult to derail it in a human service organization.
- *The benefits outweigh the costs.* While the idea is not perfect, on the whole, there are more plusses than minuses. If people think that there are more benefits, then it is easy to support the idea. Talking about the difference between short-term and long-term thinking and accounting often takes place in this frame.
- *If it saves the life of one child, it will all be worth it.* This frame unashamedly pulls at heartstrings. It says that costs might be high, but it challenges anyone to say that life, particularly an innocent child's life, is less precious than gold. Obviously, this frame can be extended to other "worthy" populations as well.
- *After what they've gone through, they deserve it.* The argument here acknowledges that the outcomes of the idea might not be fair in some sense because some people will get more than others. Yet, there is an element of fairness involved because the people who are getting more (money, services, opportunities) have also earned it by what they have gone through. Programs for veterans or the elderly are often talked about in this way.

It can actually be fun to try different frames when thinking about how to persuade others. For example, you may want to persuade the Board of Directors whom you work with that your organization should make a strategic shift in programming for your main client group, returning veterans. You know that the board has supported the programs you now run for many years, but you believe new approaches have more promise and are not being used in your city. One frame you could use is, "After what they've gone through, our clients deserve the most advanced and evidence-based programs available. That's what this new approach is—better for them and better for us, as we will be seen as the leaders in the field." Another frame could be, "The long-term benefits of the new program approach far outweigh the short-term costs of change. Here are the figures I've collected to show that. Plus, one of our largest funders will provide money for the training staff members will need."

The importance of framing in persuasion cannot be overstated. As an agency leader or manager, thinking carefully about the frame you want to use will make it much easier to persuade others to accept your ideas. On the other hand, you must not uncritically accept someone else's view of a situation. Make sure to understand what frame is being used when listening to what is being stated and proposed.

The Message

The message that is sent from the persuader to the recipient is the information that is designed to be persuasive. Here, we look at characteristics of the message, rather than content. Six general principles of persuasive messages are discussed in this section: intent, organization, sidedness, repetition and redundancy, rhetorical questions, and fear appeals. This discussion is based largely on Hoefer (2019).

Intent

In most cases, it is counterproductive to announce that you are going to try to influence someone. The moment the target hears your intent, defensive walls start going up. It is better to begin the persuasion effort without forewarning the person whose mind you want to change. There are two important exceptions to this general guideline, however. The first is when you only want to ask for small changes, knowing that the message receivers already agree with most of what you are about to say. Thus, by saying that you want to ask only for small changes, resistance is lowered. The target feels safer, knowing that you are not wanting to shake things up too much. The second exception is when your target already expects you to attempt persuasion. Thus, in many situations, it doesn't hurt to say you are going to try to influence the target's opinion, because everyone knows that is why you are communicating.

Organization

Well-organized messages are more persuasive than are poorly organized ones. There is always a temptation to neglect the preparation and organizing phase of developing your message. It is important to take the time to make your key points more salient and to ensure a logical consistency in the material.

Sidedness

Research shows that two-sided messages (those that present the position advocated and also the opposing view) can be extremely persuasive if they do two things: They must both defend the desired position and attack the other position. If the other position is mentioned but not attacked, then there is no advantage for the two-sided presentation compared to a one-sided presentation (Cialdini, 2008). The reasons for these results are that a two-sided message appears more balanced. Since most people don't think deeply about most issues, presenting the "other side" makes the presenter seem more credible. The attack on the other position and the defense of your own ideas can leave a lasting impression of having explored the issue completely.

Repetition and Redundancy

Repetition and redundancy are different, though closely related, concepts. Repetition refers to communicating the same thing over and over in exactly the same way. This is useful because people pay attention at different times. If the message is missed once, it may be seen at another time. To use a fishing analogy, you may use the same hook in the same place at different times of the day in order to catch your dinner. Redundancy, on the other hand, refers to having multiple ways of communicating similar information. A redundant message repeats the major theme of other messages, but does it in a different way. This is beneficial in persuasion because people tune into different words, images, and approaches. It is similar to having many fishing lines using different lures in the water at once—if one hook is ignored, another one may be successful.

Rhetorical Questions

The use of rhetorical questions is very effective, isn't it? Leaders who understand the science of persuasion achieve more results, don't they? Rhetorical questions are disguised statements—they stake out a position without appearing to and can be backed away from if opposition emerges. Research shows that the use of rhetorical questions can change how people think (Cialdini, 2008).

Fear Appeals

A fear appeal is a message that focuses on the bad things that will happen if you do or don't do something. The message indicates that you should do whatever it is that the persuader is suggesting in order to avoid some sort of catastrophe. When a situation is described in a way that increases fear, a natural reaction is to want to take action to protect oneself against that threat. To work, however, not only must a person feel a realistic and personal fear of negative consequences, but the appeal must also provide information about a feasible way to avoid those consequences. In other words, you can't just scare people into action. You must also guide them to safety.

Information

When you think about persuading someone on a topic, you must decide what type of information you need to present. As a nonprofit leader, your information may be as simple as stories about how an agency policy is affecting clients or as complex as a community needs assessment.

The information that you present, to be useful, can be of two types: substantive and contextual. *Substantive information* is the set of facts on which you base your arguments. *Contextual information* relates to how the situation appears to interested (or potentially interested) others—political information, if you will.

Substantive Information

Substantive information relates to what most people would call the facts of the case. Substantive information can range from singular anecdotes that are compelling and (hopefully) representative of the issue to the results of rigorous empirical research. In-between levels of quality can be found from official documents, statistical data (such as from the Census Bureau), testimony from individuals, newspapers and popular magazines, television and radio, and public meetings (Richan, 1996). We could rate the quality of these different sources of information in a conventional way, but for our purposes, the best information is the information that is most persuasive to the target. Thus, stories of individuals (particularly if they tell their own stories) are often the most persuasive sort of information because they carry a considerable emotional impact.

Contextual Information

Information about the context of a decision can be important to a target. A colleague of yours, for example, may not be convinced of the validity of your assertions until it is pointed out that your information came from the agency's chief financial officer ("I understand your skepticism about how much we can save with this change, Suzanne. I could hardly believe it myself. But these numbers come straight from the top budget person in our agency!"). Even if that one bit of information is not enough to be persuasive, it will give your statements credibility. Other contextual information in an agency setting may relate to the way other staff members view the situation, or how the issue is being discussed "around the water cooler."

Presenting the Information

Once the information is gathered, you must decide how to present it to the identified person or group. This decision has two key elements. The first relates to the manner of delivering the information, and the second to the format of the presentation.

Manner

The important elements when considering the manner of presentation are accuracy, time, message style, content, and clarity.

Accuracy

Your information must be carefully checked and fully reliable. Be sure to document the source(s) for each fact you present.

Time

With the second element, time, brevity is usually beneficial. Five minutes of your target's full attention may be all you are going to get, whether you are meeting in person, making a phone call, or having your written information read. Make the most of it.

Message Style

The choice of message style should be made after analyzing the recipient(s) you will be working with. Many different message styles may be appropriate in one setting to reach people where they are, particularly in a large group setting. Three are discussed here: positive vs. negative, private vs. public, and collaborative vs. confrontational.

Positive vs. Negative

You should decide if you are going to emphasize positive or negative appeals. In this context, a positive message means to stress the good things that will result from taking the action you are suggesting. A negative message means to call attention to the bad things that will ensue if the desired action is not taken. Some research suggests that people are more likely to want to protect themselves from negative events than to push for more positive outcomes (Cialdini, 2008). Thus, negative appeals based on what bad things will happen are more persuasive than are positive appeals describing the good things that will happen.

Private vs. Public

Information can be delivered in private (individual conversations or via written material, such as letters or briefing papers) or small-group meetings or communications, or it can be presented via larger group settings, such as staff meetings or in public venues. Research indicates that having a relationship with decision-makers that is personal and private (an individual-oriented strategy) is more effective than working in public settings (Hoefer, 2001). Still, each situation requires a separate decision to be made, because the circumstances are different.

Collaborative vs. Confrontational

Persuasion is often part of a collaborative, rather than confrontational, process. If persuasion efforts do not achieve your goals, you may, in fact, turn to confrontational tactics, but doing so too often can burn bridges to decision-makers whose support you need to achieve your goals. Remember that confrontation exists on a continuum, with gentle confrontation being a possibility as well as more forceful confrontation.

Content

A general template for any persuasive message has two elements:

- Describe the problem (including how serious the problem is).
- Tell what can be done to solve the problem.

The content of the message should, of course, be in line with the message style that was chosen. Try different frames to determine which evokes the best response. Be ready to switch to another message style and use different content if one effort begins to lose its punch. Try, however, to keep the same frame—reframing an issue is a long-term process that needs consistency over time to be effective.

Clarity

The sad truth is that communications are often unclear. For a message to be communicated clearly, the information must first be delivered using language the target can understand. Then, after receiving the message, the target must know what you want done because you have provided a clear call to action. Your audience may not agree with you or comply with your wishes, but communication has not occurred effectively if the decision-maker doesn't know what you said or what you want done.

Format

The decision relating to the format of how information is presented has three main options. It can be presented in person (such as at a one-on-one meeting with the target, a small group meeting with the target, or testifying at a public hearing), via a telephone call, or in a written form through a letter, fax, or e-mail. Each of these options has advantages and disadvantages. The choice should be made on the basis of which approach is most convincing to the target, as well as what is practical for you. Still, within each format, more effective and less effective ways of presenting the information exist.

In Person

The in-person format is generally considered the most powerful. This is because there is an immediacy and power in personal communication, where feedback can be seen and heard instantaneously, even if such feedback is nonverbal. An in-person persuasion effort also shows the most commitment, because it is the most trouble to do.

In many cases, presentations might be accompanied by a computer-based set of slides, using a program such as PowerPoint or Prezi. These programs are ideal when used to help structure the information visually; when data or other information can be presented using charts, graphs, and animation; and as a way to appeal to people with visual learning styles.

Telephone Call or Online Video Conference

A telephone or online video conference call (such as Skype or Zoom) may also carry considerable weight with people you are trying to persuade, particularly if it would be very difficult for you to make an in-person visit. Online video conferencing is much like being with someone in person, in terms of being able to see and send nonverbal information (intentionally or not). A normal telephone call can also convey much nonverbal information, including the intensity of your beliefs, the degree of confidence you have in yourself, and the depth of your knowledge, but does not convey as much information as a video-enhanced call.

Written (Letters, Faxes, E-Mail, Texts)

The written document is also a powerful tool for persuaders. Information on paper, such as in a letter or fax, often takes on more weight simply because it is connected with a material object. Use your leanest writing style, stating plainly in the first or second paragraph what the situation is and what you would like to see happen. Many busy people find themselves looking for the meat of the document immediately. Help them out by being as clear and concise as possible.

Faxes have perhaps become much less used now that e-mail has become almost universally available, but they still have their own advantages. Because a fax is essentially a letter transmitted over a phone line, anything that could be in a letter can be in a fax. The main difficulty with faxes is that you must be able to connect one phone line to another, and fax machine phone lines may frequently be in use.

Despite the ease in sending e-mail, any e-mail that is sent should be as carefully composed as a letter or prepared presentation. E-mail is now frequently read on smartphones and tablets, so it can be read nearly anywhere. Text messages, while short, may be effective in communicating key points and should be written with conscious attention to detail. While it may be tough to be persuasive in a few lines, it's worth your best efforts to try.

Written (Website Copy and Social Media)

Increasingly, websites and social media platforms are used to provide information and persuasive arguments. These resources can provide your organization's views and information to both internal and external audiences. Staff members can be kept aware of change efforts and their benefits, while outsiders can view an organization's reasons for changing (or not changing) positions and views. Reporters and others in the media may turn to such sites for background. Everyone can see your vision, mission, and guiding principles, as well as the programs you run, by turning to these sources.

In the end, the format chosen depends greatly on the way that the target is most easily persuaded. Each format, however, has advantages and disadvantages, and so, if not all are used, the format must be chosen only after careful thought.

This section has covered ways to shape your message so that it is more persuasive. There are also principles that apply to the message's senders themselves.

The Sender

No matter how you shape your message, a considerable amount of your ability to be persuasive is dependent on how you are perceived by your audience. This section emphasizes the role of credibility. To be persuasive, you must be believable. Without it, you are not going to persuade anyone. Credibility, however, is a multidimensional concept comprising three factors: expertise, trustworthiness, and likeability. Each of these is necessary, but not sufficient, to persuade people to alter their ideas or decisions. If your target already has a strong position on an issue or is distracted from paying attention to what you are saying, no shifts will occur due to persuasion. (Force or political pressure may be used to affect behavior, but that is not persuasion.)

Expertise

Expertise in an area means that you have considerable knowledge about a topic. In many cases, knowledge is power because decision makers want to achieve their goals. If you can point out, based on your expertise, that your ideas will help them avoid problems or achieve something valuable to them, you may very well be persuasive. Remember to be authentic about what you know and what you do not know. If you attempt to bluff your way in a situation, this may end up hurting you because you may be seen as untrustworthy.

Trustworthiness

Trustworthiness indicates that you are honest and lack bias (Rhoads & Cialdini, 2002). Because of this characteristic's central role in establishing credibility, leaders and advocates must be seen as trustworthy in the eyes of their targets. The best advice for establishing a reputation for trustworthiness is to simply be trustworthy: Do what you promise, don't promise what you can't or won't do, and admit when you don't know something. If you are not believed, it doesn't matter if you are an expert or not. It also won't matter if you are very likable.

Likability

The quality of likability, while perhaps not as important as expertise and trustworthiness, nonetheless has an influence on how persuasive you are. According to Roger Ailes, who has advised U.S. presidents on how to present their messages most successfully,

> If you could master one element of personal communications that is more powerful than anything we've discussed, it is the quality of being likeable. I call it the magic bullet, because if your audience likes you, they'll forgive just about everything else you do wrong. If they don't like you, you can hit every rule right on target and it doesn't matter. (as cited in Mills, 2000, p. 269)

In summary, the most important attribute you must have to be persuasive is credibility. Credibility is composed of several components: expertise, trustworthiness, and likability. Each of these can be altered to at least some degree and is important to your ability to be persuasive.

The Receiver

The receiver is the last of the four main variables in determining the approach and level of success of any persuasion effort. Successful persuasion requires different approaches to different types of audiences. The bottom line of persuasion is a bit counterintuitive, however—you, the advocate, don't change the target's mind. The only way targets can be persuaded to adopt a view or take an action is if they convince themselves of its value. Your job as a leader is to understand your targets well enough that you assist in this process. The only true way of getting what you want from people is convincing them that it is in their best interest to agree. As Bedell (2000) states, "People will do what you ask only if they believe they'll fulfill their own personal needs by doing so" (p. 22).

Conclusion

This chapter has covered a great deal of ground. The basics of persuasion have been described, along with implications for their practical use by nonprofit leaders working at all levels. Persuasion is needed by social work leaders in many circumstances, such as when working with the board, staff, and coalition partners, for example. Most people are not naturally persuasive, so the information in this chapter must be studied and practiced diligently for it to sink in. Persuasion is vital when advocating with all types of decision-makers, including those

who may hold your finances in their hands. Armed with this knowledge, you can achieve considerable progress as you work with others to accomplish important organizational goals.

Reference List

Bedell, G. (2000). *Three steps to yes: The gentle art of getting your way.* New York, NY: Crown Business.

Cialdini, R. B. (2008). *Influence: Science and practice* (5th ed.). Boston, MA: Allyn & Bacon.

Hoefer, R. (2001). Highly effective human services interest groups: Seven key practices. *Journal of Community Practice, 9*(2), 1–13.

Hoefer, R. (2019). *Advocacy practice for social justice* (4th ed.). New York, NY: Oxford University Press.

Mills, H. (2000). *Artful persuasion: How to command attention, change minds, and influence people.* New York, NY: AMACOM.

Rhoads, K. L. (1997). What's in a frame? *Working Psychology.* Retrieved from www.workingpsychology.com/whatfram.html

Rhoads, K. L., & Cialdini, R. B. (2002). The business of influence: Principles that lead to success in commercial settings. In J. Dillard & M. Pfau (Eds.), *The persuasion handbook* (pp. 513–542). Thousand Oaks, CA: Sage.

Richan, W. C. (1996). *Lobbying for social change* (2nd ed.). New York, NY: Haworth Press.

Rosenthal, A. (1993). *The third house: Lobbyists and lobbying in the states.* Washington, DC: CQ Press.

Wilson, S. R. (2002). *Seeking and resisting compliance: Why people say what they do when trying to influence others.* Thousand Oaks, CA: Sage.

Additional Resources

Bradberry, T., & Greaves, J. (2009). *Emotional Intelligence 2.0*. San Diego, CA: TalentSmart.

Cialdini, R. (2016). *Pre-suasion: A revolutionary way to influence and persuade*. New York, NY: Simon & Shuster.

HELPFUL TERMS

Call to action—an element of your persuasive measure that identifies the action you want your target to take.

Contextual information—information provided to your target about the validity or source of the substantive information in your persuasive message. Providing contextual information can strengthen your target's acceptance of your substantive information and your persuasive effort (see also *substantive information*).

Credibility—the amount that your target believes what you have to say. Credibility resides in the target, not in you—it is a judgment about you by the target.

Fear appeal—a way to deliver your message that focuses on what negatives will occur should you not do as the persuader suggests.

Framing—the process of getting a particular viewpoint accepted as the "right" way to see a situation.

Intent—a declaration to your targets that you are attempting to persuade them. Usually, declaring your intent is counterproductive, but it can sometimes be acceptable.

Manner of presentation—persuaders can choose the way they deliver their information. Elements regarding manner are accuracy, time used, message style, content, and clarity.

Message style—persuaders should choose a particular message style depending on the way the target is most likely to be influenced. Three different approaches are positive vs. negative, private vs. public, and collaborative vs. confrontational.

Redundancy—a redundant message is one that is similar to, but not exactly the same as, previous persuasive messages. It may have the same call to action, but the words and images used are different.

Repetition—Messages may be repeated in the same way to ensure that the target is aware of the message being sent.

Substantive information—information provided to your target that is directly related to the persuasive message—the facts of your argument (see also *contextual information*).

EXERCISES

1. In-Basket Exercise

Directions

Imagine you are Roberta Danzell, Chief Financial Officer for your nonprofit. Your organization's Chief Executive Officer, Beverly Johnson, knows you have recently attended a workshop on "How to be more persuasive". She wants you to lay out a "persuasion campaign" to convince the Advisory Council members to be more active in securing funds for your nonprofit. Use the information in this chapter to respond to the following memo.

Memo

Date: August 8, 20XX

To: Roberta Danzell, Chief Financial Officer

From: Beverly Johnson, CEO

Subject: Community/Business Partners Advisory Council Meeting

As we have discussed, we have a meeting scheduled between ourselves and our community/ business partners advisory council at the end of September, in about seven weeks.

One of the major items that I want to place on the agenda for the meeting is to try to bring the advisory council (AC) members to accept an increased expectation that every council member should be willing to donate financially to our organization, conduct fundraising on our behalf, and advocate on our behalf with political leaders to increase government funding to support our clients, if not the organization directly.

Research indicates that this type of support is extremely advantageous to nonprofits like us and the clients we serve. I have also investigated whether this type and level of commitment is un- usual among our set of comparable agencies. My findings are that almost all other organizations have these expectations for their Boards of Directors but not the advisory councils. Still, given the challenging situation we face financially, I would like to instigate this change, although we first will need board approval. My impression is that the board will not welcome such a change in our rules unless the AC approves it first.

What I would like from you, given your authoritative position as chief financial officer (CFO), is a three- to five-page document outlining a persuasion campaign that we can use to convince the advisory council to enthusiastically adopt this idea at the next AC meeting.

Please include, at a minimum, the following:

a. How can I frame the changes in a persuasive light?

b. Should I present all the results of my research or just the part that supports my idea? Should I appeal to their hopes and dreams for the agency and clients, or should I stress what may happen if we don't raise additional funds?

c. I'd like to hear some ideas on how adopting this new policy is in the AC's best interests.

d. Three salient points that are the most powerful talking points I have.

e. Anything else you think is important regarding how I can be very persuasive.

I don't have to tell you just how important it is for us to bring in additional funding in the next three months. Government grants are drying up, foundations are hurting, and we risk running out of money to pay staff early next year if the situation doesn't turn around quickly!

2. Name That Frame!

Read the following sentences. Which persuasion frame (listed in this chapter or not) is being used in each one?

    a. Oh, come on—it'll be fun!

    b. We went to the movie you wanted to see last time, so I think it is my turn to choose.

    c. If you can't pay me more, I'll have no choice but to find another job.

    d. I've done research on this, and the proper course of action is to do as I suggest.

    e. You've done a great job on this report! And I agree with all your recommendations except the third one. It's just a small thing I'm asking for, but could we delete that one?

    f. Don't you see—if we don't act on this quickly, the best candidates will already be hired by someone else!

    g. Haven't you noticed that other nonprofit leaders in town are all attending the Social Venture Partnership Council's meetings? Wouldn't it be a good idea for you to go, too?

Variation: Develop your own statements using one or more elements of persuasion and negotiation to use in class or in a small group. Turn it into a competition, with the person or group having the most correct answers winning a small prize.

3. Persuasion Practice

Working on your own or in a small group, write a short essay to try to persuade your instructor to change some element of the course (be sure it is something that your instructor could actually change) or your supervisor to change something at your job (again, be realistic). Then, imagine it as a one-on-one conversation. How might you change the wording or other elements of the effort between written submission and conversational delivery? (If you are in a classroom, be prepared to present this as a formal address to the class. Have several such presentations, and have everyone in the class vote on the idea that was best presented.)

4. Influencing Your World: What Works and What Doesn't?

Use the ideas presented in this book and in class for a week or two in your internship, job, and personal life. Keep a log, detailing what decisions you tried to influence, the principles you incorporated in your efforts, and what the results were. Reflect in writing or discuss in class what worked, what didn't work as well, what the circumstances were for either outcome, and what you've learned as a result.

ASSIGNMENTS

1. Look at television or radio ads through the prism of what you've read. Choose two advertisements to describe and critique using the concepts in this chapter. What elements of persuasion are being used? What's the frame? What information is presented to persuade you? What emotions are being targeted?

2. Choose a position on an issue of controversy within the field of nonprofit administration (your instructor may assist you in this). Write an essay on what the controversy is and what the two (or more) sides of the controversy are, and end with an explanation of why you believe one position is correct. Do your best to persuade your reader that you have chosen the better position using information from this book and other sources.

3. Choose a position on a controversial issue taking place in society at large. Create a short presentation to support that position. Make a video of yourself delivering this presentation. Post the video where your instructor can watch it (and possibly other students or the general public). Analyze your delivery and presentation, either in a separate video or in a written format.

Image Credits

14 Advocacy

This chapter builds directly on the previous chapter, which dealt with persuasion. Advocacy is a special case of persuasion, in that you are working to negotiate and persuade people in elected or appointed offices, rather than staff within your organization, board members, clients, peers at other organizations, and other important people in your environment. Everything covered in Chapter 13 applies directly to advocacy, although we should consider advocacy a process that extends both before and after the persuasion effort, because it involves many other tasks.

The Role of Advocacy for Nonprofit Organizations

In an insightful analysis of the role of nonprofit organizations in welfare states, Ralph Kramer (1981) indicated that being change agents "comes close to being a unique organizational competence of the voluntary agency" (p. 231). According to the Commission on Private Philanthropy and Public Needs (1975), also known as the Filer Commission, in an ambitious examination of the role of nonprofit organizations in the United States, "the monitoring and influencing of government may be emerging as one of the single most important and effective functions of the private nonprofit sector" (p. 45). These statements from over 40 years ago may not have come entirely true, partially because nonprofit managers have not been taught a systematic approach to advocacy that fits in with other skills they have had the opportunities to develop. Yet advocacy remains an important function of the nonprofit sector. Ruggiano and Taliaferro (2012) support this view, arguing that lobbying is important for nonprofits to gain the resources they need to serve the public good.

In addition to this view of nonprofit organizations being needed to voice important viewpoints, advocacy by individuals is considered an ethical responsibility by some organizations' code of ethics. The National Association of Social Workers (NASW, 2017), for example, states this explicitly:

> Social workers pursue social change, particularly with and on behalf of vulnerable and oppressed individuals and groups of people. Social workers' social change efforts are focused primarily on issues of poverty, unemployment, discrimination, and other forms of social injustice. These activities seek to promote sensitivity to and knowledge about oppression and cultural and ethnic diversity. Social workers strive to ensure access to needed information, services, and resources, equality of opportunity, and meaningful participation in decision making for all people. (Ethical Principles)

To make the obligation even more clear, in Section 6.04, NASW states four aspects of how social workers should act in terms of social and political action (see Box 14.2).

BOX 14.2 **NASW Code of Ethics, Section 6.04: Social and Political Action**

a. Social workers should engage in social and political action that seeks to ensure that all people have equal access to the resources, employment, services, and opportunities they require to meet their basic human needs and to develop fully. Social workers should be aware of the impact of the political arena on practice and should advocate for changes in policy and legislation to improve social conditions in order to meet basic human needs and promote social justice.

b. Social workers should act to expand choice and opportunity for all people, with special regard for vulnerable, disadvantaged, oppressed, and exploited people and groups.

c. Social workers should promote conditions that encourage respect for cultural and social diversity within the United States and globally. Social workers should promote policies and practices that demonstrate respect for difference, support the expansion of cultural knowledge and resources, advocate for programs and institutions that demonstrate cultural competence, and promote policies that safeguard the rights of and confirm equity and social justice for all people.

d. Social workers should act to prevent and eliminate domination of, exploitation of, and discrimination against any person, group, or class on the basis of race, ethnicity, national origin, color, sex, sexual orientation, gender identity or expression, age, marital status, political belief, religion, immigration status, or mental or physical ability. (NASW, 2017, Ethical Standards)

Prior research shows that social workers tend to be about as active in political efforts as most Americans, which indicates that the NASW code is not an especially significant aspect of their decision to advocate or not. Ezell (1991) found that managers and agency leaders tend to be more active as advocates than social workers. This is because administrators must work with people outside of the organization, and part of their work is to communicate to policymakers how political decisions impact the agency and the clients served. In addition, agency executives tend to have a greater amount of information about the organization and its needs and impact. They are often sought out to provide this information to decision-makers. This chapter should thus be of particular interest if you aim toward moving into higher levels of the organizational hierarchy.

The Six Stages of Advocacy Practice

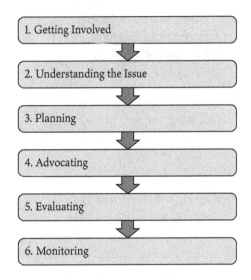

FIGURE 14-1. Six Stages of Advocacy
Source: Adapted from Hoefer, 2019.

Hoefer (2019) defines *advocacy practice* as "that part of social work practice in which a social worker takes action in a systematic and purposeful way to defend, represent, or otherwise advance the cause of one or more clients at the individual, group, organizational, or community level in order to promote social justice" (p. 3). He describes the advocacy process as a form of the general problem-solving method used in social work and other professions. Because of this, it is actually easy to explain and easy for people to understand. In direct practice work, a social worker would meet the client, assess, plan, intervene, evaluate, and follow-up.

Advocacy is much the same process, although different skills and competencies are called upon. Hoefer (2019) describes six distinct stages in his unified model of advocacy practice (see Figure 14.1). Each will be covered briefly.

Stage 1: Getting Involved

The idea of getting involved is simple: Are you going to put some of your life into trying to make a difference in a particular area, or are you not? Large numbers of Americans are not involved in political efforts at all (not even voting), much less a more difficult and time-consuming activity such as political advocacy.

Seven variables are seen as affecting the likelihood that a person will get involved with advocacy (Hoefer, 2019). These are the person's educational level, values, sense of professional responsibility,

interest, skills, level of participation in other organizations, and amount of free time. No matter your current level on all of these variables, you can increase them to some extent by consciously shaping your own environment to support growth on each variable. All agency employees, whether they are social workers or not, can be advocates to support the needs of the organization and its clients, regardless of their employee role. Employees at all levels should be able to recruit others (such as board members and clients) to support

BOX 14.3 Methods Nonprofits Can Use to Affect "Getting Involved" Variables

Education: Get Continuing Education Units or other training relating to political advocacy for all employees.

Values: Shape organizational norms by hiring people with an activist orientation.

Sense of professional responsibility: Hire professional social workers with demonstrated advocacy experience or training.

Interest: Expose staff members to results of political decisions on clients and build their sense of political self-efficacy.

Skills: Provide advocacy mentors to selected staff members.

Participation in other organizations: Assign staff members to work with coalitions or other advocacy organizations.

Time: Allow flextime or paid time to assist staff members to attend meetings and events related to advocacy efforts.

the organizational vision and services, and even to train them with the information in this and the preceding chapter.

Stage 2: Understanding the Issue

Inexperienced advocates or people new to a specific policy arena often want to move forward quickly, without taking the time to understand fully the issue(s) at hand. In particular, there is a temptation to try to understand the issue from only your own side without trying to research and appraise any other approach or perspective. Moving forward without truly understanding the issue from at least two perspectives is a mistake and may doom your advocacy effort from the start.

Hoefer (2019) lists five steps in understanding an issue. First, advocates must define the issue so that they can talk confidently within a particular frame of reference about the impacts of a problem on a particular group of people (see Chapter 13 for the discussion on persuasion frames, such as "It isn't fair" or "After what they've been through, they deserve this"). Without completing this step, there is a danger you will adopt the frame someone else has set forth rather than developing a clear sense of how you view the situation.

The second step is to decide who is affected by the issue, and how. If there is a problem, then the issue is hurting someone or a larger group of people. But it is also vital to understand who is being helped by the current situation—is it helping someone make money, or does it support the current emotional needs of a powerful person or group of people? Is the situation just "tradition" that has not been examined for some time? The third step is to decide what the main causes of the issue are. It may be impossible to determine what the ultimate cause is, but if you can determine what is causing the issue, at least at the proximate (immediate) level, it is far easier to solve the issue.

Fourth, you need to generate solutions to the issue, at least to the immediate problem. It is tempting to take the first plausible solution you come up with, but you should generate several (at least) potential solutions to have a wider variety of choices, some of which may be easier to adopt than others. You can look to other cities, states, and countries for ideas or generate additional potential solutions on your own through techniques such as brainstorming.

BOX 14.4 Methods for Developing Alternative Solutions

Brainstorming: A process of generating ideas without evaluating them right away. Save evaluation until after a set time period for idea generation is completed.

George Costanza approach: Think of how things are done now, and imagine what "doing the opposite" would be. What benefits might ensue from doing things "oppositely"?

Win-win approach: Create an alternative policy that restructures the current situation. A set of prompts and questions can be used to generate ideas.

Source: Hoefer (2019, pp. 66–71).

The fifth step in understanding the issue is to review all of the proposed solutions to estimate their impact on the problem and on social justice more broadly. Each advocacy effort requires a thoughtful decision about which solution or solutions to pursue. The ones you choose may be of different priorities, and you may trade off achieving one for having a better one enacted. Sometimes you may have to accept a bill that is easy to pass when you'd rather have a law that has a greater chance of impacting the problem.

Stage 3: Planning

Just as it is easy to want to try to solve a problem without taking the time to understand it fully, it is also easy to want to jump into action before planning adequately. Hoefer (2019) uses the analogy of using a map of getting from one place to another to illustrate planning in advocacy, which is laying out how to get from here (the current state of affairs) to there (a different and better state of affairs). Advocates can use various methods to lay out the steps in their plan, but it is important to relate the actions you take to the outcomes you want to achieve. You need to choose the precise goals and objectives of your advocacy. You also want to select an appropriate target. If you try to change Medicaid funding formulas at the local level, for example, you'll find your concerns can't be addressed at that level—it is a problem for the federal and state governments to address. Before you can advocate with your targets, you need to know who they are. Getting information about legislators and their staff members is not difficult. Elected officials almost all have websites where you can learn what their interests and positions are on issues. You can also discover their contact information, such as office address, phone number, and e-mail address.

Your advocacy plan should also include a timeline for action, perhaps tied to other stakeholders' schedules. For example, if you wait until after the legislative session is over to advocate, you may seriously delay achieving the policy change you want. Planning does not take place on its own—all the steps up to now must be completed, and the information must then be used in the planning stage. Good planning takes the information from before it and makes it possible to apply a clear set of feasible steps in the future.

Stage 4: Advocating

This is the stage where you actually contact decision-makers. Using your skills in persuading (as discussed in Chapter 13), you make your best efforts to have your target adopt (to the greatest extent possible) the ideas, plans, and positions that you put forward. You have your desire to be involved and you have your plan, based on your understanding of the issue. Advocating is simply the stage to put your plan into action. You may not have considered everything that you could have, and your plan may not be working as well as you thought it would. Then, of course, you may need to adapt your plan to better fit the changing realities before you. It is much better to adjust your advocacy plan and tactics than to abandon your values and goals.

Stage 5: Evaluating

Once your advocacy effort is completed, it is time to take stock of the results you achieved and the costs that you paid to achieve those results. It is rare when you achieve everything you started out wanting. Other participants in the policy process will want their views adopted, and your persuasion efforts may not have been fully effective. It becomes vital to judge exactly what you achieved compared to what you planned to accomplish—is it close to three-fourths of what you wanted? More like half of what your organization desired? Even less than half? This is an important part of your evaluation but not the entire evaluation.

You also need to compare what you did with what you planned to do—were you (or your group) able to meet as often as you desired with key decision makers? Were you able to round up the number of volunteers needed to make calls or write letters? If the answers are no, you'll want to examine the reasons why you weren't able to do so. If the answers are yes, you'll want to document what you did so that you'll also be able to do it again in the next advocacy effort.

The final element of the evaluation is to link your actions and your achievements. It may be you didn't do as many of your actions as you thought you would need to. If this is so, then you likely didn't achieve as much as you thought you would. But it may be that you did everything you planned to do and still didn't achieve all that you desired. In your evaluation, you'll want to analyze what happened and why you weren't as successful as you thought you would be. What lessons can you develop to improve the results of future advocacy?

Beyond the immediate results of your advocacy effort, you will want to examine the context of the policy debate. It may be you didn't get the exact policy you were working for, but you may be changing the terms of the debate (the frame used to discuss the issue). If you find key actors starting to use the same language you use when describing the problem, the population affected, or the policy options, you are winning many small victories that should be celebrated, remembered, and built on for the next time the issue is raised.

Stage 6: Monitoring

The final stage of advocacy practice is that of ongoing monitoring. You need to pay attention to the way any programs you supported are actually being run. Regulations determine much of what program staff members can do, so you will want to pay attention to the way these are written. You may find that you lose much of the gains you believed you had won if others control the way the rules are written. You also need to attend to the budgeting process to ensure that any new provisions

you supported have enough resources to do what they are supposed to do. A program that is not given sufficient funds to run itself will be crippled and ineffective, thus leading to future accusations that it should be eliminated.

Monitoring by advocates almost always takes place within the executive branch, not the legislative branch. The executive branch operates in significantly different ways than does the legislative, and skilled advocates will need to be aware that this is true. Legislators, for example, are used to being lobbied by constituents and interest groups. This is less true of people working in the executive branch, who are selected primarily for their specialist expertise and are not lobbied often in the same way that lawmakers are. Another important difference is that legislators and their staff members are well known to advocates because they have chosen to be in the spotlight. Executive branch employees, however, are much more likely to be fairly anonymous, working far from the public eye. It may be more difficult just to find out who to contact.

Does Advocacy for Social Justice Still Work?

It is no secret that the American political system has become more polarized in recent decades, with policy positions hardening into Republican and Democratic versions. The overlap between adherents to either party has decreased, so that it is difficult to reach common ground. People find they are unwilling to compromise with the "other side." It's a natural question, then, to wonder if advocacy still works. You should admit to yourself and others that advocating for social justice is not always going to be an easy sell. Still, much hangs in the balance. You are not allowed to stop trying—too much is at stake for your organization, your clients, your community, and even for you, as a social work leader. Part of your job is to inspire the others around you to make the effort to advocate.

The evidence-based approach to persuasion and advocacy is still valid. Some revisions may make advocacy efforts more successful in these contentious times. Relationships with decision-makers are more important than ever. Strangers (such as you!) are less persuasive with regard to policy and politics than are people who have a past relationship. Thus, you need to be proactive in reaching out to decision-makers, even when there is nothing that you want or need in the moment.

Listening is important. If you want to be successful, you must know what the recipient of your advocacy effort already thinks—don't just assume the political party label defines the totality of the person any more than your political party affiliation is the only important thing about you and your thoughts. As you come to have a relationship with decision-makers, you may find unexpected life experiences or ideas in common that help you provide information that supports your political position more effectively.

As difficult as it may be to accept, for some people, facts just don't matter in their deliberations. They have their view of the world, and nothing can change that. In these cases, it is a waste of effort to focus on how the recipients are wrong in their facts. The only way to successfully reach them is to engage in helping them shift their sense of identity. As you may already know, this process is difficult and a long-term commitment. It is usually better to work on your policy agenda in other ways.

It is important, however, to remember that most people in decision-making roles (including your allies, board members, and others) may disagree with your positions for reasons that are amenable to change. For this majority group of advocacy recipients, research studies provide nonprofit managers with empirical information on how to be better advocates. For example, policy-relevant information and research results are still important when lobbying. Giesler, Parris, Weaver, Hall, and Sullivan (2012) studied how local-level policymakers are influenced in their decision-making. Decision-makers at this level use "social service agency reports, social service agency staff consultation, and other [decision-makers'] opinions" (p. 236). At the state level, in Texas, research was seen as very important to legislators when voting on human services issues

(Cochran, Montgomery, & Rubin, 2010). As a social work leader, then, you want to have developed research to support your positions, even if it may not be at the level expected in graduate-level research classes (Miller-Cribbs, Cagle, Natale, & Cummings, 2010).

Two state-level comparative policy studies had very similar results as to what variables shape particular policies. Lee and Donlan (2009) found that Democratic political party control leads to higher expenditures for Medicaid; Hoefer, Black, and Salehin's (2012) results show that Democratic Party control is the primary determinant of strong teen dating violence prevention policy at the state level. This indicates that advocates in favor of stronger human services legislation may wish to help ensure that candidates from the Democratic Party are elected. Conversely, people who have another viewpoint may wish to work to elect Republican Party officials.

Dangers of Advocacy for Social Justice

The profession of social work is quick to encourage active participation to uphold social work values, but it is important to recognize that social justice advocacy is risky. It is uncommon to discuss potential harm that can occur to social workers and social work students demanding social justice. Harm ranges from incidental unpleasantness in person or on social media to losing a job or, in the worst case, enduring physical harm. Advocates who challenge established power need to be aware of the potential for being vilified or attacked. Jane Addams, often lionized within social work texts for her efforts in the Settlement House movement and peace efforts, endured vicious attacks on her work. She was regarded by many as "the most dangerous woman in America" (Sawyers, 1987, para. 1), with calls to hang her for being a traitor for her efforts to promote peace. Sawyers (1987) noted that Addams "certainly felt much pain from these attacks on herself and her work" (para. 9). Another prominent social worker, Bertha Capen Reynolds, lost her job as associate dean at Smith College in 1938 for helping unionize the staff and for being a Marxist (NASW Foundation, 2004).

Decades later, civil rights workers in the 1960s were murdered and others seriously injured by white supremacists (Taylor, 2014). This went beyond attacks on movement leaders, such as the assassinations of Medgar Evers and Dr. Martin Luther King, Jr. Many peaceful protesters were set on by police with attack dogs and firefighters with high-pressure water hoses (Library of Congress, n.d.). In 1964, the Ku Klux Klan and similar white supremacy organizations tried to terrorize others by burning African American churches and murdering three civil rights workers (Public Broadcasting Service, n.d.). In recent years, protesters for social justice have been attacked by police with pepper spray while seated passively on the ground at the University of California–Davis (Cherkis, 2011) and while peacefully protesting against a white supremacist speaker at Duke University (Shen, 2016). Getting involved with social justice, even just by making comments on Facebook or other social media, may bring unwanted attention. You may receive only a few critical comments, or you may lose friends and experience conflict with family members. If you are unlucky enough to become the target of a group opposed to your views, your account may be taken over surreptitiously, you may be bombarded with vile insults, and your ability to function online may be compromised. Death threats may be sent, not only to you but to your family members. Previous generations endured when faced with sometimes annoying and sometimes dangerous attacks because of their work for social justice, and we must also. Because social workers are called to be advocates, as a profession, we should acknowledge that we may face negative consequences and prepare for them.

Protecting Your Organization's Advocacy Campaign

Planning is essential when you anticipate policy conflict. Prevent, as much as you can, policy conflicts from becoming shouting matches and personal grudges. As you engage in advocacy, be sure to keep the following ideas in mind (Community Tool Box, n.d.).

- *Emphasize the Core Messages of Your Campaign.* Be sure you have a few solid positions that you can base your entire advocacy effort on. Develop these when you begin your advocacy effort. As you respond to attacks, remember to return to your core messages in every communication. You want to keep the controversy within the frame you developed. Map out your messages and keep to your plan. Focus on what you say about the opposition and what you say about yourself. Avoid commenting on their attacks on you or how they present themselves.

- *Study the Anticipated Opposition Before You Begin Your Campaign.* It is likely that your group has had conflicts with other groups in the past, so you can anticipate some lines of attack on your ideas ahead of time. If you understand your opponents' ideas, positions, history, and past tactics, you have a better chance to respond effectively. Opposition research will help you mobilize your best ideas in response to attacks and keep you in control of the narrative you want to present. It may be best to hold off on any response so as not to give your opponents any free publicity, but if the attack is gaining traction, you need to have a powerful answer to it.

- *Respond Strategically.* Focus on your messages and the audiences of most concern to you. You won't change the minds of opponents, so be sure to focus attention on nonactive supporters and on third parties (such as the media) who can influence the nonaligned public.

- *Track Reactions and Course Correct.* You need to determine how well your messaging is resonating. Ways to do so include using appropriate hashtags attached to your social media posts and tracking their use by others, which can be done through one or more free hashtag tracking services (Lozano, 2018). You can also use Google Alerts to inform you when key terms are mentioned online (Juraschka, 2017). Also, if calling for financial support, you can determine how many donations are being given and their amount. If your message appears to be falling on deaf ears, you will want to make changes or risk losing your advocacy effort.

Conclusion

While this is only a quick overview of the advocacy process that nonprofit leaders can use, you can see how the steps of this approach fit in well with a general problem-solving approach that emphasizes assessment, planning, intervention, and evaluation of the intervention. In addition, you must decide to get involved to begin with, and you must keep monitoring the situation to determine if the problem is improving, getting worse, or staying the same once some new proposal is adopted or if nothing is done. We also presented additional information regarding empirically supported ways to be effective in your advocacy efforts to provide more specifics for new and experienced advocates. Use persuasive techniques (see Chapter 13) as you plan and conduct your advocacy efforts.

Reference List

Cherkis, J. (2011, November 19). UC Davis police pepper-spray seated students in Occupy dispute. *Huffington Post*. Retrieved from https://www.huffingtonpost.com/2011/11/19/uc-davis-police-pepper-spraystudents_n_1102728.html

Cochran, G., Montgomery, K., & Rubin, A. (2010). Does evidence-based practice influence state legislators' decision-making process? An exploratory study. *Journal of Policy Practice, 9*(3–4), 263–283.

Commission on Private Philanthropy and Public Needs. (1975). *Giving in America: Toward a stronger voluntary sector*. Washington, DC: Author.

Community Tool Box. (n.d.). Section 2. How to respond to opposition tactics (chapter 35). Retrieved from https://ctb.ku.edu/en/table-of-contents/advocacy/respondto-counterattacks/respond-to-opposition/main

Ezell, M. (1991). Administrators as advocates. *Administration in Social Work, 15*(4), 1–18.

Giesler, F., Parris, A., Weaver, L., Hall, L., & Sullivan, Q. (2012). Sources of information that influence social service public policy decisions. *Journal of Policy Practice, 11*(4), 236–254.

Hoefer, R. (2019). *Advocacy practice for social justice* (4th ed.). New York, NY: Oxford University Press.

Hoefer, R., Black, B., & Salehin, M. (2012). Dating violence policy: Making the grade. *Journal of Sociology & Social Welfare, 39*(4), 9–24.

Juraschka, R. (2017, February 9). How to use Google alerts to monitor your small business online [Web log post]. Retrieved from https://www.hostpapa.com/blog/technology/google-alerts-monitor-small-business/

Kramer, R. (1981). *Voluntary agencies in the welfare state*. Berkeley, CA: University of California Press.

Lee, J., & Donlan, W. (2009). Cultural, social, and political influences on state-level indigent health care policy formation. *Journal of Policy Practice, 8*(2), 129–146.

Library of Congress. (n.d.). The Civil Rights Act of 1964: A long struggle for freedom. Retrieved from http://loc.gov/exhibits/civil-rights-act/civil-rights-era.html

Lozano, D. (2018, March 28). 5 free hashtag tracking tools to try in 2018 [Web log post]. Retrieved from https://www.socialmediatoday.com/news/5-free-hashtag-tracking-tools-to-try-in-2018/520120/

Miller-Cribbs, J. E., Cagle, B. E., Natale, A. P., & Cummings, Z. (2010). Thinking about think tanks: Strategies for progressive social work. *Journal of Policy Practice, 9*(3–4), 284–307.

National Association of Social Workers. (2017). *Code of ethics*. Washington, DC. Author. Retrieved from https://www.socialworkers.org/About/Ethics/Code-of-Ethics/Code-of-Ethics-English

NASW Foundation. (2004). Bertha Capen Reynolds. Retrieved from https://www.naswfoundation.org/Our-Work/NASW-Social-Workers-Pioneers/NASW-Social-Workers-Pioneers-Listing.aspx?id=474

Public Broadcasting Service. (n.d.). Murder in Mississippi. Retrieved from https://www.pbs.org/wgbh/americanexperience/features/freedomsummer-murder/

Ruggiano, N., & Taliaferro, J. D. (2012). Resource dependency and agent theories: A framework for exploring nonprofit leaders' resistance to lobbying. *Journal of Policy Practice, 11*(4), 219–235.

Sawyers, J. (1987, March 1). Jane Addams? *Chicago Tribune*. Retrieved from http://articles.chicagotribune.com/1987-03-01/features/8701160798_1_hull-housejane-addams-immigrants

Shen, A. (2016, November 3). Police pepper-spray black students peacefully protesting David Duke. *ThinkProgress*. Retrieved from https://thinkprogress.org/police-pepper-spray-david-duke-protesters-ab445022831e/

Taylor, A. (2014, May 28). 1964: Civil rights battles. *The Atlantic*. Retrieved from https://www.theatlantic.com/photo/2014/05/1964-civil-rights-battles/100744/

Additional Resources

Schneider, R. L., Lester, L., & Ochieng, J. Advocacy. *Encyclopedia of Social Work*. NASW and Oxford University Press. Retrieved from https://oxfordre.com/socialwork/view/10.1093/acrefore/9780199975839.001.0001/acrefore-9780199975839-e-10

HELPFUL TERMS

Advocacy practice—taking action in a systematic and purposeful way to defend, represent, or otherwise advance the cause of one or more clients at the individual, group, organizational, or community level in order to promote social justice.

Executive branch—interprets and implements the laws developed by the legislative branch. This is true at the national, state, and local levels (see also *legislative branch*).

Legislative branch—passes bills that may then be signed into law by the chief executive. These are then interpreted and implemented by the executive branch. This is true at the national and state levels. Local governments also have legislative bodies, although chief executives at that level operate somewhat differently than at the national and state levels (see also *executive branch*).

Proximate cause (of a problem)—the immediate identifiable cause of a current problem. Focusing on the proximate cause can give advocates something to work on, even if it isn't the "true" cause in some philosophical sense (see also *ultimate cause*).

Target—the individual or group that can make the authoritative decision that you desire.

Ultimate cause (of a problem)—the root cause of a current problem that may extend back in time and across political boundaries. It is the "true" cause of the problem but may be intractable and impossible to impact. Focusing on ultimate causes can quickly lead to demoralization (see also *proximate cause*).

EXERCISES

1. In-Basket Exercise

Directions

Imagine you are Samantha Velasquez, the Advocacy Volunteer Coordinator of your organization (choose an organization you are familiar with or one you would like to know more about). You receive a request from the Board Chairman of your nonprofit to assist in development of a plan to educate legislators on the organization's needs. For this in-basket exercise, personalize your response by finding legislators for your location. Use any human service agency you desire for Question 2c and Question 3. Be as realistic as possible when considering who should be the targets of your advocacy.

Memo

Date: September 6, 20XX

To: Samantha Velasquez, Advocacy Volunteer Coordinator

From: Kenyonne Hightower, Chair of Board

Subject: Beginning Steps for New Advocacy Efforts

It is becoming clear to us on the board that we need to become involved in the realm of educating our legislators about our organization's needs. Unfortunately, we have very little idea about how to begin. This is where your expertise comes in.

We believe that the first step is to get to know more about our legislators. We would like you to write up the following information:

1. Search for information on the following four people: one of our U.S. senators, our U.S. house representative, our state senator, and our state house representative.

2. For each of these four elected officials, get this information:

    a. The committees they serve on

    b. Their office location, phone number to speak to an aide, and an e-mail address to communicate with them

    c. Their position on one issue related to our agency's mission

3. Of these four legislators, which one do you think is the one we should start building a relationship with first? Why?

2. What's in a Name?

Discuss with one or two other people what your perceptions of lobbying and advocacy are. Would you want to tell new acquaintances that you are a "lobbyist"? Would it sound better if you indicated that your job is to influence elected officials? Why or why not? How would you like talking about your position if it were called "social justice champion"?

3. Social Media and Advocacy

While this chapter doesn't address the ways to use social media in an advocacy campaign, brainstorm with colleagues how you could use Facebook, Twitter, Reddit, Pinterest, or other social media outlets in an advocacy effort. What advantages would there be for you? What dangers might you face in doing so?

4. Give It a Try

Search the web for an advocacy organization or interest group that has views you agree with. Look on its website for information about advocacy and how you can be involved in their issue. Select one of their suggestions (don't choose "donate money"!) and tell your colleagues or classmates which one you have chosen to do. Within one week, complete this self-chosen task. Discuss what you did and how you feel about your effort with the colleagues or classmates you declared your intentions to.

ASSIGNMENTS

1. The seven variables related to a person's getting involved with advocacy are the person's educational level, values, sense of professional responsibility, interest, skills, level of participation in other organizations, and amount of free time (Hoefer, 2019). Give yourself a grade from A to F on each variable. Discuss why you think this is so. Create a plan to improve each area where you have a grade of B or less.

2. Choose a human services issue that is of interest to you. Write a one- to two-page letter that you can send to a legislator that presents your ideas on this issue. Review your letter in light of the information on persuasion discussed in Chapter 13. Send it.

3. Select an existing human services program. Find information on how its budget has changed over the past five years. Relate this to the change in need for the program. Write a short paper (two to three pages) summarizing the information and examining whether you believe the budget has been adequate or not. If you feel particularly passionate about this topic (or for extra credit, if your instructor agrees), schedule an appointment with an appropriate target to explain why you believe the budget needs to be increased, decreased, or remain the same.

Image Credits

Fig. 14.1: Richard Hoefer, "Six Stages of Advocacy," Advocacy Practice for Social Justice. Copyright © 2019.

Img. 14.1: Copyright © 2014 Depositphotos/Wavebreakmedia.

Img. 14.2: Copyright © 2016 Depositphotos/Ellandar.

Img. 14.3: Copyright © 2015 Depositphotos/Under_verse.

Img. 14.4: Copyright © 2013 Depositphotos/Iqoncept.

Img. 14.5: Copyright © 2018 Depositphotos/Artursz.

Img. 14.6: Copyright © 2017 slowking4, (GFDL v1.2) at: https://commons.wikimedia.org/wiki/File:Womens_march_washington,_D.C._1216834.jpg. A copy of the license can be found here: https://www.gnu.org/licenses/old-licenses/fdl-1.2.html.

Img. 14.7: Copyright © 2015 Depositphotos/Gustavofrazao.

15 Putting the Pieces Together

In the previous chapters, we have looked at many aspects of human services administration. Figure 15.1 shows the four-quadrant model first displayed in the book's Preface, along with the trends affecting social work organizations (from Chapter 1). The figure also includes the leadership theories and skills from Chapter 4 to remind us of the breadth of topics addressed. In Part I, we began by looking at the context of human services and the values and theories that underlie our work in this sector. We explored what being a social work leader entails in Chapters 4 and 5, looking at leadership and the importance of personal communication skills in Part II. In Part III, we looked in more detail at the four quadrants of human services administration functions. In Quadrant I, we examined functions that are task-oriented and internal to the organization. The specific topics covered were strategic planning in Chapter 6; program planning, logic models, and evaluation in Chapter 7; and budgeting and finance in Chapter 8. As we moved to more externally oriented tasks in Quadrant II, we explored issues of fund development and grantwriting in Chapter 9 and marketing in Chapter 10. Quadrant III skills are those that are internal and people-oriented. In this section, we examined issues of human resources in Chapter 11 and board relationships in Chapter 12. Finally, in Quadrant IV, we moved to people-oriented and externally focused functions to learn about persuasion in Chapter 13 and advocacy skills in Chapter 14. As you look back across the topics covered, you will find that a common denominator in almost all the functions of human services administration is the ability to form and maintain relationships.

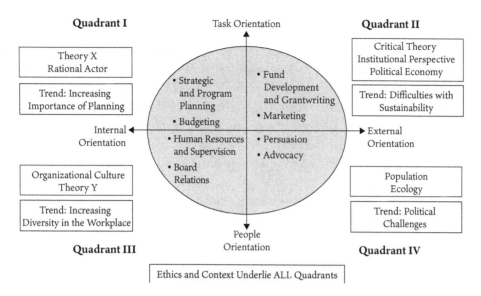

FIGURE 15.1. A Four-Quadrant View of Leadership, Trends, Needed Skills, and Linked Theory

Building Relationships

Human services leadership and administration is about forming relationships at all levels. Relationships are vital for dealing with funding sources, regulatory agencies, the general public, boards and commissions, referral sources, staff, clients, and all other stakeholder groups related to the organization. *Relationship* is a term of great historical significance in the social work literature (Johnson & Yanca, 2010) and in other disciplines, as well. While it is often used in relation to the direct service worker–client dyad, it is of equal importance in administrative practice. Perlman (1979) describes

relationship as "a catalyst, an enabling dynamism in the support, nurture and freeing of people's energies and motivation toward problem solving" (p. 2). This definition well describes the tasks of human services administrators.

The importance of administrative relationships is documented in a study of 37 companies from 11 parts of the world, in which Kanter (1994) found that relationships between companies grow or fail much like the relationships between people. Kanter reported that when relationships between organizations were built on creating new values together, rather than on a mere exchange arrangement, both partners considered their alliance a success. True partners valued the skills that each brought to the relationship. The same can be said for all levels of nonprofit administration. Social work administrators understand intuitively the importance of relationships. Relationships are key to our professional identity. Skinner (2018) incorporated the rise of Internet-powered communication into this conclusion, adding further power to the idea that relationships are keys to success.

As noted earlier in the book, Hoefer (2009) refined the ratings of 37 skills, attitudes, and knowledge areas needed for social work administration into four categories: people skills, attitudes and experiences, substantive knowledge, and management skills. Of these four, "people skills" are the most important set of skills for the nonprofit administrator. Management competencies are not a substitute for core social values and interpersonal skills. Denhardt (2015) advises public administrators not to define their role or gauge their actions based solely on business values and market-based approaches, but rather on democratic ideals such as citizenship, community, and participation in decision-making. We echo this advice for social work leaders and promote using the NASW (2017) Code of Ethics for guidance.

Although it seems at times that our entire society now embraces the neoliberal idea that everything (including human services) is a market that must be run with only thoughts of profit and efficiency in mind, we believe that such ideas must be tempered. Combating human need is still the reason for social work and human services.

As we were finishing this book, the story of a "lunchroom lady" named Bonnie Kimball from New Hampshire emerged in the press. When a young student did not have cash on hand to buy lunch and was $8.00 in arrears, this woman allowed him to take food items at that time, upon his promise to bring funds the next day to erase his debt and pay for the food. She was fired for this breach of the rules. After considerable negative publicity ensued for the privatized lunchroom catering service and the public school district contracting with it, she was offered her job back, but she (and others who had quit in protest) no longer wished to work there (Chavez, Riess, & Kaur, 2019). The superintendent of the school district stated, "First and foremost, it is our goal to do right by our families, community, students and employees at the Mascoma Valley Regional School District. The events of these past few weeks and the feedback I have received from parents has given me considerable pause" (Chavez et al., 2019). What impresses us in this story is the willingness of Ms. Kimball (and others) to stand up for what they felt was right for the children they interacted with, even at the cost of their jobs.

Human services administrators of all types, but especially social work leaders, must find the way to do right by their clients and communities. While it may not be easy to maintain this spirit, due to some of the negative trends pointed out earlier, relationship-building and maintenance with all stakeholders is something to strive for. It is your ticket to success as a social work leader. It is also what will enable you to continue in your career over the long run.

The Joy of Administration

Edward Deming, the father of total quality management, often promoted the idea that every employee should be able to achieve joy at work and that joy would lead to improved quality and a high-performance organization. "Management's overall aim should be to create a system in which everybody may take joy in his work" (Neave, 1990, p. 36). Deming's instruction at the time was not research-based, but it has been echoed in the past few years as those in the field of positive psychology have explored psychological wellness rather than illness. The

emerging subfield of positive organizational behavior (POB) is attempting to apply the concepts of positive psychology to the workplace (Youssef & Luthans, 2007).

A roadblock to the study of joy is the lack of an operationalized definition of the concept. It is not a clearly definable emotion and is expressed in a variety of ways by different individuals (Hoskote, 2009). Joy is not the same thing as happiness. Happiness often requires a series of events to occur, and when those events end, happiness may disappear. In contrast, joy is long-lasting and can be recalled at will by the person who has experienced it (Lazarus, 1991). After an extensive literature review, and based on the findings of her interviews with health care professionals, Manion (2003) defined joy as "an intensely positive, vivid, and expansive emotion that arises from an internal state or results from an external event or situation. It may include a physiologic reaction, an expressive component, and conscious volition. It is a transcendent state of heightened energy and excitement" (p. 653).

Manion's approach is comprehensive but not easily operationalized. Watson and Hoefer (2016) adopted a definition of joy provided by William Schutz (1967):

> Joy is the feeling that comes from the fulfillment of one's potential. Fulfillment brings to an individual the feeling that he can cope with his environment; the sense of confidence in himself as a significant, competent, lovable person who is capable of handling situations as they arise, able to use fully his own capacities, and free to express his feelings. (p. 15)

Watson and Hoefer (2016) used this description of joy because it focuses on administrative tasks: coping with a difficult environment, building a sense of self-confidence through competence, handling situations by using one's own capacities, and expressing feelings appropriately. Social work has a rich history of seeking to build on strengths rather than building on weaknesses. Saleebey (2008) argued that for macro practitioners to focus only on deficits would further marginalize oppressed communities and groups. Likewise, in social work administration, we need more focus on the positive aspects of leadership and administrative practice. In teaching administration, we should follow the lead of positive psychology in embracing the idea that "what is good about life is as genuine as what is bad and therefore deserves equal attention" (Peterson, 2006, p. 4).

Fredrickson's (2002) work in positive organizational psychology found that negative emotions are undone by positive emotions such as joy and amusement. Positive emotions were found to promote resilient coping in the midst of adversity. Positive emotions, such as joy, broaden people's mindsets and promote unique and creative lines of thought or action. Being more creative allows one to push the limits for bringing innovative ideas to fruition (Fredrickson, 2002).

Little research has been conducted in the area of the joy of administrative social work practice. In fact, there is little research on the topic in any related discipline. The most extensive work has been in the area of POB, which attempts to apply the concepts of positive psychology to the workplace (Youssef & Luthans, 2007). Currently, the literature relating POB to social work leadership and administration is almost nonexistent, but we believe it is vitally important to create it.

One of the assignments that we give to the students in our social work administration class is for them to go into the community and interview an agency executive director. During a class discussion of the student's interview experience, one of the students made a very interesting comment. She said that she was fascinated when the administrator she was interviewing began to talk about the joys of being a human services administrator. During the next class after the interview, the student said, "You teach us about the challenges and the tasks of administration, but we don't hear about the joys of being an administrator." This comment led to a modification of the assignment and the beginning of a research project to explore the "joys of human services administration." The early results of this exploration, with 20 executive director interviews, have revealed several themes. We will review here the joyful aspects of being a social work leader that current administrators mentioned in their interviews (seen in Box 15.1).

BOX 15.1 6 Ways Social Work Leaders Find Joy in Their Work

- Making a difference in people's lives
- Mentoring staff
- Finding meaning in work
- Being an advocate
- Giving and receiving recognition
- Seeing it in their (your) eyes

Making a Difference in People's Lives

Without exception, the human services administrators said that the greatest joy of their job was knowing that their agency was making a difference in people's lives. If an administrator has true passion and a heart for the people served by the organization, he or she will find joy in the work. As you consider where you will expend your time and energies in your career, be sure that you have passion for the people served and a belief in the mission of the organization.

Mentoring Staff

The second most common source of joy identified by the human services administrators was helping their staff to grow and to advance in their careers. Several talked about people who had been mentors in their lives, and they now found joy in helping others to reach their career and professional goals. As you advance in your career, remember those who have served as your role models and mentors. Remember your responsibility to be a mentor and to help others to meet their professional goals.

Finding Meaning in Work

Some of the administrators had come to the human services field by way of the business world. In their interviews, they talked about the difference in the setting and what that difference meant to them. One said, "At my other job, we were concerned about money. Here, we are concerned about helping autistic children learn to speak."

Being an Advocate

Other administrators said they found joy in advocating for their clients who could not advocate for themselves. In most cases, they spoke of being an advocate at the community level and seeing that services were available for their client populations. Many who had come from direct services spoke of feeling they could help more people as an administrator than they could as a direct service provider. Many saw their work in the community of human services as a function of advocating for the people served by their organizations.

Giving and Receiving Recognition

Moments of joy come when respondents see staff and volunteers get the recognition they so richly deserve. Joy is found when everyone comes together to provide needed assistance to agency clients. Joy also comes about when receiving compliments from others about one's department.

Seeing It in Their (Your) Eyes

Several students commented that when they asked the question, "What brings you the most joy in your work?" they could see a physical change in the administrator's facial expression. "Their face lit up," or, "I could see the passion in their eyes," were common observations made by the students. Find a position that will be so important and meaningful to you that others can see it in your face when you talk about your work.

Conclusion

As we bring this book to a close, we want to emphasize the positive aspects of social work leadership and administration. Educators must take it upon themselves to balance descriptions of the difficulties of human services administration with the joys of the work, as well. The contradiction between only describing how awful being an administrator is and exhorting students to become administrators needs to end. Education on the positive elements of leading a nonprofit should be included in all course work touching on administration topics. Doing so helps students thinking about getting their education in management to see that leaders help people in many ways, even if not in the same ways that their direct practice colleagues hope to.

Focusing on joy is also a way to keep qualified administrators in the field and to attract new and talented people to the work. Nonprofit organizations can help their managers and administrators find and focus on these elements to delay or prevent ongoing high levels of stress, burnout, and early retirement from the field.

As a social work leader, you will want to master each of the areas discussed in this book. While the tasks and skills are important to your success, much of your success will be related to your ability to form and maintain relationships with the stakeholders of the organization. You will be the face of the organization in the community you serve. Serving as a leader will no doubt bring great challenges, but it can also be a fascinating and rewarding career that will bring you great joy.

Reference List

Chavez, N., Riess, R., & Kaur, H. (2019, May 17). A lunchroom worker fired after letting a student take food for free just got offered her job back. She won't take it. *CNN*. Retrieved from https://www.cnn.com/2019/05/17/us/lunchroom-employee-fired-offered-job-trnd/index.html

Denhardt, R. B., & Catlaw, T. J. (2015). *Theories of public organization* (7th ed.). Stamford, CT: Cengage.

Fredrickson, B. L. (2002). Positive emotions. In C. R. Snyder, & S. J. Lopez (Eds.), *Handbook of positive psychology* (pp. 120–134). New York, NY: Oxford University Press.

Hoefer, R. (2009). Preparing managers for the human services. In R. J. Patti (Ed.), *The handbook of human services management* (pp. 483–501). Thousand Oaks, CA: Sage.

Hoskote, R. T. (2009). *The dynamics of joy in work* (Doctoral dissertation). Retrieved from ProQuest Dissertations and Theses database. (UMI No. 3401322).

Johnson, L. C., & Yanca, S. J. (2010). *Social work practice: A generalist approach* (10th ed.) Boston, MA: Allyn & Bacon.

Kanter, R. M. (1994). Collaborative advantage: The art of alliances. *Harvard Business Review, 27*, 96–109.

Lazarus, R. S. (1991). *Emotion and adaptation*. New York, NY: Oxford University Press.

Manion, J. (2003). Joy at work!: Creating a positive workplace. *The Journal of Nursing Administration, 33*(12), 652–659. doi:10.1097/00005110-200312000-00008

National Association of Social Workers (NASW). (2017). *Code of ethics*. Retrieved from https://www.socialworkers.org/About/Ethics/Code-of-Ethics/Code-of-Ethics-English

Neave, H. R. (1990). Deming'88* .Part 1: Win-win, joy in work, and innovation. *Total Quality Management, 1*(1), 33–48. doi:10.1080/09544129000000004

Perlman, H. H. (1979). *Relationship: The heart of helping people*. Chicago, IL: University of Chicago Press.

Peterson, C. (2006). *A primer in positive psychology*. Oxford, UK: Oxford University Press.

Saleebey, D. (2008). *Human behavior and social environments: A biopsychosocial approach*. New York, NY: Columbia University Press.

Schutz, W. C. (1967). *Joy: Expanding human awareness*. New York, NY: Grove Press.

Skinner, P. (2018). *Collaborative advantage: How collaboration beats competition as a strategy for success*. London, UK: Robinson.

Watson, L. D., & Hoefer, R. A. (2016). The joy of social work administration: An exploratory qualitative study of human service administrators' positive perceptions of their work. *Journal of Social Work Education, 52*(2), 178–185.

Youssef, C., & Luthans, F. (2007). Positive organizational behavior in the workplace: The impact of hope, optimism, and resilience. *Management Department Faculty Publications, 36*, 774–800.

Image Credits

INDEX

ABOUT THE AUTHORS

Richard (Rick) A. Hoefer, PhD, is the Roy E. Dulak Professor for Community Practice Research at the University of Texas at Arlington (UTA) School of Social Work. He publishes frequently regarding social work leadership, nonprofit administration, advocacy, social policy, grantwriting, and program evaluation, and he teaches in those areas at the BSW, MSW, and PhD levels. He is a consultant in private practice, helping nonprofit organizations become more effective and efficient as they achieve their missions. He is a member of the National Association of Social Workers (NASW), the Council on Social Work Education (CSWE), the Association for Research on Nonprofit and Voluntary Action (ARNOVA), the International Society for Third Sector Research (ISTR), and the American Evaluation Association (AEA). Dr. Hoefer is the founding and continuing editor of the *Journal of Policy Practice and Research*, an award-winning teacher, and recipient of the NASW Tarrant County (Texas) Social Worker of the Year award.

Larry D. Watson, PhD, is retired from the UTA School of Social Work faculty. He continues to conduct research and publish in the area on nonprofit administration and social policy. Prior to joining the faculty of the UTA School of Social Work, he served as the president and CEO of Methodist Mission Home in San Antonio, Texas, and was executive director of Catholic Family Services in Amarillo, Texas. He is the former president of NASW Texas and currently serves on the National NASW Board of Trustees. He also serves on PACE, the political action committee of NASW, and has served as chair on TPACE, the state-level political action committee. He was honored by the Dallas Chapter of NASW for Lifetime Achievement in Social Work.

CPSIA information can be obtained
at www.ICGtesting.com
Printed in the USA
LVHW061440280223
740589LV00009B/750

9 781516 598748